ADOPTED **TERRITORY**

ADOPTED **TERRITORY**

Transnational Korean Adoptees and the Politics of Belonging

Eleana J. Kim

Duke University Press
Durham and London 2010

Printed in the United States of America on
acid-free paper ∞

Designed by Heather Hensley

Typeset in Warnock Pro by Keystone Typesetting, Inc.

Library of Congress Cataloging-in-Publication Data
appear on the last printed page of this book.

This work was published with a publication subsidy
awarded by The Academy of Korean Studies Grant,
which is funded by the Korean Government
(MEST, Basic Research Promotion Fund).

TO MY PARENTS

Contents

Acknowledgments

First and foremost I express my greatest gratitude to the many adoptees who tolerated my presence and questions, welcomed me into their lives, and contributed their words and experiences to this ethnography. I have appreciated many of them not only as crucial interlocutors but also as cherished friends and colleagues. Much of what I have learned about Korean adoption has been due to the indispensable and foundational research of Tobias Hübinette and from my innumerable conversations with Kim Park Nelson, whose friendship represents one of the many rewards of my fieldwork experience. The everyday reflections, opinions, advice, and ongoing friendships of Me-K Ahn, Jackie Aronson, HyoSung Lee Bidol, HyoJung Bidol, Sarah Kim-Tomcek, Deann Borshay Liem, Lisa Hanson, kate hers, Hosu Kim, Hollee McGinnis, Sarah Park, KimSu Theiler, Jane Jeong Trenka, and Maya Weimer have informed my thinking and encouraged me in countless ways.

Susan Soon-Keum Cox early on saw the value in research on the first generation of adult Korean adoptees, and I deeply appreciate her willingness to let me volunteer for the first Gathering conference in 1999 and her subsequent generosity with her time and extensive knowledge. When I first began the Korea portion of my research in 2001, Mihee Nathalie Lemoine was an expert guide and welcoming friend. Along the way, I was lucky to meet fellow researchers and adoptees engaged in their own fact-finding missions, including HyoJung Bidol, Su-Yoon Ko Burrows, Tammy Chu, Kelli Donigan, Amy Harp, Pam Jost, Eun Yung Fairbanks and JaeSik Kauffman, Jenny Na, Lene Myong Peterson, Elise Prebin, and Kim Stoker. At the Overseas Koreans Foundation (OKF), Jeannie Hong's assistance, cooperation, and friendship were crucial to my research and own sense of belonging in Korea. I was very lucky to find Kim Do Hyun, a fellow researcher and a dedicated advocate for adoptees, managing KoRoot when I returned to Korea in 2004, and to coincide with Dae-won Kim's tenure at Global Overseas Adoptees' Link (GOA'L). I hope that some of the wisdom and insights I gathered from conversations with both Dae-won and Reverend Kim have found their way into these pages. Other staff and volunteers from International Korean Adoptee Services (INKAS), OKF, and GOA'L who helped educate me on the intricate dynamics of adoption in Korea include Jung AeRee, Hellen Ko, Ma Kyung Hee, Kim Jong Hyock, and John Hamrin.

This book first began as a dissertation project in the Anthropology Department at New York University under the guidance of Faye Ginsburg, who offered invaluable mentorship and instruction from the beginning of my graduate school career. Fred Myers, Rayna Rapp, and Lok Siu contributed their sage advice as committee members at crucial moments in the fieldwork and writing process. I was also particularly fortunate to have supportive encouragement and critical feedback from Laurel Kendall and Toby Volkman both during and after the dissertation phase.

The moral support and intellectual solidarity of friends at New York University and beyond helped see this project to fruition. Great thanks to Amahl Bishara, Kristin Dowell, Danny Fisher, Aaron Glass, Sherine Hamdy, Leo Hsu, Jessica Cattelino, Elise Andaya, Shanti Avirgan, Julie Chu, Cheryl Furjanic, Bill Horn, JongBum Kwon, Lauren Shweder, Lisa Stefanoff, Ruti Talmor, Pegi Vail, Daniel Kim, Hijoo Son, Sue-je Gage, Nicola Kountoupes, June Hwang, and especially Susie Rosenbaum.

This project was funded by a number of institutions, including the James West Memorial Fund Fellowship for my preliminary research in Korea in 2001 and the Social Science Research Council's International Dissertation Research Fellowship, which funded the American and Korean segments of my fieldwork during 2003 and 2004. Research in Korea was supported by the Fulbright Institute of International Education and made possible by the daily behind-the-scenes assistance provided by then director Horace Underwood and the staff at the Fulbright office in Seoul. At New York University the Institute for the History of the Production of Knowledge (IHPK) and the Dean's Dissertation Grant provided essential funding to support me during the writing process. Thanks to Troy Duster,

Mary Poovey, Eileen Bowman, Aaron Panofsky, and Emily Cohen, and especially to Emily Martin at IHPK. Finally, the Center for Korean Studies at the University of California, Los Angeles, provided a home for me during my Korea Foundation postdoctoral fellowship, and I am particularly appreciative of John Duncan's gracious hospitality. I've found a warm and stimulating intellectual community at the University of Rochester where I've been able to see this book to completion. I extend my heartfelt thanks to Tony Carter, Ayala Emmett, Robert Foster, Thomas Gibson, and Daniel Reichman for their exceptional collegiality, and to Ro Ferreri for her tireless work on our behalf.

I benefited immensely from the feedback offered when I presented this work to various audiences at the University of British Columbia; Brown University; University of California, Los Angeles; University of Toronto; University of Illinois, Urbana-Champaign; University of California, Berkeley; Wellesley College; University of Minnesota; and University of California, Irvine. I also extend my appreciation to the anonymous reviewers at Duke University Press, one of whom revealed herself to be the esteemed Elaine Kim. Ken Wissoker supported this project from the beginning and shepherded it expertly into production. Thanks also to Mandy Earley and Rebecca Fowler for their administrative support and for answering all my nagging questions. I'm also grateful to Brenda Reeb and Katie Papas at the University of Rochester Rush Rhees Library, and David Klassen at the University of Minnesota Social Welfare History Archives for their assistance with archival materials.

George Drake of the Korean War Children's Memorial Project kindly shared his recollections, connections, and extensive archive. The late Mrs. Oak Soon Hong and her daughter Juli Eisenberg graciously invited me to their home to conduct an interview, as did Susan T. Pettiss. I thank them each for enduring long conversations with a researcher struggling to grasp the events and cultural realities of 1950s South Korea and America.

Chapter 1 first appeared in the U.S.-Korea Institute at SAIS Working Paper Series (WP 09–09), and a version of chapter 5 was published in 2007 in *Anthropological Quarterly* 80 (2) (spring). I thank both editors for permission to reprint the contents of those articles here. I also appreciate the willingness of the artists whose work appears in these pages for allowing their images to be reproduced. "Calling Card" by kate hers (Kate Hershiser) is reproduced with permission from Yeong and Yeong Book Company. Finally, I acknowledge the Strategic Initiative for Korean Studies for awarding me a generous publication subsidy grant.

Alissa Quart, Molly Larkey, Ing Lee, and Sridhar Venkatapuram deserve special mention for their countless acts of kindness over many years, as does my extended family in Korea and New York, especially Hyeryun, SungHae and Sungsook, Sungwook, and Yeongseop. My mother, father, and brother have bolstered me with just the right balance of sympathy and cajoling discipline. My mother's courage and steadfastness and my father's boundless curiosity and profound humanism have been enduring sources of inspiration and nurturance for me. This book is dedicated to them. Finally, Rick Snyder's daily sustenance of inestimable love, intellectual clarity, and incomparable wit merits so much more than words can express.

Notes on Transliteration, Terminology, and Pseudonyms

ROMANIZATION

I follow the McCune-Reischauer system for the romanization of Korean words, and the Korean convention of family name first. Exceptions are made for names of places (e.g., Seoul) and people with commonly recognized English transliterations (e.g., Syngman Rhee).

ADOPTION TERMS

Since the late 1990s, the term "transnational adoption" has gained currency among academics—a move that is largely a result of the theoretical interest in transnational processes related to "globalization." The vast majority of these adoptions could also be described as transracial adoptions, a term that came into usage around the adoptions of black and mixed-race children into mostly white families in the United States during the 1960s. In chapter 1, I follow the dominant conventions of the adoption profession by using "intercountry" or "international" adoption interchangeably. In Korea, the terms "foreign adoption" (*kugoe ibyang*; as opposed to domestic adoption, *kungnae ibyang*) or "overseas adoption" (*haeoe ibyang*) are most commonly employed to denote the movement of children from Korea to the West, and the latter resonates with the contemporary interest in diasporic or "overseas" populations. I refer to transnational adoption from the Korean perspective as "overseas adoption." Regarding the children born to Korean women and fathered by American or United Nations soldiers I follow the conventions of the period, which also reflect the preoccupations of Americans and Koreans regarding these hybrid children—"mixed race" in the United States, and "mixed blood" (*honhyŏl*) in Korean.

Certain terms have become commonly used among adoptees and adoption professionals to describe the "adoption triad" comprised of birth parents, adoptive parents, and adoptees. The genitors of the child, who may have been called "natural" or "real" parents in the past, are now often referred to as "birth parents" or "biological parents." Some adoptees use the Korean words "omma" (*ŏmma*) or "omoni" (*ŏmŏni*) to refer to their Korean mothers, whether or not they have been reunited. I employ "birth parents," and "natal parents" interchangeably to refer to adoptees' Korean parents.

Adult Korean adoptees in Europe and the United States began designing the form and content of Korean adoptee culture and identity in the 1990s, and the lexical conventions that have been taken up suggest the heterogeneity of adoptee social practices. The adoptee Sunny Jo created the acronym KAD for "Korean Adoptee," a form that she further defines in her essay "The Creation and Rise of KAD as a Separate Identity and Nation" (2004). The acronym KAD is often used in online communities, such as on Korean Adoptees Worldwide, the electronic mailing list that Jo manages, but most adoptees I met and talked with used "adoptee" or "Korean adoptee" to describe themselves and their community. Similar to the domestic United States adoptee activists who promote the use of "adopted person," some Korean adoptees preferred to use the term "adopted Korean" because of their concern about the infantilizing and diminutive construction of "adoptee" that connotes for them the ways in which adoptees are often construed as perennial children. Others I've met in the Minneapolis Twin Cities area reverse the conventional construction of "Korean adoptee" to highlight their Koreanness by referring to themselves as "Korean, adopted" (usually in contradistinction to "Korean Koreans"). Meanwhile, adoptee activists in Korea invented the acronym OAK for "overseas adopted Korean," which was then taken up by the Korean government's Overseas Koreans Foundation for their adult adoptee programs. Adoptees who have returned to live in Korea also sometimes eschew the common construction *ibyanga*, which means adopted child, and refer to themselves as *ibyang* (adopt) or *ibyangin* (adopted person). I elect to use "Korean adoptee" and "adopted Korean" interchangeably, as they are the terms in most common usage among adoptees. As this brief foray into adoptee naming conventions suggests, the "global community" of adoptees is not a unitary object but rather is composed of subsets of regional and online groups with distinct histories and concerns even as they have become increasingly coordinated under the broad umbrella of the Korean adoptee global network.

THE KOREAN PENINSULA

Given the complex geopolitics of the Korean peninsula, it is necessary to qualify my choice of language when referring to Korea. "Korea," in common English usage, most often denotes "South Korea" or the Republic of Korea (ROK), thereby implicitly undermining any legitimacy the North Korean state (DPRK) may have as a representative of the Korean people. For reasons of style over politics, I follow this convention throughout. At other times I use "Korea" in quotes to indicate a reified notion that conflates place, culture, and identity, and I use South Korea (without quotes) to indicate the specificity of the South Korean state (ROK) and its bounded geopolitical territory.

PSEUDONYMS

All organizations in this book are referred to by their real names. Most of the adoptees who appear in this dissertation are public figures known within the adoptee community, and they requested that their real names be used in lieu of the conventional assignment of pseudonyms. I reserve the use of pseudonyms for adoptees who are not active in formal organizing activities and who do not have a recognizable role in the community. I also chose to assign pseudonyms in cases where I draw upon adoptees' personal experiences that are not directly related to their work in adoptee organizing or community building.

Abbreviations

AAAW	Asian Adult Adoptees of Washington
AKA–SF	Association of Korean Adoptees–San Francisco
AKA–SoCal	Adopted Korean Association–Southern California
AKConnection	Adopted Korean Connection
AKF	Adopterade Koreaners Förening (Adopted Koreans' Association)
AKF	American-Korean Foundation
ASK	Adoptee Solidarity Korea
AVEC	Adoptes Vivant en Corée (Adoptees Living in Korea)
BKA	Boston Korean Adoptees
CCEJ	Citizens' Coalition for Economic Justice (Kyŏng Sillyŏn)
CPS	Child Placement Service
EKL	Euro-Korean League
ESWS	Eastern Social Welfare Society
GAIPS	Global Adoption Information Post Services
GOA'L	Global Overseas Adoptees' Link
ICA	Intercountry adoption
IKAA	International Korean Adoptee Associations
InKAS	International Korean Adoptee Services
ISS	International Social Service
ISS–AB	International Social Service–American Branch
KAAN	Korean American Adoptee Adoptive Family Network

KAVA	Korean American Voluntary Associations
KoBel	Korean Belgium Association (formerly EKL)
KSS	Korea Social Service
MAK	Minnesota Adopted Koreans
MIHWAF	Ministry for Health, Welfare and Family Affairs, South Korea
MOFAT	Ministry of Foreign Affairs and Trade, South Korea
MOHW	Ministry of Health and Welfare, South Korea
OKA	Overseas Koreans Act (Chaeoe Tongp'o Pŏp)
OKF	Overseas Koreans Foundation (Chaeoe Tongp'o Chedan)
SWS	Social Welfare Society

Introduction

Understanding Transnational Korean Adoption

In May 2006, coinciding with South Korea's second annual "Adoption Day," the National Assembly member Ko Kyung Hwa unveiled a proposal for the reform of adoption legislation. Her proposal's main item was a plan to discontinue the nation's overseas adoption program, a fifty-three-year-old social welfare policy that spanned nearly the entire history of the Republic of Korea. A few months later the government announced major expenditures for a range of adoption-related projects, all of which were directed toward promoting domestic adoption, such as monthly subsidies for parents who adopted children, state coverage of adoption fees, a loosening of eligibility requirements so as to include older parents and single individuals, and the implementation of "adoption leave" (*ibyang hyuga*)—the adoption equivalent of maternity leave. In addition, to encourage "domestic adoption first" and provide an opportunity for domestic adopters to be located, children would be deemed ineligible for overseas adoption for a period of five months (with exceptions made for children with congenital disabilities) (C. Park 2006).

This announcement received plenty of media coverage in the South Korean press, but its repercussions were felt well beyond the nation's borders. In the United States and Europe, expectant parents who were waiting for their referrals—assignments of a child by a Korean adoption agency—were informed by their local adoption agencies that they might experience further delays in placements, and, in anticipation of the imminent end to the program, some Western agencies refused to accept any more applications for Korean adoptions. On electronic discussion boards, parents spoke of "switching programs," meaning that they would seek to adopt from another country such as China. This transnational ripple effect was not without precedence, and some social workers reportedly believed that it was just another predictable installment in a long series of aborted plans by the South Korean state to end overseas adoption, which has been a continual source of shame and embarrassment for the nation (Lewin 1990; Chira 1988b).

In fact, a similar constellation of events took shape in the 1970s when South Korea announced the suspension of foreign adoptions due to censure by the North Korean government, which vilified South Korea's commodification of children as the logical end point of capitalism. As a consequence, adoptions to Scandinavian countries were disrupted between 1970 and 1975 and only resumed following "intense lobbying" by European governments (Hübinette 2004). American agencies and adoptive parents also reportedly lobbied their local politicians to pressure South Korea to keep the program going, and again in the late 1980s and mid-1990s announcements of plans to end adoption to the West were typically accompanied by vocal concerns by politicians, social workers, and parents on both sides of the Pacific about child welfare and doubts about Korea's ability to provide families for its needy and abandoned children.

That one nation's domestic social welfare projects can so profoundly affect the lives of individuals in the West is characteristic of transnational adoption, which now takes place within a neoliberal global economy, a transnational public sphere, and an international human rights regime nominally held to the standards laid out in 1993 by the Hague Convention on Protection of Children and Co-operation in Respect of Intercountry Adoption.[1] These transnational intimacies and engagements now extend to children throughout the world, with parents and agencies in the global North holding nations in the global South accountable to often ethnocentric and classed notions of "family" and culturally embedded standards of the child's "best interests" (Howell 2007; Stephens 1995).

South Korea, which in 2007 ranked as the world's thirteenth largest economy in terms of GDP, represents an exception among the so-called sending countries. This exception stems from the fact that it has the longest history of overseas adoption, and its advanced medical services and streamlined process ensure healthy infants within a short period of time, thereby earning it the reputation as the Cadillac of adoption programs. It is also exceptional in that its demographic profile shares the same highs and lows of other so-called advanced industrialized nations, which are the typical "receiving countries"; that is, it has been among the "lowest-low" fertility countries since 2001 (with the lowest birthrate in the world in 2008),[2] and it has skyrocketing rates of abortion and divorce along with rising rates of infertility. Dire economic predictions based on the shrinking workforce and the aging population mirror those of other affluent nations, yet South Korea is unique in that it sends children abroad for adoption. These paradoxes have reached new extremes—local jurisdictions have instituted monetary incentives to married women to conceive more offspring even as single mothers are provided below-subsistence-level welfare subsidies to raise their children.

Given the precipitous decline in the birthrate and the dark future it has forecast for the nation's fiscal health, it is not surprising that adoption would reemerge as a topic of some political concern. At the same time, however, with an annual average of 2,200 children adopted overseas since the 1990s, the connection between population decline and overseas adoption must be regarded as being largely symbolic. Like the heated debates between adoption advocates and adoption foes, discourses around the "adoption issue" (*ibyang munje*) in Korea have been more often marked by bald polemics rather than nuanced analysis. Over the past few decades, both in the West and in Korea, adoption has been the subject of highly polarized gazes ranging from a jaundiced perspective that views it as a neoimperialistic perpetuation of gender, race, and class-based inequalities on a global scale to a blindly sentimental perspective that sees it as an incontrovertible good or a necessary humanitarian rescue of the world's neediest orphans.

This latest elaboration of familiar debates is, however, notably different from the preceding ones in that there is now a triangulation of voices: Korean lawmakers and Western adoption agencies have been joined by adult Korean adoptees who are actively contributing their opinions on the moral and ethical value of adoption. The voices of some of these adoptees have been considered to be excessively unruly (and, it seems, quite threatening) by advocates of adoption, including agency social workers and adoptive parents. In August 2006, based on information from a retired Korean social worker who was a longtime liaison with Korean agencies,

Children's Home Society of Minnesota (CHSM) announced that a small but vocal group of "unhappy" adoptees living in Korea was influencing the government to prematurely end overseas adoption. Along with the Pennsylvania-based agency Welcome House, CHSM sent out urgent requests to adult adoptees, whom they referred to as the "silent majority," asking them to write letters to assembly member Ko in support of international adoption. Moreover, they detailed how these letters could effectively describe one's "positive experience growing up as a Korean adoptee in this country" in order to counteract the voices of adult adoptees "who have been vocal in describing their negative adoption experiences."

In the end, Ko's proposed legislation died on the table and quickly receded from public view.[3] The letter writing campaign, however, produced its own unintended outcomes and controversies. Adoptees, adoptive parents, and adoption agency social workers, some of them also adoptees, sparred and debated as well as deconstructed and supported each other's opinions in discussion boards, electronic mailing lists, and blogs. Conversations took place in person at adoption agencies, adoptee organization meetings, and among friends, in which adoptees and others deliberated over the politics of Korean adoption, the role of American agencies in the affairs of other nations, and CHSM's strategy of driving a wedge into the adoptee community by forcing adoptees into artificial oppositions of positive or negative, grateful or ungrateful, and for or against adoption.

As these events suggest, Korean adoption is a highly contested, transnational field that encompasses a range of nations, institutions, ideologies, laws, technologies, media, and social groups that hold stakes in its reputation and future. In this book I tell the story of Korean transnational, transracial adoption from the perspective of the adult adoptees who came of age in Europe and North America in the 1970s, 1980s, and 1990s, a period commonly associated with globalization. As the pioneers of both transnational and Asian transracial adoption, these children represented a "social experiment," the outcomes of which were subject to intense scrutiny and debate since the practice began in the mid-1950s. Korean adoptions, determined to be largely successful by social workers and academic experts in the 1950s and 1960s, expanded dramatically in the 1970s and paved the way for subsequent waves of adoptions of children from the developing world into white Western homes. Transnational or intercountry adoption was regarded during the Second World War as a radical but temporary solution to child displacement wrought by war and its attendant social dislocations. By the 1970s, largely due to the success of the Korean model, transnational adoption became an institutionalized social welfare practice in many nations and a naturalized "choice" for individuals in the Euro-American West.

I began my research at a time when a significant contingent of the first waves of Korean adoptees had come of age, and when a recognizable and self-conscious community, consolidated out of disparate spaces of social activity and discourses, was beginning to give normative shape to a collective "Korean adoptee identity." I frame adoptee discourses and social practices as a "counterpublic," a form of performative "world-making," in the words of Michael Warner, in which adoptees "recognize themselves . . . as already being the persons they are addressed as being and as already belonging to the world that is condensed in their discourse" (2002: 82). The "world-making" of this counterpublic is constituted through a range of circulating discourses and a shared social imaginary and is also made manifest in particular sites of collective action. This book offers a historical and ethnographic analysis that seeks to answer the following questions: What can the emergence of the adoptee counterpublic tell us about dominant categories of belonging—kinship and citizenship—in the context of globalization? How do adoptees negotiate personhood in light of the heightened geneticization of identity and Western paradigms of the liberal individual? How have adoptee migrations and returns challenged the "nation" and its attempts to mobilize diaspora politics in the pursuit of its global aspirations?

In Euro-American societies, adoption has long raised fundamental questions about the connection between procreation and reproduction, the balance of nature and nurture, genetics and environment, and the biological and the social in constructions of personhood and identity. These questions have become more pronounced in the context of biogenetic advances and assisted reproductive technologies, such that formerly naturalized associations between kinship and family and between procreation and reproduction have loosened and become decoupled. Given these developments, Marilyn Strathern proposed in 1995 that we could soon be witnessing an era of "more kinship, fewer relations" (357), in which genetic information alone, rather than actual social relations, could be the basis of self-knowledge. Adult adoptees in my study suggest otherwise. For them, questions about kinship and identity are not limited to biogenetic information and cannot be divorced from social relations. To put it another way, biogenetic information such as knowing whether one has a predisposition for prostate cancer cannot answer the historically contingent question of why one was sent for adoption. Some adoptees may fixate on genetics due to concerns about heritable disease and mortality, but for many of them, their origins are constructed out of socially grounded notions of kinship, citizenship, and histories of connection and disconnection.

As I show in the subsequent chapters, the Korean adoptees I met made it clear to me that, for them, questions of kinship and identity are intricately connected to broader political-economic and historical processes. The adoptees in my study would not deny the significance of biological connections or genetic information to their conceptions of self, but their views on that significance have altered over time and continue to shift with the ongoing movements of the adoptee counterpublic that exist in dynamic relation to South Korean modernity and globalization. Against views that might dismiss adoptees who seek out "roots" as being overly wedded to individuated, essentializing, and biologistic modes of thinking, my research on the Korean adoptee counterpublic suggests that adoptees construct identities out of kinship knowledge that is eminently collective, contingent, and most of all, social.

ADOPTED TERRITORY

In summer 2003 I was spending my second year in Korea working as a counselor for an annual cultural tour hosted by the South Korean government. On the third day of the program I was asked to distribute meal tickets to the thirty-odd adoptee participants during the short break between afternoon events. I was hurrying down the dimly lit hallway of the hotel in Suwon where we had arrived earlier that day when I ran into Garrett, a twenty-year-old university student from the Netherlands. He was sitting on a low couch next to the elevator at the end of the hall. After only a few days, Garrett had already distinguished himself within the group with his shaved head, cheerful demeanor, slapstick humor, and well-appointed wardrobe. Just the day before he had told me that he felt 100 percent Dutch, and we had a somewhat strained conversation about the politics of assimilation and new immigrants in Europe. Now he was sitting by himself at the end of the hall and shyly asked if I had time to join him.

As I sat down he said he knew that I was researching Korean adoption, and he wondered if I could explain to him why adoption is still continuing from Korea. I told him that the majority of birth mothers today are young unmarried women and teenagers and that a lack of adequate sex education and the stigma of single motherhood are a few of the contributing factors. I became aware that in my attempt to keep my answer simple and neutral I was succeeding only in presenting it in an overly intricate fashion. Garrett, however, seemed barely to have heard my winding explication. Instead, he proceeded to tell me about his visit to his adoption agency that day with a group of other adoptees who wanted to view their adoption files. Afterward, the agency social workers invited the group to lunch nearby. Since there were too many people to fit into one car, Garrett volunteered to stay behind to be picked up on a second run. Because it was raining outside he went back into the lobby to wait, during which time he saw an infant receiving a visa to be adopted to the United States. He suddenly began to weep, saying he couldn't understand and it felt so weird to see that. He said it broke his heart to have come all the way back to Korea to see another little baby leaving.

Garrett had been adopted as an infant by well-off parents. He identified completely as a member of his Dutch family and nation, and he was cultivating an international identity—he loved to travel and his closest friends were exchange students at his university. I have no doubt that Garrett, if asked, would say that he had a "positive experience" as an adoptee. But his act of witnessing a child's preparations to leave Korea set in motion more ambivalent feelings about adoption and its necessary prequels of abandonment and relinquishment—emotions that, it should be clear, fall outside the epistemological purview of quantitative outcome studies and compilations of "positive" and "negative" experiences.

Compounding the complexity of these feelings were the seeming contradictions between Korea's rapid ascent toward advanced nation status and its continuing reliance on international adoption. Many adoptees like Garrett grew up imagining Korea as a third world country in which "underdevelopment" made their adoptions necessary interventions, without which they might not have survived and for which they should be grateful. When they arrive in Seoul and witness the modernization miracle of shiny, high-tech South Korea firsthand, however, the discrepancy between the ongoing practice of overseas adoption and Korea's globalized modernity can be striking and unnerving. For Garrett, his adoption made sense in a setting where third world deprivation was answered by first world charity. When this equation fails to add up, dominant logics of adoption as necessarily in a child's best interests also seem to break down. Garrett was not alone in struggling with the question of why adoption from Korea continues after more than fifty years, as well as with the question of how to understand his life in relation to postmodern Korea and the phenomenon of transnational adoption. In fact, a growing number of adult adoptees are confronting the political and social realities that structured their lives, which have been largely obscured by hegemonic narratives of rescue and opportunity.

Transnational, transracial adoption is often invoked as the actualization of ideals of humanitarianism and the promises of multiculturalism, and adoptees are regarded as potential representatives of postnational cosmopolitanism. Yet adoptee narratives and social practices point toward the limits of these discourses in a world in which categories of race, nation, and family and their frequent conflations continue to structure the lives of individuals in powerful ways. Adoptees embody and expose the contradictions of the global. They are like holographs—turned one way, they appear to be among the most privileged of cosmopolitans, turned the other, they are the ultimate subalterns as "orphaned" and "abandoned" children. For anthropologists, adoptees are "good to think" because of the complex ways in which their lives blur naturalized categories of biology, society, nature, nurture, and native and alien. They are also, however, important to listen to for what they have to say about adoption as a global system embedded in market rationalities and as a transnational system of child welfare.

This book is an ethnography that stays close to the words and performances of its interlocutors. In it I do not pretend to offer prescriptions about the best practices in adoption, and I do not intend it to be read as a guide for adopting parents. I argue for the importance of understanding adult adoptee narratives and articulations of personhood as socially and historically specific responses to common experiences of displacement and disidentification. In contrast to the majority of existing studies on Korean adoption, which are concentrated in fields of psychology and social work and which take an individuated view of adoptees, this ethnography applies the tools of the anthropological trade to offer an examination of "adopted territories"—networks of adoptees and their activities, situated in a range of virtual and actual locations, that comprise the transnational Korean adoptee counterpublic.

FROM INTERNATIONAL ADOPTEE OUTCOMES TO TRANSNATIONAL ADOPTION STUDIES

Through the attempted reduction of an adoptee's life to positive and negative experiences, the CHSM letter-writing campaign noted above revealed the tendentiousness of the moral debates that typically circulate around adoption as a form of child rescue or as a form of exploitation. Moreover, the enlistment of adoptees with "positive" experiences to fight the moral battles of agencies against an imagined "unhappy" minority of adoptee foes reinforces the dominant constructions of adoptees as either well adjusted or maladjusted, happy or angry, and, consequently, assumed to be correspondingly for adoption or against adoption.

This binary logic mirrors that of the majority of psychology and social work outcome studies, which have thus far dominated transnational adoption as a field. These studies attempted to measure the mental health or "adjustment" of children and adolescents adopted transracially and transnationally, and they are limited by their tendency to disembed the phenomenon of transnational adoption from its relevant historical, social, and political contexts. Moreover, these studies' findings rely upon a developmentalist framework that understands adoptee adjustment and acculturation to be part of an individualized process of moving from "preadoption" traumas of loss and biological rupture into the "postadoption" phase of adjusting to normative kinship structures (middle class, heterosexual, and nuclear). The majority of these studies, for the most part based on samples of one hundred or fewer, determined that transnational adoptees are no different from and sometimes are better adjusted than domestic adoptees, as well as in comparison to nonadopted siblings (for an overview of these studies, see Altstein and Simon 2000).

The power of these findings as "expert knowledge" is often mobilized to support the so-called positive view of transracial adoption, despite problematic assumptions, methods, and measures. Most of the studies conducted throughout in the 1970s and 1980s, for instance, were based on reports about the children by their adoptive parents and focused on "adjustment" and "self-esteem" while studiously avoiding issues of racialization. Dong Soo Kim's study from 1978 was the first to suggest contradictions between the "positive outcomes" of adolescent adopted Koreans and the fact that they "were extremely concerned with their physical appearance," and tended to "reject their own racial background" (482). As Kim provisionally concluded, "The so-called good adjustment of these children is being accomplished at the cost of their unique ethnic cultural heritage and identity, partially reinforced by parents' innocent, yet inapt, expectations" (485). These concerns, however, were not raised again until the 1990s when a new crop of studies turned attention to "ethnicity" and "race" but tended to essentialize or conflate them, sometimes collapsing them with uninterrogated notions of "culture" (R. Lee 2003).

By the mid-2000s, a growing number of anthropologists, sociologists, and humanities scholars began examining the social, cultural, and historical implications of transnational adoption. Drawn to the ways in which these migrations pull into proximity far-reaching political-economic forces with the intimate realms of kinship, this work has come to constitute a distinct subfield (e.g., see Volkman 2005b; Dorow 2006; Howell 2001, 2007; Yngvesson 2001, 2002, 2003, 2005; Anagnost 2000; Eng 2003; Gailey 2000; Park Nelson, Kim, and Peterson 2007; Riley 1997; Bowie 2004). This qualitative and ethnographic work attends to the ambiguities and ambivalences of transnational adoption and offers interpretive models of adoptee subjectivity that are more multiple and complex than might be suggested by the previously existing studies.

In addition, these scholars are attuned to the global circulations engendered by adoption as a form of child migration and therefore refer to these adoptions as "transnational" rather than "international" or "intercountry" adoptions. These adoptions are transnational in that, as Toby Alice Volkman notes, they "entail ongoing, crisscrossing flows in multiple directions, in space that is both real and virtual" (2005a: 2). And although children are adopted overwhelmingly from poorer countries to wealthier ones, suggesting a unilinear movement and assimilation process, like other migrants (see Basch, Glick-Schiller, Blanc 1994), they have instigated a range of subsequent mobilities—of information, people, goods, and services—from and to the so-called sending and receiving nations that are shaped by (and, in turn, shape) new globalizing trends and transnational processes.

Most of the studies to date have privileged the perspectives of adoptive parents to examine how racial difference is negotiated and conflated with "cultural" difference within the family and how parents rewrite family scripts to naturalize the "artificial kinship" of adoption (Modell 1994; Howell 2007). Anthropologists in particular have been interested in how the "biological" and the "social" are negotiated against the backdrop of multiculturalism and globalization, especially when the child's foreign origins are racially marked.

Another line of inquiry examines the processes through which the child in transnational adoption is constructed as an object of desire and exchange. Sara Dorow and Barbara Yngvesson both deconstruct the stark separation of the adoptee's life into "pre" and "post" adoption phases, from the "birth country" to the "adoptive country." In their accounts the transnationally adopted child must be viewed as being fully embedded in and embodying cultural worlds and social relations, with values and meanings attaching to her as she passes across borders of nation and family. Otherwise, those prior histories and relationships risk being marginalized, erased, or devalued in her radical transformation from needy third world orphan to privileged first world citizen. My analysis draws particular attention to the symbolic power of the figure of the orphan and the material effects it has had on the lives of adult adoptees.

In the practical and legal procedures of adoption, much bureaucratic and emotional labor is directed toward the severing of networks and connections in order to produce an "eligible orphan," who then is free to be exchanged and transformed through Euro-American models of kinship into someone's as-if genealogical child. American and international legal paradigms reinforce this notion that adopted children are orphans through the privileging of plenary, or "hard," adoptions that wholly replace and erase original parents with adoptive ones. In American immigration law, children must be "eligible orphans" to enter the United States as "immediate relatives" of the adopting parents under the family reunification provision.[4] This legal fiction protects the custody rights of the adoptive parents and ensures that the natal parents hold no legally valid claims to the child upon which to base their own family reunification petitions. Symbolically and legally, then, the erasure of the natal parents and the cutting of prior social relations have long been prerequisites to rendering a child adoptable. This severing and erasing process not only produces a child who is legally and socially "free" to be incorporated into another kin network but also reduces the child's complex origins—social, political, and cultural—to generic categories.

As Esben Leifsen argues, this process of making children into orphans in transnational adoption suspends "the unique value of the person, which makes her or him incomparable and not exchangeable" (2004: 193) and replaces a plurality of relationships with social discontinuities and a singular relation. In effect, a child is rendered adoptable (rescuable) and also vulnerable to commodification. But as Sara Dorow cogently notes, "Transnationally adopted children are not bought and sold, but neither are they given and received freely and altruistically; the people and institutions around them enter into social relationships of exchange, meaning, and value that are both caring and consumptive." This close imbrication of commodification and care can make it difficult to distinguish between the "caring-parent" and the "consumer-parent" or between humanitarian and egocentric motivations (2006: 17).

A key part of this dynamic is the object of desire—the third world orphan, which is a powerful symbol in global public culture that gathers together the humanitarian and commodity logics of transnational adoption. The humanitarian orphan erases and neutralizes the political-economic realities that lie at the root of abandonment and adoption (see chapter 1); it also, however, highlights the commodification of bodies and the gross inequalities that fuel the transfer of children from poor countries to families in wealthy nations. For adult adoptees, the "orphan" thereby invokes a paradoxical set of associations of adoption with opportunity and oppression, with having been saved or sold, especially as they negotiate the moral values of adoption in the context of South Korea's rapid economic development and the particular circumstances of their lives.

Working out these questions often involves a process of "return" or excavation of personal history and past lives. As Barbara Yngvesson (2002) argues, the legal fiction of the orphan demanded by plenary, or "clean break," adoption leaves behind an excess of relationships that "enchains" the child's givers and recipients and "haunts" adoptee subjectivities (see also Dorow 2006).[5] These can be thought of as the constitutive outside (Butler 1993)—comprised of obscured or excerpted social relations. In this way, adoption not only makes children into orphans, but, over time, produces missing persons,[6] and the resulting narrative discontinuities have proven to be central to the social imaginary of Korean adoptees whose expressive cultures and discursive practices often explore "loss," and the challenge of constructing identities and places of belonging out of bits and fragments.

In the second half of the book, I examine adoptee "returns" to the so-called birth country—voyages that are now considered to be an expected stage in the adoptee lifecycle. It was, in fact, adult Korean adoptees who transformed the view of international adoption as a one-way journey from "sending" to "receiving" country into a two-way transit. Many adult Korean adoptees describe how, during their childhood and adolescence, "Korea" was actively relegated to the past—within the temporality of their own biographies and also within the temporality of a modernist development teleology—as the sign and symbol of their difference and as a boundary between their unknown pasts and their present realities. The lives of adoptees coincided with Korea's emergence as one of the "Asian Tiger" economies and with intensifying flows of Korean goods, media, and people moving through the countries where the adoptees had been raised. The project of return—or, as one adoptee told me, of attempting to "fill up the hole that is Korea"—has been enabled by globalizing flows and postmodern "time-space compression" (Harvey 1990).

Rather than viewing these returns as a retrogressive turn to "biology" in an attempt to replace the "inauthentic" relations of adoptive kinship, however, my research suggests that returns are part of a range of counterpublic discourses and practices through which adoptees mediate and perform kinship. In the chapters that follow, I focus my attention as an ethnographer on the spaces and moments in which the significance of being adopted from Korea is foregrounded and heightened, and where what I call "adoptee kinship"—a form of solidarity based upon radical contingency rather than biologically rooted certitudes—is made.

"IT'S A NETWORK AND IT'S NOT REALLY A NETWORK": THE TRANSNATIONAL KOREAN ADOPTEE COUNTERPUBLIC

The tour on which I met Garrett was one of many sites that compose a transnational field of adoptee cultural production that has been emerging since the late 1980s. I started my preliminary research at the Gathering of the First Generation of Korean Adoptees, a conference in 1999 that is frequently referred to as the beginning of the international Korean adoptee community. Since 1999 I have been tracking adult adopted Korean social practices and cultural productions on the Internet and at conferences, local adoptee group meetings, film screenings, and other events.

When I started formally interviewing adoptees in early 2003, the majority of those I met who were involved with adoptee organizing had only intermittent contact with other groups, and often had never met in person. Yet they were connected to each other through flows of information and a shared imagination of the international dimensions of the adoptee network. Some adoptees expressed politicized views on adoption and engaged in critiques of "the system," whereas others were content to meet socially and make new friends. Given the scattered locations and lack of direct communication among my interlocutors, during the course of my fieldwork I continually asked them, by phone, email and in person, in Minneapolis, New York, Seattle, and Seoul, how they viewed these collective adult adoptee social formations—did they believe that a community, network, or movement of adoptees existed? If so, how did they know that it did?

By the time I left the field in late 2004, these questions were no longer pertinent, as the word "community" circulated with increasing fluency and fluidity. On the heels of the International Gathering of Korean Adoptees conference (commonly referred to in short as "the Gathering") in Seoul in 2004, many were actively discussing their "community," its boundaries, and its futures. Since then, the International Korean Adoptee Associations (IKAA) has been established as the official representative for the adoptee "global network," which links some ten thousand adoptees from a dozen organizations around the world. Tackling the multiple and heterogeneous sites of this project ethnographically required a traveling methodology in order to address the question of how a shared sense of personhood was established among spatially dispersed, highly diverse individuals.

Toward this goal I found the framework of "counterpublics," "social imaginaries," and "public intimacy" (Warner 2002; Fraser 1992; Habermas 1989; Taylor 2002; Rapp and Ginsburg 2001; Berlant 1997) to be useful in my conceptualization of how new media technologies and mobilities of the postmodern age facilitated the "production, distribution, and regulation of particular kinds of images, norms, and knowledges across political spaces" (Ong 1999). Also, I drew inspiration from Kay Warren's multisited and engaged methodology in her study of Pan-Maya activists and in so doing chose to focus ethnographic attention on central figures and events rather than attempting to present a "totalizing account of the movement" (Warren 1999: 28). The counterpublic framework helps me to highlight the fact that the adoptee social imaginary exists in diacritical relation to dominant publics—whether in the United States, Europe, South Korea, or an increasingly transnational public sphere. The adoptee counterpublic also exists within a broader field of transnational adoption, which includes adoption agencies, adoptive parents, Korean social workers and legislators, and NGOs, but it does not exist in parallel with one single state authority. It is "counter" in that it has remapped the boundary between public and private by bringing intimate narratives and expressions of adoptee subjectivity into multiple national and transnational public spheres, with different effects in different locations. For instance, in the second half of the book I discuss the work of activist adoptees who are engaged in a social movement to gain legitimate belonging and citizenship in South Korea. These projects have relevance to evolving conceptions of the Korean nation and democracy, thereby rendering adoptee counterpublicity in South Korea more clearly legible in liberal political terms (Fraser 2005).

Conducting an ethnography of a deterritorialized social formation presented me with particular methodological challenges. I chose to focus my attention on American adoptee groups, but in Korea and at adoptee-related events I also had a chance to meet many European adoptees. Rather than following particular individuals, I designed a multisited project that followed adopted Korean circuits, cohabited their spaces, tracked their discourses, and observed their practices. I had perhaps more mobility and flexibility than most adoptees to travel and spend extended periods of time in a variety of locations, yet I was also constrained by my "nonadoptee" status and my exclusion from "adoptee-only" spaces. From my position as a Korean American nonadoptee outsider, I came to understand how adoptees, who shared a feeling of always being an outsider or misfit, inverted normative terms of social belonging and personhood to construct themselves as insiders (Goffman 1963). And by tracking the mobilities of and interconnections among adoptees, I discovered not only how online communication facilitated adoptee networking but also how face-to-face encounters, especially at major conferences, were vital to the production of what is widely referred to as the "Korean adoptee community."[7]

I spent a total of six years trailing and tracking the adoptee community, with a concentrated period of fifteen months of fieldwork in the United States and Korea. Seven months were spent conducting in-depth interviews with core members of American adult adoptee organizations in Minneapolis, New York, Los Angeles, Chicago, and Boston. The adoptees in my study regularly traveled across the country to meet each other at gatherings and conferences, participated in electronic mailing lists, and visited Korea on motherland tours. In addition, many of them also attended the Gathering conference in Seoul in 2004. By being situated at key moments and locations and mirroring their movements and practices, I was able to witness how adoptees travel and cross paths and, through these transitory moments of intense sociality, construct normative forms of belonging and identification in a transnational circuit (Rouse 1991). In total, I formally interviewed forty-one Korean adoptees who were active in community building and activism, and I had contact with dozens more, through informal interactions at collective events.

In Seoul I conducted research in a more spatially coherent yet complex urban field composed of expatriate adoptee social networks, adoptee advocacy organizations, and government-sponsored motherland tours. A total of eleven months of fieldwork in Korea involved volunteering at the Overseas Koreans Foundation (OKF), a government-run agency that was established as part of the government's proactive cultural and economic globalization policy that sought to reach out to ethnic Koreans worldwide. I was a volunteer for their annual motherland tour for adult adopted Koreans for three years, and I also volunteered with three adoptee-advocacy NGOs in Korea. I conducted interviews with social workers, adoptee advocates, European and American adoptees and adoptee activists, and Korean NGO volunteers.

Thanks to the generosity of funding institutions, I enjoyed a modicum of transnational mobility for a short time, but in the process I faced the dilemma of belatedness—the anxiety and actuality of missing ethnographically rich and conceptually crucial moments because I seemed so often to be in transit, even if that meant a half-hour subway ride between two locations within the sprawling metropolitan area of Seoul (Passaro 1997). My ethnographic practice shares similarities with Andrea Louie's "mobile anthropology" (2004) in which she herself became the subject of research, and also with Louisa Schein's "itinerant anthropology" (1998) in which she positioned herself as a nexus and translator between translocal sites. But eventually I came to think of what I was doing as "roving" because it conveys my experience of the disjunctive nature of multisited ethnography—the indecisive pull in multiple directions at once.

It was in Korea that I began to question how my own peregrinations and the circulation of my written work not only mapped but in some ways also constituted the transnational connections that comprise the global network and shaped how it was understood. My project initiated a series of collapses—not only between "field" and "home" (Gupta and Ferguson 1997), thereby implicating shared discursive consciousness ("when they read what we write"; Brettell 1993), the dialogic construction of knowledge, and the "writing machine" of representational excess (Marcus 1999) —but also between myself as a roving researcher and my increasingly siteless field, which seemed to be recursively (re)constituting itself around my own transnational movements.

This concern became heightened at moments when it seemed I was the sole link between the sites I was examining, and when I considered that the groups and individuals I knew had themselves never met face-to-face. But I also knew that there were other linkages that I didn't know about or was unable to witness firsthand. Part of this fieldwork vertigo was an effect of being in the network (Riles 2001; Latour 2003) and participating in the production of its artifacts and also in collective representations and performances in which the global scale and scope of "the community" were made to seem real and palpable. The main aesthetic form for the adoptee network is the list (Riles 2001)—that is, lists of objectives for the network, lists of organizations that compose it, the countries in which adoptees live, their names, the adoption agencies which placed them, and so forth. I also participated in the production and reproduction of lists (Overseas Koreans Foundation 2004) and thus in the representation of the community to itself as well as through engaging adoptees in discussions about the community, whether it exists, and why it's important. Verification of the community manifested in the adoptees' talk of the community as something that was already there prior to their discovering it.

The impossibility of grasping the network as a social totality was also expressed by Liselotte Birkmose, a key organizer of the 2004 Gathering. As she told me, "It's a network that's not really a network, honestly speaking." The deterritorialized adoptee network in its unrepresentability and lack of an "outside" has come to take on the same features of the "network" as an analytic metaphor. Bruno Latour (1993) describes networks as intermediary arrangements between local and global, composed of partial views and pathways. As an imagined transnational series of relations, "the network" affords no one person a privileged view of it, but many people are engaged in sustaining and reproducing it through local actions. As I traced the movements of adoptees, I could more clearly imagine my own views and pathways.

When I returned to New York, the field as network was still with me, or rather it was there to be dipped into daily through a phone call via Skype to an adoptee friend in Korea or an online instant messsaging chat, through the various adoptee conferences that were being planned or held in the United States, Europe, and Korea and through my writing and presenting at those conferences, or at colleges and universities where adoptees attended my talks. As I participated at one location, putting information and opinions into circulation, my words entered into a dialogic and polyvocal field, and I also began to take on force myself—as translator, transmitter of information, and producer of knowledge.

In effect, this ethnography is bounded by time and in space through its focus on what I learned from interviewing and socializing with adoptees in a variety of locations and contexts using a range of mediated technologies. It centers on the years between 1999 and 2004 and is bookended by the first and third Gathering conferences. These events are historic ones that have made the adoptee community visible to itself and that have created spaces for adoptee subjectivity to be performed and discursively produced. My ongoing connections and collaborations with adoptee activists and scholars has also informed my revisions to this work as I've become associated with a growing cadre of Korean adoption researchers, many of whom are adopted. My ethnographic representation of the adoptee counterpublic is, therefore, undeniably partial (Clifford 1988) in both senses of the word—it is constrained by physical limitations imposed on my roving methodology and it is informed by my positioned views on Korean adoption that have been deeply shaped by my relationships with adoptees.

I caution against viewing the Korean adoptees in this book as being representative of the broader Korean adoptee population. Transnational adoption is a highly contested practice in American and transnational public spheres and adoptees are not exempt from moralizing discourses about children's best interests and the best practices in adoption. Aside from insisting upon a more nuanced understanding of adoptee experiences rather than reducing them to quantifiably positive or negative outcomes, I encourage readers to approach this book as an ethnography that attempts to understand an emergent social formation and not as a portrait of "Korean adoptee identity." I resist the taxonomic desire to catalogue adoptees within the rubrics of the Asian American or Korean American communities. Rather than taking adoptee "culture" or "identity" as my object of analysis, therefore, I examine the social imaginary of Korean adoptees as it emerged in the midst of particular historical conjunctures, ideologies, and technologies. Even as some adoptees are engaged and invested in strategic essentialist definitions of collective identity (Spivak 1988), I frame these representations as situated, performative acts directed at broader publics and structured by particular political projects.

Against "outcome" studies that aim to provide recommendations that support or denounce international adoption as a child welfare system, I draw attention to the deep ambivalence that characterizes many adoptee narratives. This is an ambivalence that allows one to say with confidence and without contradiction that one is happy to have been adopted and that one cannot imagine a different or more loving family, but also that these joys coexist with a sense of loss and sadness for people, places, and experiences barely remembered or never known. It also allows for the adoptees who were raised in abusive or dysfunctional homes to be able to express their rage and also their desire to find better, less drastic, solutions for children in need. As one adoptee put it to me, adoptees live within the dialectic of loss and gain, and it is this dialectic, I argue, that produces the ambiguous figure of the transnational adoptee and that deserves focused analysis. Adoptees' split temporality and shape-shifting transnationality encompass the complexities and contradictions of the global and also illuminate the ways in which we all negotiate contingencies of personhood out of insufficient and mutable categories of the biological and the social.

A NOTE ON THE ADULT ADOPTEE

My research is organized around what might seem to be a culturally constructed and variable distinction between children and adults. As I argue in this book, adoptee conferences are ritual-like performances that consecrate and institute adoptees as adults. Therefore, in choosing to focus on and to use the term "adult adoptee," I follow what has become a convention among adoptee organization leaders. The "adult" in "adult adoptee" refers to chronological age, which generally hews to the distinctions made between minors and adults in national legal conventions. The importance of age in determining who can participate in adoptee activities is reflected in how national and cultural conceptions of adulthood have been

Table 1 Korean children adopted overseas annually (1953–2008)

YEAR	NO.	YEAR	NO.	YEAR	NO.	YEAR	NO.	YEAR	NO.	YEAR	NO.
		1960	638	1970	1,932	1980	4,144	1990	2,962	2000	2,360
		1961	660	1971	2,725	1981	4,628	1991	2,197	2001	2,436
		1962	254	1972	3,490	1982	6,434	1992	2,045	2002	2,365
1953	4	1963	442	1973	4,688	1983	7,263	1993	2,290	2003	2,287
1954	8	1964	462	1974	5,302	1984	7,924	1994	2,262	2004	2,258
1955	59	1965	451	1975	5,077	1985	8,837	1995	2,180	2005	2,010
1956	671	1966	494	1976	6,597	1986	8,680	1996	2,080	2006	1,899
1957	486	1967	626	1977	6,159	1987	7,947	1997	2,057	2007	1,264
1958	930	1968	949	1978	5,917	1988	6,463	1998	2,443	2008	1,250
1959	741	1969	1,190	1979	4,148	1989	4,191	1999	2,409		
	2,899		6,166		46,035		66,511		22,925		18,129

Note: The total number of overseas adoptions between 1953 and 2008 is 162,665.
Sources: Data from Hübinette 2005; South Korean Ministry for Health, Welfare and Family Affairs (MIHWAF) 2009

incorporated into international adoptee activities. For instance, at the Gathering conference in Seoul in 2004, the age eligibility for participants from North America and Australia was set at twenty-one, whereas for adoptees from Europe it was set at eighteen. This difference between European and other adoptees was based loosely on legal drinking age, which tends to be lower in European countries (sixteen to eighteen) than it is in North America and Australia (eighteen to twenty-one), and also on a rather ill-defined notion of maturity and perception of readiness.

Following these definitions of adulthood, the adoptees that I met and who were my principal interlocutors were among those born or adopted between 1953 and 1986. In that thirty-three-year period, approximately 103,000 Korean children were adopted overseas, out of an estimated total of 162,665 (table 1). Adoptions during the 1970s alone accounted for 46,000 of those adoptions, and the annual rates continued to climb in the 1980s with a total of 66,511 adoptions in that decade. The majority of these children were sent to the United States, France, Sweden, Denmark, Norway, and the Netherlands, with fewer numbers of children going to Belgium, Australia, Germany, Canada, and Switzerland (table 2). Hence, during the period of my fieldwork, the great majority of the adoptees who

Table 2 Korean children adopted overseas by receiving country, 1953–2008

PRIMARY COUNTRIES (1953–2008)		OTHER COUNTRIES (1960–1995)	
United States 1953–2008	109,242	New Zealand 1964–84	559
France 1968–2008	11,165	Japan 1962–82	226
Sweden 1957–2005	9,051	Okinawa 1970–72	94
Denmark 1965–2008	9,297	Ireland 1968–75	12
Norway 1955–2008	6,295	Poland 1970	7
Netherlands 1969–2003	4,099	Spain 1968	5
Belgium 1969–95	3,697	China 1967–68	4
Australia 1969–2008	3,359	Guam 1971–72	3
Germany 1965–96	2,352	India 1960–64	3
Canada 1967–2008	2,181	Paraguay 1969	2
Switzerland 1968–97	1,111	Ethiopia 1961	1
Luxembourg 1984–2008	561	Finland 1984	1
Italy 1965–2008	383	Hong Kong 1973	1
England 1958–81	72	Tunisia 1969	1
		Turkey 1969	1
		Other 1956–95	113
		Total	163,898

Sources: Hübinette 2004; South Korean Ministry for Health, Welfare and Family Affairs (MIHWAF) 2009

participated in adoptee events and the majority of my informants were between twenty and forty and had been raised in the United States or in Scandinavia. Women tended to outnumber men in most activities by around two to one, which reflects the greater numbers of girls adopted during those decades.

In the United States, the largest wave of adoptee migrants coincided with the post-1965 expansion of Korean immigration to the United States, and Korean adoptees comprise an estimated 10 percent of the total Korean American population. Since the 1960s, agencies based in Minnesota, Oregon, Iowa, and Pennsylvania have been active in Korean adoptions (S. H. Park 1994: 166–67). At the peak of adoptions from South Korea in the 1980s, there were thirty-three United States agencies coordinating adoptions from the four designated overseas adoption agencies in Korea. The states with the highest concentrations of adopted Korean children are those in proximity to the adoption agencies that have had the closest ties to Korean agencies. Therefore, the majority of children were placed in the Midwest (Minnesota, Wisconsin, Iowa, Nebraska, Michigan, Montana, South Dakota), the Pacific Northwest (Oregon and Washington), the Northeast (New York, New Jersey, Massachusetts, and Vermont), and the West (Utah and Idaho), with very few in the Southwest or in the South.

Adoptee groups have been established in metropolitan centers with concentrations of adoptee residents, including Stockholm, Copenhagen, Oslo, Paris, Brussels, Amsterdam, New York City, Los Angeles, San Francisco, Minneapolis, Seattle, Portland, Chicago, Boston, and Seoul. According to IKAA, ten thousand adoptees are members of the dozen organizations that fall under its umbrella. Thus, out of the roughly one hundred thousand Korean adoptees worldwide who are over the age of eighteen, an estimated 10 percent are associated with the broader adoptee community.

BEING A NONADOPTEE

In the chapters that follow I foreground my own status as a nonadoptee because it was a key limitation in my relations with adoptees, even with those who welcomed me as fictive kin as an honorary adoptee or as someone who'd been "adopted by adoptees." As I discuss in chapter 4, adoptee social practices are organized around shared storytelling, which composes adoptee collective histories. As a nonadoptee, I have no story to tell, except in response to the question that is inevitably asked by adoptees and nonadoptees alike: How did you get interested in studying adoption? The question itself often begs for a personal story—that an intimate or family member is adopted, for instance—and when I do start to tell "my story" I often get the impression that the answer, or lack of a relevant answer, is a disappointment to the listener.

My story, then, begins with my being a second-generation Korean American woman who, like many adoptees, first got wind of what was then an emergent Korean adoptee counterpublic while surfing the Internet. It was July 1999 and I was surprised and intrigued by the numbers I read on the Website of the Korean American Adoptee Adoptive Family Network (KAAN): 140,000 Korean children have been adopted worldwide since the end of the Korean War, mostly to white families in the West. I soon learned that the numbers were closer to 150,000 or 200,000, and given the scale of this migration I was perplexed by the fact that I had never heard of it before. Upon further reflection I realized that I had known in passing a few adoptees in my childhood but they existed on the periphery of my consciousness; that is, they were remembered not as adoptees but as Tommy or Mary who were adopted from Korea and whose parents were white. In finding Websites for adult adoptee organizations and watching the films of adult adopted Korean artists, I began to suspect that there was a progressive and politically minded set of adoptees coming of age and forming a social movement. What I found was that most adoptees were engaged in journeys of self-exploration rather than in activism per se, but that there was a latent tension around the politics of adoption, notably its pros and cons—the very tension that came to the surface in the anecdote that opened this chapter.

Even if my story about how I became interested in adoption was not particularly compelling for the adoptees to whom I recounted it, I was clear about my goals and intentions: I was interested in the agency and social mobilization of adoptees and not in compiling and analyzing personal biographies, which are the object of much pop psychologizing and voyeuristic fetishization in the media and in the academic world. Thus, my interviews with adoptees, although they may have covered the vital stats of their adoption histories (i.e., when they were adopted, to where, and from where), focused on adoptees as social actors and their participation in and views on the emergence of Korean adoptee cultural and political identity.

Despite my outsider status and my inability to tell the right kind of story, my friendships and rapport with adoptees were clearly built upon shared generational consciousness, experiences of racialization in the West, and educational and class dispositions. In Korea, many adoptees are themselves immersed in ethnographic explorations of Korean culture and investigations of the history and practices of the adoption system. Thus, I shared with some of the most activist of adoptees a common intellectual project—namely, scrutinizing Korean adoption as a field of practice and constructing Korean adoption as an object of knowledge. Part of my "circumstantial activism" (Marcus 1998) has been to locate and make accessible information about the historical and cultural contexts of Korean adoption, thus helping to provide a critical history for adoptees, many of whom also lack basic details of their personal histories.[8] What follows is a provisional attempt in this direction.

SITUATING KOREAN TRANSNATIONAL ADOPTION

Adoption from South Korea has continued uninterrupted for more than five decades and constitutes the longest and largest such program in the world. Until the mid-1990s, on an annual basis the nation was sending more children overseas than any other country. According to the South Korean Ministry for Health Welfare and Family Affairs (MIHWAF), between 1953 and 2008 a total of 161,665 children were adopted into families in more than twenty-nine different countries, with the vast majority sent to North America and Western Europe (tables 1 and 2).[9] The reasons for adoption are complex and have shifted over the course of the past half century, and at every stage they have been shaped by conjunctures of state control over population and the management of bodies (Foucault 1990), gendered practices of moral persuasion and coercion (what Ann Anagnost [1997] in the context of China's population policies calls "euphemized violence"),[10] and the unevenness of Korea's fitful modernization—all of which help to determine "who is considered to be in the national body and who out of it" (Ginsburg and Rapp 1995: 3).

Unwittingly implicated in cold war geopolitics and policies of a global developmentalist regime (Escobar 1995), these legally designated "orphans" were actually victims of poverty, social dislocation, and gender inequality. They were escorted onto planes and emerged at arrival gates around the Western world to be embraced by new families, given new names, and enter entirely new social worlds. More than 75 percent were adopted into American families, with the rest going to families in Western Europe, Canada, and Australia. Overseas adoptions steadily increased throughout the 1960s and 1970s, from 638 in 1960 to nearly 6,600 in 1976. The peak was in 1985, with more than 8,800 adoptions in that year alone, and reductions in adoptions since 1989 have leveled off to approximately 2,300 children per year in the decade of the 1990s.

As I describe in chapter 1, the first adoptions from Korea were part of an emergency effort to rescue war orphans and "mixed-blood" GI children (*honhyŏla*) in the aftermath of the Korean conflict. Overseas adoption, however, continued well past the initial crisis phase and quickly transformed into a surrogate welfare system that Western observers at the time believed was encouraging the relinquishment of children (Chakerian 1968). As Korea industrialized, large numbers of abandoned children were

Table 3 Adoption circumstances of overseas adopted Koreans, 1958–2008

YEAR	ABANDONED	BROKEN HOME	SINGLE MOTHER	TOTAL
1958–60	1,675	630	227	2,532
1961–70	4,013	1,958	1,304	7,275
1971–80	17,260	13,360	17,627	48,247
1981–90	6,769	11,399	47,153	65,321
1991–2000	225	1,444	20,460	22,129
2001	1	1	2,434	2,436
2002	1	0	2,364	2,365
2003	2	2	2,283	2,287
2004	0	1	2,257	2,258
2005	4	28	2,069	2,101
2006	4	5	1,890	1,899
2007	11	2	1,251	1,264
2008	10	126	1,114	1,250
Total	29,975	28,956	102,433	161,364

Source: South Korean Ministry for Health, Welfare and Family Affairs (MIHWAF) 2009

a consequence of rapid economic and structural transformations and cold war era population and development policies intended to build national stability. In the initial decades, poor and working-class women, widows, or single mothers gave up children due to poverty and social stigma. In addition, men living outside of the extended family structure were unable to raise children on their own, and they relinquished children due to divorce and a patriarchal family head system (*hojujedo*) that granted sole legal custody to fathers. Since the late 1990s, middle-class and working-class young women and teenage girls have constituted the great majority of birth mothers (table 3). It has been argued that Korea's international adoption system not only retarded the development of domestic adoption and child welfare policies, but also provided a quick-fix solution that has been complicit in the social disenfranchisement of Korean women (Sarri, Baik, and Bombyk 1998).

In industrializing South Korea, propaganda campaigns, sterilization programs, the promotion of emigration, and international adoption were all part of a more universal state project to check population growth in the name of modernization and economic development. The demand from the West for adoptable children coincided with the concerns of the Korean state, thereby making Korean adoptions appear to be a viable solution to the nation's immediate social welfare problems. Offering economic relief from demographic pressures, these adoptions were also valued as literal "foreign relations" by creating intimate links between Korea and Western nations. Whereas transnational adoption developed out of a confluence of biopolitical and geopolitical interests in Korea, from the perspective of the receiving countries, transnational adoption offered a (new) reproductive technology—one that has become an increasingly commodified "choice" existing alongside a number of other, stratified consumer options for would-be parents.

Transnational Adoption as Stratified Reproduction

According to the demographer Peter Selman (2007), the total global transfers of children nearly tripled from a mean annual rate of approximately sixteen thousand children in the 1980s to nearly forty-five thousand in 2004. Related to trends in delayed childbearing and reduced fertility in the West, this expansion was most dramatic in the United States. The legalization of abortion, welfare support for and social acceptability of single parenthood, a domestic shortage in white babies available for adoption, and the power granted to birth mothers in "open adoptions" have been directly related to the increase in demand for transnational adoptions. Bringing a needy third world child into a first world home, once considered to be a gesture of humanitarianism, has now become an option of last resort in which the world's youngest and healthiest infants are highly sought within a broader field of new reproductive technologies (Lovelock 2000). Media reports and adoption agency social workers reproduce the idea that parents suffering from infertility turn to adoption after they have exhausted their own financial or physical capabilities in the quest for genetically related children. A closer look, however, reveals that humanitarian motives and egocentric desires are often more complexly intertwined in the choices that adoptive parents make, both in the past and at present.

Transnational adoption conforms to what Shellee Colen identified as "stratified reproduction," a "transnational, highly stratified system" in which "physical and social reproductive tasks are accomplished differentially according to inequalities that are based on hierarchies of class, race, ethnicity, gender, and place in a global economy, and migration status and that are structured by social, economic and political forces" (1995: 78). In other words, global inequalities determine the scope of women's reproductive choices and the distribution of reproductive labor, often serving to reproduce the stratifications on which those inequalities are based. The production of intimate kin relations out of stark economic and political asymmetries and the intensification of these inequalities in the global "free market" constitute the mundane and troubling heart of transnational adoption.

For instance, the ability of women in the West to choose to adopt from overseas is based upon the constrained choices of underprivileged women in developing countries who often have few options but to surrender their children for adoption (Perry 1998; Cornell 1999). Critics of international adoption (Masson 2001; Perry 1998; Hollingsworth 2003) view transnational adoption as a flawed system that encourages the exploitation of third world women's labor in lieu of reforming the structural inequalities that force women to give up their children. Moreover, the children who benefit from international adoption represent but a tiny fraction of the millions of needy children around the world who struggle for basic survival. In the case of Korea, one might argue that the nation's modernization miracles complicate the characterization of Korean adoption as a form of stratified reproduction. Yet just as a few hundred African American mothers send their children to Europe and Canada every year for adoption, imagining a better, less racist future for their children outside of the United States, the Korean women who relinquish their children today are, despite the nation's wealth, located in subordinated class, race, and gender positions that structure their abilities to mother their children and that render it imaginable and even desirable to send their children to Europe or the United States for a "better life."

Stratifications of gender and race are unmistakably reproduced in transnational adoption, which has been predominated by Asian female children. Especially in light of the condemnation in 1972 by the National Association of Black Social Workers of placements of black children in white homes as cultural genocide, the adoption of Asian babies has been construed as a safe choice for financially able Americans to adopt more "flexibly" racialized children who not only are more easily assimilated but whose birth parents are less likely to make claims on their children (Dorow 2006). As the transracial adoption of black and Native American children came to a virtual halt in the early 1970s, transracial transnational Korean adoption rapidly expanded and became fully installed as an institutionalized practice.

Claudia Castañeda critiques the ways in which the transnational transracial adopted child is appropriated as a sign of racial harmony or multicultural idealism, and thus "becomes the global" (2002: 104). This utopic, colorblind approach reduces the child's racialization to a flexible and optional "racial makeup" that is dehistoricized and made to be culturally insignificant (94). The relative flexibility of a child's racial makeup is also, however, largely dependent upon global hierarchies of race that intersect gender and age categories. For instance, model-minority myths about Asian immigrants coincide with predominant views of infant Asian girls as most likely to be accepted in white homes and communities. In contrast, older black boys in foster care have been stigmatized as the least "redeemable" (Dorow 2006) and most risky. The disregard of racial difference in Asian adoptions is reflected in social work terminology, which reserved "transracial" for black-white placements and "international" or "intercountry" adoptions for adoptions across national borders.

The shifting tides of American adoption ideologies have had ripple effects on Korean adoptions, both international and domestic, over the past five decades. From the 1950s through 1970s, the "sealed and secret" adoptions promoted in American contexts provided the model for modern Korean adoptions, in which legal relinquishment was accompanied by the cutting of any prior familial ties (Modell 2002). When the adoptee rights movement and birth mother groups in the United States first began advocating for openness in adoption in the 1970s they paved the way for "open adoptions," the form that is most prevalent in the United States today. Views on adoption and the importance of kinship knowledge shifted dramatically from pathologizing adoptees' desire for knowledge about origins to stigmatizing adoptees' disinterest in seeking out their origins. During this tumultuous time in American adoption, however, Korean adoptions, along with most international adoptions, remained "closed," and Korean adoptees have only just begun to make headway in their struggle for rights to information. Transnational adoptees who seek information about their natal families are no doubt influenced by the shift to openness in domestic American adoptions, and the difficult and painful searches undertaken by Korean parents and overseas adoptees suggest that desire for kinship knowledge and potential relationships is potently informed by both Euro-

American and Korean ideologies of blood and a belief in its ability to authenticate identity.

The intense privileging of blood in Korean kinship ideology marks adoption with "the dual stigma of illegitimacy and infertility" that long characterized American adoption (Wegar 1997). In 1977, the anthropologist Mark Peterson described cases of secret surrogate arrangements and of adoptive mothers in Korea disguising themselves to look pregnant in order to make the adopted child seem "natural." Because of this, birth mothers in Korea, now given a choice, reportedly prefer to place children internationally in the hopes of meeting them again in the future, which is less likely to happen if the child is adopted into a Korean family. Thus, even though recent press reports about openly adoptive families are suggestive of changing attitudes toward adoption in Korea, the primacy of blood and patrilineality in Korean kinship are continually cited as major hurdles to the opening of Korean adoption. Indeed, given the low figures in domestic adoption statistics, one must assume that the majority of adoptions that take place in Korea continue to be arranged outside of the adoption agency system. These facts suggest to some observers that Confucianism continues to retain a strong hold on Korean perceptions of legitimate kinship, and that only blood can substantiate family relations. Attitudes toward adoption provide lenses onto contemporary conceptions of family and kinship in Korea, where modernization and Confucian values are often counterposed and considered to be in conflict.

Transnational Adoption and Korean Child Circulation

In studies of Korean kinship, traditional or customary Korean adoption typically refers to a practice that came into prominence during the seventeenth century with the institutionalization of a neo-Confucian orthodoxy in the middle of the Chosŏn period (1392–1910). As Peterson (1996) argues, this form of agnatic adoption (*suyang*) developed during the "Confucian transformation" in which legislative codes permitted only male patrilineal relatives of a younger generation (typically agnatic nephews in their adulthood) to be adopted. Whereas adoptions in the earlier Koryŏ period had been largely concerned with the inheritance of property, these agnatic adoptions were motivated by social norms of patrilineal descent and continuity of ancestral rites (*chesa*) (Deuchler 1992). According to Peterson, this standard for aristocratic (*yangban*) lineages gradually trickled down and became the ideal model for family and social organization across class strata. This neo-Confucian turn in Korean law and society involved a radical conversion from bilateral kinship structures to patrilineal ones, from uxorilocal and ambilocal to patrilocal residence, and from equal inheritance for sons and daughters to inheritance based on primogeniture. Prior to the seventeenth century, women, wives' relatives, and nonkin adoptees could have inheritance rights. With the ascendance of primogeniture, agnatic adoptions became the norm and women's status was reduced through their exclusion from ancestral rites and inheritance. A woman's value became wholly dependent upon her ability to bear a son for her husband's lineage.

Agnatic adoptions of adult male heirs may have become hegemonic, but evidence exists of other social classes engaging in alternative forms of child circulation and fosterage (Roesch-Rhomberg 2004). For instance, peasant families adopted young girls as daughters-in-law (*minmyŏnŭri*) as a strategy of inheritance and marriage (Seth 2006; Kim Harvey 1983; H. O. Park 1998) and some Korean families adopted unrelated children, sometimes to provide care for childless elderly couples and sometimes as servants or slaves (Kim and Henderson 2008; Deuchler 1992). These diverse practices lead Kim and Henderson to assert that "the currently pronounced common belief that the Korean traditional family is based on blood ties and never had space for outsiders is far from the historical situation in the Chosun Dynasty, which was surprisingly more open and benevolent than modern 'traditional attitudes'" (16–17).[11]

Thus, despite historical evidence that Koreans adopted unrelated children before the seventeenth century, most of the South Koreans that Peterson met in the 1970s understood adoption only in neo-Confucian terms, and they found American adoptions of nonrelatives to be "incomprehensible" (1977: 83). Until the 1990s, sex ratios at birth and adoption statistics reflected intense son preference among Koreans, especially as government initiatives to restrict family size encouraged many women to use sex-selective abortion, secret adoptions, or overseas adoption as family planning strategies in their pursuit of a son.

More recently, the social transformations related to industrialization—massive rural to urban migration, the rapid nuclearization of the family, and the precipitous decline in the birthrate—have helped to reduce the significance of ancestral rites, the preference for having sons, and, concomitantly, agnatic adoption. The anthropologist Eunhee Kim Yi's research on the changing Korean family reveals how the nuclearization of the family has promoted stronger bonds between natal parents and their daughters, who are more highly valued and less likely to be treated as outsiders. Sons are no longer considered to be dependable supports for parents in their old age, and as such "the old practice of adopting a son from agnates has almost disappeared. None of those who had only daughters told me about plans to adopt a son. This decline in the practice of adoption shows that the importance of *jesa* [ancestral rites] has weakened. But it also reflects changes in the perception of the relationship between the mother and the son. In responses to questions about adoption, people often comment that even their own son does not want to live with his old parents and that people want to give property to their own daughter, the blood child, rather than to distant agnates" (2001: 24). As this brief survey suggests, the factors that constitute modern or traditional Korean gender identities, kinship relations, and adoption are continually under construction (Kendall 2002). Even though adoption and extramarital births retain a strong social stigma, publicly acknowledged adoptions (*konggae ibyang*) are slowly gaining visibility in the Korean media and have become something of a trend among young celebrities. Adoption (*ibyang*) in Korea has thereby ceased to refer to agnatic inheritance and instead indicates Western-style agency-facilitated adoptions of nonrelative children, the majority of whom are infant girls.

Transnational Adoption as Transnational Biopolitics

As Faye Ginsburg and Rayna Rapp note, "Throughout history, state power has depended directly and indirectly on defining normative families and controlling populations" (1991: 314). In modernizing South Korea, control of the population was a key concern of the developmentalist state. One could very well consider the first adoptions of mixed-blood children to be a form of "state racism" (Foucault 1997) in the context of President Syngman Rhee's official nationalism that drew upon an ideology of "one people" (*ilminjuŭi*) to buttress his own authoritarian claims to legitimate leadership.[12] The ideology of "one people" borrowed its power from anticolonial era nationalist historiography that posited Korea as an ethnically homogeneous nation based on unbroken ancestry and shared bloodline (Shin 2006). In this context, children of mixed parentage presented a polluting element and also a public relations problem in the midst of cold war hostilities, as they offered clear evidence to North Korean communists of South Korea's dependency on and subordination to postwar American occupying forces (see chapter 1).

In addition to functioning as a mechanism of population control and securing national loyalty through state racism, adoption became a source of foreign capital early during the postwar reconstruction. Between 1951 and 1964, the number of abandoned children at orphanages increased from 715 to 11,319—a remarkable figure that suggests, as Richard Weil notes, that the "presence of efficient foreign adoption facilities encouraged the abandonment of children" (1984: 282). It could well be argued that orphanages (which were largely funded by Western relief organizations), and, later, state-subsidized adoption agencies, functioned as a surrogate welfare system and a conduit for foreign exchange. The period between 1960 and 1975 in which urbanization, education, female employment, and the availability of contraception contributed to the rapid decline in fertility —from 6.3 to 4.2, thus representing "one of the fastest national fertility transitions in recorded history" (Repetto 1981: 3)—also witnessed the rapid amplification of adoptions overseas, from 638 adopted children in 1960 to more than 5,000 in 1975.

These startling statistics, coupled with the propinquity of money and children in transnational adoption and the attendant implications of human trafficking, have made Korea's overseas adoption program a target of criticism throughout its history. The program also played into cold war antagonisms between North and South Korea, when Pyongyang first began its repeated criticism of the South Korean government's liberal adoption policies in 1959. These criticisms reached a peak in the early 1970s and undoubtedly helped to motivate South Korea's decision to reduce the numbers of foreign adoptions and encourage domestic adoption by instituting the Five Year Plan for Adoption and Foster Care (1976–1981) (Sarri, Baik, and Bombyk 1998).[13] Negative reviews also arrived from South Korea's capitalist friends and neighbors when the nation's pride in hosting the 1988 Summer Olympics in Seoul was tainted by reports in the American press asserting that children constituted Korea's "largest export" (Chira 1988a). In 1989, with most countries sending less than one tenth of 1 percent of live births abroad, South Korea was still sending 1 percent of live births (Kane 1993).

In the midst of the most scathing media critiques in the 1980s, it was reported that Korea was making $15 to $20 million per year on adoption, and that the adoption business had become a cost-effective way of dealing with social welfare problems (Herrmann and Kasper 1992; Rothschild 1988; Sarri, Baik, and Bombyk 1998). The cost of international adoptions has increased exponentially since they began, which leads many to question the "not for profit" nature of adoption agencies and to suspect that financial motives lie behind the purported altruism of adoption as a social welfare project. In the first two decades of adoption, prospective parents were responsible for only the immediate costs of immigration documents, medical clearance, and airfare. Today, the average cost for a Korean adoption is around $15,000, and an estimated $6,000 is collected by the Korean agency, which totals $35 million per year when calculating the foreign adoption placements of all four agencies (K. S. Kim 2004). The public welfare services diverted by the state to the four government-approved overseas adoption agencies—prenatal care for unwed mothers, homes for disabled children, and preadoption foster care—are funded by revenue earned from overseas adoption placements.

Whether or not the government actually profited directly from the adoption of its Korean children, as some believe (Rothschild 1988), it is hard not to view Korean children as victims of a misogynistic and patriarchal developmentalist state that encouraged fertility reduction and outmigration as solutions to overpopulation (Moon 1998). As more stories of birth parents surface in the Korean media and from adoptees who are reuniting and learning the circumstances of their relinquishments, a picture of how agencies functioned as agents of biopower has emerged in which hegemonic familist ideologies combined with Eurocentric notions of the child's best interests. The close intertwining of welfare facilities and adoption agencies suggests the existence of a system that was geared toward the efficient processing of children for adoption rather than toward the preservation of existing kinship relations.

Even if adoptions offered economic benefits or alleviation of social welfare burdens for the Korean state, they also continued to symbolize South Korea's dependency on Western aid. Throughout the 1960s and 1970s attempts were made to develop alternative solutions to child welfare, including long-term foster care and domestic adoptions. Shortly after Park Chung Hee's coup d'etat, the Ministry of Health and Social Affairs launched a movement to deinstitutionalize the child welfare system and encourage the raising of children in families. Called "Every Person Should Raise an Orphan" (Koa han saram sik mata kirŭgi undong), this 1962 initiative began by requiring government workers to adopt one child each. This program had mixed results and was eventually discontinued, but efforts to encourage domestic adoption were outlined in special adoption legislation in 1976 (Social Welfare Society 2004).

In the 1980s, these programs were abandoned under the military regime of Chun Doo Hwan. During this decade, overseas adoptions were radically expanded and rationalized as part of an emigration and civil diplomacy (*min'gan oegyo*) project, with unrestricted numbers of children being sent to the West "to improve relations between South Korea and the receiving countries" (S. H. Park 1995). The negative press generated by these adoptions during the 1988 Olympic Games stemmed the tide, and since then international adoptions have been tightly tied to domestic adoption placements through a "quota system." The number of domestic placements made by each agency in any given year determines how many international placements will be permitted in the following year. Since then, domestic adoptions have fluctuated between 1,000 to 1,500 placements per year, and these rates are still considerably lower than those of overseas adoption. Because of the difficulty in placing children domestically, adoption advocates argue that Korea is not ready to suspend its international adoption program, and they insist that Koreans must first begin by changing their Confucian attitudes toward adoption even as they promote conservative versions of best families. Implicit in these views are universalizing paradigms of childhood and children's best interests that paternalistically construe non-Western governments as morally flawed and "incapable of running their own societies" (Pupavac 1998: 6).

Transnational Adoption and Neoliberal Family Values

Attitudes toward adoption not only provide a window onto beliefs and practices of kinship in Korea but also reflect the stratifications of gender and class that accompanied South Korea's rapid yet uneven process of modernization. By the end of the 1950s, the numbers of children categorized as mixed blood began dwindling and full-Korean children constituted the majority of overseas adoptees. Many of these might be more aptly described as economic orphans who were relinquished in large part

Table 4 Overseas adoptions by gender and disability, 1955–2008

YEARS	NO. OF CHILDREN	MALE/FEMALE (%)	HEALTHY/DISABLED (%)[1]
1955–1957	1,216	n/a	n/a
1958–1960	2,532	29.0/71.0	37.3/62.7
1961–1970	7,275	31.1/69.2	71.6/28.4
1971–1980	48,247	35.9/64.1	90.5/9.5
1981–1985	35,078	45.4/54.6	79.9/20.1
1986–1990	30,243	46.6/53.4	69.2/30.8
1991–1995	10,974	50.1/49.9	55.4/44.6
1996	2,080	56.7/43.3	55.0/45.0
1997	2,057	54.6/45.4	61.9/38.1
1998	2,249	57.5/42.5	62.4/37.6
1999	2,409	57.0/43.0	65.8/34.2
2000	2,360	60.3/39.7	73.1/26.9
2001	2,436	55.9/44.1	69.5/30.5
2002	2,365	58.3/41.7	65.0/35.0
2003	2,287	59.8/40.2	71.6/28.4
2004	2,258	61.3/38.7	68.8/31.2
2005	2,101	64.4/35.6	64.9/35.1
2006	1,899	66.0/34.0	62.5/37.5
2007	1,264	57.1/42.9	60.4/39.6
2008	1,250	61.8/38.2	91.4/8.6

Sources: Ha 2002; South Korean Ministry for Health, Welfare and Family Affairs (MIHWAF) 2009
[1]Children are categorized as "normal" (*chŏngsang*) or "disabled" (*changae*) in South Korean government statistics. In the past, the categories were "normal" and "abnormal" (*pichŏngsang*) with the latter category inclusive of mixed-race children. In the recent past, children in the disabled category have included those with a range of conditions, from relatively minor and/or treatable conditions to more severe, congenital diseases.

due to extreme poverty and a lack of social service options. A preference for sons was evident in the sex ratio of children adopted throughout the 1960s and 1970s, during which time between 60 and 70 percent were girls. But since the 1980s, as the average family size shrank and the main cause for adoption relinquishments shifted from poverty to out-of-wedlock births, gender ratios have become nearly evenly balanced (tables 3 and 4). In addition, because domestic adopters have shifted their preferences from boys to girls in the last decade, an excess of boys is now being adopted overseas.

Whereas the women who relinquished their children in the 1960s and 1970s tended to be poor factory workers, as South Korea's economic boom took off in the 1980s, unmarried college-age women were releasing their infants. In the late 1990s, an increasing trend in teen pregnancies supported the supply of adoptable children. Today, nearly all the children adopted overseas are infants born to unwed mothers in their late teens and early twenties. The births take place in "homes for unwed mothers" (*mihonmo chip*) run by the adoption agencies, and the babies are cared for by agency-paid foster mothers until their departures to their Western families (W. J. Kim 1994).[14]

In 2008 the government announced to great fanfare that, for the first time in history, domestic placements in 2007 had exceeded those of international ones, thereby suggesting that the "domestic adoption first" programs had been effective and that international adoption would soon be regarded as a thing of the past. A closer look at the numbers, however, suggested more complicated circumstances. Korean domestic adoptions had been on a steady decline since 1999, and the 1,300 placements in 2007 actually represented a low point in domestic adoption. Indeed, it was the restrictions placed on international placements rather than an increase in domestic adoptions that accounted for the historic shift. It would seem that the exigencies of statistical targets were being privileged over the welfare of needy children. The celebration over the numerical reversal diverted attention away from the state's longstanding reluctance to devote more resources to social welfare, including protections for women and children, programs to prevent unplanned pregnancies and child abandonment, and economic support to single mothers.

At this writing, the future of Korean adoption remains uncertain given Korea's economic instability and sensitivity to international opinion. But the "problem" of adoption (*ibyang munje*)—a question of national pride—is continually attributed by journalists and policy officials alike to the tradition-bound blood obsession of Koreans (*hyŏlt'ongjuŭi*), who, it is argued, need to become more open to Western forms of adoption. State policies are likewise premised on the notion that residual Confucian values stand in the way of solving the adoption problem, and that abandoned children constitute a cultural problem rooted in the refusal of Korean citizens to take responsibility for their children. In presuming that domestic adoption is the only solution to the overseas adoption problem, policymakers and cultural observers discount the possibility of birth mothers keeping and raising their children, as a growing number reportedly would choose to do, if they had the necessary financial and social support.

There are an estimated eighteen thousand children currently living in welfare institutions and an estimated ten thousand children born to unmarried women in Korea each year. South Korean and international adopters can only partially alleviate the problems of all abandoned Korean children, a situation that creates hierarchies of desirability and disability—perfect infants and "waiting" or "special needs" children. Public education campaigns encouraging greater receptiveness to domestic adoption have been instituted by adoption agencies in South Korea, and increasing openness among parents of adopted children has helped to reduce some of the stigma of adoption in South Korea. Yet familist ideologies that spurn nonnormative, nonnuclear family arrangements continue to conspire with entrenched patriarchal values and conservative sexual moralities in the "euphemized violence" that governs and constrains the reproductive choices of single women.

In effect, state policies reinforce the conservative family values that disparage motherhood outside of marriage. For instance, under the "domestic adoption first" policy initiative, "singles" (*toksinja*) became eligible to adopt children, thereby allowing never-married, divorced, or widowed individuals to qualify as parents. In the context of Korea, where Confucianism and blood ideology are often blamed for the adoption problem, extending adoption rights to those who are already nonnormative householders might appear to be a solution that embraces a liberalized view of the family. At the same time, however, the policy implicitly reinforces the censure of extramarital sex and motherhood by creating a hierarchy of singles—those who are parents through adoption and rewarded with state subsidies versus those who are single mothers outside of marriage and therefore less deserving of provisions that might make it economically feasible for them to keep and raise their children. Recent experiments in group living and innovative fund-raising practices by independent unwed mothers' homes represent a few responses by these women and their advocates to help them raise their children in the face of social stigma and inadequate welfare support. As such, they are producing new kinds of households based on communal living and childcare arrangements that are minimally dependent upon the state, but, unlike single adopters, their efforts go unrewarded and uncelebrated.

These developments are occurring alongside the emergence of new postmodern representations of gendered identity in postmodern South Korea. A prominent example of these new identities is the "Miss Mom" character that has appeared in various domains of public culture. She is financially independent, sexually empowered, and unencumbered by tradition (Lankov 2008). In these narratives, unwed motherhood is framed as a choice for privileged women who reject marriage but embrace maternity. Thus, the shameful, secretive *mihonmo*, which literally means "not yet married mother," is now accompanied by its neoliberal doppelganger, the *pihonmo*, which means "unmarried mother," but that connotes self-fulfillment through sexual freedom and class-based entitlement. Whether these images of emancipated pihonmo will further marginalize actual mihonmo (who do not enter into motherhood based on choice but through what might appear to be residual forms of patriarchal oppression and victimhood) or whether they will foster the acceptance of alternative kinds of parenting and family life is an open question. What is clear, however, is that neoliberal rationalities and global imaginaries are increasingly influencing the value placed on women's reproductive choices and capacities.

THE STRUCTURE OF THE BOOK

This book is organized into two sections. In the first section, I situate Korean adoption and the emergence of the Korean adult adoptee counterpublic within the political and economic transformations of the late twentieth century. I describe in detail in chapter 1 how adoption to the United States developed in the immediate aftermath of the Korean War. In chapters 2 and 3, I contextualize adoptee personhood by analyzing how common experiences of alienation and disidentification with dominant categories of kinship and citizenship serve as the grounds for the adoptee social imaginary. In chapter 4, I bring ethnographic focus to adoptee counterpublic activities at the Gathering conferences, which become the sites for ritual-like performances of categorical and collective adoptee personhood. In part II, I shift the focus and location of analysis to South Korea. I examine the South Korean government's recognition of adoptees as "overseas Koreans" in chapter 5, by closely analyzing problems of cultural citizenship that confront adoptees who live and work in Korea. I extend this analysis in chapter 6 to consider the relationship of returning adoptees and the Korean NGOs that emerged in the late 1990s to help them. The concluding chapter unpacks the figure of the humanitarian orphan in order to show how it continues to influence the political subjectivity of adoptee activists and their attempts to intervene into hegemonic discourses about adoption and child welfare.

Part I

1

"Waifs" and "Orphans"

The Origins of Korean Adoption

Bertha Holt's *The Seed from the East* (1956), an account of her husband Harry's pivotal role in the history of international Korean adoption, offers this vivid summary on the back cover: "Korea . . . 1954 . . . Thousands of children suffered in crowded, understaffed and poorly supplied orphanages—children, it seemed, that no one wanted. But God gave one couple a heart to love these children. This most ordinary family—a lumberman with a heart condition, a farming wife and six children—changed the world when they adopted eight Korean-Amerasian children. The story of the Harry Holt family testifies to God's ability to use ordinary people to bring about extraordinary change. Intercountry adoption flourishes today, largely because God used the faith and determination of the Holts to adopt homeless children into families of their own." This is, in fact, the story that is conventionally told about the origins of Korean overseas adoption.[1] Not only a narrative of Christian charity and divine selection, it is also one of the "extraordinary" capabilities (even if God given) of "ordinary" individuals. The key characters in this story are thousands of needy children, a quintessential American frontier figure, and a Christian God. Bertha Holt, Harry's "farming wife," penned *The Seed from the East* (1956) and also *Bring My Sons from Afar* (1986),[2] both of which borrow their titles from verses in the Book of Isaiah. These are the primary texts that compose the legendary story of Harry's efforts to bring Korean children to families in the West.

It is undeniable that Harry Holt played an instrumental role in helping intercountry adoption to flourish, and for many in Korea the Holt name is virtually synonymous with overseas adoption and child welfare.[3] Yet, fifty years later, the mythic stature of Holt as represented in Bertha's books and by Holt Adoption Agency (now Holt International Children's Services) is being challenged by many who are critical of how international adoption developed into a quick fix for the problems of child welfare in the global South and a solution to childlessness in the North (see Sarri, Baik, and Bombyk 1998).

The construction of adoption as an expression of humanistic altruism is perhaps most easily defended by those who benefit from the discrepancies in economic, social, political, and gendered power between Western parents and those elsewhere. Yet some of those beneficiaries, the adoptees themselves, have developed penetrating critiques of contemporary adoption. Dismayed to know that Korea continues to send an average of five or six babies abroad every day, they consider Holt's humanitarian mission to be an example of another quintessentially American figure—the missionary as cultural imperialist (Bruining 1989; Hübinette 2004; Nopper 2004; Trenka, Oparah, and Shin 2006).[4]

These negative views of Holt, while informed by contemporary cultural politics, are not, however, entirely new. Holt was, from the beginning of his child-rescue crusade, a controversial figure in the media and the object of vigorous opposition by professional social workers and child welfare specialists in the United States who found his "unorthodox" placement methods to be dangerous for the children he transplanted and for the families that received them.[5] In addition, although Korean children dominated worldwide international adoption placements well into the early 1990s, this phenomenon can only be properly understood in the context of the international adoptions from Europe and Japan that evolved directly out of the Second World War and American geopolitical ascendance in the early years of the cold war. The patriotic pronatalism of 1950s America —which linked American cultural citizenship and national security with parenthood and the nuclear family (May 1988)—combined with a middlebrow internationalist ethos (Klein 2003) that encouraged everyday Americans to imagine themselves as participants in world events are also important to my analysis of how international adoption came to be a rationalized and institutionalized practice around those first Korean placements. The concerns that social workers, anthropologists, psychologists, and others voiced in the initial years of international and transracial adoption resonate in the debates that continue to be waged over the benefits and costs of adoption today.

I begin this chapter with a discussion of how Korean children figured in the American social imaginary by examining the images and articles from American print media in the 1950s in which the "Korean waif," as the object of sentimental attachment and rescue for American GIs, frequently appeared. These "waifs of war" and military "mascots" were among the first to be adopted, oftentimes by American soldiers or their extended families. Although it was the appearance of "mixed-blood" children as a social welfare problem that spurred the Korean government to pursue international adoption as an emergency measure, the first adoptee-mascots were by and large full-Korean boys.[6]

The American press was especially influential in provoking sentimental reactions among Americans, many of whom responded to media images of orphans and "mixed-race" children by contacting the Korean government to donate money, clothing, and toys to orphanages or to inquire about how to adopt these children into their families. I place this phenomenon within the context of American adoption policy and practice of the time, wherein a rationalized social work institution (Herman 2002; Berebitsky 2000) along with a shortage of available white babies led to stringent requirements for infertile American couples who wanted to participate in the postwar baby boom. The adoption of mixed-race Korean American children thus became another alternative for so-called childless couples, especially those motivated by Christian values.

The collapse of egocentric motives into altruistic discourses, combined with an American sense of entitlement and cultural superiority, can be clearly gleaned from the letters written by hopeful couples in America to representatives of the Korean government in the 1950s. I examine the documentation of two cases from South Korean state archives that clarify how Americans articulated their desires for Korean children and how the South Korean state helped to facilitate adoptions in the early years. For it was not simply the desire of Americans that made these adoptions possible but also the accommodating role of the first South Korean administration. The Korean government was concerned about establishing legal procedures for the efficient removal of children from Korea and was perhaps equally invested in fortifying its international reputation. As I show, the South Korean government under President Syngman Rhee capitalized on the sentimental power of Korean orphans to further its diplomatic and foreign relations interests, especially with the United States. Finally, I describe how the establishment of adoption agencies and technological infrastructures by the 1960s made possible, and even necessary, the replacement of dwindling numbers of mixed-race children with full-Korean children. These economic and social orphans are the children who constitute the great majority of Korean adoptees today.

TRANSPLANTING CHILDREN

Prior to the large influx of children from Korea, evacuees or refugees from European countries affected by the Second World War constituted the largest number of foreign children brought to the United States. Some of these transplanted children stayed permanently in American families, whereas others were repatriated after the war. In total, the United States Committee for the Care of European Children facilitated the entry of 4,177 children from Europe into American families between 1940 and 1952 (Close 1953).[7]

Meanwhile, in postwar Japan, the occupation of United States military forces during reconstruction resulted in thousands of Amerasian children born out of the often temporary liaisons between American servicemen and Japanese women. Between 1952 and 1975, more than two thousand children from Japan were adopted by servicemen or foreigners in Japan and overseas (Goodman 2000: 148),[8] but these first transracial intercountry adoptions did not become the object of media attention that the Korean mascots or war orphans would soon become—perhaps due to Japan's ambivalent status as a former adversary as well as discomfort about American boys "sleeping with the enemy." The Japanese-American Joint Committee for Help to Mixed-Blood Children was established to offer aid to the estimated six thousand such children and their mothers (Asbury 1954),[9] and Pearl Buck's Welcome House, the first transracial adoption agency, brought Amerasian children to America as part of a liberal, antiracist, anticommunist project. For Buck, these "children without a country" were the responsibility of Americans who had the moral duty to nurture them as well as the patriotic duty to save them from the scourge of communism.[10]

Predictably, the United States military occupation of South Korea led to sexual relations between American soldiers and local women.[11] The South Korean government estimated that there were one thousand mixed-blood children in the immediate aftermath of the Korean War. At that time, the majority of children in the orphanages and hospitals were full Korean, with mixed-blood children primarily concentrated around the 38th parallel, close to the American military units. American media reports featured images of these children from 1954 onward and thereby incited sudden and unexpected interest among American couples and individuals who wrote to Korean consulates, the Korean government, the UN ambassador, and even directly to the president of South Korea to request information about how to adopt a Korean orphan. In the face of postwar chaos and the humanitarian crisis of thousands of orphaned and abandoned children, both full Korean and mixed, the Korean government moved hastily to establish an adoption law and to pursue overseas adoption as a solution to its immediate social welfare needs.

KOREAN WAIFS AND THE MASCOT PROBLEM: AMERICAN SOLDIERS FATHER KOREAN CHILDREN

The surrender of Japan in 1945 seemed to promise liberation and a long-awaited opportunity for self-determination for Korea, which had suffered thirty-five years of brutal colonization under the Japanese. Following the war, however, the cold war superpowers quickly negotiated the distribution of Japan's former colonies, and Korea, given its strategic geopolitical location, was divided into two occupation zones. The half north of the 38th parallel was under the immediate influence of the Soviet Union, and the southern half was under the protection of the United States. The arbitrary division at the 38th parallel, scrawled hastily on a map in 1945, led to the establishment of two opposing states by 1948. As such Korea was turned into a political hot zone, and the stage was set for the first military conflict of the cold war, with North Korea supported economically and militarily by the Soviets and China, and South Korea by the UN and the United States.

The three-year war that ravaged the tiny peninsula resulted in ten million separated families and left half a million widows and tens of thousands of orphaned or needy children in South Korea alone. An estimated thirty-six thousand American troops died, and as many as three million Koreans on both sides had perished by 1953 when the military stalemate restored the boundary at the 38th parallel and set the two nations on a course of cold war hostilities and competing nationalisms for decades to come.

Without the devastation wrought by the war and the subsequent United States military occupation, Korean adoption would probably not exist today. In 1954, Susan Pettiss, assistant director of the International Social Service–American Branch, alerted her fellow social workers, "Let's face it, international adoptions are here to stay." And a year later, a study on adoption published by the United States Children's Bureau in 1955, under the subheading "Intercountry Adoption," made explicit the connection between United States postwar interventionist policies and its international welfare responsibilities: "As long as it is necessary to maintain approximately a million and a half men in the military overseas what happens to the children of these men becomes a social and a political problem" (Children's Bureau 1955: 38).

Children left homeless or orphaned during the war were constructed in the American media as objects of humanitarian concern and became major beneficiaries of overseas charity following the war. Moreover, their welfare was key to an American postwar communist containment policy that sought to use humanitarian aid as a means of building good will among the Korean people. The thousands of mixed-race children who were born to Korean women and fathered by members of the armed forces quickly became a highly visible social welfare and publicity problem for both the new South Korean government under President Syngman Rhee and for the newly hegemonic United States, which was concerned about maintaining a reputation as the embodiment of democratic ideals in the "free world."

For the United States, these "GI babies" or "UN babies" presented a possible weapon that the communists could seize upon in the ideological battle to discredit the United States and its cold war expansionism.[12] Bob Pierce, the founder of World Vision International, an evangelical Christian aid organization that first began its international humanitarian projects in Korea, explicitly used the adoption of mixed Korean children as part of an anticommunist, Christian propaganda program. Ironically, however, it was the solution of overseas adoption that led eventually to North Korea's scathing criticism of South Korean "traitors" who sold children to American "slave traders . . . divided among capitalists and plantation owners" (*Washington Post* 1959).[13]

South Korea was the largest development project in the world after the end of the war, with the United States being the primary orchestrator of the nation-building project—a principal objective of which was to create a viable anticommunist state in Asia (Ekbladh 2004: 19). In addition to $200 million donated annually by the United States, as well as costs for maintaining its military bases and troops, American money flooded in from voluntary aid groups, sectarian organizations, and individual donors.[14] Many of the initial fundraising and donation drives were devised by American soldiers and chaplains who wrote home to families, churches, and local newspapers asking for food, clothing, or other supplies for orphanages that they had helped to set up. According to a 1954 report by the Christian Children's Fund, Armed Forces Aid to Korea (AFAK) had by that time built fifty orphanages as part of an anticommunist goodwill project, and the Korea Civil Assistance Command (KCAC), staffed by the United States army, took care of 65 percent of the material needs of orphanages (Asbury 1954).

Americans at home joined the effort by engaging in a number of aid "operations" for Korean children that were widely publicized. The most famous was Operation Kiddy Car, the evacuation in 1950 of one thousand children from Seoul to Cheju Island at the beginning of the war. Colonel Dean Hess, a Catholic priest turned fighter pilot, was credited with saving these children, and he wrote a memoir that became the Hollywood feature film *Battle Hymn* in 1956.[15] Other examples include Operation Santa Claus, an army-initiated Christmas clothing drive for orphanages, and Operation Winter and Operation GI, which converted American women's knitting work into interventionist relief projects. Operation Giftlift brought Christmas presents in 1952 to the children in the Cheju Island orphanage from members of the air force stationed in Japan. The transportation en masse of Korean children out of Korea also borrowed from the militarized connotations of the word "operation": World Vision's Operation Stork and Harry Holt's Operation Baby brought planeloads of children to the United States in late 1956.

In addition, Korean waifs and orphans often appeared in reports recounting the charitable deeds of American soldiers.[16] A *Christian Science Monitor* article, "GIs Clothe South Korean Waifs," from October 1953 contains a photo showing a small Korean toddler with an American soldier holding a sweater up to her shoulders (figure 1). The first paragraph reads:

1. "GIs Clothe South Korean Waifs," *Christian Science Monitor*, 17 October 1953.

"American soldiers—who once called all Koreans 'gooks'—now are engaged in a number of projects which indicate that affection and respect have largely replaced their earlier skepticism. Many GIs who find Korean customs confusing and Korean politics unsavory are putting their efforts into the most promising of many unofficial relief activities: aid for South Korea's ragged, appealing children. For these soldiers, the tattered waifs with the beguiling faces are the most understandable feature of the Korean scene." As this article suggests, American soldiers were able to overcome latent or blatant racism and cultural skepticism by focusing on humanitarian efforts for beguiling children. The waifs of war were often represented as orphans and Korean relatives were rarely, if ever, mentioned in these press accounts. Rather, as shown in the article's photo the benevolent American soldier stood in as a parental figure, thereby crossing racial and cultural moats of confusion by taking on a paternal role to provide for and clothe the needy third world child.

American servicemen are thus ambiguous figures in the history of adoption from Korea. On the one hand, they fulfilled a paternalistic role as the main supporters of orphanages and conduits for charitable donations from concerned Americans at home. On the other hand, many of them abrogated their actual paternal responsibilities as fathers to children who were subsequently abandoned due to the dual stigmas of illegitimacy and miscegenation. These children made up the first wave of intercountry adoptions from Korea. This Janus-faced nature of the American military occupation—exploitative and humanitarian—has characterized the neocolonial relationship between America and Korea since the 1950s. As Nancy Abelmann and John Lie write in describing the role of the United States in South Korea: "Through military and civilian contacts, the United States became at once an object of material longing and materialistic scorn, a heroic savior and a reactionary intruder" (1995: 62).

The metonymic association of the United States with "heroic saviors" took material form in American newspaper images that portrayed servicemen arriving at airports after the end of their tours of duty in Korea—with young Korean boys, or mascots, in tow. These reports, first appearing in 1952, described how Korean boys and girls were adopted by the GI's parents and sometimes by the soldier himself. Through perseverance and personal connections, servicemen cut through "red tape" during a period when Korea itself had no international adoption policy or legislation and when race-based immigration policies in the United States effectively barred all Asians from entry (excepting limited quotas for Chinese, Indians, and Filipinos).[17] As Nancy Ota notes, many of these early adopters received special clearance through the military and filed private congressional petitions that may have functioned like "rewards for meritorious service," or else were considered uncontroversial because they were based on a notion of familial relationship, even if not one of blood (2001: 229).[18] Married couples in the armed services constituted a major proportion of adoptive parents in the first few years, as their itinerant careers made it difficult for them to conform to standard adoption agency protocols and requirements for domestic adoption (Children's Bureau 1955: 7–8).[19] But there were also the numerous cases of bachelors adopting Korean boys and girls, thereby leading one international social worker to fret, "Frequently we receive requests for assistance in adopting Korean boys (and girls!) from United States servicemen who are single. You know the mascot problem well! We usually suggest they discuss with Mrs. Hong [director of the

2. "Korean Waif Becomes Real American Boy," *Los Angeles Times*, 10 January 1953.

Korean agency] how they would help these Korean youngsters to get an education in Korea. We believe these children are often over 10, therefore not eligible under the Refugee Relief Act Section 5. We hope she can refer these servicemen to relief agencies and arrange a method of financial contribution and social planning."[20]

A case culled from American newspaper archives reveals the unfortunate and more complicated story of one of these so-called mascots. Brought over at the age of three, Lee Kyung Soo, renamed Lee Paladino—a plump, dimple-cheeked Korean boy—was featured in newspaper articles that chronicled his first few years in his adoptive country. Adopted by Vincent T. Paladino, a navy chief boatswain's mate, Lee was found on a "muddy Inchon street," according to the *Los Angeles Times* profile entitled "Korean Waif Becomes Real American Boy" (figure 2). The initial difficulty in acquiring a United States entry visa for Lee made his arrival at the Idlewild airport, along with his baptism and his first day of school, even more picturesque and newsworthy (*Los Angeles Times* 1953a; see also

Chicago Daily Tribune 1953 and *New York Times* 1953, 1954). However, the final story in the archive is not accompanied by a photo of the perpetually smiling boy mimicking his proud adoptive father. Rather, it conveys a very different narrative of "becoming American": Lee was relinquished to the state when his father married and "friction" developed between Lee and his stepmother. Sent to a foster family, Lee, at the age of nine, ultimately ended up being formally adopted by his adoptive grandparents (*New York Times* 1958).

In the immediate postwar period, fictive adoptions of mascots, especially boys, and the conception of children with Korean women were both ways in which American men "fathered" Korean children, and they index the ambiguous forms of intimacy that emerged out of the neocolonial encounter between South Korea and the United States. Early adoptions of mascots by single men and the abandonment of Korean women and their mixed-race children are both non-normative expressions of paternalism (men being maternal on the one hand, and engaging in illicit sex, on the other). These relations soon gave way to ones that conformed to more normative views of sexuality and the nuclear family, inflected by American Christianity, in which adoption practices were feminized and children were framed as humanitarian orphans, rather than as children abandoned by their American fathers.

"A KOREAN ORPHAN FOR YOU"

In the years following the Second World War, American paternalism on the global stage, characterized by cold war era expansionism and worldwide militarization, was matched on the domestic front by maternalism in the form of "adoption"—whether fictive as in child sponsorship, or real as in the case of intercountry adoptions. As Christina Klein argues, sponsorship programs such as that of Christian Children's Fund came to be seen as part of the fight against the encroachment of communism in Asia and as a means by which Americans could "identify with the nation as it undertook its world-ordering projects of containing communism and expanding American influence" (2003: 159). The historian Arissa Oh explicitly links the success of Harry Holt's religiously inspired mission to what she calls "Christian Americanism"—a "fusion of vaguely Christian principles with values identified as particularly 'American'—specifically, a uniquely American sense of responsibility and the importance of fam-

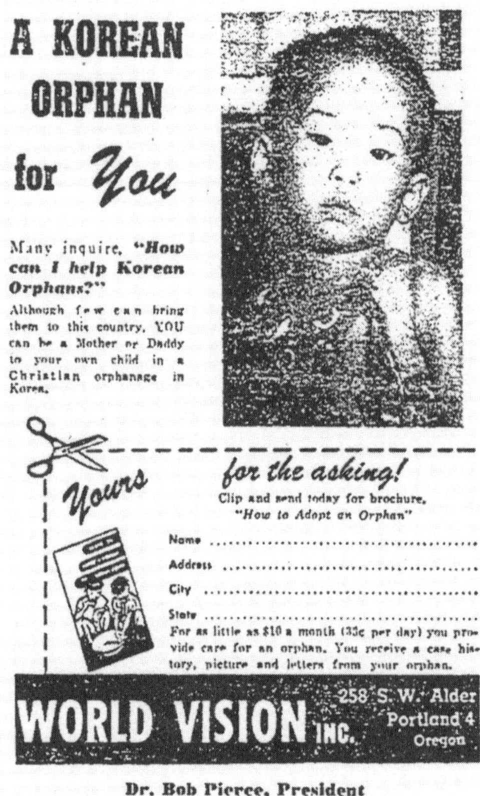

3. World Vision advertisement, "A Korean Orphan for You," *Los Angeles Times*, 17 January 1956.

ily. . . . It equated being a good Christian with being a good American" (2005: 175).

Christian Americanism, anticommunism, and adoption were closely tied in the decade of the 1950s, which witnessed a proliferation of the word "adoption" in appeals for sponsorship and long-distance fostering of Korean waifs and orphans. Aid organizations made pleas to the American public to adopt orphanages, schools, or other institutions as a means to encourage greater numbers of individual donations. In a World Vision advertisement from 1956 (figure 3), the conflation of charity, commerce, and family in the word "adoption" is clearly legible: "A Korean Orphan for You: Many inquire, 'How can I help Korean Orphans?' Although few can bring them to this country, YOU can be a Mother or Daddy to your own child in a Christian orphanage in Korea. . . . Yours for the asking! Clip and send away for brochure, "How to Adopt an Orphan."

The hucksterish quality of the ad lends it a ring of populism but also suggests that in pro-family 1950s America being a "Mother or Daddy" to a Korean orphan was what everyone else was doing. The exchange of personalized letters, information, and money involved in fosterage from afar helped to feed American imaginations about these children, and, as Klein argues, " 'adoption' linked political participation and political obligation to feelings of pleasure, love, and domestic fulfillment" (2003: 159). In fact, the effectiveness of using the language of adoption to promote sponsorship became apparent when sponsors began petitioning to make their figurative adoptions real by bringing "their child home."

HOW TO ADOPT KOREAN BABIES

"How to Adopt Korean Babies" was the title of an article that appeared in *Ebony* magazine in September 1955 (figure 4). With images of a dozen Korean-black mixed babies, the article painted a bleak picture of these children as ostracized and stigmatized in Korea, where "racial purity is a deeply entrenched social fetish" (31). In a climate of hostility toward them and their mothers, these babies were often found abandoned or left at orphanages: "For both political and humanitarian reasons, officials of the U.S. State Department hope that these children will find homes in America. Not only would the youngsters benefit enormously by coming to the U.S., but, in the words of a Foreign Service aide in Korea, their adoption 'would effectively counteract any drop in America's prestige in that part of the world.' "[21]

The *Ebony* article instructed interested individuals to contact the State Department for information about the Refugee Relief Act (RRA; or Public Law 203).[22] This act was passed by the United States Congress in August 1953 and allowed for four thousand orphans (younger than ten years of age) from any country with oversubscribed quotas to be adopted in the United States by American citizens. Set to expire on 31 December 1956, the RRA did not confer citizenship but rather made provisions for nonquota immigrant visas for "eligible orphans." Although it did not specify particular countries for eligibility, given the restrictive and discriminatory immigration laws of the time "nonquota" meant that special provision was being given for "oriental" children.[23]

Hal Ok Chin, 2, a chubby, curly-haired girl, has been in orphanage for about a year. She is in good physical condition. Child has a twin brother in same institution who is still extremely weak, as result of neglect and prolonged malnutrition.

Chung Ho Lyu, 2, was left in banana box on railroad right-of-way leading to Seoul. Korean farmer rescued him shortly before train roared across spot where baby had been abandoned. Healthy, alert orphan is receiving good care at foundling home.

HOW TO ADOPT KOREAN BABIES

Three hundred Oriental-Negro foundlings are available for adoption by Americans

THE CUDDLESOME, wistful-eyed children on these pages are the least loved boys and girls in Korea. They are war babies, offspring of Oriental-Negro romances that flowered between battles and faded with the first hint of armistice. They and nearly 300 others like them are wards of foundling homes in Korea where they will be cared for until more suitable arrangements can be made for them.

It is doubtful that any of these youngsters will find sanctuary in their native land. There, as in other Oriental countries, racial purity is a deeply entrenched social fetish. The child of mixed origin is regarded as inferior and unclean. Koreans tend to ostracize them and their mothers. So strong is the prejudice against these youngsters and the women who conceived them that hundreds of desperate mothers abandoned their half-Negro babies in rice fields, left them to starve in bombed-out streets, or thrust them upon American hospital authorities.

For both political and humanitarian reasons, officials of the U. S. State Department hope that these children will find homes in America. Not only would the youngsters benefit enormously by coming to the U. S., but, in the words of a Foreign Service aide in Korea, their adoption "would effectively counteract any drop in America's prestige in this part of the world." Under the U. S. Refugee Relief Act, eligible orphans may be adopted by qualified American families virtually for the asking.

Al Ki Pak, 1, was abandoned in back yard of Korean farm house. Hoping that baby might be identified by her parents, farmer turned it over to U.S. authorities.

Sa Il Kim, 3, a twin, is undergoing treatment to build up his physical condition. His mother deserted him in rice field. She later claimed baby but could not care for him.

Man Soo Chung, 2, was brought to orphanage by mother who could not support him. Refugee Program will admit orphans through Dec., 1958.

Continued on Next Page 31

4. "How to Adopt Korean Babies," *Ebony*, September 1955.

The passage of this legislation led to a concerted effort by the South Korean government, the International Social Service–American Branch (ISS–AB), and other various individuals and organizations, including Holt, to find a way to get Korean children to the United States before the December 1956 deadline.[24] Before its expiration, President Eisenhower approved an emergency measure to allow an additional 659 orphan visas in order to prevent "tragic family separations" (*Christian Science Monitor* 1956). Subsequent legislation extended the availability of these nonquota visas and raised the age limit from ten to fourteen, until a permanent immigration law for "eligible orphans" was enacted in 1962.

In Korea, overseas adoption developed out of a humanitarian crisis and in a legal and social policy vacuum. At the time, Korea lacked even a formal domestic adoption law and had nothing resembling a social welfare system. In fact, social welfare in Korea today is largely based on the models provided by Western humanitarian organizations after the war, and it was profoundly influenced by American social work consultants who designed programs and trained women in the field (see Choi 1995). In addition, a number of Korean adoption agency workers received social work training in American universities.

In the following two sections I draw upon documents from government and International Social Service archives to outline how adoption from Korea was largely shaped by two forces: an internationalizing social work profession in the United States and the desire of the Korean government to solve its social welfare problems through intercountry adoption. By reading across domains of foreign policy, social work, and personal letters I examine how legal codes and the child's best interests were negotiated transnationally during the earliest years of Korean adoptions, and I look at how notions of development, altruism, and opportunity were articulated in ways that echo many of the discourses that dominate discussions of international adoption today.

The Market at Home

How is it that images of Korean children halfway around the world were able to enliven the parenting desires of so many white Americans? To answer this question, one needs to take into account how ideologies of family and nation intersected with the dominant adoption practices of the day. In a postwar cultural climate wherein patriotism and pronatalism were conflated, domestic adoption petitions increased twofold between 1945 and 1955, compared to the previous decade.[25] Reflecting a demand for (white) children among white middle-class Americans who longed to participate in the postwar baby boom, this sudden reversal in the balance between supply and demand led to important shifts in child welfare policy and social work practice. Some agencies reported that prospective parents outnumbered available children by as many as ten to one, and in 1955 the *Washington Post* found that children were being bought and sold for up to $2,000 on the black market (Edstrom 1955: 29).

Because couples were "clamoring for children to adopt" (Gallagher 1958), the social work profession in America was finding itself under attack, not only for being the gatekeepers to a couple's potential happiness and fulfillment as parents but also for screening procedures that many couples felt were discriminatory and unnecessarily prying.[26] In addition, "independent adoptions" were proliferating as a result of a diminished view of the adoption profession in the public eye. Under these pressures from a powerful segment of the population—white, middle-class heterosexual couples—social workers gathered forces to discuss how to relegitimize their profession and alter public opinion while safeguarding the rights of the child—a social responsibility, they argued, that they were uniquely qualified to bear given their specialized experience in casework.

John Ehrenreich argues that social work, since its professionalization during the Progressive Era, has been considered a low-status "feminine" occupation, and "as a consequence, social workers were (and remain to this day) extremely defensive about their professional status and were unusually preoccupied, even obsessed, with the problem of making social work 'scientific,' of defining a 'knowledge base' for the field" (1985: 57). This defensiveness became pronounced among adoption workers in the mid-1950s (see also Berebitsky 2000 and Gill 2002). Their knowledge base was grounded in the experience of matching children and families, and their authority rested on the conviction that they, unlike doctors or lawyers involved in independent adoptions, were uniquely trained in the theories and practices necessary for ensuring good child placement and "scientifically perfect" families (Berebitsky 2000: 154).

Matching had been a central preoccupation since the advent of the adoption profession in the nineteenth century, when both children and parents were analyzed according to criteria of class, race, religion, intelligence, and personality. Religion was often used as a basis for matching and was also required by law in some states, thereby presenting setbacks for couples in mixed-religious marriages and also for Jewish parents (see Herman 2002). In accordance with the dominant ideology that bound adoption to secrecy, matching was crucial to ensure that the child would fit into the family without any seams of illegitimacy that could expose the child to the shame of fictive kinship.

In the 1920s and 1930s children were the ones subject to "scientific" scrutiny, and they were probed for their intelligence and suitability for parents who had the luxury to indulge in eugenic demands in a wide-open baby market. By 1945 the tables had turned, however, as the number of desiring parents far exceeded that of available babies. In addition, in the affluent years of postwar America, notions of child development based on environment rather than genetics coincided with an increasingly child-centered family culture where the possibilities offered by full-time mothering and proper nurture trumped fears of inherited traits (see Herman

2001b). In this new era of child welfare, no child would be deemed unadoptable from the outset. Rather, as social workers argued, it was a matter of finding the right family for each child instead of finding the right child for any family. This relatively child-centered ideology put social workers in a new role—that of determining the fitness of families.

Therefore, by the 1950s prospective parents were being screened economically, emotionally, and psychologically for their abilities to parent a child. According to a report by the Child Welfare League of America, "the adoptive parents must have good health, a stable marriage, exhibit a degree of maturity, and must have evidenced some ability to adjust to the reality of their childlessness. They must be able to see the child as a human being with his own personality, who needs love and affection and a sense of 'belonging'" (Gallagher 1958: 10). Agency workers closely monitored adoption placements, which were considered to be provisional until a six-month to one-year period of observation had elapsed. The social worker was key to ensuring that the placement was suitable and that the relationships between parents and children were adequately cemented. During this provisional supervisory period, the social agency stood in as the legal guardian and protector of the child whose adoption would not be finalized without proper observation and full agency approval. Another important role the agency played was safeguarding the identity of the birth mother, who was guaranteed confidentiality so she could leave the stigma of an illegitimate birth behind her and return to a life of middle-class respectability.[27]

As might be expected, the family model that the social work system privileged and rewarded was white, middle-class, and heterosexual.[28] In addition, promoting this model was framed as a social responsibility: "Upon adoption, in the 1940s and 1950s, fell the burden of affirming the composition of the family: homogeneous in looks, tastes, and temperament. The goal of fitting a child into her family was a stated aspect of policy; unstated was the equally important goal of fitting the family into the social order" (Modell and Dambacher 1997: 18–19). Beyond looks, tastes, and temperament, the screening process privileged ethnic, racial, religious, and intellectual similarity. Couples who demonstrated adherence to conventional gender roles were looked upon approvingly while working mothers were frowned upon. This quest for "best" families, as argued by Brian Gill (2002), was tacitly guided by a notion that collapsed "normality" with "normativity," unreflectively pursuing an ideal type based on the biologically related family. Thus, the experience of social workers was cited as invaluable for ensuring that the adoptions would be successful. Yet the legitimizing discourses that the profession produced were at odds with an increasingly dissatisfied consumer base that would seemingly go to any lengths, legal or not, to satisfy the desire for children, wherever they might be found. For couples who were childless or who wanted to have more children but were too old or lacked the stability, money, status, lifestyle, or education that social workers seemed to demand of prospective adoptive parents, the images of needy orphans halfway around the world must have seemed like a godsend.[29]

Enter Korean Adoption

The first reported civilian adoption of a Korean "war baby" by an American was finalized in December 1953. On 21 December an article in the *Los Angeles Times*, "First Korean War Baby Brought Here by Nurse," described how the baby, abandoned at birth, "joined the hundreds of other war babies born into similar circumstances—unaccepted by Koreans and unwanted by their American fathers." The nurse who adopted her had been the director of nurses at the Seoul Sanitarium and Clinic, a hospital run by Seventh Day Adventist missionaries. She stated that there were fifty Amerasian children in that hospital alone. The article led to more than six hundred requests by letter and telegram to the Seventh Day Adventist hospital for information about how to adopt a Korean war orphan (Kim, Shaefer, and Mills 2003: 116).

The requests were passed on from George and Grace Rue, Seventh Day Adventist missionaries and the directors of the hospital, to Francesca Rhee, the Austrian wife of President Syngman Rhee, in early 1954 and, that same year, from First Lady Rhee to Hong Oak Soon, a foreign-trained nurse who had been in charge of the Nursing Bureau under the United States military government before the war. As Mrs. Hong told me, Francesca Rhee sent a big sedan to pick her up, handed her the stack of letters, and asked her to read them and then implored her to figure out a way to handle the situation. The Korean government could not offer any financial support, so Mrs. Hong went to each of the foreign aid organizations to ask for money to help set up an adoption agency.

Child Placement Service (CPS; Han'guk Adong Yanghohoe), nominally supported by the Ministry of Health and Social Affairs, thus became the first South Korean government-approved adoption agency in January 1954. It was set up to deal exclusively with overseas adoption. Various foreign voluntary associations gave it administrative support and it received start-up money from the American-Korean Foundation (AKF), a nonsectarian organization established in 1952 that was a main source of foreign aid to Korea well into the 1970s. As an organization, CPS worked with the Adoptions of Orphans under Public Law no. 203 subcommittee, which was formed under the Child Welfare Committee of the Korean American Voluntary Associations (KAVA) in August 1954. The International Social Service, a Geneva-based organization, had been a major contributor to the refugee relocation programs after the Second World War and had helped to arrange adoptions of children from war-torn European countries to the United States. Because of this prior experience ISS–American Branch was approached by KAVA and CPS with requests to act as the main liaison for CPS as it tried to set up proper channels for the transfer of children from Korea to the United States.[30]

Even before the cease-fire in 1953 and the establishment of CPS, the issue of mixed-blood children was recognized and being addressed by the South Korean government. In 1952, for instance, it was reported in the *Dong A Daily* that the Ministry of Social Affairs was researching the total number of mixed-blood children with the intention to arrange for their "separate accommodations" (*ttaro suyong*) (*Dong A Ilbo* 1952). And in 1953 police bureaus across the country were instructed to examine the situation of mixed-blood children by categorizing them according to color: white, black, and yellow (*hŭk paek hwang sam saek ŭro pullyu hayŏ chosa*) (*Dong A Ilbo* 1953).

Furthermore, as soon as the United States Congress passed the Refugee Relief Act (RRA) in 1953, Phyllis Woodley, secretary to President Rhee, attempted to establish channels with an organization in the United States to facilitate adoptions. Her letter in November to Dr. Howard Rusk of the American-Korea Foundation stated, "We desperately need help from some source—an authority who will be recognized by American authorities here—to receive these requests and deal with them expeditiously on the spot. We need to meet this quota as far as we can, for it is clear there are enough American couples who want to adopt these children."[31] Meanwhile, in response to a hesitant query from the South Korean ambassador to the UN, Ben C. Limb (Im Byung Jik), President Rhee wrote, "We are most anxious to send as many of our orphans to the States as possible. In particular we desire to have adopted those children of Western fathers and Korean mothers who can never hope to make a place for themselves in Korean society. Those children should appeal to Americans even more than Koreans."[32]

President Rhee had significant interest in promoting Korean adoption abroad, and his office exerted considerable effort to locate specific children requested by American couples. According to CPS's successor organization, Social Welfare Society, President Rhee's ideology of "one nation, one race" (*ilguk, ilminju*) and a particular form of postcolonial Korean ethnonationalism (*tanil minjok chŏngsin*) made the situation of mixed-blood children an urgent concern for the government (Social Welfare Society 2004: 39).

TECHNOLOGIES OF INTIMACY: TRANSFORMING THIRD WORLD ORPHANS INTO FIRST WORLD CHILDREN

Even before the *Los Angeles Times* article in December 1953 the Korean consulates in Los Angeles and San Francisco had been receiving letters from all over the country inquiring about the procedures for adopting a Korean child. In fact, throughout the 1950s and 1960s TV and print media appearances of American adoptive families with recently arrived Korean children would spur new waves of public interest, as evidenced by letters sent to the consular offices and ISS, which often cited media reports. Also, Americans sent monthly monetary donations of $10 to sponsor children in orphanages, which were deposited into the government's Orphan Aid Fund. Like other groups involved in sponsorship programs organized by religious charities, the Korean government would arrange for specific children to be the beneficiaries of individual sponsors, and then they sent photos and information about the child to the sponsor. Sometimes these arrangements also led to adoption petitions.

An article in the monthly women's magazine *McCall's* in October 1953 featured an American knitting drive for the children in the Cheju Island orphanage. "Operations Winter" was organized by members of the General Federation of Women's Clubs and the American Legion Auxiliary Group (figure 5). At least three inquiries to the Consul General about Korean war orphans mentioned the article as inspiring a desire to adopt Korean children. The article, "Warmth for the Orphans of Korea," led one

UNATIONS

Nearly a thousand orphans evacuated from war areas in Korea are sheltered on Cheju Island, where they survive on what we send them

Warmth for the Orphans of Korea

American women's knitting project will help save children's lives

MILLIONS of American women, members of the General Federation of Women's Clubs and the American Legion Auxiliary, will be knitting sweaters and afghans this fall to make it a merrier Christmas for the homeless in Korea.

Sweaters for the children and blankets for their families will be made from scraps and reclaimed wool, as well as from new skeins, all as part of a major "Operations Winter" project of the Federation and the Auxiliary. Apart from this project, members of these organizations will continue to send used clothing, mittens, blankets and food through American Relief for Korea.

The idea for using scrap yarn originated less than a year ago. Mrs. Georgia M. Cragin of Washington, *(Continued on page 18)*

5. "Warmth for the Orphans of Korea," *McCall's*, October 1953.

couple to wonder "if we couldn't give love and a home—our love and our home" to one of those Korean orphans.[33] The handful of letters received in late 1953 were sent from Connecticut, Iowa, California, Michigan, and Texas, and they express a range of different motivations and requests in terms of gender and age, with one woman writing, "My husband and I would like very much to place a Korean War Orphan in our family and in doing so, eliminate a small part of the world's suffering." Many of these families had "natural" children, and couples sought to add children of a certain age to round out their families or give playmates to their children. Typical requests included, "We want a girl about 6 or 7 years old. Can you help us find her?" or "My little girls have always wanted a little brother so I would prefer a little boy, but either would be alright."[34]

Love at First Sight

One case from the presidential archive of Syngman Rhee illustrates how eagerly the Korean government tried to accommodate requests of American parents, many of whom wrote to the Consul General in California or addressed their letters directly to the president. Known for being a staunch anticommunist, Rhee was a recognizable figure in the American media as a Christian who had been educated in the United States and who had a European wife. Many people addressed their correspondence either to the president or the first lady, or to both, and they often identified themselves as fellow Christians. In addition, they sometimes aligned themselves with South Korea or the Rhees in the fight against the communist threat.

On 23 October 1953 Mrs. Casey from Forsyth, Missouri, sent to the Korean consulate in San Francisco a handwritten letter in which she enclosed a clipping of the *McCall's* article about the knitting drive. Like many of the other requests for orphans, Mrs. Casey hoped that she and her husband, childless after nineteen years, could have a child adopted into their home in the Ozarks in time for Christmas. And, like others who were inspired by media reports of needy Korean children, Mrs. Casey and her husband wanted to adopt the child they saw in the photo—a little girl whose face they circled, noting, "the child in circle is one we are writing about."

"We are poor people so couldn't give luxury as the rich of this country have, but we have a small farm, and could give a child food, clothing and an education. From what I have read and heard, perhaps we would be able to do much more for her, than could be done in your country under present existing conditions, which I surely hope will improve rapidly as possible." Mrs. Casey includes a postscript: "Surely by looking at this picture the people in charge of these children will be able to identify this child. If she is still in the home she is the baby we would like to have."[35]

Mrs. Casey's letter was forwarded to the office of the president, which then got in touch with the Cheju Island orphanage to locate the little girl. Within a month, information about the child, Sul Ja Kim, had been sent to the consul general's office, with a letter to the Caseys: "Sul Ja KIM was born on 7th August, 1950. Her parents are unknown but are presumed to have been killed during the first part of the Korean War. She entered the orphanage on 1st December, 1950. The child is of gentle and social nature and has normal and balanced growth. She had measles on October, 1953, but is in good health."[36] A photo of Sul Ja and a list of required documents necessary to process her adoption were included along with the letter. In these early days of adoption, aside from the paperwork necessary to certify the child as an orphan and to acquire a passport and a visa, the biggest obstacle was arranging transportation. Interested parents who knew army personnel returning from Korea could arrange for them to escort the child, but it was otherwise difficult to find someone to take care of an unaccompanied child and it was expensive to pay for the airfare.

The correspondence between the Caseys and the presidential office continued for one year as Mrs. Casey tried to find a way to bring Sul Ja home. The Caseys, who owned a 150-acre farm, had no liquid assets to pay for transportation or other fees. As Mrs. Casey explained, "We could take a child and divide what we have with it, give it anything it would need, but we have no large amount of cash. I hope there is some way you can help us get the baby over here. Surely there will be some way when she needs us so much and we want her so very much."[37] Through persistence and luck Mrs. Casey was granted a special favor by an American army general stationed in Korea, and by February 1954 the Caseys were assured that Sul Ja would be delivered to them. Yet in October 1954 the Caseys were informed by telegram that Sul Ja's father had appeared at the orphanage to retrieve her.

Despite the information provided in the orphanage documents, not only did Sul Ja have a living parent but she also had a twelve-year-old biological sister who was staying at the same orphanage. Devastated, Mrs. Casey questioned the legality of annulling the adoption, as she and her husband had "amounts of documentary evidence that she had been released last March. We even have a receipt for her passport. Do you not believe that a release signed in the beginning of such processing as we have had to undergo should in all fairness still be in effect when the child is ready to come to us?"[38] She then questioned the paternity claim of the Korean father, who, she finds it hard to believe, took four years to find his daughter, and perhaps does not have her best interests in mind: "I can't help feeling Sul Ja's father would be unselfish enough to sign Sul Ja's release so that she might enjoy the benefits of life in America. She would have both a mother and a father also, and we do love her very dearly, in fact we do not see how we can give her up."[39] And in a follow-up letter she asks, "How will the persons who deprived her of a home here in America feel when they fully realize what they have done?"[40]

The president's secretary conveyed condolences to Mrs. Casey, saying, "Sul Ja's father has proved his paternity and will not release the child. We have been unable to persuade him to let her go to you." He goes on to suggest that they try to adopt another child, recommending a UN baby: "These children will, we believe, more easily fit into the American way of life as they are usually intelligent and quite attractive and would probably be more easily accepted into the society of your community. It is these children and not the Koreans who will find it difficult to make a happy life for themselves in our country. We will of course, if you so desire it, locate a suitable Korean girl for you."[41] The Caseys were eventually offered a girl of similar age to Sul Ja but mixed race, but the case was handled by CPS and no further documentation was found in the presidential archive.[42]

Becoming a Daughter

Another contested case suggests some of the broader cultural and structural assumptions at play in the transnational exchange of children. The Manleys, a married couple from Pacoima, California, who had adopted a Korean girl after sponsoring her through a local school, wrote to President Rhee asking for a "great big favor."[43] A friend who had been enlisted in Korea had "found another little girl"—called in this letter "Miss Chang, Chong Ja"—before leaving Seoul in January 1959, and he had arranged for her adoption through Holt Adoption Agency. The child, however, did not want to be adopted or removed from her foster family. Due to this unforeseen circumstance, Mrs. Manley wrote to the president, appealing to him as a Christian: "Please. Please. But God's will be done. Please know we only want this child to love [and] to give a chance to go school to dance [and] learn music [and] to raise as our own beloved daughter along with our own Mary Oh, who just arrived, 1 month ago today."

The office manager at Holt attested that they had met with the child and her guardian and decided that the case was closed, as the guardian was unwilling to release the child. Although the foster parents had made an agreement with the army officer who had acted as a proxy for the Manleys, the child herself was unwilling to leave her foster parents, to whom she had grown attached. The Ministry of Health and Social Affairs investigated the family and determined that, contra what the Manleys suspected, the child was not being coerced or controlled by the foster parents, and was not being exploited as a servant. The ministry then wrote to Mrs. Manley to explain that "constant efforts have been made to persuade Miss Chang, Chong Ja to change her mind by the foster family, village neighbours, and school teachers but in vain, as she stubbornly resists to give in." In July 1959 the Manleys were informed that there was nothing further to be done.

In response, Mrs. Manley took off the kid gloves and put aside Christian fellowship to make a claim based on "fair play": "Perhaps he [their enlisted friend] feels as I do someone who paid more may have got her. Now I loved Korea the things I read about your President Rhee. I get the papers from Seoul every week, I and my Church have sent many things money yet. . . . Now we are going to sponsor another orphan. . . . I feel if they signed a release she should come. . . . Our countries are friends but I want to know where Korea stands on fair play. And I have lots of friends and some[,] may I say[,] influence."

The health minister then responded as follows:

> I thank you for the humanitarianism expressed in your letter. . . . Although we previously made a decision to close the processing of Miss Chang Chong Ja's adoption on the grounds that the child refused to be adopted by anyone other than her present foster parents, we brought her to Seoul to further consider the matter. We continued our efforts to persuade her to become your daughter through a series of tests and counsellings by a team of case workers, consisting of a social worker, a psychologist, and a psychiatrist of the Social Child Guidance Clinic, which is one of the best child counseling centers available in Korea. The result is that she has changed her mind and wants to go to you as your daughter. It seems that until she talked to professional social workers in an absolutely free atmosphere she did not realize how fortunate she would be to be adopted into a happy home like yours.

The "fortunate" future of Chong Ja was predicated on the poverty and chaos of Korea in the postwar period, which fueled prevalent desires among many Koreans to pursue the American dream. In Korea in the 1950s and 1960s the citizens' duties to the country were emphasized by the state in concert with ideologies of nationalism and anticommunism. A 1955 letter from a government official in Korea to a minister with a Korean delegation in England questioned the "cliché or fad with us that emigration is a good thing without any question." He asserted the importance for "right-minded and able-bodied Koreans to remain home and contribute to the rebuilding of the nation in every way possible. . . . All patriotic people should stay home at least until this national crisis is over."[44]

Yet contradictory desires and resentments coexisted with a sense of duty to the new nation and its rebuilding. Scraping by under conditions of extreme poverty and social dislocation, many Koreans sought opportunities to go abroad, especially to America. In 1966 the Korean American novelist Richard E. Kim, upon returning to Korea, recounted the resentful reaction he received from those who were not as lucky as he was: "I know lots of students who went to America. Like you. And they don't come back. I am not mad at you. I am not mad at them either. I don't blame them. If I could get away, hell, I wouldn't come back either. But I know I can't. . . . Just stand outside the Bando hotel at noon and watch the lucky ones boarding the buses to the airport to fly out of the country, and watch those who are sending them off, sick with envy. Every kid I know wants to get out" (cited in Abelmann and Lie 1995: 60).

Emigration to the United States was two tiered—namely, privileged exchange students and underclass military brides (Abelmann and Lie 1995: 60). Ahead of both of these groups however, were the orphans who received first priority for visas from the United States diplomatic office (*Dong A Ilbo* 1955). In this context, Chong Ja's refusal to be sent to America was most likely considered to be a foolish squandering of an invaluable opportunity, one that many other Koreans would have eagerly pursued.

These cases highlight the biopolitical and geopolitical logics of South Korea's adoption policy in the postwar period. Adoption served as a way for the state to regulate its mixed-blood population through the management of bodies and sexuality (Foucault 1979) and to simultaneously maintain good will with American citizens. Borrowing from Didier Fassin's critique of humanitarian action, I argue that adoption was a "politics of life" in the sense that it gave "specific value and meaning to human life" and implicitly involved the "selection of which existences it is possible or legitimate to save" (2007: 500, 501). The Korean government undertook research to locate and assess the actual number of mixed-blood children, as well as the number of women living or in relations with UN or American soldiers. Adoption became a way of purifying the population by regulating mixed-blood children as well as the illicit sexuality of their Korean mothers, and social workers became the main actors in executing this project of family planning and population control.

Hong Oak Soon herself traveled to the DMZ to locate children and convince mothers that it was better for everyone if they were to send their children to be adopted by Americans who wanted them. Some Amerasian adoptees of the war generation with whom I've spoken can still recall encounters between Korean social workers and their Korean mothers who were convinced to send them for adoption (see Han 2007). According to one fifty-year-old Korean American adoptee, Korean mothers "were told all sorts of things." His mother, who was a singer, was told that her son would be adopted into a musician's family, "and therefore . . . she'd give me up . . . [for] a future as living a life she would want for me." It is not unimaginable to assume that similar arguments may have been presented to Chong Ja about her own best interests and the opportunity for education and material comforts that she would waste by refusing the offer of love and the chance to be a daughter to the American family who wanted her.

The cases of Sul Ja and Chong Ja present discordant moments that bring to light cultural assumptions and social structural relations. In both cases, assumptions about opportunity, entitlement, and familial ownership were rhetorically mobilized by desiring Americans in their attempts to adopt the children they had decided were theirs. The desire of Mrs. Casey and Mrs. Manley to adopt a child was initially framed as a humanitarian gesture of aid and altruistic solidarity with Korea, but under the threat of the adoption's dissolution both women resorted to the language of litigation, a typically American response to perceived wrongs. Moreover, both women drew upon universalizing ideologies of children's best interests, buttressed by American exceptionalism. These cases additionally suggest the lengths to which the Korean government was willing to go in terms of effort and resources to fulfill the requests of these desiring parents.

As contested cases they also bring to the surface the boundaries between legitimate and illegitimate kinship and how parental claims could be mobilized ("she would have both a mother and a father also") or delegitimized ("someone who paid more may have got her") by individuals and the state. The strikingly hybrid nature of these negotiations—personalized attention from the Korean government to help individual Americans produce nuclear families—crossing traditional boundaries of public and private, and, moreover, national borders, suggests the peculiarities of transnational adoption as a reproductive technology.

In the case of Sul Ja Kim, despite the fact that her adoption had been all but promised by the president of Korea himself, the appearance of the Korean father (one wonders what might have happened if the mother had shown up) trumped all other claims to the child. In the case of Chang Chong Ja, her relationship to her foster family was not, apparently, legally binding and could therefore be contested (as a utilitarian or exploitative relationship of slavery, rather than of familial love, or as temporary rather than permanent) and thereby undone through threats of legal action, adult persuasion, and expert opinion. In both cases it becomes clear how arbitrarily the lives of these girls were decided by the contingencies of war, international relations, government intervention, the American media, and ethnocentric notions of a happy home.

The communications scholar Lisa Cartwright describes how the "global social orphan" was constructed in American media accounts of Romania's crisis in child welfare in the early 1990s. The collapse of physical, cultural, and personal distance between spectator and sufferer made possible by the circulation of images in the media provoked American couples to travel to Romania, "thereby playing out the collective fantasy of direct transnational crisis intervention and becoming parents as an act of humanitarian aid." As she notes further: "News and its compelling visual evidence had become vehicles for intimate encounters and for private, even familial, transformations involving bodies and intimacy" (2005: 195).

As the Casey example suggests, the American media in the 1950s also functioned to produce fantasies of rescue that inspired Americans to action through an imagined collapse of distance between themselves and the children represented in photographs and on film. Indeed, the founder of World Vision, Bob Pierce, actively mobilized visual technology, and he was "a pioneer of Christian documentary film, combining evangelical concern, humanitarian political and social activism, and motion pictures" (Hamilton 1980). In fact, one of Pierce's early films was the original inspiration for Harry Holt to rescue children from Korea.[45] Through images in magazines like *McCall's* and in documentary films such as those produced by Pierce, what Cartwright calls the "global politics of pity" brought a sense of moral urgency to saving children across the world by bringing them directly into the privatized world of the home. Moreover, the motivations of parents were buttressed by new legal frameworks and promises granted at the presidential level.

Transnational adoption is a phenomenon that may be precipitated by a social crisis of the welfare state and actualized through the extraordinary abilities of ordinary people, but, as these examples illustrate, its full elaboration as a system depended upon the coordination of a range of technologies: national family and immigration legislation; expert knowledge and universal notions of children's best interests; missionary, development, and humanitarian charitable projects; the circulation of images and the production of transnational imaginaries and affects; and the availability of international communication and transportation technologies. In the case of Korea, although Holt arrived early on to "save" UN and GI babies, his rescue mission's success was predicated on these "technologies of intimacy" as well as the convergence of South Korean geopolitical interests and biopolitical concerns.

FROM MIXED BLOOD TO FULL KOREAN: FOREIGN AID, DIPLOMATIC RELATIONS, AND NATION BUILDING

The "mixed-blood" children of war were not only considered by the South Korean government to be a major liability in its nation-building project and cold war campaign for sovereign legitimacy but also they were recognized as vehicles for accruing economic benefits through American largesse. In contrast to the language of benevolence used to characterize (white) American interest in Korean children, a South Korean official described in a letter to the Korean diplomat in England how UN soldiers from Ethiopia who had fought in Korea had been "pestering for adopting a number of war orphans." As he goes on to explain: "We have so far resisted their importunity on the ground, though not so explicitly said, that we have no diplomatic mission in Ethiopia and that the Government, being these poor orphans' natural guardian, would be irresponsible if it gave them without being sure of protecting them."[46] Although the statement is probably consistent with government policy, it belies what was a more significant concern—namely, the ways in which "these poor orphans" could act as channels for foreign aid from wealthy nations. Ambassador Im makes this explicit in a letter to President Rhee summarizing a UN conference on the topic of "maintenance of obligations," in which the financial redress for women and children abandoned by foreign occupation troops was discussed: "While these meetings go on, and while we should be alert on what can be done through this for the benefit of our girls and their children, we shall also keep in mind the larger aspects of national interest such as intercountry adoption and military aid we continue to receive and keep our diplomatic relations in proper attitude."[47] The ambivalent role of women and children in South Korea's nation-building project—devalued and dehumanized at home but revalued as objects of desire abroad—precisely demarcates the ways in which South Korean biopolitics dovetailed with its geopolitics. The regulation and normalization of the population was effectuated through a convergence with international relations. Adoption thereby became a form of transnational biopolitics in which domestic population problems were converted into diplomatic solutions—what policy rhetoric later referred to as "civil diplomacy" (*min'gan oegyo*).[48]

Although mixed-race or mixed-blood children were the initial objects of concern, by the late 1950s the population of abandoned mixed-blood children in institutions was rapidly declining as the rate of child abandonment among the general Korean population soared. The shift in Korean adoption from mixed-blood war orphans to full-Korean social and economic orphans is crucial to understanding how Korean children became enrolled in an aggressive modernization policy that leveraged poor Korean families and the lives of their children for national security and foreign policy goals. The interest and demand for Korean war orphans exploded in the United States, especially after Holt's widely publicized adoption of eight children in 1955, and with the establishment of Holt Adoption Agency in 1956 competition among the existing agencies in Korea heated up by the beginning of the 1960s. A dwindling supply of adoptable mixed-race children had by then led to practices such as baby hunting and financial remuneration to Korean mothers who were counseled by adoption agency workers to relinquish their children.[49] These measures were justified by the widespread belief that Korea's monoracial culture held no future for these mixed-race children, especially as they reached school age.[50]

Nevertheless, a growing number of these mothers were choosing to keep their children, as the possibility of reuniting with the child's father was no longer simply a vain hope: marriage petitions filed by American men stationed in Korea multiplied up to eighty per month in the late 1950s and 1960s. Moreover, the existence of mixed-race children had became normalized in "camptowns" (*kijich'on*)—areas surrounding American military bases where prostitution was prevalent—and some optimistic observers at the time noted signs of greater acceptance by local communities and the public at large. By 1962 there were no mixed-race children living in baby homes or orphanages, yet demand for these children continued to be high among Americans who either had no other options for having children or were determined to save a Korean child, or both. Under the Park Chung Hee administration (1961–1979), social workers and the Korean government grappled with the reality that international adoptions could only provide a temporary solution to the problem of child abandonment, and a range of programs was implemented to encourage family preservation, to tackle the root causes of child abandonment, to integrate mixed-race children into mainstream public schools, and to promote foster care and domestic adoptions.

With increasing numbers of children abandoned and institution populations exceeding capacity, one of the initiatives made by the government was the Home Returnee program. It was estimated that more than 70 percent of children in orphanages had living parents, and under the program they were to be sent back home. It was then discovered, however, that many of these children were actually "ghost children" who not only had parents but also were not even in residence in the orphanages. Many were sent to the orphanage for basic schooling, as a form of day care, or else existed solely on paper to pad the roles of the institutions. Despite these and other measures, a peak of 11,000 cases of abandonment was reached in 1964 (in comparison to 755 in 1955), and by 1968 there were 70,000 children in six hundred institutions, with most considered to be unadoptable due to older age, poor health or disability, or unattractiveness. By 1965, 70 percent of children being sent overseas were of full Korean parentage, and from 1967 the number of countries they were sent to was expanding to include the Scandinavian nations, Holland, Australia, and Canada. Thus, even as the supply of mixed-race children dwindled and the urgency of their welfare abated, the number of children sent overseas was rapidly increasing.

Holt Adoption Agency, with its vertically integrated system of orphanages, baby homes, medical services, and adoption administration, was able to move children quickly and, relative to ISS and KAVA, was less concerned about the need for developing indigenous solutions to Korea's welfare needs. Holt was, in fact, identified by Korean and American social workers as a "contributory factor to the increase in adoption; [Holt] brings in substantial money to Korea [and] sets a precedent of how Korea can transfer its welfare responsibilities to other countries."[51] This transfer of welfare responsibilities took place in the context of Korea's cold war era fixation with national security. With 2 percent of the national budget spent on social welfare, and more than 40 percent on national defense, welfare institutions were entirely dependent upon sponsorships, and directors of orphanages and baby hospitals held on to as many sponsored children as possible in order to ensure the continuous flow of money from foreign organizations. This situation became exacerbated as sponsorships began flagging in the late 1960s and early 1970s. The organization CPS, which functioned as ISS's partner, was caught between American social work standards for placement and the competitive situation on the ground. Locating mixed-race children in need of adoption and securing their adoptability meant taking on guardianship and supporting them in foster care until they could be matched to an appropriate American family. With insufficient funds for foster care offered by overseas sponsors and government subsidies, the only solution for CPS was to expand its intercountry adoption placements. Thus, contradictory pressures converged—the political and ethical necessity to contract the number of overseas placements in order to prevent further dependency on intercountry adoption, and an economic necessity to expand the program to European countries, where relatively lax standards meant faster placements than the United States, in order to make ends meet.

ISS social workers were ambivalent about the organization's role in Korea because of their belief that long-term planning for the social integration and acceptance of mixed-raced children should take priority over "forced emigration, under the guise of inter-country adoption."[52] Eventually ISS left Korea because it viewed its role in intercountry adoption as compromising its commitment to promoting universal standards of child welfare. Children in Korea were being abandoned for reasons of racism, poverty, and a lack of social welfare services, a situation that ISS considered to be counterproductive to the goal of creating indigenous solutions for children in need. Moreover, the displacement of social welfare funding onto adoption agencies that could bring in foreign exchange made the continued presence of ISS in Korea a cause for serious concern. As an observer from Korea stated in 1966, "In Korea today where there is strong need for foreign exchange, I am inclined to think that agencies are assessed by the Ministry in terms of dollars they bring into Korea. The quality of service or service rendered is only secondary."[53]

The transfer of financial responsibility from government to agencies was formalized through the 1975 adoption law. A quota system was installed in which a ratio of international to domestic placements had to be met by each agency. Although it seemed to be an attempt to encourage domestic placements and to reduce overseas adoptions, in actuality, because of the cultural resistance to Western-style adoptions in Korea, the adoption agencies were unable to fulfill the domestic adoption quota.[54] In lieu of domestic placements, the government required agencies to provide social services for children and families. As Patricia Nye, ISS's East Asian Branch supervisor, wrote in a report in 1976, "in this sense, the Korean government is transferring the cost of social service to adoption agencies with overseas income, or to the adoptive parents."[55]

CONCLUSION

The waifs and mascots who were adopted by returning servicemen after the war gave way to the orphans who were adopted by Americans in increasing numbers starting in the late 1950s. The great majority of these children were not actually orphaned but had living parents who either relinquished or abandoned them. The orphan label, despite its inaccuracy, however, framed these children as desperate for material aid and rescue. It also effectively disconnected them from prior historical and social contexts, thereby freeing them to be saved through incorporation into new families, which was the primary means by which they also became citizens of new nations.

Liisa Malkki argues that children function as a "tranquilizing convention" in the international community by serving to depoliticize highly political contexts (cited in Bornstein 2001). In the case of humanitarian interventions in particular, children are, she writes elsewhere, "sentimentally valued as beings who are nakedly and purely human," and thus transcend "national and other categorical identities and differences" (1994: 54). Orphaned children and children in need, especially since the turn-of-the-century sentimentalization of the child (Zelizer 1994), have been romanticized and construed as icons of humanistic identification, sentimental desire, interventionist rescue (cf. Briggs 2003), and Christian internationalism, especially in contexts of devastation and disaster—which was demonstrated by Westerners clamoring to adopt children from countries ravaged by the Southeast Asian tsunami in 2005 and from Haiti after the 2010 earthquake.

In this historical account of the early period of Korean adoption I have suggested how Korean children functioned as "tranquilizing conventions" during the war by helping American soldiers in Korea and everyday Americans at home make sense of the first conflict of the cold war and converting what might have been viewed as postwar occupation into a humanitarian intervention. My research also suggests that the South Korean state construed actual children as potential mediators of intimate relations between states. In fact, these two processes are fundamentally linked in Korean adoption—the sentimentalization and depoliticization of children as orphans and pure humanity also made them available to be dispatched as sons and daughters who could link people and nations in their roles as ambassadors and bridges. This connection between transnational biopolitics and geopolitics illuminates the ways that the Korean and American states leveraged differential values of human life across enormous scales—from that of individual bodies to international political relations. These articulations of biopolitical and geopolitical projects depended upon a coordinated set of technologies that mobilized a "global politics of pity" that objectified children as orphans, identified them as adoptable, and transferred them to new families.

As depoliticized figures of humanitarianism, Korean orphans provided opportunities for intimate diplomacy through international adoption. They also served as vehicles for economic aid. First in the form of international child sponsorship, then through adoption agency fees, the exchange of money for children between economically privileged and disadvantaged parties in transnational Korean adoption highlights the discomfiting association of adoption with the commodification of persons and social relations and the threat imposed by the "corrupting" market on the authenticity of intimate relations (Zelizer 2007). Following Erica Bornstein (2001), adoption, like sponsorship, is at root tragically ironic. It produces senses of shared humanity and closeness yet it also reinforces and magnifies the economic disparities between individual beneficiaries and their local communities, as well as between those who give and those who receive. It thus simultaneously produces closeness and distance, identification and difference, common humanity, and base inequality. And it is in and through these exchanges that the conspicuous discrepancies between developed and developing nations that make child exchange seem necessary, or in the child's best interests, are reproduced and reinforced.

The imbricated hierarchies of wealth, race, and political power upon which international adoption is based have in the present produced deeply ambivalent feelings among the adult adoptees themselves. As objects of humanitarianism, beneficiaries of capitalism, and symbols of development, their lives in many ways embody the tragic irony that Bornstein describes. In the chapters that follow I explore what these adoptees as adults have made of the ironies of international relations.

CODA

"GIs and the Kids, A Love Story: American Armed Forces and the Children of Korea, 1950–1954" was a photo exhibit organized by George Drake, an emeritus professor of sociology at Washington State University, a Korean War veteran, and the adoptive parent of a Colombian child. Drake is also the founder of the Korean War Children's Memorial in Bellingham, Washington, along with the online project, www.koreanchildren.org. The exhibit, on display in a medium-sized ballroom at the MGM Grand Hotel in Las Vegas in 2005, presented images of Korean children—"war orphans"—who were the most vulnerable victims of the three-year conflict. It also included images of American servicemen who offered aid, solace, and companionship to many of these children. As described in the brochure accompanying the exhibit: "In preparation for action in the Korean War, American servicemen had to be taught to aim a gun at another human being and shoot to kill. They did not have to be taught to offer solace to a crying child, feed a hungry child, treat an injured child or seek shelter for a homeless child. That came with being an American."

The photographs, culled from more than two thousand photographs and eighteen hundred documents located in archives in the United States and overseas, were organized into a historical narrative beginning with the outbreak of war on the Korean peninsula and ending with examples of mascots who were informally or actually adopted by their military friends. Newspaper articles and photographs told the stories of these orphans found deserted and traumatized on roadsides by American military battalions. Further images showed children involved in Operation Kiddy Car—the evacuation of nearly one thousand Korean children before the invasion of Seoul in 1950—and other images depicted their everyday lives in orphanages, such as Boys Town, which had been set up or supported by American soldiers. Still other photos included images of smiling American men and happy Korean children at Christmas parties and other entertaining activities that the soldiers hosted for orphanage children.

Associated with the exhibit was a dinner and awards ceremony for war veterans. This event's master of ceremonies was Terry Moore, a former Hollywood starlet who had been on the USO circuit and who was known for being once married to Howard Hughes. Although Moore's career as an actress was short lived, she was widely recognized as a popular pin-up in the 1950s. On hand, too, to present awards to the war veterans was Jane Russell, also a popular 1950s pin-up and former wife of Howard Hughes, as well as a long-time advocate for children. Russell had adopted a child from Ireland in the 1930s, and she was also the founder of WAIF (World Adoption International Fund), the fundraising arm of the ISS–American Branch.

Among the honored guests was Grace Rue of the Seventh Day Adventist Hospital. She was accompanied by some of her "children" who had been raised at the Seventh Day Adventist orphanage or adopted into Seventh Day Adventist families in the United States. A major figure from the cold war, Buzz Aldrin, the former astronaut of the Apollo 11 mission and second man to walk on the moon, was also a special speaker. These figures had been invited to acknowledge the principal honoree of the evening, Army Chaplain Russell Blaisdell, who had been in charge of Operation Kiddy Car. Although Colonel Dean Hess became the star and celebrity who took the credit for the operation, it was in fact Colonel Blaisdell who had orchestrated the rescue mission. Setting this historical record straight has been a primary motivation for George Drake, who continues to invest his time and personal savings into the memorial project despite ongoing difficulties in finding willing sponsors. Aside from other servicemen from the army and the navy who had helped, in various ways, the children of the Korean War, other attendee-participants included several Korean "war orphans," as they were called. Two of these individuals, now adults in their fifties, were on the Operation Kiddy Car airlift.

The ceremony involved the presentation of certificates of appreciation by the war orphans, who expressed their gratitude to the veterans receiving the commendations for saving children like them. They in turn received certificates from George Drake for their participation in the event. There was an underlying tone of Christian religiosity to the event, including a prayer offered by Chaplain Blaisdell and many invocations of God as the source and inspiration for the humanitarian efforts of these individuals. The execution of the event was predicated on a shared belief in American family values and the ability of innocent children to help adults overcome cultural and political barriers, or "moats of confusion" (*Christian Science Monitor* 1953). What was also necessary was a belief in the orphanness of the orphan—that is, in his or her essentialized lack of social or biological ties. This event and personal narratives of other U.S. veterans of the Korean War underscore how the *generic* humanity of the children allowed U.S. soldiers to redeem their own *particular* humanity as Americans whose acts of charity reinstated their personal and national moral exceptionalism in the context of a dehumanizing war.

The orphans who attended the event were all mixed-race individuals who spent time either on the streets or in welfare institutions. One woman I spoke with remembered very clearly the constant hunger she experienced while living at the orphanage, and she described eating rosebuds, which, even at her young age, she knew to be a nutritious source of vitamin C. Another homeless orphan had been living on the streets and had been set on fire by a gang of boys because of his mixed-race appearance. I also met the blond-haired, blue-eyed infant who had been found at a Korean orphanage and fostered by the crew of a United States Navy ship until his adoption by an American military doctor.

Each of the orphans expressed their heartfelt thanks for the humanitarianism of the veterans, and even though they hadn't been saved directly by the servicemen at the ceremony, they thanked them for "literally saving" many other children. The sentimentality of the event produced and reproduced the myth of the orphan, which was performed symbolically by the actual orphans but only made sense in direct relation to the elderly veterans they were helping to honor. Roland Barthes in his critique of the Family of Man photographic exhibit suggests how visual representations of "humanity" serve to evacuate history and difference: "Everything here, the content and the appeal of the pictures, the discourse which justifies them, aims to suppress the determining weight of History: we are held back at the surface of an identity, prevented precisely by sentimentality from penetrating into this ulterior zone of human behaviour where historical alienation introduces some 'differences' which we shall here quite simply call 'injustices'" (1957: 101). In the GIs and the Kids exhibit it was not the humanity of children or of "orphans" saved from death or social ostracism that was being commemorated but rather the humanity of American servicemen as Americans. This metanarrative of American exceptionalism, righteousness, family values, and charity was imposed rhetorically on the bodies of Korean children through the photographic exhibit, and in the award ceremony it was reenacted through a ritual coproduction.

George Drake is intent on bringing to a wider public's attention the underacknowledged efforts and contributions made on behalf of Korean children by what he calls the American "army of compassion." Even while recognizing the real impact that these men and women had on the lives of Korean children, I was struck by how the other types of intimacy that emerged during the war—relationships between Korean women and foreign soldiers—were absent at the award ceremony, thereby suggesting that the myth of the orphan disallows recognition of the social, historical, and biological connections that produced the mixed-race orphans of Korea. Indeed, one adoptee of the war generation whom I interviewed was particularly dismissive of the project precisely on these grounds, saying, "They were the ones who abandoned us!"

Perhaps, though, it is the ability to embody both orphanness and adopteeness that characterizes what I describe in the next chapter as Korean adoptee "contingent essentialism." Thomas Park Clement, who was the mixed-race child set on fire by a gang of street children, lived on the streets of Seoul in the years at the end of the war and was later adopted by a wealthy American family. He went on to become a successful inventor of medical instruments and today he is CEO of a multimillion-dollar business that manufactures equipment for the medical industry. He self-published a memoir in 1998 and has been active in the adult adoptee community since he was first introduced to other adoptees at a conference in 1997.

Toward the end of the awards dinner Clement was invited to the stage to present Jane Russell with a commemorative certificate, and after a long night of countless invocations of the word "orphan" he was the first to introduce the word "adoptee" into this discursive arena. In acknowledging Jane Russell's lobbying of Congress to pass early international adoption legislation, Clement stated that "There have been over two hundred thousand total Korean . . . orphans adopted across the world. And there are over one hundred thousand here in the U.S." Pausing before he uttered the word "orphans," he went on to make explicit the historical connection between the humanitarian work of American soldiers in the 1950s and the existence of two hundred thousand Korean children adopted around the world today. He continued by saying, "In the U.S., I personally know thousands of Korean adoptees. Many of them are presidents of companies, some of them are doctors, too many of them are lawyers [audience laughter] . . . some are VPs of fortune 500 companies. . . . I'm not sure if you knew that what you were involved in would affect so many people and give them such an opportunity, and it is an honor to present this to you."

Clement delivered a model-minority narrative of Korean adoption, highlighting the successes of adoptees and the opportunities granted to Korean orphans through international adoption. In doing so, he also was able to apply his social capital to present an adult face to Korean adoption against the infantilizing figure of the orphan. In fact, in an article published shortly after the event Clement commented wryly, "I think it's funny to be introduced as a 'war child' or 'war orphan' since I am now in my mid-50s. That makes me one of the oldest children on planet Earth, I would think" (2006: 39).

Given Clement's own personal history, which spans from the Korean War period to present-day adoptee community building and activism, his statement to the Las Vegas audience that there are "over one hundred thousand here in the U.S." served to resignify the timeless images of "orphan" children of the past by connecting them to the live presence of adult adoptees today. Clement himself projects ambivalence: he is a successful businessman and an exemplar of American capitalism who also goes by the name "Alien" in adoptee circles; he has set up an informal suicide hotline for adult adoptees; and he avers that all adoptees are haunted by ghosts. Thus, Clement's statement is suggestive, if only indirectly, of other, more complex, histories surrounding the sentimentalized love story of Korean war waifs and American GIs.

2

Adoptee Kinship

I first met Thomas Park Clement at the Korean War Children's Memorial event in Las Vegas, but I was already familiar with his name as well as his online username Alien. Whereas many adoptees invent email addresses out of English transliterations of their Korean names, Clement simply used Alien, which, as he related to me in an email, refers to the designation he found on his immigration papers as a child: "That was my first encounter of the Alien kind. . . . And then it fit. Alien as in 'alienated.' . . . It is more and more befitting because I did not fit into the white neighborhood I grew up in. Someone even tried to petition the neighborhood to keep us from moving in because of me." He added that, as a multiracial person in the adoptee community where "most of the KADs [Korean adoptees] are 100 percent Korean . . . I don't even fit in there. Although they accept me with open arms, I do not look like most of them."

Clement's personal history is, like others of his generational cohort, composed out of a dramatic trajectory from "Korean war orphan" to model-minority "American." Clement might also be considered a celebrity adoptee—one of a handful who has been featured in the South Korean and Korean American media as a particular success story.[1] As he recounts in his memoir *The Unforgotten War: Dust of the Streets* (1998), Clement believes he was born during the start of the Korean War and recalls being abandoned around the age of four or five. A missionary eventually found him and brought him to an orphanage where he stayed until 1959, the year that the Clement family in North Carolina adopted him at the age of seven.

I had called Clement for an interview at his office at Mectra Laboratories, Inc., a medical equipment manufacturing company of which he is the founder and CEO, a few days before emailing him about his online moniker. At the time he was in the process of publishing the memoirs of the Norwegian Korean adoptee Sunny Jo, an activist and the founder of Korean Adoptees Worldwide, which, with its more than one thousand members, is the largest and most active electronic mailing list for Korean adoptees. A dozen or so American members of Korean Adoptees Worldwide had recently spent a weekend at Clement's house in Indiana, and as we talked on the phone he forwarded to me via email a copy of an article he authored about the Las Vegas memorial event. The article was scheduled to appear in *Korean Quarterly*, a Twin Cities–based periodical published by parents of adopted Korean children that covers Korean American and Korean adoptee news. The multiple arenas in which Clement was involved during summer 2005 represent just a few of the many locations and types of adoptee cultural production and social activity that have emerged over the past decade.

When I asked Clement how he first got involved with adoptee-related community building, he recounted to me the following: "It was in 1997. . . . I Googled 'Korean adoptee' and I got all these hits. And that was an amazing thing because I had lived here [in the United States] for so long, and I had never met one, and you get the feeling that you're the only one. And to get all these hits on this topic; so I clicked on the first one, and the first one I clicked on was Crystal Chappell, do you know her?" I knew of Crystal Chappell as HyunJu Chappell, an adoptee organizer who in 2002 had given a presentation about adoptee networking at a conference commemorating the centennial of Korean immigration to the United States (Chappell 2004). Around 1997, when she was living in the Bay Area, she co-founded the adoptee organization Association of Korean Adoptees–San Francisco (AKA–SF). After getting in touch with Chappell through her personal Website, Clement was invited by her to the Second Annual Global Korean Network Winter Conference in Los Angeles, where four other adoptees had been invited to speak on a panel called "The Korean-American Adoptee Experience" (Global Korean Network of Los Angeles 1997). It was at the Global Korean Network conference that Clement, as he put it, first "met another one." In fact he met more than one, as Global Korean Network brought around sixty adoptees, from the United States and Europe, to Los Angeles in February 1997.

The conference, entitled "Re-defining the Korean Identity and Culture in Light of the Global Korean Diaspora," signaled a growing interest among first- and second-generation Korean Americans in building historical consciousness, ethnic pride, and collective cultural and economic power through the fostering of ethnic identification among Koreans around the world. This was a significant event for adoptees, who according to the conference literature had been "long-ignored members" of the Korean American community (Global Korean Network of Los Angeles 1997). Now they were being invited to participate in the redefinition of a "global Korean diaspora." But its significance for the adoptee participants extended beyond their symbolic recognition as "Koreans" in that it gave them an opportunity to meet together as a group to begin discussing the possibilities of building a global network of Korean adoptees.

Clement's brief narrative, condensed even further here, provides some key characteristics of the "Korean adoptee community," as it came to be referred to by adoptees during the course of my fieldwork. My version of Clement's narrative highlights four aspects of Korean adoptee social practices: self-consciousness about not fitting into dominant categories of race, family, and nation; the ability to access and capitalize on the Internet's networking potentials; the significance of conferences as face-to-face meeting grounds and sites of self-objectification where adoptees construct quasi-public representations of themselves for themselves and broader audiences; and the recognition of adoptees as part of the diaspora by native and overseas Koreans.

In this chapter and the next I delineate the first two aspects of the emergence of the adoptee "community," and in chapters 4 and 5 I turn my focus to the third and fourth aspects. Based upon interviews with American and European adoptees in Korea and the United States, in this chapter I outline the ways in which common experiences as racially other children in white majority families and communities shaped the "moral careers" (Goffman 1963) of adoptees involved in adoptee organizations and activism.[2] In conclusion I introduce the terms "adoptee kinship" and "contingent essentialism" to offer a framework for understanding how adoptee personhood converges around expressions of nonnormative, unnatural, and alien origins and is based on shared histories of displacement rather than on naturalized solidarities of blood, ethnicity, or territorial belonging.

I should note that I avoid attempting to delineate a sociological or psychological profile of a typical adoptee. Rather, I am interested in teasing out the particular ways in which adoptees articulate a sense of ontological distinctiveness through a process of "disidentification" with normative categories of personhood and social belonging (Lowe 1996). In other words, the identity of adoptees is not reducible to an ideal type such as that of diaspora (Safran 1991), but rather is an ongoing production of a shared social imaginary that has taken on transnational dimensions. The adoptee counterpublic is organized around a discursive process of identity construction in which adoptees endeavor to define themselves as a group that is distinct from others that might share demographic or biographical similarities but whose members, as nonadoptees, cannot share in the "separate ontological category of humans" (Patton 2000: 6) that many adoptees feel that they inhabit.[3] Rather than take this category as a given, however, I focus on its emergent character—namely, the ways in which it has been substantiated through a process I refer to as "contingent essentialism." Adoptee identity is at once essentialized as something natural and also construed as something cultural or socially constructed. It thus takes on biological associations despite the inherently nonbiogenetic basis of adoption.

In what follows I draw on interviews I conducted with adoptees active in regional groups and international conferences and on participant observation at adoptee-related events conducted between 1999 and 2005. The counterpublic links disparate strangers whose generationally specific experiences serve as the basis for collective personhood. Out of alienations, displacements, and liminal states adoptees project a categorical identity that is now recognized in broader social fields and publics. This categorical identity is continually performed, negotiated, and contested, and in subsequent chapters I examine how requisite exclusions and negotiations of internal divisions complicate the institutionalization, consolidation, and stabilization of the "Korean adoptee community."

MEDIATIONS OF KINSHIP

Transnational Korean adoptees who, like Clement, are unable to fit normative categories of personhood, demonstrate how identity and kinship are forged at the blurred intersections of the biological and the social, and how particular kinds of information that others may take for granted—about origins, birth, genealogy, blood, culture, and race—are radically contingent but also crucially constitutive of identity (Strathern 1999; Carsten 2007). Without such information, knowledge of the self, social personhood, and cultural citizenship could all be considered compromised, whether in Korean or Euro-American contexts (cf. Strathern 1999). Moreover, information about origins in adoption is often controlled, managed, and distributed by institutions, including adoption agencies, families, and governments, and circulates in highly limited pathways. Although the information itself does not guarantee the answer to existential questions, the secrecy and limited access often associated with this information heightens its significance to personal self-completion especially for those actively searching for answers (Carsten 2007).

In this context, it is noteworthy that adoptees have appropriated new media technologies—Internet chat rooms, electronic mailing lists, blogs, social networking sites, video streaming, and the like—to create spaces where the "narrative urgency of those compelled to tell what might be termed their *un-natural histories*" (Rapp and Ginsburg 2001: 543) can be publicly released. Against normative models of personhood and family life these forms of "mediated kinship" have counterdiscursive power and are productive of "public intimacy"—that is, "potential sites of identification and even kinship that extend beyond the biological family" (Rapp and Ginsburg 2001: 534). Adoptees share stories, compare personal histories, and negotiate their individual and collective identities as Korean adoptees in a variety of spaces, both actual and virtual. In doing so they rework ways of doing and knowing kinship in increasingly public domains beyond the domestic or private, thereby producing new kinds of social identities and intimate relations. From this perspective, kinship is not a preexisting truth that is discovered or found, but rather a set of relationships actively created out of social practice and cultural representation.

What I call adoptee kinship is a form of public intimacy that extends relatedness beyond "biological" and "adoptive" family and is a response to what Rayna Rapp calls "the late modern pathologizations of personhood, gender and kinship" in the context of increasingly stratified forms of reproduction. As she writes, "Ironically and dialectically, experiences with nonnormative, pathologized reproduction can also provide the material for self-reflection and mobilization of new social and political identities" (2001: 469). Korean adoptees, who are themselves the products of "non-normative, pathologized reproduction" are actively engaged in just such mobilizations.

These mediations of kinship take place within the context of other emergent processes—the rise of biomedical subjectivity (Novas and Rose 2000) and technologies of the self (Foucault et al. 1988)—that have brought on the contemporary mandate to "know thyself" and have made adoptees' quests for origins and search for birth parents increasingly normative and expected, especially in light of ongoing movements for adoptees' rights to information in the United States (Modell 1994; Carp 1998). Thus, self-help, therapy, and self-empowerment discourses, the geneticization of identity (Finkler 2001) and the medicalization of adoptee experience through conditions such as Reactive Attachment Disorder (RAD), constitute the backdrop to shifting conceptions of adoptee personhood in the West. Paradigms of secrecy have been increasingly displaced by the injunction to search for and know one's genealogical and cultural roots, thus indicating the degree to which kinship knowledge has become central to personhood in general and to adoptee personhood in particular (Carsten 2007: 409).

ALIENS

The standup comedian Amy Anderson converts her adoption history into a vehicle for laughter in routines such as the following: "I was born in South Korea . . . and then I was adopted by Swedish people in Minnesota [audience laughter]. . . . It's kinda like being raised by wolves, except for they're white people, you know what I mean?" The humor that a mainstream audience might find in this story is evoked by the heightened disjuncture between South Korea and Swedish people in Minnesota in which racial and national boundaries are crossed and made analogous to cross-species kinship. It is an unnatural and surprising juxtaposition, but Anderson also injects a critique of conventional ways of understanding adoption and race by inverting expectations—here, instead of the nonwhite person being likened to animals, as is common when adopted children are compared to domestic pets, for instance, it is the Swedish people who are like wolves. Anderson's standup routine, like Clement's use of the name Alien, highlights the defamiliarizing effect that the body of the transnational, transracial adoptee has on the American family and nation. The visibly different adopted child is at once normal—its adoption interpellates and normalizes the child into the heart of the nation as a member of a white nuclear family—but also unnatural and out of place—the child's racial difference indexes her foreign origins and implicitly links her to groups that have long histories of being culturally and economically excluded and marginalized. It is this particular conjuncture of the profoundly normal (a person with the name Amy Anderson who is a member of a midwestern American family) and the surprisingly unnatural (a South Korean person raised by Swedish people) that provides comic fodder for Anderson and that distinguishes Korean adoptees from other Asian Americans.

An additional distinction between adoptees and other Asian Americans is the fact that adoptee names, such as Amy Anderson, Kimberly Taylor, or Peter O'Brian, often produce "cognitive dissonance," as the journalist Mark Hagland put it to me. He explained, "We look different from what people think we will look like, and we are different from what people think we should be." This cognitive dissonance renders adoptees conspicuous in racialized terrains where names and phenotypes are expected to "match," with clear lines of connection among accepted categories of place, culture, and identity (see Gupta and Ferguson 1992). Adoptees learned in their early childhoods that their names and faces "do not go together" and the continual experience of inadvertently disrupting culturalist and racialized expectations may help explain why it has become commonplace for adoptees as adults to reclaim or incorporate their Korean names into their American names, sometimes trying on different combinations and permutations for fit. Some have said that they are tired of having to deal with invasive questions from strangers (whether they've longed for their "real" parents; if they've met them; if they have been to Korea, and related questions) and thus take on a Korean surname. Although few legally alter their names, many more use their Korean names as online tags or email user IDs, and others use "Western" and Korean names alternately, depending on the situation. As Sunny Jo explains, "By legally reverting back to their Korean name at an older age, and/or using it in their email addresses and computer ID's, adult KADs are using the Internet as a vehicle to reclaim their lost heritage" (2004: 64).

Adoptees' Korean names, however, are not always artifacts of authentic origins. More often than not they are of ambiguous provenance, perhaps selected by Korean kin, but just as likely made up by orphanage directors or adoption agency workers. Like their names, their birth dates and places are also subject to uncertainty, especially for those who were foundlings. In some cases, birth dates were recorded according to the lunar calendar, thus adding more confusion to the mix. Hence, for many adoptees, origin stories are unstable fragments of received information. Adoptees who have searched for or found natal family often discover that the few bits of data that they possessed about their pasts are, in fact, fabrications or inaccuracies. They find that they are one or two years older or younger, for instance, or that they were never true orphans, or that their names had been changed more than once along the process of moving between orphanages and agencies.

On adoptive kinship, Janet Carsten writes, "where *birth* does not imply certainty, endurance or solidarity, it is emptied of most of the symbolic meaning it has in the dominant discourse of kinship, and time itself has a key role in producing new meanings for kinship" (2004: 15). This is certainly true for many Korean adoptees, and it has been documented in autoethnographic films such as *Passing Through* (Adolfson 1998) and *First Person Plural* (Borshay Liem 2000), in which adoptees who search for Korean family discover that their "true" families are the ones that raised them and that the "diffuse enduring solidarity" of kinship needn't be restricted to relations grounded in biogenetics but can be created out of shared intimacies (cf. Weston 1991) and through the accretive effects of everyday care and nurturance (see E. Kim 2001).

Blood, however, is in many social contexts still a potent vector for measuring relatedness and personhood, and it has gained greater force in conjunction with the molecularization of identity in a postmodern biomedical age (Nelkin and Lindee 1995; Finkler 2001).[4] Those without blood knowledge may thus be construed as incomplete because they lack basic information about social, cultural, and biogenetic origins. These connections among personhood, kinship, and origins may have something to do with the feeling that a male adoptee raised in the American South described to me as "being like a cartoon character, floating on a white page, without a background or a context."

In similar terms Marilyn Strathern extrapolates from the legal and cultural conundrums presented by in vitro fertilization the links between knowledge and Euro-American notions of the individual. As she writes, "The quest for facts about the way the world works, and in issues of procreation the role accorded to 'blood' and 'actual' facts, is also part of the Euro-American quest for self-hood: self-knowledge is considered foundational to personal identity, and that includes knowledge about both birth and parentage" (1999: 68). These interlocking equations among kinship, knowledge, and personal identity are demonstrated in the significance accorded to the celebration of birthdays and the recounting of birth narratives in Euro-American culture. By reflecting and reproducing sentimental attachments to biological or biogenetic origins they authenticate one's identity. Hence, adoptees are understandably cautious or cynical about investing emotional significance in a name or date that may have originated in an impersonal bureaucratic procedure, and adopted children and parents today often celebrate the adoptee's "arrival day" or "gotcha day," which in many instances have as much or more significance than birthday commemorations.

Related to this uncertainty about origins is the feeling of incompleteness that adoptees, both in-race and transracial, domestic and international, commonly describe as having a hole in one's soul or, in the words of the adoption activist Betty Jean Lifton (1994), a sense of "genealogical bewilderment." According to adoption specialists, loss and grief are inescapable aspects of the adoption experience for all members involved in an adoption. Birth parents lose their child, adoptive parents experience the pain of infertility and the loss of the biogenetically related child they could never have, and adoptees are haunted by the loss of their natal parents and lack of genetic knowledge. This model of loss has become a dominant paradigm in social work and in psychological and popular cultural understandings of adoption and adoptee subjectivity, and it often is rightly criticized for fetishizing origins and promoting genetic essentialism. The reversal of prior models that advocated secrecy and pathologized adoptees who longed for biogenetic connections as maladjusted has been so complete that adoptees who may not want to find their roots or who are not involved in a search of origins are often viewed as being repressed or in denial (Modell 2002; Carp 1998; Herman 2008).

In Korean adoptee narratives loss has emerged as a common theme (see, e.g., Borshay Liem 2000; Trenka 2005; Bishoff and Rankin 1997; Cox 1999), and for some, loss of biogenetic connections and genealogical knowledge is frequently accompanied by or conflated with a longing for cultural roots. This tendency to elide cultural heritage with biological connections has been especially prominent in contemporary transnational adoptive family practices, facilitated by flows of information and cultural products associated with globalization.[5] For Korean adoptees, essentializations of Koreanness are constructed out of physical or psychological traits presumed to be ethnically specific and inherited genetically by the adoptee (physiognomy, ethnopsychological tendencies, food preferences, etc.) or as culture never acquired but presumed to be deeply embodied and rendered inaccessible to the adoptee. Many adoptees, especially those adopted at older ages, believe that they have an emotional block that prevents them from learning the Korean language, for instance, and others harbor feelings of inadequacy for failing to act or think like a Korean.

The loss associated with an essentialized Korea and Korean culture is materialized in the common trope in Korean adoptee narratives about childhood or adolescent aversion toward other Asians or Koreans. For many of these adoptees the project of creating a coherent self in an "as-if" family as an "as-if" white person was undermined by their own material embodiment. The Asian or Korean body of the adoptee itself destabilizes the coherence of self-identity, and the split between an internal white identity and an external Asian body is often expressed in Korean adoptee autoethnography through the metaphor of mirrors. Mirrors, like family snapshots that are prominently featured in adoptee films and videos, encompass the conundrum of the adoptee's divided subjectivity. Both present visible evidence of the adoptees' incontrovertible racial difference from her family and peers and also provoke questions about inherited traits and family resemblances. They index the "haunting" of adoptee histories (see Dorow 2006) and the multiple temporalities and possible lives that are contained in and referenced by the adoptee's body.[6] They also represent, retrospectively, the "false race consciousness" of adoptees who recall vigilantly avoiding their own reflections, or else if they did look in the mirror they could only see a white person staring back.

Although Holt Adoption Agency started the first culture camp for adoptees in 1976, another common narrative among adoptees describes their unwillingness to attend culture camps or Korean cultural classes as adolescents because of the desire to deny or repress their difference from family and peers. Because these activities were not integrated into everyday family life, culture camps, like mirrors or snapshots, highlighted adoptees' difference when they were particularly preoccupied with fitting in. As Kari

Ruth, one of the founders of Minnesota Adopted Koreans, wrote, "I did attend high school with about eight other adopted Koreans like myself, but I was only friends with one. The rest of us usually tried not to associate with one another. That Asia-phobia thing. It was like looking in the mirror" (1999: 77).

This "Asia-phobia" is coupled with or compounded by an anxiety about ethnic authenticity. Adoptees of the first wave in the 1950s and 1960s were not likely to feel as if they had "ethnic options" (Waters 1990). Rather, they expressed insecurity about being misrecognized as Asian even as they knew that they were not white. As Mark Hagland told me, "We all have issues about authenticity. I used to call myself a fake Korean, and Korean Americans real Koreans. . . . I felt intimidated." And David Nakase, the president of AKA–SoCal and a mixed-race adoptee in his early fifties who was raised in California in the 1960s, described reading a psychological outcome study about Korean adoptees when he was in his twenties: "One of the things the person observed was that the kids were generally fearful of Asians. [laughs] It's funny, but when I read it, it rang true. They were nervous around other ethnic minorities like myself because it's so obvious that you don't fit, and I don't think the acuteness of that—at least for me—it hasn't really diminished with age."

DISIDENTIFICATION

The misrecognition of adoptees whose socialization as white is at odds with their racialization as Asian is, following Judith Butler, an instance of disidentification—that is, an "uneasy sense of standing under a sign to which one does and does not belong" (1993: 219). Lisa Lowe describes disidentification as a "space in which alienations, in the cultural, political and economic sense, can be rearticulated in oppositional forms. . . . It allows for the exploration of alternative political and cultural subjectivities that emerge within the continuing effects of displacement" (1996: 103–4). Certainly, adoptees' social practices can be seen as forms of disidentification with dominant narratives of race and nation, but they are arguably more multiple and shifting than that of other minority subjects because they are caught not only between homogenized cultures and nations but their own families cross those categorical divisions. Adopted Koreans experience a misfit identification with the dominant white mainstream as well as with dominant ways of being Korean or Korean American, and this alienation structures their senses of national, ethnic, and familial belonging as well as their alternative politics and cultural subjectivities. As David Nakase recounted his feelings when accompanying his elderly mother, aware of how "strange" it must appear to others: "What's this Asian guy doing with this old lady?" There is a constantly shifting boundary for adopted Koreans in their negotiation of ethnicity that positions them uncomfortably, sometimes within, sometimes outside of, existing cultural scripts for being American, Korean, and Korean American.

Adoptees in some contexts may identify completely ("I'm 101 percent Danish," one adoptee told me) yet in other contexts begin to see the arbitrariness of their relationships. One female college student enrolled in a class on Asian American cultures that described the steps of ethnic identity development in terms of binaries between "oppressors and oppressed." As she stated, "[In this model,] white people are victimizers and people of color are victims. I'm being oppressed by white people, who are my parents. That was too much."

The mis-fit with dominant national, ethnic, and cultural models is the grounds for creating a space where, as more than one adoptee has stated, "there's less explaining to do." For adoptees who came of age before pluralist multiculturalism replaced earlier models of full assimilation, meeting other adoptees can feel like recovering adolescence. As Mark Hagland noted: "None of us had real peer groups growing up. When we found each other, it was an electric thing." For another adoptee from the American South, the process of getting to know other adoptees was "like taking off rose-colored glasses, seeing how the world really is. . . . Maybe people really do think I'm Korean!" Another adoptee in her forties had no idea that other adoptees existed until she found out about a local adoptee group in southern California: "I didn't even have to say anything, all these emotions came out that I never even knew I had."

For a female adoptee in her twenties it was about feeling "safe," whether in the context of other adopted Koreans or other internationally adopted people. She described attending an adoptee dinner at the annual conference sponsored by the Korean American Adoptee Adoptive Family Network where questions that in other contexts might highlight her difference and novelty were, among other adult adoptees, a point of instant connection: "I sat down, and within like five minutes people were talking about if they searched for birth parents, if they met their birth parents, what kind of experience that was. . . . [They said,] 'Tell me about your life . . . what was it like to meet your birth parents?' With these people you could get in depth without feeling invaded."

CONTINGENT ESSENTIALISMS

> What would be the real cause for people wanting to come together and identify? That's an ongoing problem in the world and society as well. How do you overcome the fact that we are all individuals and all coming from different places? Given that we're all disparate individuals, what are the overarching commonalities in our experience?—DAVID NAKASE, PRESIDENT, AKA–SOCAL

In the chapters that follow I examine the practices of place and boundary making that constitute adoptee identity politics in which negotiations of internal differences help to produce and constitute community. In this chapter I unpack the profound sense of shared personhood and self-sameness that is frequently articulated in adoptee discourses. A particularly suggestive comment was made by the president of the Swedish adopted-Korean organization, Adopterade Koreaners Förening (AKF), Daniel Kim, when in a speech addressed to an audience of adoptees at AKF's tenth anniversary celebration, he remarked: "I have a family in Sweden and a family in Korea. You are my third family. It's important to take care of each other because we are a family, and I could be you, you could be him, he could be her." As someone who has reunited with his Korean parents, Daniel offers a model of kinship that is not exclusive but additive, transnational, and expansive. In addition, his message highlights a central point of this chapter, namely that "adoptee kinship"—relationships of intimacy and identification actualized through and necessitating continued practices of care and reciprocity—is founded on the arbitrariness and contingency of adoption histories, and the fact that "I could be you, you could be him, he could be her." Hence, adoptee family is based on a peculiar mix of inalienability and substitutability that recalls the ambivalent origins of adoptees who may be viewed either as either precious gifts or exchangeable commodities.

Other adoptees employ different metaphors and models for describing the often-instantaneous affective ties among adoptees. Susan Soon-Keum Cox described the peculiar bond that adoptees share as being akin to that of other groups of people who have uncommon life experiences. I asked her over coffee in Eugene, Oregon, if she could talk about the bond I had heard so many adoptees claim to share, or if it was, as many said, "beyond words."

> It is beyond words, but I would imagine it's similar to other people who have any other common, profound experience. If you are a cancer survivor, if you . . . [are] a POW, obviously, these are very extreme and bad examples, but . . . [it's that] the experience is so unique that it's hard to explain to someone else who hasn't had it. . . . Even if it's someone who has a very negative view of their adoption experience or someone who has a very positive view of their adoption experience, [the key is] being with others who are, you know, just like me. I mean, those are the words that you just hear over and over. Those are the words that are the natural expression that people have about it. And I think, perhaps people think that we sit around and talk about it all the time, when in fact that is the magic—you don't have to discuss it at all; it's just deeply and profoundly understood without words.

Thus, adoptees do not share one singular and momentous historical event from which they draw their collective memory. Instead, their adoption narratives often describe common experiences of profound isolation, liminality, and survival. As the journalist Mark Hagland, adopted as an infant with his twin in 1961 to a family of German-Norwegian Lutherans in Milwaukee, Wisconsin, told me in an interview in November 2003:

> Growing up in Milwaukee [it felt like] I was a Martian who landed in a spaceship, and then I discovered there were other Martians, and they were having Martian conventions! So it's very intense and powerful because none of us had a peer group, and we didn't identify as Korean Americans or usually even as Asian Americans and yet we were discriminated against and singled out and identified, usually in a negative light. So for us now it's amazing. It's like a club that you can only join by circumstances of your birth and your life, because you have been born in Korea and adopted either to the U.S. or another country outside Korea. And it's pretty amazing, you know.

Thomas Park Clement articulated his sense of group membership in this way: "First of all, to be a member—you are a member whether you want to or not. If you are a Korean adoptee then you're enlisted. Whether you're connected through the Net or through friends, you're still a member because you have the credentials, the life experience; you share the same ghosts." Kim Park Nelson, then a board member of AKconnection, responded to my question about the negotiation of differences among adoptees by saying, "There's no difference, in my mind, that trumps . . . the adoptee identity. Obviously not everyone has had the same experience, but everyone has had the same experience of being born in Korea, and through whatever process this happens to you, you end up here. . . . That is a common experience, and I think that that will continue to be a common experience no matter how culturally sensitive your parents are kind of trained to be or how multicultural our society becomes. It will always be part of it."

Adoption "credentials" confer membership: Cox gives it a mystical, naturalized, and romantic framing, whereas Hagland sees it as an exclusive club. Park Nelson characterizes it as being grounded in a primary experience, and Clement as an inescapable haunting. These diverse articulations suggest that the fact of adoption, irrespective of particular experiences, constitutes a shared substance, which in turn invites comparisons to inalienable ties of relatedness often attributed to kinship as reckoned through blood and biogenetics—"I could be you, you could be him, he could be her."

These potent statements about the shared belonging of adoptees were reinforced by the accounts of "nonadoptee" Korean Americans I have met in adoptee social spaces. These individuals have expressed surprise or displeasure at being made to "feel as if [they] don't belong," as one Korean American friend told me after she accompanied me to an adoptee event in Seoul. It is precisely this inversion of normative signification—wherein the marked term is no longer the adoptee but rather the nonadoptee—that constitutes adoptee kinship based on "contingent essentialism." Contingent essentialism is distinct from the biologism or genetic essentialism that characterizes much of the public discourse about adoptees and their "real" origins, identities, or families. The often powerful bonds of relatedness that adoptees claim to share are not based on a common desire for pure "origins" as presumptions of genetic essentialism would suggest but rather on a shared acknowledgment of the instability and uncertainty of origins and the involuntary forfeiture of historical and cultural connections, whether one thinks of oneself as an alien, a foundling, an orphan, or a kidnapped child.

ADOPTEE KINSHIP

Adoptees are transnational migrants yet they confound conventional categories such as refugee, immigrant, or exile by sharing similarities with each of these types but not entirely conforming to any one of them. They are eminently and incompletely transnational—their lives straddle two nations, two families, and two histories—yet they typically lack the social, cultural, and economic capital to flexibly take advantage of new global transformations (see Ong 1999). Even as they are symbolically revalued as potential economic and cultural bridges and ambassadors by the Korean state, in their everyday lives, whether in Korea or in their adoptive countries, cultural citizenship and national belonging are often felt to be tenuous and incomplete. While the Korean state has extended recognition to adoptees as "overseas Koreans," thereby enfolding them into an official vision of the Korean diaspora (see chapter 5), this relationship is far from uniform for all adoptees. Moreover, the term "diaspora" is infrequently used by adoptees to describe themselves or their collective identity, in part because the significance of Korea—which can be both a site of longing and of trauma—is too unstable and polyvalent to provide a sense of home or true locus for their imagined connections.

Thus, although these adoptees may share similarities with other diasporic populations, rather than cultural identity or diaspora—which have provided useful heuristics for describing emergent social formations in light of shared histories of migration and displacement from a homeland—in my analysis I reroute diaspora through kinship to describe what I perceive to be a new form of personhood characteristic of the adoptee social imaginary. Adoptees' common experiences of disconnection, disidentification, and displacement from a real or imagined Korea and Korean family, expressed as loss, involuntary exile, a fact of life, or good fortune, bind these disparate individuals to a shared identification as a Korean adoptee. As articulated in a post by an adoptee to the electronic list Korean Adoptees Worldwide (K@W): "It's a bittersweet thing to know someone else has feelings that exactly mirror yours, sweet because it feels like you've met kin in emotion; bitter because this bond is based on the loss we share." Given the heightened symbolic load of their origins, national, cultural, and biogenetic roots are often conflated and reciprocally reinforcing, yet the often painful encounters of adoptees with incomplete transnationality disrupt essentializing and biologically rooted discourses of diaspora and hybridity (cf. Helmreich 1992). This incomplete transnationality helps to illuminate the ways in which transnational groups of all types must forge identifications across national boundaries in ways that fit their own circumstances in order to fill in the gaps of incompletion and to construct models of personhood against existing norms.

Rather than an ethnography of adoptive kinship or adoptees as a diasporic formation, therefore, I propose an ethnography of adoptee kinship that is distinguished by but not reducible to a specific generational consciousness (Mannheim 1993 [1952]). The production of adoptee kinship can be seen as a response to the lived contradictions that adoptees have experienced as racially "other" children assimilated into the normative Western nuclear family. As adults they found themselves straddling the assimilationist era in which they were socialized and the newly regnant era of multiculturalism and globalization. Self-exploration through shared storytelling is central to adoptee social practices and can be seen as a performative negotiation of self and world (Ginsburg 1989). Through these stories adoptees attempt to make sense of their past lives, and they also engage in the construction of a moral vision that includes a sense of entitlement and responsibility to participate in debates about the ongoing practice of transnational adoption as a form of child welfare and social reproduction.

Transnational and transracial adoption presents challenges to adoptees and their families that adoption agencies have only recently been addressing openly, in part as a reaction to the critical and sometimes troubling testimonies of adult adoptees. Whereas in the past a color-blind approach was tacitly encouraged, thus permitting the reproduction of the "as-if genealogical" myth of normative adoptive kinship (Modell 1994), adoptees' racial difference, although often suppressed in the family, produced dissonance in social contexts beyond the boundaries of the family and immediate community. The psychologist Richard Lee terms this phenomenon the "transracial adoption paradox" in which adoptees, despite being racial or ethnic minorities, "are perceived and treated by others, and sometimes themselves, as if they are members of the majority culture (i.e., racially White and ethnically European) due to adoption into a White family" (2003: 723).

For some adoptees this paradox is not felt to be a contradiction at all. One twenty-year-old adoptee from Connecticut described how she was "always ready" to be subject to racist comments yet knew when she went home that she was not different from her family and that she was "white." For others, however, experiences of alienation and racialized exclusion disrupt the smooth conflations of family-race-nation that transnational adoption is supposed to effectuate. As I discuss in the next chapter, adoptees' as-if genealogical kinship relations do not always guarantee their as-if membership in the dominant racial category, and neither does it secure their cultural citizenship in the nation. These gaps in the dominant discourse of adoption have produced spaces of disidentification and the grounds for adoptee kinship.

Kinship, therefore, is not simply a way for me to reference the particular form of intersubjective intimacy that adoptees have produced among themselves. Rather, it also allows me to suggest how adoptees' experiences with nonnormative family forms have laid the ground for alternative forms of personhood. Not unlike the forms of gay and lesbian kinship identified by Kath Weston (1991), the ways in which adoptive kinship "queers" or defamiliarizes normative conceptions of family and identity contribute to the production of the adoptee counterpublic.

For adoptees, social practices and cultural production are the vehicles through which they articulate what Erving Goffman called "moral careers," an understanding of the self as explained by past experiences and as an effect of one's present position (Goffman 1963).[7] Adoptees share stories of alienation and racial exclusion and also invest in a shared collective identity as a Korean adoptee through participation in conferences and membership in adoptee associations. Adoptees who identify as a Korean adoptee take the bonds among adoptees to be natural but also recognize the necessity of reproducing those bonds through community building. Thus the community is reified as a priori, out there, and waiting to be discovered but it is also something that International Korean Adoptee Associations and other adoptee organizations actively produce and perpetuate through their self-conscious networking and place-making practices. Community, like culture or kinship, therefore, cannot be taken to be natural or preexistent but rather it is an effect of contingent performances and world-making practices (Warner 2002). The adoptee counterpublic is constituted by the circulation of discourses and the performances of a collective identity that articulate a form of personhood otherwise absent or misrecognized in dominant public spheres.

3

Adoptee Cultural Citizenship

We seek to break a certain silence—silence from our land of origin, silence from the lands we now inhabit—tongues tied by racism, some external, some painfully internal; tongues tied by social mores, codes, and contradictions; tongues tied by colonialist myths of rescue missions and smooth assimilations.—TONYA BISHOFF AND JO RANKIN, *SEEDS FROM A SILENT TREE*

The child-centered adoption practices of today encourage transnational adoptive families to think of themselves as multiracial or multiethnic, and the most progressive adoption advocates strongly suggest that families assimilate and integrate into racially diverse neighborhoods. In the past, however, it was the children who were expected to meld into racially homogenous communities. Multiculturalist ideologies now frame transnational adoption as an opportunity to enrich or expand the scope of family and nation, but the first waves of Asian adoptees were inserted into Euro-American homes with the assumption that their foreignness would *not* pose a threat to hegemonic definitions of family or nation. Indeed, one might ask how it was possible that these early Asian adoptees failed to alter local or national understandings of race and culture given the radical nature of their placements at a time when laws banning Asian immigration and interracial marriages had long been in place in the United States.

A possible answer to this question lies in the power of the family as a normalizing institution. Whereas refugees and other immigrants become interpellated as citizens through a variety of biopolitical institutions (Ong 2003b), in the case of transnational adoptees their material and affective membership in the national polity—"cultural citizenship"—is primarily accomplished by and within the family. Another clue lies in the "flexible" racialization of Asians, especially in the American national imaginary (Dorow 2006), in which the transracial adoptions of black children are considered to be comparatively risky and highly controversial, especially following the censure in 1972 of transracial placements by the National Association of Black Social Workers.

Even as liberal, color-blind paradigms hopefully assumed that adoptees would seamlessly acculturate to family and nation, however, the topic of their futures did draw some concern in the early years of Asian international adoption. The International Social Service (ISS) in fact opposed the expansion of postwar South Korean adoption from mixed-race to full-Korean children because of what they considered to be insurmountable racial hurdles in pre-civil-rights era America. After the experimental placement of forty-six Chinese children from Hong Kong in the mid-1950s, ISS convened in 1959 a symposium of experts, including social workers, psychologists, and anthropologists, to discuss the issue of Asians adopted by white families in the United States (International Social Service 1960). Although it was determined that most of the children had a good chance of being accepted into their local communities due to their positive adjustment to their adoptive families, participants at the symposium repeatedly returned to an urgent question: Given the legal and cultural prohibitions against miscegenation, who would they marry when they grew up?

At the heart of this question is the issue of social reproduction and race: after assimilating into their families, schools, and churches, would adopted Asians be able to participate in the (heterosexual) reproduction of family and nation? Or would their racial difference preclude them from integrating into the social fabric? Would they become isolated outcasts or delinquents? The symposium was unable to resolve the question of the future marriage prospects of adoptees, but my point here is not to lay to rest those experts' concerns but rather to highlight the broader apprehensions about transracial, transnational adoption that the question of marriage reveals.[1] The assumption that participation in normative forms of social reproduction symbolized by marriage would resolve the adoptees' problematic belonging to the nation exposes the tacit acknowledgment that family and other institutions might fall short of fully "naturalizing" the race of the nonwhite adoptee. Yet even as current statistical evidence of marriage preferences and dating patterns of adult adoptees could be interpreted as signs of their "successful" assimilation into white families and communities (the majority of adult adoptees surveyed report being in heterosexual relationships with white partners), these metrics cannot explain the development of powerful forms of adoptee kinship since the early 1990s.

The attempts by adoptees to articulate their experiences required breaking the multiple silences that surrounded their personal adoption histories, both in their adoptive countries and in Korea. As neither native nor immigrant, adoptees existed in partial relation to dominant categories of national belonging in ways that conventional measures of marriage trends, educational attainment, and socioeconomic status could not capture. Whereas in the previous chapter I outlined adoptee kinship as a shared habitus produced out of common experiences of being "unnatural" members of normative families, in this chapter I address adoptee cultural citizenship and the problematics of national belonging in the context of globalization.

Cultural citizenship refers to everyday forms of belonging that are distinct from legal-juridical forms of inclusion instituted by formal citizenship. It refers to the ways in which structures of inclusion are also structures of exclusion and how citizenship is experienced as partial, stratified, and differentiated (Siu 2003). It also refers to the ways in which individuals become citizens through a dialectical process of "self-making" and "being made" via institutions of governmentality and within contexts of global capitalism (Ong 1996, 2003b). As Aihwa Ong notes, immigrants are valued differentially through "processes of explicit and implicit racial and cultural ranking pervading institutional and everyday practices" (1996: 740). For adoptees, their families were the main institutions through which they became naturalized and normalized as members of their adoptive nations. From childhood, however, daily contradictions between their identifications as white and their misrecognition as Asian or Korean brought into painful relief the ways in which their cultural citizenship was tied to histories of racist exclusion that distinguished them from their parents and peers. Moreover, as I describe further in this chapter, as adoptees came of age a lack of multicultural capital hindered their ability to participate in social contexts where ethnicity and cultural identity had suddenly become valued aspects of social personhood and belonging. Global flows opened up new possibilities for adoptees to engage in transnational practices with respect to Korea and other diasporic Koreans, yet they were comparatively ill equipped to engage in "flexible citizenship" (Ong 1999) or to capitalize on their cosmopolitan potential. These dynamics of inclusion and exclusion provide the basis for the adoptee social imaginary and the production of new spaces of authentic belonging. My intention in this chapter is to historically situate the emergence of the adoptee counterpublic, but my larger point is that, like problematic kinship narratives, problematic narratives of national belonging structured by global capitalism and influenced by the proliferation of identity-based social movements shaped the horizons of adoptee organizing in the late 1990s and early 2000s.

Beginning with a historical overview of adult adoptee associations, which first began forming in the 1980s in Europe and in the early 1990s in the United States, I show how, like many other identity-based movements in late modernity, adoptee organizations emerged at the conjuncture of new media technologies, normative models of self-making and self-knowledge, and new kinds of social organization. The Internet transformed what were relatively autonomous local and regional groups into a self-conscious network of individuals and groups and provided virtual spaces for the production and performance of Korean adoptee personhood.

KOREAN ADOPTEE TIME-SPACE COMPRESSION

There is no question that the acceleration of global circulations of people, commodities, ideas, and capital associated with globalization created new conditions of possibility for adult adoptees to imagine themselves as part of diasporic and transnational worlds, not only in relation to Korea—which largely came to them in the form of immigrant communities, food, consumer products, and media—but also in relation to each other, with adult adoptee presences in at least fifteen different nations.[2] Regional groups that were dispersed and disconnected in European capitals and American metropolises in the late 1980s were, by the early 2000s, increasingly coordinated as a self-conscious network of adoptee organizations, conferences, and individuals in interconnected fields of cultural production.

A cyclical regularity to the adoptee social calendar now exists, with motherland tours in Korea planned during the summer months, mini-gatherings in the fall and spring, the annual KAAN (Korean American

Adoptee Adoptive Family Network) conference in July, the GOA'L (Global Overseas Adoptees' Link) conference in August, the Gathering conferences every two or three years, and the ongoing daily email messages on Korean Adoptees Worldwide and other electronic mailing lists. This cycle is typically punctuated with announcements of smaller conferences, artists' exhibitions, workshops, and regional organization meetings in Europe, the United States, and South Korea. In addition, in conjunction with the Gathering conferences, "leadership meetings" among representatives of adoptee associations in Europe and the United States have taken place since 2003. These groups formally inaugurated the adult Korean adoptee network in 2004 with the establishment of International Korean Adoptee Associations (IKAA). Comprised of ten affiliated organizations, IKAA provides the organizational structure for the Gathering conferences. It also serves as a virtual forum for adoptees by linking their ten thousand-odd members who constitute 20 percent of all adult Korean adoptees.[3] The network and its members have become even more explicit and expansive with the proliferation of online social networking technologies that mediate publicly and privately, on a daily, or even minute-by-minute basis, adoptee relationships, social practices, and cultural production, whether through personal messages, group announcements, or advertisements for art exhibitions, film screenings, political actions, and conferences.

Undoubtedly, the mid-1990s revolution in home computing and the Internet was the key factor in the development of a reflexive recognition among adoptees of their global presence and interconnectedness. Moreover, the collapse of space and the acceleration of time associated with developments in communications and transportation technologies increasingly helped to bring the past of Korea into the present lives of adoptees. Air travel to Korea became economically affordable for more adoptees at the same time that the South Korean government and adoption agencies began to promote touristic travel to the birth country as a necessary part of the adoptee lifecycle. The adoptee counterpublic readily conforms to Benedict Anderson's model of an imagined community (1991) in that it depends upon a shared language (English) and is conditioned by the mass circulation of media that permits individuals in geographically distant locations to imagine themselves as connected to each other and existing in the same time-space as others who are having similar and simultaneous experiences. In this regard adoptees have come to marvel at their own diversity in language, nationality, and culture but can still share a powerful sense of kinship and belonging. As one Swedish adoptee told me, "It's about knowing you're not alone, but also not alone in any part of the world."

PARTIAL VIEWS OF THE ADOPTEE NETWORK

There is no official history that recounts adoptee associations and their origins, and the chronology I present here, based upon my interviews with adoptees from a variety of organizations, does not pretend to be a totalizing account. Rather, I provide a skeletal outline of partial views and pathways (Latour 2003, 2005) in order to highlight the ways that particular adoptee organization leaders imagined the community as a network. This account of their narratives implicates my work in the production of the adoptee social imaginary in that through seeking out particular social, political, and economic connections I became engaged in their very production and reproduction. My narrative is, therefore, one of many that might be written. I present here a relatively linear narrative that attempts to give shape to the multiple and ephemeral nodes of the network, but I also foreground the inherent gaps in the interviews and the contexts into which I attempt to situate them.

European Pioneers

Adoptees have been organizing regionally since 1986, the year that Mattias Tjeder, then eighteen years old, founded Adopterade Koreaners Förening (Association of Adopted Koreans, AKF). I met Mattias in August 2004 on the Overseas Koreans Foundation's Summer Cultural Awareness Training Program for Overseas Adopted Koreans—a government-sponsored motherland tour. We had just spent a few hours on the eastern coast of Korea touring the Unification Observatory where we peered through binoculars to catch a glimpse of North Korea. Back on the tour bus heading back to Seoul, as the other participants slept off another late night of drinking and socializing, I asked Mattias to tell me how he first started AKF.

In response Mattias stated that he had grown up in the suburbs of Stockholm, where he had known only one other adoptee in middle school. Then in 1985, at the age of seventeen, he "began wanting to know [his] background." This desire led him to a taekwondo school as well as to a Korean language class offered at a school run by Korean immigrants that was initiated for the enculturation of their own children. It was at the school that Mattias met four or five other adoptees. Encouraged by the South Korean embassy in Stockholm, he drew upon this small network with the goal of establishing an association for adult adoptees. Within one month, simply by word of mouth, thirty adopted Koreans had gathered. A year later AKF was featured on television, and out of that publicity it grew to more than one hundred members. As Mattias explained, "We had no idea how many adoptees were in Sweden . . . there was a Swedish Korean War veterans' association that had adoptive parents as members, and there was an association for Korean immigrants, and also the Adoption Center [an international adoption agency]. All of them wanted to be our mother association, but we decided early on that the organization was only for adoptees. We didn't want any one else to decide what we should do; we wanted to be free. We restricted the membership rules and definition [to adoptees only] and recruited people off the street." There are an estimated nine thousand Korean adoptees in Sweden, which makes it home to the largest national concentration of Korean adoptees in Scandinavia. Since 1986, according to Mattias, more than nine hundred adult members have passed through AKF. In 1989 he was invited to a three-week "homecoming" program, sponsored by the South Korean government, on which he met other adoptees from Europe. Some of these adoptees were inspired by Mattias to start their own organizations once they returned to their adoptive countries.

Mattias's account of how AKF was inaugurated resonates with the origin stories of other groups in which isolated adoptees discover each other in the metropolitan centers of Europe and the United States. Like AKF, many other organizations were first established with the help of ethnic Korean immigrants and then quickly restricted their membership to adoptees only as an assertion of autonomy and self-determination. In addition, AKF had two sister organizations, one started by Chilung Brunnegård in Göthenburg and one in Malmö started in 1988 by John Hamrin and another adoptee he met through a posting on a university bulletin board. John explained to me, over coffee and cake at the CoEX mall in Seoul in 2004, that before the Internet made it possible to publicize a group such as theirs the means of building membership often meant spotting and approaching adoptees in a crowd: "You can pick them out—adoptees going alone, acting different, or two adoptees together, speaking Swedish, not Korean or something else, or they have friends who aren't Asian." The members of

AKF-Malmö decided that the group would be restricted to adoptees born in Korea, and they even turned away an Indian adoptee.

According to John, for the Malmö group there was no local Korean immigrant presence (meaning there were no restaurants or other community groups). Because of this, he noted, "we tried to look by ourselves; someone who took lessons in Korean taught Korean. We had cultural events, discussion groups, and included Swedish traditional things. We tried to have a balance and tried not to scare people off by being too political." Malmö is twenty minutes from Copenhagen, Denmark, where a group of adoptees had formed Korea Klubben in 1991. Danish adoptees had been gathering informally at Korea House, a restaurant run by the Korean immigrants Ko Mee Rim and his wife. Ko was a former Olympic coach in taekwondo; he also ran a taekwondo school and his wife offered Korean language courses for adoptees. Members of the Malmö group also joined in these activities.

One of the adoptees that Mattias met in Korea in 1989 was Mihee Nathalie Lemoine, who started the Euro-Korean League (EKL) in Brussels in 1991. Like the adoptees in Sweden and Denmark, the founding members of EKL met at a Korean language class—this one run by a Korean immigrant church. They began socializing together on a weekly basis before deciding to organize formally. When Lemoine moved to Seoul in 1995 the organization became transnational, and the adoptee social imaginary began to take on broader dimensions.

By the 1980s South Korea's rapid modernization and increasing competitiveness in the global economy had helped it shed its postwar reputation as a poor third world country defined by its dependence upon the United States. When it was granted the honor of hosting the 1988 Summer Olympics, media images of Korea were televised worldwide. These images offered adoptees an opportunity to view their country of birth as contemporary and coeval with the West and allowed them to imagine returning to a place that had been largely consigned to distant fantasies or daydreams. Not only were images of Korea circulating globally but also products and people brought Korea into greater proximity with the everyday lives of adult adoptees.

Another key development was the discovery of adult adoptees by South Korean civic activists who were beginning to conceive of the Korean diaspora as an integral part of their globalization and democratization agendas.

In 1992 Kim Do Hyun, a South Korean Presbyterian minister, was assigned to serve as an ecumenical coordinator between Swiss and Korean-Swiss churches by the Federation of Swiss Protestant Churches, a sister organization of his church in Korea. Given the small population of Korean immigrants in Switzerland, Kim was instructed to reach out to adoptive families with children from Korea. In the process he was introduced to adult adoptees, including Kim Dae-won (Jan Wenger) who was adopted from Korea in 1968. Following the suicide of a Swiss Korean adoptee in 1993, both Reverend Kim and Kim Dae-won recognized the urgent need for a support group for adoptees. Together they established Dongari, which is the Korean word for "social circle." Within this group they organized an annual dinner, a self-help group for adoptees, and social events like ski weekends and picnics. They met once monthly, and the Korean church assisted with cultural events that introduced adoptees to the language, culture, and foods of Korea.

One year after the founding of Dongari, Reverend Kim worked with the South Korean NGO Citizens' Coalition for Economic Justice (CCEJ) to network with adoptees in Europe for a conference in Düsseldorf, Germany. The "Conference of Korean Adoptees in Europe" brought more than fifty adoptees together for the first time, and, as Mihee Nathalie Lemoine wrote on the Website for the Korea-Belgium Association, they began to learn about the different circumstances posed by racism and the politics of national inclusion in other European countries:

> Through those interactions we have learned that in Sweden, about 10 Korean adoptees demonstrated in front of the Korean Embassy in Stockholm for the first time ever to ask for recognition. Currently some adoptees are doing research on the real purpose of the initial adoptions between Sweden and Korea, advancing that it's related with Nazism. Some Danish-Korean adoptees complain about the strong racism in their adoptive country and are even scared to be listed with their Korean-Danish names, while many others see no problems. Most of the French-Korean adoptees feel a sense of great pride in being French, and view the adoptive situation with a French sense of justice and criticism.

Around the same time a growing number of adoptees were returning to Korea to live, teach English, or to study Korean. With CCEJ's support and encouragement adoptees in Korea attempted to start an organization in

Seoul to build a global network, but this effort ran aground due to personality conflicts and power struggles. In the end the group Global Overseas Adoptees' Link was formed by a group of a dozen adoptees living in Seoul with the intention of providing a home base for adoptees returning to Korea (see chapters 5 and 6).

Two years after the Düsseldorf conference, CCEJ worked with the Global Korean Network to stage the Korean diaspora conference that Thomas Park Clement attended in Los Angeles. At that time there were three Korean American adoptee organizations—Minnesota Adopted Koreans in the Twin Cities, a group in New York called Also-Known-As, and the Association of Korean Adoptees of Southern California (AKA–SoCal). Kim Dae-won had already set up two online lists, the private for-adoptees-only list Dongari and the public list Uri Nara (our nation). Through these lists he was in touch with adoptees from the United States, including members from AKA–SoCal, which began its own Website and online chat board in 1998.

American Adoptee Identity Entrepreneurs

In the United States, adoptees were scattered across a wider geographic expanse than in the European countries. Minnesota is home to more than ten thousand Korean adoptees and has the highest number per capita of adoptees in the nation, so it is not surprising that in 1991 Minnesota Adopted Koreans (MAK) became the first officially established Korean adoptee organization in the United States (Meier 1998).[4] Like its European counterparts, MAK had ties to the Korean immigrant community in the Twin Cities. It was founded with the help of the Korean Institute of Minnesota (KIM), a school organized by a Korean immigrant church for second-generation and adopted Koreans (*Korean Quarterly* 1998). Despite the early establishment of MAK, many adoptees who were raised in Minnesota and in the Midwest report having little to no knowledge of the existence of other adoptees, or, if they did, they actively avoided the few Asians or adoptees in their communities and schools.

A few years before MAK officially formed, the adult adoptees Mi Ok Bruining and Eileen Thompson were trying to network among adoptees in the Boston area; in Southern California David Nakase and Steven Morrison held informal meetings with other adult adoptees. These groups all formed prior to the mid-1990s explosion in home computing and the

Internet, and as such relied upon word of mouth, direct mailings, and media publicity to fill their ranks.

Unlike their European counterparts for whom spotting other Korean adoptees was relatively easy in the homogeneous settings of Scandinavia and northern Europe, networking and recruiting among adult adoptees in the United States presented challenges. Not only do their white names seldom give them away in school rosters or phone books but also their Asian appearance is less conspicuous in metropolitan settings with sizable Asian ethnic or immigrant populations. Adoption agencies often only have contact information for adoptive parents, which may also be out of date. Some adoptees who tried to start organizations in Europe and the United States faced resistance from agencies that, because of privacy concerns, were reluctant to help adult adoptees network with each other. The group MAK dissolved in the late-1990s without ever setting up a Website, but its successor organization AKConnection (established in 2000) made the Internet a central part of its recruitment strategy.

In December 2003, over dinner with the board of AKConnection at Seoul House restaurant in St. Paul, Mark Traynor, a former board member and the technical expert of the group, articulated the importance of the Internet for reaching adoptees:

> One of the differentiating factors was . . . the availability of the Internet; it's a huge tool. Everyone pretty much uses the Internet. You can type in "adopted Korean," and you're going to get something. Whereas three or four years ago . . . the only way to get in touch was they had these mailing lists, [they] paid a lot of money to make these labels, and then they sent out mailings. . . . You really gotta work to find an organization like that. Whereas now, I'm sitting at home at 1:30 in the morning, you know, I remember that I'm adopted Korean, and I'm thinking, you know [laughter], I'm serious, we've all been there.

As other board members laughed sympathetically at Mark's characterization of the closeted adoptee, sitting at home and offhandedly searching for "adopted Korean" online, they echoed him, saying, "Yeah, we've all been there."

Tawni Traynor, Mark's spouse and then president of the group, added the following comment: "I know that that's where [the Website] really serves its purpose. Because people aren't ready to come out in the open, they're not ready to come to an event. But they can read adoptee stories and find out there's a lot of adoptees out there and find out there's stuff going on. Eventually they'll be thinking, and they're going to be ready. It takes a while." In other words, the adoptee counterpublic was constituted by adoptees actively engaging in public intimacy or silently lurking, but still imagining themselves as being addressed by the circulating discourses of other adoptees "out there."

The online chat board run by AKA–SoCal was an early form of networking for adoptees in Europe and the United States, and its actual-world organization was active in publicizing the existence of adult adoptees in the Southern California area and nationally. After Los Angeles and its sizable Korean immigrant presence became a televised spectacle of racial dystopia during the 1992 Rodney King uprising, it was reported in the Korean ethnic media that the city had become a magnet for runaway Korean adoptees (cited in Hübinette 2005: 208). Whether or not this was true, adoptees in the Los Angeles area began meeting and organizing shortly thereafter. Jo Rankin had grown up in San Diego and was a founding member of AKA–SoCal. Eventually she met Basil Zande, a Korean adoptee from Switzerland, and his second-generation Korean American wife, SoYun Roe, and in 1994 they turned their casual conversations and mutual interests in adoption issues into an official organization. Rankin was instrumental in recruiting adoptees to come to the 1997 Global Korean Network conference, and in July 1999 Roe curated "Snapshot," an exhibit at the Korean American Museum to coincide with the first annual Korean American Adoptee Adoptive Family Network (KAAN) conference. Acknowledging that the adoptees had "come of age," the Snapshot exhibit was the first of its kind to focus on Korean adoptee history and experiences.

On the East Coast, Hollee McGinnis, an adoptee from Westchester County in New York state, started the group Also-Known-As in New York City in 1996. After graduating from college she met a few other adoptees through a Korean-American community service organization and also through a self-realization workshop, where she first began thinking about forming an organization for transnational adult adoptees. The organization's name, Also-Known-As, refers to adoptees' dual lineages—as Hollee McGinnis, aka Lee Hwa Yong, for instance. In 2000 in New York City the group sponsored a screening of the adopted Korean filmmaker Nathan Adolfson's *Passing Through*. After the film, a discussion was led by the group's president, Peter Savasta, who grew up in an Italian American neighborhood in Queens. At one point in the session he described how as a youth he had been known as the "Italian kid," adding further that adoptees "feel completely American, yet outside, people say things like, 'You speak English very well,' or, 'where do you come from?' We're not completely American because of our appearance, but we're not Korean culturally."[5] Savasta underscored the significance of producing social spaces for adoptees to be both in a social context that they often feel requires them to choose one over the other: "We are sitting on the fence, trying to create a space for ourselves. If you can get enough people on that fence, you can collapse it and take from both, move between the two sides."

Whereas many adoptees had always felt a sense of alienation from both white peers and Asian others, this sentiment was by no means universal. Some had never experienced their identities as problematic until comparing stories with other adoptees, which then provided an opportunity to reflect on their own ethnic socialization. In October 2004 the president of Boston Korean Adoptees (BKA), Jen Strong, told me about how she first met other adoptees through a posting on the Internet in 1998. Adopted as an infant in 1971 and raised in Cape Cod, Strong attended a preppy New England boarding school. She said that meeting other adoptees helped her to retrospectively understand her own experience as a nonwhite WASP: "I never really realized that the questioning I did when I was in my late teens, like, well, I'm a Protestant, but I'm not a White Anglo Saxon Protestant, so I guess I'm just a 'P.'" She laughed, and continued by saying, "I can't really say I'm a WASP. I didn't realize at the time that I was doing that because I had been adopted transracially so I was going through all the identity questioning."

When Strong was twenty-five her mother met by chance a Korean adoptee who was the son of the harbor master at a Cape Cod marina, and she told Jen about it: "So when she was telling me this story, a little light bulb went off in my head. 'Oh, there must be other adoptees my age, not just the little kids I see in the mall with white parents, but people my age.'" While surfing the Internet she found some Websites related to Korean adoption, and in 1998 she came across an announcement inviting adoptees living in the Boston area to a dinner meeting. She went to the restaurant where twenty adoptees also showed up. That was the beginning of BKA.

Adult Korean adoptee organizations now exist in Belgium, Canada,

Denmark, France, Holland, Luxembourg, Norway, Switzerland, Sweden, the United Kingdom, Germany, Australia, and Korea, and in at least a dozen American states, including California, Illinois, New York, Oklahoma, Oregon, Massachusetts, Minnesota, Washington, Texas, Hawaii, and Vermont. Although only the oldest and largest groups are permitted to be members of IKAA, all are considered to be part of the global network of adoptee associations. Even as the Internet provided the means for more efficient recruiting and information sharing among adoptees, conferences offered the opportunity for large numbers of adoptees to meet face to face. They quickly became sites for the materialization of the network and the self-objectification of adoptees for themselves and for wider publics.

NEW MONUMENTS

I began my research in 1999 in Washington, D.C., at the International Gathering of the First Generation of Korean Adoptees (now known simply as the Gathering), which is widely recognized as the beginning of the international adoptee community. For adoptees who went to the Gathering it was the experience of being among so many other adoptees that was affectively compelling and symbolically resonant. Cheryl Scimeca, a former member of AKA–SoCal, told me how, since it was to be her first trip to the nation's capital, she had planned to visit historical monuments after the conference. But after witnessing the sheer number of adoptees who'd gathered together, her attention shifted: "I had no interest afterwards. I was like, 'Who the hell cares about monuments? I've just met over four hundred adoptees in one room' . . . and I never thought we could do that, so that was more amazing and monumental than seeing [any] stupid American monument."

Scimeca actively disidentified with the nation and its "stupid monuments" in favor of identifying with an emergent subculture of adoptees. Yet the adoptee counterpublic was predicated not merely on the spectacle of its own members, who had gathered together for the first time, but also on "an awareness of its subordinate status" in relation to a dominant, normative public (Warner 2002: 86). As they collectively explored their similarities and differences, a growing sense of ownership over their own experiences developed. Thus, although participants at the Gathering frequently remarked on the need for more scientific and statistical research to help them understand the broader significance of the similarities and differences among them, also gaining force was a desire to exercise their "voice," "break a certain silence," "tell their own stories," and claim moral authority over international adoption.

The "first generation" referred to in the title of the first Gathering followed the sociological convention of designating a generation as a thirty-year interval. As such it included adoptees between the ages of twenty-one and fifty who were born and adopted between the 1950s and 1970s. Although within that generation there are several waves of adoptees—roughly periodized by decade, beginning with the Korean War orphans in the mid-1950s, the second wave of adoptees in the 1960s, and the third wave in the 1970s—a defining feature of this large group is that they grew up under the banner of assimilation and today find themselves in the era of globalization and multiculturalism. Moreover, the counterpublic defined itself in contradistinction to Korean diasporic formations and to a new generation of adoptive families who became highly visible and vocal in the late 1990s and early 2000s as adoptions from China expanded dramatically (Volkman 2005b).

Thus, just at the moment that adult adoptees were claiming agency over their own histories and beginning to formulate a language to describe their experiences, ethnic Koreans, adoptive parents, and agency social workers were actively seeking to frame adoption in ways that many adoptees felt further silenced them. As mentioned in chapter 2, by the late 1990s diasporic Korean community leaders, even when they attempted to include adoptees, often neglected the significant ways in which their experiences diverged from the typical Korean immigrant experience. Whereas Koreans in the West often framed them as long-lost members of the Korean community and looked upon them with a mixture of guilt, pity, and probing curiosity, adoptive parents and adoption social workers seemed to impose a whitewashed version of adoption as a highly successful social experiment. Especially in light of the popularity of the Chinese adoptions that inaugurated a new wave of international adoptions to the West, parents adopting children from Asia were anxious to hear about adult adoptee experiences. They viewed adoptees ambivalently as experts who were transnational adoption's pioneers and as object lessons of the previous generation of adoptive parents' unenlightened views on culture and adoption (Brian 2007). Adoptee collective personhood has thus been shaped in relation to nonadoptee others who attempted to appropriate adoptee experiences into their own authoritative discourses about the meaning and significance of transnational Korean adoption.

Adoptive Parents

From adult adoptees' perspectives, adoptive parents, like social workers, are seeking to define and diagnose adoptee issues with what adoptees view as an objectifying and instrumentalizing agenda. As Maureen Grimaud put it, "The problem is that adoptive parents are trying to define what an adoptee is, and the adoptee is saying, 'No, no, no, no, no, we're in a whole different class that nobody has been able to define, and we are ourselves are still trying to define who we are. So, how can you tell us what we are, what we think we know, or what we think we are, when we don't even know?' So therein, I think, lies the miscommunication between the two."

Some adoptees such as Sunny Jo, who has been engaged in not a few flame wars with adoptive parents on her electronic mailing list K@W, explained how the accessibility of knowledge in the postmodern era has become the grounds for asserting authoritative accounts of the meaning of adoption, against the personal narratives of adoptees themselves: "Some of the current adoptive parents really scare me. Our parents . . . , I mean, they were ignorant because there wasn't a lot of information around. But the current ones, they think they know everything because they've read all this information that's available. [They're] totally obnoxious, like, we know that, we know better. And often to adult adoptees who've lived it."

This condescension from a new generation of adoptive parents has been potently articulated online, especially in response to the postings on adoptee personal blogs and on electronic mailing lists and news feeds where adoptive parents seek out the words and perspectives of adult adoptees. These new parents may find, however, that what they hear is disturbing, angry, or an affront to their own moral vision and reproductive choices. In their responses to adoptees' views, implicit or explicit assumptions often posit a causal relation between an adoptee's negative adoption experience and his or her negative views on adoption. For Sunny Jo, the conflation of personal difficulty with political attitudes is a false one: "That's the argument, but that's not reality. They think, oh, if you're against adoption, you hate your adoptive parents, you have a bad relationship with them, and you had a shitty life. No, it's actually quite the opposite—it's often people who have a very good relationship with adoptive parents and have had an okay life, but [they] start to question. Because they've had the support of adoptive parents, they've had the support to actually think critically."

Since the early 2000s, adopted children from Asia, especially those in families of middle-class to upper-middle-class urban professionals, have been, in the late capitalist age of super-parenting, inundated with cultural heritage. Often they are integrated from a young age into communities of other adopted children and adoptive families, sent to culture camps, and regularly travel back to their birth country. In contrast the Korean adoptees of this so-called first generation were adopted into a range of families within the broad swath of the American middle class, from lower to upper middle. They resided primarily in the Midwest, in suburban and rural areas, and very frequently were the only Koreans or Asians, aside from adopted siblings, in their neighborhoods and schools. A narrative that has come to dominate transnational adoption discourses since the 1990s distinguishes the first generation Korean adoptees from foreign children adopted today by the fact that they and their parents lacked the information about birth country and birth culture and the support services from adoption agencies, known as postadoption services, that are now widely available.

Adoption agencies and the new generation of adoptive parents with children from Asia focus on the progressive choices they have made to inform themselves and to educate their children in their cultural heritage. They contrast their proactive parenting with that of the parents of adult Korean adoptees, and while there may be some truth to this comparison many adult adoptees feel that this attitude of enlightenment disguises a defensiveness among adoptive parents who may be comfortable with providing cultural heritage in the form of multiculturalist consumer practices but who are also deeply uncomfortable with issues of racial difference and their own white privilege. Thus, although adult adoptees acknowledge that the racialized exclusions that mark Asian experiences in the United States may be ameliorated through cultural exposure, they insist that exposure through consumption is not enough. Adoptees see white parents' inability to grasp histories of racism and experiences of racialized minorities in the United States as a problem of white privilege, which also blinds them to the inevitability that their children will fit into the nation differently than they do.

In effect, despite the fact that adoptive parents today have more resources to learn about adoption, multiculturalism, and identity development, adoptee organizers believe that transracial adoptee personhood is a form of embodied difference that they alone are uniquely qualified to discuss and to fully comprehend. Eileen Thompson, a trained social worker who counsels adoptees and college students in Boston, explained how little things had changed since her childhood in the 1970s: "When I meet these groups at KAAN and places like that, I would like to be able to think that all the things I was subjected to growing up—I would like to feel like kids these days [adoptee youths at KAAN conferences] don't have to deal with it, but it's not true—you hear the same stories. It's like a time warp. . . . And I don't expect that anyone gets through unscathed."

Adoptees like Eileen see adoption agency professionals and adoptive parents today as being overly invested in a narrative of progress and change that considers the problems of the previous generation of parents —namely, their failure to recognize the importance of cultural identity and racial difference—as having already been addressed and resolved. Adoptees in this way articulate counternarratives to the dominant story of transnational adoption as the realization of multiculturalism's promises of a truly pluralist society. Indeed, this generation demarcates the positive and negative limits of transracial, transnational adoption—exemplifying both the potential for interracial harmony and the failures of color-blind ideologies. Many adoptees feel that the discourses of pluralism and colorblindness that may have encouraged and celebrated their parents' choices to raise a nonwhite child hampered their own identity formation because they were left isolated when faced with the realities of racial difference and discrimination.

The tensions between adult adoptees and the new generation of adoptive parents are perhaps most keenly felt by adoptees who are also parents. Mark Hagland employed the analogy of Kosovo to describe the embattled relationship between adult adoptees and adoptive parent organizations such as KAAN. Not only is the struggle over the politics of representation and the legitimization of opposing ideological positions but also, ultimately, it is over the recognition of adult adoptee agency. Mark sees himself as a bridge person and is able to identify with the desires of adoptive parents to guarantee their children's happiness, but he also acknowledges the necessity of adoptee self-identification and self-articulation:

> Now, being a parent, I totally empathize. I want my child to hav perfect life and I want to protect her. . . . Today's parents are so mu better educated than our parents were, but they almost bend over backwards, you know; they get the kids to the culture camp when they're four years old, they take the taekwondo, they get them a *hanbok* [traditional Korean attire] when they're two years old, it's like too much, you know. I think that's where . . . the self-identification and the self-articulation comes in. Because we have always had other people tell us who we are. And we kind of need to say who we are ourselves. For me, it's not a matter of hostility or resentment or pushing back. For some it is. . . . And that is totally legitimate. Once we find that we can empower ourselves, you can't take it back. So maybe there is that little bit of ferociousness there.

Korean Americans

Aside from tensions between adult adoptees and new adoptive parents, adult adoptees also had to negotiate relations with other diasporic Koreans. Whereas adoptive parents and agency workers embraced culture in their attempts to address transnational adoptees' difference, often by using culture as a proxy for race, ethnic Koreans embraced a racialized view of being Korean that subsumed culture into race.

In the United States, the Immigration and Nationality Act of 1965 lifted discriminatory national-origins quotas and made it possible for Koreans to settle in the United States in unprecedented numbers. Around the same time, South Korean population policies actively encouraged the emigration of its citizens, including adoptable children, to ameliorate the demographic pressures on economic growth and stability. Thus the peak years of Korean adoption in the 1970s and 1980s coincided with the rapid increase in Korean migrations to the West. Adoptees who attended college in the 1970s and 1980s had few opportunities to meet second-generation or 1.5-generation Korean Americans (those who emigrated as young children or teenagers) among their classmates, although exchange students from Korea may have been their first exposure to ethnic Koreans. For those who attended college in the 1990s and early 2000s, however, a growing cadre of Korean exchange students as well as a nascent or well-developed Korean American student subculture made it more likely that they would meet "real" Koreans. Korean student associations mushroomed on college campuses around the country in the 1980s and 1990s, and the annual Korean American Student Conference (KASCON) was inaugurated in 1987. In addition, Christian college groups such as Campus Crusade for Christ developed vibrant Korean American presences.[6]

These spaces provided meeting grounds for young second-generation Korean Americans to congregate around shared cultural values and social networks. Like the second-generation South Asian college youths that Sunaina Maira has written about, Korean American college youths also engage in symbolic ethnicity and invest in forms of cultural nationalism and tradition based on "nostalgia without memory" (2002: 113).[7] These social boundaries and distinctions based on cultural markers and ethnicized knowledge could, however, have the effect of implicitly excluding other Korean Americans, especially adoptees, who were unschooled in Korean ways. In 2003 Sarah Dankert, recently graduated from Barnard College, told me that a Korean American male friend who did not know she was adopted told her that he had recently broken up with his girlfriend because "she was too much of a Twinkie, she was too white." This flippant comment raised for Sarah the culturalist, racialized, and gendered expectations that surrounded her—"I was like, 'Oh, what if he finds out I'm white?' That's the kind of mentality and it's so hard core." That this brand of race politics, which excludes adoptees as inauthentically Korean, informs stereotypes of adoptees held by some Korean Americans became clear to me after meeting a Korean American from California while socializing with a group of adoptees in Seoul. In his attempt to establish rapport with me he made clear distinctions between us and them: "They're so white bread, aren't they?"

LOCATING "KOREAN ADOPTEE CULTURE"

The rise of identity politics on United States college campuses and in social life at large offered new opportunities for Korean adoptees to encounter Asian Americans and Korean Americans. For some, however, these experiences served only to heighten feelings of liminality and disidentification. Adoptee authors have employed metaphors of tightropes or pendulums to capture a feeling of suspension between two reified cultures—Korean and American.[8] For others, even the image of a pendulum swinging between two irreconcilable locations was an overly optimistic rendering of what was experienced as a painfully static in-betweenness. Adoptees who experienced rejection by ethnic Koreans and rejection from white peers or family might have simply felt stuck in a cultural nether land. A number of adoptees spoke of how their interest in exploring their "Korean half," whether related to searching for Korean family or exploring cultural roots, was disparaged by or considered threatening to their white peer group and their adoptive parents.

Unlike second-generation ethnic Americans for whom cultural awakening or interest is often grounds for strengthening family ties and belonging, for transracial adoptees this assertion may instead be the grounds for greater individuation and differentiation from adoptive family. Not a few adoptees described how traveling to Korea and potentially searching for one's natal family introduces a threat to their kinship bonds with adoptive parents, usually mothers. Coming out as an Asian, Korean, or adoptee for some meant disrupting multiple myths of the as-if genealogical family, of love trumping racial difference, and of the well-adjusted adoptee. As Kim Park Nelson writes, "If family harmony is dependent upon adoptees' understanding and agreement that race doesn't matter, the insistence that racial difference does matter can upset this balance, sometimes in extreme ways" (2007: 203).

This crucial stage in the adoptee journey is one marked by disidentification in which they recognize that they fit neither the dominant monoracial constructions of America as white nor ethnocentric constructions of Koreanness, whether among South Koreans or Korean Americans. In this context, meeting other adoptees who are "just like me" has been articulated by many adoptees as life transforming. Adult adoptees of the "first generation" lacked role models and some are thereby especially keen to provide the support and mentorship for each other that their parents and other institutions could not. As one adoptee at the Gathering in 1999 said, "This [the conference] is a statement to parents that we didn't get what we needed then and we're getting it now."

Adopted Korean groups in Europe and the United States, since the late 1980s and early 1990s, have been identifying and addressing what adoptees need by providing spaces for virtual or actual dialogue, circulating information about Korea and adoption, and educating adoptive parents or mentoring younger adoptees. Some groups are mainly social and focus on the importance of private spaces for talk and peer counseling, whereas others invest in the broader circulation of counterpublic discourses into the public sphere with book readings, film screenings, cooking classes, informational sessions, conferences, and mentorship programs. Like most voluntary associations, many members of the groups' leadership struggle with maintaining attendance and membership. Further, the organization can be like a revolving door with adoptees entering and leaving without giving back to the growth of the organization once they've fulfilled their personal goals for joining the group, whether to address emotional or psychological difficulties related to adoption, to make adoptee friends, or simply to satisfy curiosity.

The adoptee organization presidents and board members I met in 2003 had stayed on in their positions for consecutive years and spoke of anticipated burn out because there was no one willing or able to replace them.[9] The commitment to providing a space for adoptees to congregate was, however, universally expressed by those involved with adoptee organizing. Even when faced with the frustrations of apathetic members or an uneven turnout at events, the board members I spoke with felt that they fulfilled an important, sometimes urgent, need for adoptees who would otherwise have few alternatives for emotional and psychological support. Fellowship, mentorship, and networking are key terms in adoptee organizing discourse, and adoption agencies now recognize that these activities and mentoring relationships are essential to postadoption services. Despite this acknowledgment, as volunteer organizations, adoptee groups often struggle to survive, and they depend upon the long-term commitment of a few key individuals.

In October 2003 at a well-attended dinner meeting and reading by the adoptee author Jane Jeong Trenka organized by Also-Known-As, I spoke with Joy Lieberthal, then president of the group and a social worker at an adoption agency in New York. She explained to me in passionate terms how she wanted to reach the "thousands of other adoptees who don't come to these events, and the thousands of other parents who don't come." For Joy, Also-Known-As provides a necessary alternative source of support for adoptees who find adoption agency programs targeted only for young children, or who might seek counseling from a therapist who lacks expertise about adoption-related issues, and who therefore might end up in unhealthy intimate relationships because of internalized racism and confused ethnic and racial identifications.

In contrast to their American counterparts, adoptees in European countries constitute the majority of ethnic Korean immigrants. As noted earlier, connections to Korea for European adoptees were often mediated by one or two first-generation immigrants who took an interest in adoptees as fictive kin in the homogeneous racial landscapes of Scandinavia and Western Europe. These Korean migrants were part of the new waves of immigration to Europe in the 1980s and 1990s, but they were largely overshadowed by larger and more politically controversial waves of refugees and labor migrants from the Middle East, Africa, and Eastern Europe. Many adoptees distanced themselves from these stigmatized immigrant groups—whose difference was framed as a problem of assimilation and incommensurate cultural values rather than race and who were the target of virulent xenophobias and extremist forms of nationalism. The differences among European and American adoptees and the differences among adoptees from different European countries with respect to race, culture, and nation are well beyond the scope of my study, but the fact that European adoptees also had to contend with the problematic of cultural citizenship should be obvious. Fully assimilated into predominantly elite families, European adoptees could simultaneously feel secure in their national belonging due to their class privilege—for instance, by speaking "more perfect Danish" than other Danes—yet also be subject to constant misrecognition as a foreigner, that is, an immigrant, which signified the poor, uneducated, and culturally other. Although some adoptees associated with immigrant communities in Europe, many more existed as "almost, but not quite" white European (Bhabha 1994).

For European associations, especially before widespread Internet access, creating connections between adoptees and Korea was a central pursuit. At the twentieth anniversary conference for the Swedish association AKF, Lena Kim-Arctaedius addressed a question about the organization's future: "It's about generations—for our generation we felt more Swedish than anything else. The younger generation has greater contact with older adoptees and Asian culture. They don't come to AKF for Korean culture—they can listen to K-pop and watch a Kim Ki Duk film [on the Internet]—so one of the main activities we do is not sought after so much." This statement points toward a more general trend among adult adoptee groups—as global flows made Korea more accessible to adoptees and their parents the focus shifted from Korean culture to Korean adoptee culture.

This distinction came up when I asked the AKConnection board if they included Korean culture in their programs. As Tawni Traynor responded, "We don't know how to do that. . . . We eat together; we know the food. We ourselves don't know the culture that well." Her husband, Mark, added, "The events are focused on adoptee things, things that no one—you can probably go to University of Minnesota and take a class in Korean. But you can't go [anywhere to take a course on being an adoptee] that's why it's the unique environment to talk to someone about why you can't say *annyong-haseyo* ["hello" in Korean] correctly."

Mark emphasized his point by giving his pronunciation of annyong-haseyo a particularly flat Midwestern flavor, which amused all of us. Despite the parodic tone, however, his comparison offers a more sobering insight. One can take a class in Korean language and culture but there is nowhere to take a class in being an adoptee. Adoptee knowledge cannot be so directly transferred because it is lived and embodied knowledge grounded in inauthenticity—the inability to speak Korean correctly, for instance—that is distinctively shared by adoptees. Adoptees, especially those over thirty, straddle eras characterized by assimilationist and pluralist models of cultural belonging. They lack multicultural capital in a relatively new context in which race and ethnicity are actively foregrounded aspects of social and political identity, and knowledge of one's roots and heritage grants social value and personhood to immigrants and people of color. Thus adoptee contingent essentialism connects inauthenticities and disidentifications of race and ethnicity as well as the uncertainties of adoption histories.

As Kim Park Nelson, another board member and Korean adoption scholar, added, "The organization does a lot to support adoptee culture, if that exists. There's more emphasis on that [than on Korean culture]." I then asked the board if they agreed that there is something like an adoptee culture, to which Mark responded: "It's funny . . . hearing all three of those people [three other board members who'd been expressing their expectations of the upcoming adult adoptee conference in Seoul] saying that the reason they want to go to Korea is that they want the experience of being around a lot of other Korean adoptees. . . . Because, when you grow up, at least myself, and don't know any other adoptees . . . well, I'm trying to hang out with Koreans, and it's not working out too good, and I'm trying to hang out with these [other] people, and it's not working out too good. When you are in a group of Korean adoptees, you definitely feel like—that, to a certain degree . . . that's your race, or whatever you want to call it." Tawni then seconded his description, saying: "That's your people."

NEW NORMS AND AUTHENTICITIES

Mi Ok Song Bruining calls the instantaneous bonds of adoptee relatedness "instimacy." This instant intimacy and sense of belonging, however, can mask internal differences, status distinctions, and exclusions within the community. Predictable vectors of difference exist in terms of class, gender, sexual orientation, and disability, and these intersect with others specific to Korean transnational adoption: race and racialization, relationship to Korea, attitudes toward birth family searches, and political views on adoption.

Most adoptees I met who participated in adoptee "real-life communities" shared common backgrounds in terms of class and education, and the conference circuit and travels to Korea have become privileged zones that are available to individuals with the financial means and flexibility to participate. Sunny Jo explained to me that in the online world there is greater diversity than in the real-life communities of organizations or conferences that are, she states, "kind of selective in their scope. They are catering mainly to a middle-class, professional, university-educated base. For someone who is not from that background I think it's often very difficult to get a foothold in those real life groups. I know people I've met on the Internet who have been former prison inmates or former homeless [people] or drug abusers. They said, 'Well, I didn't feel welcome in the real life groups because I didn't have the same background, I didn't talk like the other people, didn't think like them, because my experience was so different,' but they say on the Internet it's easier, it's more accepting. Maybe because they can be more anonymous, it's not like they have to stand up [and say] 'Hello, I'm a prison inmate.'"

In fact, in response to a board member who marveled at the "instant" connection she had experienced with European adoptees, Kim Park Nelson cautioned, "It's been very alienating for some people. They feel like there should be that [instant connection], but they don't—'oh I feel like I should be relating to you really well, because we're both adopted, but I don't.'" Park Nelson has been sensitive to the creation of adoptee orthodoxies not only as an academic but also as someone who was initially put off by racialized attitudes among adoptees in their twenties who disparaged first-generation immigrants and disapproved of interracial dating. Her partner is white and she realized that this would be a liability in building rapport with other adoptees: "I found out on the first day [of the conference] that there's this very anti-white dating sentiment around. So I'm like, oh shit, here I am with my white boyfriend; as soon as I thought that, that's awful, why would I even question my own relationship for a minute because of this? . . . I really started thinking in a more focused way about articulating, not so much defending, my relationship, but contesting the idea that there's one adoptee identity, and if you're not in it you're somehow less authentic. It took me a whole year, from being, 'Huh, people actually think this,' to being able to say something about it."

The internal diversity of adoptees and adoptee experience has been acknowledged at conferences like the Gathering that explicitly project an image of adoptee unity, yet over the past several years certain vectors of experience have become dominant optics through which adoptees view themselves and identify each other, thereby creating new statuses and developmental trajectories. For instance, typical questions that adoptees asked each other reflected the ways that they identify each other and themselves as Korean adoptees: When were you adopted? Where did you grow up? Have you gone to Korea? Have you searched for your birth family? These questions correspond to what have become normative stages in the adoption journey.

These stages include meeting other adoptees, traveling to Korea on a motherland tour, meeting foster parents or visiting orphanages, searching for and possibly finding relatives, living in Korea for an extended period, having children, or adopting from Korea oneself. Adoption social workers frame these rites of passage as part of the adoption journey. The adoption journey is a "technology of the self" (Foucault et al. 1988) that provides a model of adoptee subject formation that is progressive and developmental, as well as somewhat predictive but still open to variation and revision. Adoptees who are new to the adoption community and the adoption journey are often referred to as "first timers" who gain more knowledge and expertise as they proceed on their journey. First timers refers to adoptees who have never been to an adoptee conference or participated in an adult adoptee activity, or have only recently come out as an adopted Korean and are thus considered to be inadequately racialized, perhaps still thinking of themselves as white.

The term "first timer" was also used by "long timers" in Korea to refer to adoptees who were in Korea for the first time since they left as children, and it connotes the assumption that they would be more emotionally fragile than those who had already undergone the initial culture shock and demystifications of their expectations of return. Certainly not all adoptees follow the same trajectory, and some adoptees never meet another adoptee until they travel to Korea or they may find a birth family but never join an adoptee group. The journey might therefore be described as a gradual opening up and extension of the adoptee into broader fields of racial and ethnic identification, across local, national, and transnational scales. The journey as metaphor for identity development thus offers a narrative framework in which a heroic protagonist recovers personhood by making connections between past, present, and future, but the destination is less important than foregrounding the ongoing constructedness of the self. The journey captures the ways in which adoptees' desire to "repair the broken narrative" (Tomes 1997)—to achieve the wholeness or plentitude promised by the truth of origins—is predicated on its own impossibility. It is a therapeutic model that foregrounds indeterminacy but also frames the process of identity construction as an agentive one grounded in an individual search for greater knowledge of the self, whether in striving for coherence or embracing fragmentation (see E. Kim 2001).

Racialization, age, and life cycle experiences also have distinct effects on how identifications are articulated and constructed. Adoptees of the first wave who are now in their forties and fifties, some of whom are of mixed ethnicities, often viewed the younger cohort, those in their twenties and thirties who grew up in greater proximity to multiculturalism and globalization, as luckier because it was easier for them to explore and connect to Korea or Korean Americans. Whereas they were more likely to identify with their adoptive parents' ethnic heritage as German-Norwegian or Italian, for instance, the younger adoptees often demonstrated greater flexibility around ethnic identity, especially those who met other ethnic Koreans in college, who moved to more diverse neighborhoods or urban centers during or after college, and who spent time visiting or working in Korea.

Maureen Grimaud described this group as the "AKA generation" in reference to adoptees who are active in Korean adoptee associations and thus have more opportunities to learn about Korean culture. Grimaud, who was adopted in 1963 at the age of two to a "farm family" in rural Minnesota, felt that her generation was already beyond the point at which they could undo their racialized identifications. She had attended the first Gathering in Washington, D.C., and then became a regular participant in what is known as the "mini-gathering" phenomenon—that is, the informal get-togethers for adult adoptees in various cities across the United States that attract anywhere from two dozen to more than one hundred adoptees every six months. When I called Grimaud at her home in South Carolina, she explained, "It's taken forty-two years to get out of the white shell, and resoundingly, we all felt white. We didn't feel the least bit Korean. Being raised in a really small white community, isolated . . . When you grow up that way some things are hard to get out of your mind."

The exchange of information about birth family search provided one of the strongest motivations for adoptees to seek each other out. Jen Strong pointed out that in the late 1990s she perceived a strong assumption among adoptees that everyone would at some point want to search for their Korean family—and if one didn't then it was assumed that one was "in denial." She also became tired of always having to eat Korean food when she socialized with adoptees, and she wondered, "Can't we go to an Italian restaurant?" She went on to describe how the expansion of the community in numbers has now forced a broadening of "what's normal." As she explained: "But since then, though, I've noticed for the past two years or so, that attitude is going away, as people now realize that you can't, there's so many of us, that you can't just say oh we're all like this, or we're all like that. And a lot of people now have matured in their viewpoints, to see, it's ok if you don't want to search, a lot of people don't, or it's ok if you do, there's nothing wrong with you. I think our sense of what's normal has been broadened. And I think overall people have become more accepting."

The most divisive issue among adoptees is that of international adoption itself in its positive and negative moral valences. Debates about transnational adoption often construe it as either a humanitarian expression of altruism or an egocentric act that capitalizes on the disempowerment and disenfranchisement of third world women. Adoptees themselves often are asked to weigh in on the debate—"Are you for or against?" Indeed, I was also frequently asked to represent my own views on adoption when discussing my research with adoptees, given the polarized ways in which all research and authoritative knowledge is appropriated to support pro- or anti-adoption points of view.

The divisiveness of this topic for adoptees reflects the lack of consensus in national and transnational publics about the costs and benefits of transnational adoption as a system embedded in a broader history of Western imperialism, American hegemony, and stratified reproduction. Adoptees who oppose the system that produced them, however, have until recently been pathologized as angry, maladjusted, resentful, or otherwise irrational by adoption agency social workers and adoptive parents, as well as other adoptees. On the opposite side, adoptees who are pro-adoption may become active in reproducing the institutions of Korean adoption as volunteers at orphanages, camp counselors, adoption agency consultants, or adoption agency workers.

Of course, these reductive and absolute binaries obscure what are, in fact, much more ambivalent and shifting feelings about Korean adoption as a defining event in one's own life and as a fifty-year-old system. But it is precisely the contingent aspect of adoption and the adoptee's lack of agency in his or her destiny that makes it such a fraught topic. As I explore in greater detail in the next chapter, my research revealed that the articulation of feelings about one's individualized experience as an adoptee was actively encouraged as a therapeutic exploration of identity, yet discussions about the structural politics of international adoption were often viewed as divisive and undermining of community. For instance, an initial attempt to found a group in Chicago ran aground when some adoptees wanted to make it explicitly political and others were interested in cultural activities and socializing.

CONCLUSION

Adoptees present an implicit challenge to essentialized notions of identity in which isomorphisms of place, space, and culture (Gupta and Ferguson 1992) reduce the multiple vectors of difference and power that compose subjectivities to knowable and homogeneous cultures. Kinship, race, and nation are all hybrid frameworks that organize social personhood and gain explanatory and normative force through their purported rootedness in biology and blood even as they are understood to be social constructions. Biogenetic metaphors often gain force from gendered ideologies of family and link genealogical relations to naturalized forms of belonging, whether to an ethnic or racial group or to a national territory (McClintock 1995; Malkki 1995; Carsten 2004), but adoptees' migrations expose the fault lines of these naturalized discourses.

For adoptees, cultural citizenship has proven to be eminently problematic, as their racial difference has marked their distant and different origins in racialized landscapes in which Asians in the United States (and Europe) have historically experienced what Devon Carbado calls "racial extraterritorialization," which encapsulates a state of "inclusion in American citizenship and exclusion from American identity" (2005: 638). Adopted as orphans who were severed from natal origins and made "free" for adoption, these children of "pure humanity" were resignified as American or French citizens, and they were brought back into the "national order of things" (Malkki 1994) through their legal incorporation as "immediate relatives" or "as-if genealogical" sons and daughters. But the security of that identity was consistently undermined by the prevalent conflation of racial difference and foreignness, thereby revealing the fiction that equates citizenship with nationality. Adoptees' daily confrontations with the problematics of belonging suggest that dominant epistemes of personhood and self-making—kinship, race, and nation—continue to be powerfully salient despite the breakdown of biogenetic definitions of family, the defunct myth of the biological basis of race, and the predicted erosion of the power of the nation-state under globalization. The answer to "who am I?" is thereby frequently pursued through a search for origins—whether birth family, racial and ethnic community, or birth country. In Korea and among Koreans, however, adoptees confront another set of ethnocentrisms and naturalized categories that implicitly discount their complex histories. Many now locate home in translocal virtual and actual spaces where adoption rather than procreation is the "fact of life" (Strathern 1999) that provides proof of inviolable inclusion.

Adoptees' liminality has been appropriated by artists and academics who are drawn to the poststructuralist implications of their familial, racial, and national boundary crossing (Eng 2003). Yet in practice adoptee personhood is more often than not produced and normalized through the sharing of individual experience, which is often performed in order to authenticate adoptee contingent essentialism. As I explore in the next chapter, the dominant model of selfhood at play in adoptee conferences is a liberal one based on notions of self-actualization through narrative activity, in which adoptees' ability to witness and affirm each other's experiences was seen as an important stage in developing a healthy adoptee identity. In this way, the organizing efforts of adoptees share clear similarities with other identity-based movements among disenfranchised or marginalized groups. Increasingly, however, common experiences of marginalization and alienation, especially in Korea, have been connected to broader projects for social recognition, including mobilizations for adoptees' rights to information and reform of adoption policy and practice.

4

Public Intimacies and Private Politics

In May 2005 I visited White Dot Studio, a storefront gallery on the Lower East Side of Manhattan, to meet the filmmaker and conceptual artist KimSu Theiler. Her installation "Let Me Introduce Myself" had been on display in the gallery for three weeks, and this was the final day before it would be coming down. The installation as a whole was visually spare and comprised primarily of text. The sole image on display appeared on single-channel video projected onto the storefront window of the gallery. That image, shot from a fixed camera angle, showed a pair of hands scanning an article in a Korean newspaper, and it was accompanied by an audio track of a Korean woman translating the contents into English. One could hear the Korean woman saying that KimSu's film *Great Girl* (1993) had been screened at the Korean Cultural Service in New York in 1996. She read statements that KimSu had made in an interview in which she discussed being adopted from Korea at the age of four, her memories of living in an orphanage, and her family in the United States.

The remainder of the installation piece was a literal remediation and rematerialization of a two-week-long email correspondence KimSu had with a person claiming to be her half brother. We learn in the first email he sent to her that KimSu's maternal aunt in Korea had read the newspaper article that appears in the video and relayed the information to KimSu's mother, who then sat on the information for a few years. Eventually the aunt, frustrated by her sister's inaction, told her nephew, KimSu's half brother, about the existence of his older sister. The half brother decided, two years later, to contact her by sending her the email depicted in the installation.

Although minimalist in form, the installation was surprisingly evocative. Five portable DVD players were hung across the gallery wall, alternating with large white sheets of parchment paper (figure 6). The words from KimSu's brother's emails, which had been translated into somewhat awkward English by a friend, were reproduced on the thick paper through meticulous pin piercings (figure 7), and KimSu's emails were presented on the DVD monitors with magnifying plexiglass screens clamped to their sides (figure 8). The tiny holes composing the words of her brother's letters recalled the raised dots of the Braille alphabet, and because of the lighting they were difficult to decipher. The effect of the texture heightened the viewer's desire to touch the paper as if it were indeed Braille and as if through touch the holes could be rendered into more legible words.

On the DVD monitors words from KimSu's emails appeared slowly one letter after another as if they were being typed in, but at a pace too slow for comfortable reading. When the words filled up the screen they would disappear and the letters would begin filling in from the top again, thereby making it impossible to go back and recover what had been read just a second before. In addition, although the viewers clamped to the screens magnified the words, they also distorted them, thus forcing the viewer to rock forward and back and side to side to get a proper angle to read each word on the screen. Both the paper and the screens produced the effect of being pulled in and pushed away, and as such served as a metaphorical embodiment of the emotional cast of the letters as well as the elusiveness of memory and the limits of language.

In one exchange KimSu expresses her shock at having learned of her brother's existence. To this he responds, "Well, how about me?" His life has also been radically altered by the knowledge of having an older sister, and it has been made more difficult because he has had to keep this knowledge secret from the rest of his family. As they cautiously negotiate their new relationship to each other as strangers who are relatives, by comparing inherited features and sharing intimate thoughts, her brother expresses the hope that they will "become a family like friends."

KimSu's construction of the reading and viewing experience foregrounds the gaps and disconnections in translation, understanding, and knowledge that often characterize transnational adoptee reunions with

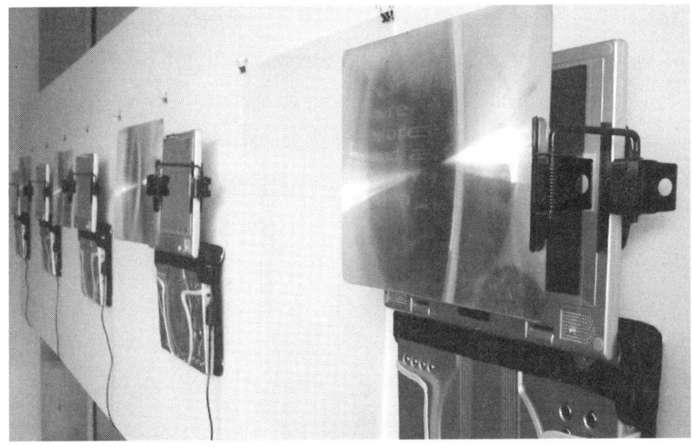

6. KimSu Theiler, "Let Me Introduce Myself," installation view. (Courtesy of the artist)

7. KimSu Theiler, "Let Me Introduce Myself," detail view. (Courtesy of the artist)

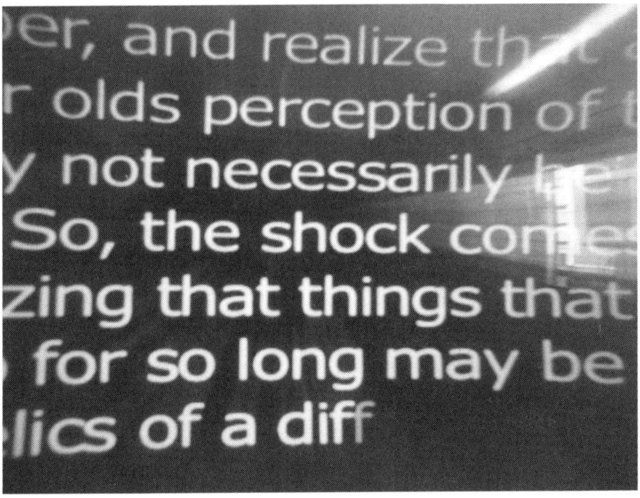

8. KimSu Theiler, "Let Me Introduce Myself," detail view. (Courtesy of the artist)

birth family. Whereas technological advances facilitate the flow of communication by allowing, for instance, the instant transfer of photographs between KimSu and her brother, by reinscribing these exchanges through the use of both extremely low-tech manual labor (pin pricks) and high-tech mediation (DVD players), KimSu produces literal interference in the consumption of this information. Like the electronically attached photographs that "didn't come through," as documented in one of KimSu's emails to her brother, the work highlights the holes and distortions in even the most advanced forms of technologically mediated communication, especially in the case of transnational family reunions that must traverse significant temporal, cultural, and geographic expanses.

KimSu and I chatted as other people entered the gallery, some of them friends and some just curious passersby. While she talked with them, I turned back to the installation to read more of the work, and I was captivated by its taut execution and affecting power. KimSu told me that after the communication with her Korean brother she had not wanted to talk about the experience with other people. Instead, she preferred to present through her artwork the exchange as it happened. "This is all there is," she told me matter of factly.

KimSu's reaction to my telling her about my research was, like her installation, arresting for me—albeit in a different way. When she introduced me to family friends who'd come in from Long Island to see the gallery show, she told them, "She's doing research on Korean orphans, like me." I had never heard of an adoptee refer to herself as an orphan, even though, as an adoptee friend reminded me, some of them, including himself, may actually have been orphaned. In KimSu's case, she had information about her Korean family and held onto vivid memories of her time spent in an orphanage, especially of her mother coming to see her every day, which granted her special status among the other children there. This sense of singularity seems to be something that she has retained, but unlike other adoptees for whom being "the only one" is often described as an experience of profound alienation from the "normals" (as Erving Goffman calls normative subjects in his sociological treatise on stigma), for KimSu it seems that this singularity is bound up with her identity as an artist.

KimSu's striking and perhaps faux naive utterance of the term "Korean orphan" indexed her willful refusal of identification with the adoptee world—even though she has had her film *Great Girl* screened at adoptee events, she had no sustained contact with other adoptees. It also called forth the extent to which I had grown acculturated to the norms of the adoptee social imaginary when I recoiled at the infantilizing valence of the word. Moreover, KimSu's statement and my reaction to it highlighted the fact that identifying as a Korean adoptee has become a politically engaged choice that is tied to contemporary politics of recognition and the production and circulation of counterimages and counternarratives (which includes KimSu's creative works) to the dominant trope of the Korean orphan.

THE PROBLEM WITH ORPHANS

On another hot and humid late summer afternoon in Seoul, a week before the 2004 Gathering conference was scheduled to begin, I had just met up with the long-term president of the Danish adoptee association, Liselotte Birkmose, for lunch near the four-star Ambassador Hotel where the conference was to take place (figure 9). Liselotte, who was also a key planner of the second Gathering in Oslo in 2001, had spent the past few weeks in Seoul preparing for this Gathering. She was working closely with Jeannie Hong, the director of adoptee affairs at the Overseas Korean Foundation (OKF), which was also the main sponsor of the Gathering and of adoptee activities worldwide.

As we walked down the quiet side streets behind the hotel to find a restaurant Liselotte told me, "We've decided to ban war orphans." What she meant was that the planning committee had decided that there would not be any war orphan imagery in the conference materials or programs. She added that there would likewise be no mention of Korea as the motherland. Because the Korean War and the motherland directly link adoptees to Korea historically and metaphorically, they serve as a symbolic link among adoptees. Yet war orphan imagery, as I described in chapter 1, performs a kind of representational violence that evacuates the historical specificity and political realities of adoptees. The trope of the motherland in turn sentimentalizes and biologizes adoptees' ties to Korea, and it imposes a nationalist logic and an inalienable ethnic identification on what is a much more complex and ambivalent relationship. These two overdetermining figures are like barnacles that cling to the representations of adoptees in official rhetoric of Korean government officials and especially in Korean media reports. Both of these stereotypes also incarcerate adoptees as children, whether in relation to the international order of nations, as is

9. "Welcome, Adoptees, to Seoul, Korea!" The 2004 Gathering at the Sofitel Ambassador Hotel, Seoul, South Korea. (Photo by author)

the case with the humanitarian image of the orphan, or in relation to the Korean nation-state, in the case of the motherland.

Because of Liselotte's somewhat strident remark I became alert to the symbolic struggle in which the conference planning committee was engaged over the collective memory of adoptees. They had shouldered the responsibility of representing the diversity of the community to adoptees themselves as well as to the Korean government and the public at large. Creating this image of unity and collective pasts and futures was a major project for the Gathering. In the end, although images of war orphans did appear in the conference program and printed matter, they were confined to explicitly historical narratives where they indexically represented the child victims of the Korean War rather than merely metonymically standing in for adoptees as a whole.

In this chapter I explore the Korean adoptee counterpublic through an ethnographic analysis of the Gathering conferences, which have become major events for the consolidation of the transnational Korean adoptee social imaginary. Refusing the orphan label is a key part of claiming cultural citizenship and social legitimacy for these adoptees, as is the creation of social spaces of authentic belonging. At these public events, adoptees assert their adult agency through metaphors of kinship and contingent essentialism, and they establish physical boundaries to define the community against other groups that might challenge their claims to autonomy—adoptive parents, adoption agencies, and ethnic Koreans. Yet conflicts over the shape of adoptee counterpublicity demonstrate how potentially divisive political differences among adoptees have been managed and contained.

TRANSNATIONAL PUBLICS AND PUBLIC INTIMACY

The Gathering has emerged as the main forum for the collective production of Korean adoptee history and shared memory. As nonhierarchical and relatively unstructured events, adoptee gatherings might be seen as being marked by the immediacy of "communitas"—or what Victor Turner (1969) defined as a liminal state that precedes the entry into structure. Turner's framework is useful for considering how people in small-scale settings, especially those whose marked subjectivities are stigmatized or marginalized, engage in ritualized behavior that levels status distinctions and provides spaces for alternative social relations (see Robins 2006).

Michael Warner's recent elaborations of publics and counterpublics (2002, 2005), which draw from Jürgen Habermas's work (1989) on the bourgeois public sphere, offer a broader conceptual framework than that developed by Turner for grasping the role of stigma and marginalization in alternative social imaginaries and relatedness beyond the face-to-face community. For Warner, counterpublics exist in the shadow of a cultural dominant (2002: 86), and they are unrecognized or illegitimate with respect to normative institutions and rules of decorum. The identities of participants are transformed by their engagement in these counterpublics, which themselves hold transformative potential in mediating new forms of sociality and "public personhood." In contradistinction to the rational-critical discourse recognized by the state and normative publics, counterpublics traffic in expressive-poetic performances of corporeality that cut against the grain of what is considered germane in most settings.

In a similar vein, Rayna Rapp and Faye Ginsburg (2001), following Lauren Berlant, examine what they call "public intimacy" in the disability community in terms of the mediations of kinship that open up possibilities for expanded models of citizenship and sociality. Like the communities of disability that they examine, adoptees also exhibit an elaborate life in cyberspace—including organization Websites, electronic mailing lists, social networks through sites like Facebook, and a growing presence in the blogosphere—and their subjectivities are likewise organized around embodied difference. The marginalization of adoptee perspectives in the public sphere compels their own "narrative urgency" to tell their "unnatural histories" (Rapp and Ginsburg 2001: 552). Rapp and Ginsburg along with Warner engage with questions of citizenship that encompass general notions of belonging to a national body, relations to state institutions, and political and social recognition. For them the "cultural dominant" exists within a national frame, even if the reach of the specific mediations of counterpublicity or public intimacy may extend well beyond the boundaries of the nation-state.

For Korean adoptees, counterpublic activities take place within a more complex set of transnational and diasporic relations that stand in dialectical relationship with multiple cultural normativities and dominant publics. There are both conservative and progressive aspects to adoptee counterpublic activities. In spaces such as the Gathering conferences the notion of community can be viewed as disembedding complex social identities from local politics, thereby risking the imposition of essentialized norms and ethnonationalisms (adopteeism) as a response to existential uncertainties. This tendency complicates assumptions about adoptee social practices as being inherently resistant or progressively transformative of existing power structures. In contrast, other adoptees, especially in Korea, have been engaged in progressive projects aimed at reforming transnational adoption, yet these attempts reveal a key limitation to adoptee counterpublic activities—namely, the lack of a corresponding state to which adoptees may present interventionary claims (see Fraser 2005).[1] As I describe in this chapter and in subsequent ones, some adoptees living in Korea have been directing their political projects toward the South Korean state as they increasingly identify their needs and rights as being integral to questions of belonging and recognition within the frame of the nation-state.

Under IKAA, the Gathering conferences have become opportunities for adoptees to objectify themselves and to provisionally suspend time and space and locate a sense of home in their own liminality. As the conf program states, "Between two worlds, we find ourselves floating. Bu not alone; this is our *community*. The significance of this trip will be everlasting. It is both a journey into our past and a milestone as we move forward." The planning committee structured the Gathering as a symbolic rite of passage for adoptees, notably by transforming them from childlike orphans into *adult* adoptees who not only are independent and autonomous but also gain strength in numbers. As Susan Soon-Keum Cox stated in her plenary speech, "This Gathering in Korea is our opportunity to return to our motherland, not as the orphans who left so long ago, but to return as proud independent adults." Further, following Pierre Bourdieu (1991), the Gathering conferences are socially significant as "rites of institution" that consecrate adoptees as a distinct category and naturalize the boundary between adoptees and nonadoptees.

The conference speakers clarified the goal of the event as the production of collective adoptee identity by employing discourses of self-actualization, self-empowerment, and collective ownership of history and memory. As I hint at in the previous chapter, much of this sense of collective identification has been effected through the construction and exclusion of adoptee others—namely, adoption agencies, adoptive parents, and other ethnic Koreans—who provide clear indication of the sources of paternalism that, like the figure of the orphan, have continually haunted adult adoptees. The amount of emphasis placed on the assertion of adoptee empowerment and independence is proportional to the degree of infantilization and dependence that adoptees feel is imposed upon them. Thus, active boundary making works to exclude those parties that hold vested interests in defining and delimiting adoptees and their social value. Adoptee conferences set the boundaries of the community through the deployment of "strategic essentialism" (Spivak 1987), which is often articulated as an ethos of "FOR adoptees BY adoptees," as stated in the 2004 Gathering program, and the construction of "adoptee-only" spaces.[2] Whereas the IKAA leadership saw their project as devoted to the celebration of adoptee identity and considered as their main goal the public recognition of adoptees as adults, others, guided by a concern for social justice, wanted to mobilize the political agency of the counterpublic to intervene into dominant Korean representations and discourses about adoption.

I outline the particular ways in which a collective sense of personhood and belonging was encouraged through the production of specific temporalities and spatial relations at the Gathering conferences. Conference organizers framed the Gathering as a rite of passage that transforms participants, who often express feelings of isolation, from orphan children into the new social category of the adult adoptee and members of the adoptee global network. The Gathering conferences have succeeded in presenting the public face of the community and have materialized the network as an ontological reality. The conferences are heterogeneous sites of heightened emotion and affect that articulate diverse histories and subjectivities into a normative vision of adoptee identity that is then projected into multiple public spheres. Yet, as I show, the network and the community it purports to represent are effects of specifically located social practices, often shot through with difference, ambiguity, tension, and conflict.

INVENTING TRADITIONS IN THE NON-PLACE OF THE HOTEL

The cultural "inauthenticity" and lack of multicultural capital that mark adoptee subjectivities are reflected in the material culture of the Gathering conferences, which are overwhelmingly text based with few symbolic artifacts. The cover of the 2004 Gathering program, for instance, was a tastefully designed, somewhat austere collage with white cutouts of flying cranes against a flat background of narrow stripes composed of running lists of the fourteen countries where adoptees currently live: Australia, Belgium, Canada, Denmark, France, Germany, Holland, Korea, Luxembourg, Norway, Sweden, Switzerland, the United Kingdom, and the United States.[3] The Gathering logo is a simple Korean yin-yang symbol in black and white with the Korean word *tahamgge* (all together) superimposed over it. Although typical images of transnational adoptees feature Asian children in colorful traditional costumes, eating with chopsticks, or waving national flags, the majority of the visual representations at the Gathering were comprised of snapshots of adoptees socializing, dancing, or having discussions, without any obvious markers of cultural distinction.

In terms of material culture one might say that the lack of such cultural displays in the adoptee counterpublic is an aesthetic appropriate to their histories of displacement, and those artifacts that they do have—adoption agency paperwork and referral photos—take on a heavy symbolic load. Adoptee artists often draw upon the symbolism of these documents as impersonal bureaucratic forms that hold clues to their distant and irretrievable pasts (E. Kim 2001). As I elaborate below, the visual culture on display at the Gathering conference suggested how the diverse individual and collective temporalities of adoptees condition particular representational strategies that at once acknowledge the particularities of personal biographies and also invent tradition out of the very recent past by tracking the origins of community from the advent of adoptee associations in the 1980s and 1990s and the first Gathering conference in 1999. Instead of presenting a reified culture as the social glue that binds adoptees together, the Gathering constructs a particular spatiotemporal location in which adoptees can perform their shared personhood largely through shared stories and talk.

The opening ceremony at the 2004 Gathering included welcoming remarks by Liselotte along with Tim Holm on behalf of the planning committee, greetings from representatives of eleven adult adoptee organizations around the world, and messages of support from Korea's First Lady and the South Korean Minister of Health and Welfare. Susan Soon-Keum Cox, the principal force behind the first Gathering in 1999, delivered a speech that framed the Gathering as part of a collective journey:

> Some of you were at the first Gathering in Washington, D.C., in 1999, and it was a historic coming together of the first generation of adoptees. As we stood on the steps of the U.S. capitol for a group photo, it was clear that we had become a global community. Two years later, the second Gathering in Oslo brought us together again, and the deepening and strengthening of us as a vocal community was becoming stronger and more evident. And this was also the genesis of the shared feeling that there would be a Gathering in Korea, and that as a community of adult adoptees we would make the journey to Korea here together. And so we are here.

Cox's speech and the multimedia presentation that followed both installed a temporal framework that permitted adoptee participants to recognize a common past and invoke a shared future. As clearly stated in the speech, the Gathering conferences are symbolic and material sites for the collective performance of the adoptee counterpublic:

> This Gathering is about community, commonality, and our shared history and future. It is not to highlight individuals or individual accom-

> plishments, but to join together, supporting and celebrating all of us. The Gathering demonstrates that no one person is more notable or significant than another. This Gathering in Korea is our opportunity to return to our motherland, not as the orphans who left so long ago, but to return as proud independent adults who represent many adoptive nationalities, but who will *forever* be connected to the country where we were born. This Gathering, like our individual adoption histories, belongs to us. It is *our* journey, *our* connection and a vision and dream, and the commitment must be carried forward by our energy and enthusiasm. For all of us it was that first journey from Korea that took us to our adoptive lands, countries and families, but it was also the life journey that brought us here today back to Korea and back to each other.

Cox explicitly framed the Gathering as a homecoming for adult adoptees who are now able to claim ownership and agency over their own histories and journeys, of which the community, as symbolized by the Gathering, was now an integral part. Following Cox's speech, which received a rousing response, Todd Kwapisz, a member of the planning committee, introduced a multimedia presentation about the adoptee community, which he explained was developed so that the audience would "be able to reflect on our journey and where we are going in the future."

The presentation was in the form of a digitized slideshow compiled from images that had been donated for use by adoptees and adoptee groups in the United States and Europe. It offered a historical narrative that began with the Korean War, and ended with title card announcing the 2004 Gathering. The opening section, "War in Korea!" featured black-and-white images of the war and the first adoptions of mixed-race orphans. The second section, marked by a shift in the soundtrack from dramatic drumming to acoustic guitar music, opened with a title card, "Birth of a Community," that juxtaposed the words "friendship," "understanding," and "mentorship" with images of teenage adoptees learning traditional Korean fan dances, martial arts, and tea ceremonies at Korean adoptee heritage and culture camps in the 1980s. The third section included the photo, mentioned in Cox's speech, of adoptees standing together on the steps of the United States capitol at the first Gathering. The accompanying text described the 1999 conference as "beginning a tradition of adoptees coming together and creating community." Having established the first Gathering as the tradition of the community, the presentation then showed a sequence of photos from the second Gathering along with the title card "The tradition continues in Oslo, Norway."

At the conclusion of the presentation, snapshots of adoptees socializing together at mini-gatherings in the United States and adoptee association events in Europe were shown to visually represent the community in action. These images were accompanied by the following text: "Friends are the most important ingredient in the recipe of life . . . community . . . friendship . . . connections . . . unity . . . camaraderie . . . acceptance . . . and the tradition continues . . . Korean adoptee Gathering 2004, Seoul, South Korea." Many of the participants at the Gathering might have recognized themselves or their friends in those photographs, and the slow zoom-ins and fadeouts of the lyrical slideshow may have helped them recall nostalgic memories of socializing at mini gatherings, outings, and conferences.

Based on Liselotte's initial comment to me regarding the "ban" on orphan images, one could say that Cox's speech and the multimedia presentation worked in concert to dislodge the orphan figure as the iconic representation of adoptees by replacing it with another set of images, narratives, and collective memories—namely those of *adult* adoptees in the active formation of what the planning committee in the conference program dubbed a "Global Community," based now on a set of identified and recognizable traditions. The slideshow inscribed the Seoul Gathering as the culmination of the community and the journey, thereby enrolling the spectators as members of the community and participants in the journey at the very moment that they watched the narrative unfold. Whereas the first Gathering had been framed as an opportunity to discover who adoptees are as a collective group and was marked by a sense of staking out uncharted territory, the third Gathering, in contrast, projected a sense of certitude in who adoptees are as well as in the existence of the community itself, which was framed historically and temporally around a common past, a shared present, and a projected future.

The Gathering conferences, mini-gathering weekends, and conferences sponsored by the Korean American Adoptee Adoptive Family Network have been the main sites for the self-objectification and self-exploration of adoptees. Invariably these events take place in corporate hotels, which seem to be ideal locations for building a transnational and deterritorialized adoptee consciousness and for the siting of adoptees' own, in the words of

James Clifford, "traveling cultures." Marked by an ambivalence "as sites of dwelling *and* travel," traveling cultures conjure rootlessness and exile as well as exploration and escape (1997: 31). The hotel is one of the "non-places" of supermodernity described by Marc Augé (1998), a liminal and ephemeral space through which people pass for a limited number of days before returning "home." Adoptee conferences highlight specific similarities among adoptees and allow for a restricted and relatively controlled exploration of differences, therefore providing a safe zone in which adoptees can interrelate before they return to their "real" lives. Further, with their events scheduled at regular intervals they provide temporal continuity for the "community," and they also become sites for the expenditure and accumulation of economic, cultural, and social capital. Adoptees who are active in conference projects, for instance, have earned reputations as their names circulate in a widening range of locations.

Hotels are hybrid private-public spaces that are at once exceptionally intimate (hotel guest rooms) and exceedingly performative (lobbies and ballrooms). This hybridity is fitting given both the inwardly and outwardly oriented concerns of counterpublics, which, as Nancy Fraser notes, "have a dual character." "On the one hand," she continues, "they function as spaces of withdrawal and regroupment; on the other hand, they also function as bases and training grounds for agitational activities directed toward wider publics" (1992: 110).

Located in a secure built environment marked by transience, the conference is also a site of exclusion and privilege where entry of the public at large is policed through registration fees and name tags. The centrality of hotels to adoptee conferences presumes a common class status and disposition among adoptees—who, if not cosmopolitan global citizens, have at least a modicum of disposable income and flexibility in their schedules to travel to conferences, especially those halfway around the world—implicitly barring from participation those who lack surplus time and capital. The impressive sacrifices that some adoptees have made to attend these conferences, however, attest to the great significance they hold as collective rituals.

Through the production of particular spatiotemporalities the Gathering conferences provide opportunities for adoptees to express and reflect on their collective identification. At the 2004 Gathering, because of the heightened emotions and presumed vulnerability of adoptees, some of whom are telling their stories for the first time, conference organizers spent a significant amount of energy monitoring the boundaries between adoptee-only and public spaces. Adoptee-only spaces were tightly monitored in order to protect adoptees from voyeuristic researchers, reporters, and social workers, but they also restricted the publicness of adoptee talk to private spaces. The performances of collective identification were largely choreographed by the planning committee, which presented a mature and successful image to the Korean government and the Korean public. Journalists were only permitted to speak with adoptees who had given express, written consent to the Gathering organizers to be approached by the media. Some adoptees who voluntarily spoke with reporters were closely watched by planning committee members, who insisted that adoptees needed to be shielded from the exploitative schemes of Korean journalists. As I discuss in chapter 6, the media circus at the Gathering was a cause of concern for organizers and adoptees alike, but in some cases, adoptees felt that the organizers' attempts to limit their exposure to reporters was excessively controlling and even paternalistic.

PUBLIC INTIMACIES: "YOU GET TOGETHER IN A ROOM AND TALK? WHAT'S SO SIGNIFICANT ABOUT THAT?"

On the first night of the 2004 Gathering, adoptees, sponsors, volunteers, and journalists filed into the hotel's main ballroom for the evening reception. It was a casual affair and most adoptee participants were dressed in T-shirts and cargo pants, knit tops and skirts—appropriate attire given the summer heat and humidity outside. A serpentine line had formed around the buffet, which offered the standard fare for events such as this: an array of Korean food, crudités, mini sandwiches, sticky-rice delicacies, fruit, and sushi. Near the front of the room where a stage had been set up I found a place to sit with some adoptee friends from Seoul, and we watched the intense mingling going on around us. There was the nun from the Won Buddhist temple who had been a long-time supporter of adoptees in Korea being greeted by Jeannie Hong, the director of adoptee affairs in the international exchange bureau of the Overseas Koreans Foundation. Deann Borshay Liem, who had directed the personal documentary *First Person Plural*, was also there, shooting footage for her next project, which was to be a social history of adoption from Korea.

I noticed a well-dressed man sitting near the center of the room, whom I recognized as someone I had met several months earlier. He was from Scandinavia and had been studying at the Yonsei University Korean Language Institute with a Danish adoptee whose boyfriend I had met earlier in the course of my research. We had all shared a meal together in one of the many barbeque restaurants in Shinch'on, the area around Yonsei University. During our meal I described my research to the group, and the Scandinavian adoptee told me that after his Korean father passed away his sister had been fostered by and eventually adopted into a Korean family whereas he was adopted overseas. After our meal we went to a traditional Korean wine house, where we drank old-fashioned unrefined rice wine (*tongtongju*) and talked about English education in Scandinavia, Korean Buddhism, learning the Korean language, and living in Korea. At one point in the evening the adoptee offered to introduce me to his sister to interview her for my research.

I approached him and asked if he remembered me, and he said, "Oh, yeah, of course." I sat down with him and said that I was curious to hear more about his Korean sister. He proceeded to recount to me his adoption history in an engaged if somewhat rehearsed manner, and at the end of it he said, "So, how about you, what's your story?" At that moment I realized that he had been acting out of mere politeness when he said that he remembered me—he had, it seemed, mistaken me to be a fellow adoptee in this adoptee-dominated space. I apologized and stammered, "Oh, no, I don't have a story." I showed him my conference badge, which had "researcher" printed on it, and explained to him that I wasn't an adoptee but that I was doing research on Korean adoption and was at the Gathering as a volunteer and researcher. He said, "Well, I guess it's hard to tell here, one assumes that everyone is an adoptee." It was true, for when I looked around again at the congregation of four hundred to five hundred people there were "Korean Koreans," whom one could spot relatively easily from their dress, decorum, and speech, and then there were the rest—mostly in their twenties and thirties—in groups of a few people to a dozen, socializing mostly in English but also in French, Dutch, Swedish, Danish, and Norwegian.

I felt unsettled after my aborted exchange with the Scandinavian because my inadvertent blending in the adoptee universe had resulted in failed reciprocity. In this context, moreover, as a nonadoptee I had no story to tell, or at least not one that was relevant. It was clear, however, that this was not the first time the Scandinavian had told his story, and it was also clear that this exchange of stories is constitutive of the adoptee counterpublic. A year later in Portland, Oregon, I met with Todd Kwapisz, who told me about his view of the importance of the Gathering:

> What makes this conference so unique is . . . there isn't really anything *tangible* about [it]. You get together in a room and talk? What's so significant about that? . . . for some strange reason whenever you go to these conferences, adoptees want to talk, and most likely all you hear are the same topics over and over. But these are the topics that really resonate in our community. These are the topics that are really important to our community, and these are the topics that we face every single day of our lives. And so . . . we make no apologies for that whatsoever. It's just, that's the reality of the Gathering.

This characterization of the Gathering as being mostly comprised of just "talk" does not, however, convey the extent to which many nonadoptees—especially researchers, social workers, adoptive parents, adoption professionals, and journalists—who are explicitly excluded from these adoptee-only venues, long to listen in. In fact, the first Gathering foregrounded the research potential of adoptee workshops, yet, in doing so it failed to anticipate the latent antagonisms among adoptees toward expert knowledge producers.

BECOME WHAT YOU ARE: FROM FOBS TO LONG-LOST SIBLINGS

In September 1999 I was granted permission by Susan Cox to volunteer at the first Gathering conference. I drove down on a Friday afternoon from New York to Washington, D.C., where I arrived at the downtown Hilton Hotel before the start of the conference. I was assigned to help out at the registration desk, where my duties were to check off adoptees' names from the preregistration roster and to give out name tags and conference guides. The volunteer working next to me was an adoption agency social worker who was also an adoptive parent with a daughter in attendance.

There was excitement and electricity in the air. For some it was a reunion, as adoptees who'd met years before at summer culture camps reconnected; for many others, however, it was the first time they had ever met another adopted Korean, or even, in some cases, another ethnic Korean. As one tall, thin male adoptee told me, "I came out of curiosity to see other Korean people. Are all Koreans tall and skinny? I didn't know!" Another adoptee described the experience of being among so many other adoptees as "*sur*-real": "Everyone looked FOB [fresh off the boat] to me, but once they started talking, they sounded like a long-lost sister."

From behind the reception desk the adoptive parent volunteer and I marveled at the diversity of names among the adoptees and the fact that they were from all over the world. Indeed, it was amazing that they were all there together—the self-proclaimed historic nature of the event was palpable. Reproduced in the conference program were images for each participant: the first photo showed the face of an infant or young child and the second a more recent headshot. The participants' adoptive names were followed by their Korean names, and the accompanying information included their date and place of birth, the adoption agency that placed them, their adoption arrival date, where they lived now, and their professions. In some instances, short personal statements were included with the basic information. In reading these portraits I was struck by how representative the adoptees were of mainstream America in terms of residence (thirty-six states represented) occupation (engineers, teachers, accountants, hairdressers, social workers, psychologists, nurses, artists, consultants, students), and family names (McGowan, Garcia, Murphy, Richards, Peters, Taylor, Steiner).[4]

Following the opening ceremony the adoptees were divided according to year of birth into different discussion groups, with each of the discussion groups to be facilitated by an adoption agency social worker. The Gathering committee had sent out a questionnaire to registered participants before the conference, from which they had collected 167 responses. The findings were announced during the opening plenary and became the basis for discussion in the group sessions. As the reception area cleared out, the adoptive parent volunteer suggested that we sit in on a session, to which I readily agreed. We entered a random room and sat in the back. Most of the sixty-odd adoptees in the group were sitting in a scattered pattern facing the center and front of the room. The facilitator in the group was a white adoption agency social worker, and she first asked those in attendance to tell her why they had decided to come to the conference. As they did so she wrote their responses in a list on the white board at the front of the room.

I cannot relate fully what happened in that workshop session, but listening to the testimonies of adoptees, some of whom were articulating their feelings about adoption for the first time, was an eye-opening and heart-stirring experience for me, as many adoptees expressed painful emotions and some recounted traumatic life experiences. When I spoke with adoptees at the 1999 Gathering, many hoped for more research on adult adopted Koreans in order to help them to contextualize the broader significance of the similarities and differences they were just beginning to discover among themselves. In recognizing that the conference itself was a kind of research, some adoptees I spoke with considered a scientific or generalizable outcome study to be a necessary and sorely lacking resource for their own self and group understanding.

Yet what quickly became recognized as the most significant and unprecedented outcome was that the adoptees should be the subjects of their own history rather than having adoption agencies, psychologists, social workers—and anthropologists—making judgments about how they, as part of a daring "social experiment," have fared. Since then as adult adoptees have become the object of heightened scholarly attention (by nonadoptees and adoptees alike) there has also been a mixed reception among adoptees to the notion of research, especially that by nonadoptee researchers.[5]

As I show in the rest of this chapter, my inability to participate in adoptee world-making by engaging in the public intimacy of talk and storytelling limited my access to some adoptee spaces. Despite this, what I attempt to unpack is the ways in which my own outsider status revealed the distinctiveness of adoptee personhood. If adoptee conferences are like rites of passage for adoptees who, through talk and testimony, become initiated as adult adoptees, the rite itself can be seen as instituting the boundary between adoptee and nonadoptee (Bourdieu 1991).

In my conversations with Liselotte Birkmose she explained her perspective on constructing adoptee spaces in a way that resonates with Bourdieu's discussion of how rites of institution sanction and sanctify a difference "by making it exist as a social difference, known and recognized as such by the agent invested and everyone else" (1991: 119). In May 2005 at the twentieth-anniversary conference of the Swedish adoptee group AKF in Stockholm, Liselotte made the following statement to me: "My idea has always been to create the structure, but inside this structure people can have [freedom]. I don't like to have *one* idea of people or of our community. That's also [the case] in Korea Klubben [the Danish adoptee group]; we have these different activities and we create the forums and set up the structure, and within this people can just be *who they are.*" Liselotte's statement echoes that of Bourdieu, who says of rites of institution: "'Become what you are.' That is the principle behind the performative magic of all acts of institution" (1991: 122). The magic of institutional acts, however, requires economic resources, intellectual labor, and material design to appear natural and to provide the space where people will feel free to "just be who they are."

MAKING THE GATHERING, DESIGNING ADOPTEES

The first Gathering conference was the brainchild of Susan Cox, who as a mixed-race child during the Korean War was adopted at the age of six through Holt to a family in Oregon in 1956. She became a regional celebrity at the age of eighteen when she was crowned the Oregon State Dairy Princess, and a few years later, at the age of twenty-four, she was invited to be the first adoptee on the board of Holt Adoption Agency. In 1983 she was hired to be on the Holt staff, first working in fund-raising and then later as a policy executive. Cox's original idea was to bring adoptees together on a trip to Washington, D.C., to visit the Korean War Memorial. Although she wanted the event to be a collaboration and not simply a reflection of her own vision, it was clear that she held strong views on the significance of the conference and the image it would project:

> When we designed the first program, I wanted there to be some formal activities, some informal activities. . . . it was really important to me that we go to the Hill [Capitol Hill], that we go to the [South Korean] embassy, that we have things that really demonstrated that we had come into our own. [Also,] because there was a lot of debate about how much it would cost and what we could do to keep the costs down, I wanted to make sure that it was at a nice hotel [and] that you didn't come and then stay in some crummy little place somewhere.

Ensuring that reporters and the South Korean ambassador came to the event was, for Cox, crucial to her goal of legitimizing adoptees as "an accomplished community" and demonstrating that they "were not orphans anymore." Cox worked closely with Todd Kwapisz, who at the time was in charge of culture camps at Holt, to design a conference program with an eye to maximum symbolic value. Cox wanted "lots of visuals," the most important of which would be the before and after photos that framed pictorially a narrative of adoptee lives by mapping the disjunction from one location and name—one identity or one set of possible identities—to another. Cox told me that she felt that the media would be attracted by the graphic quality of the photos, which required little verbal explanation. As noted above, the photos were accompanied by information about the adoption circumstances and present lives of the adoptees. These descriptors were used by the adoptees to introduce themselves to each other and to remember and reconstitute their fractured histories. In addition to creating the conference program, Cox edited an anthology of adoptee writing, *Voices from Another Place* (1999), which was made available at the conference.

Having a "Korean component" to the conference was also important to Cox. She found the ambassador from South Korea to be ideally suited to address the adoptees, because he was the "first politician . . . from Korea that didn't apologize and say, 'Oh, you poor dears, you poor little orphans.' We were not orphans in his mind." Finally, because Cox worked for Holt, she wanted to make sure that other adoption agencies were involved: "Instead of saying this is a Holt event, which would then *alienate* the other agencies, [we wanted] to say that this is an *adoptee* event and we as adoptees are inviting *you* to come." Yet the invitation she extended to the adoption agencies proved to be a source of acrimony for some of the adoptee participants, and it brought to the surface significant tensions between adult adoptees and the agencies that placed them.

Mi Ok Bruining, who was adopted to Rhode Island at the age of six in 1966, elaborated on this tension while I chatted with her in the kitchen of Eileen Thompson, a board member of Boston Korean Adoptees. Mi Ok reluctantly acknowledged that the 1999 Gathering helped Korean adoptees become recognized nationally and internationally, but she also considered the conference to be "a showcase of how well we turned out. We were basically placed on parade, and we were a media blitz on all the positive elements of what were considered successful adoptees." Mi Ok and others interpreted this focus on accomplishment and success as a cooptation of adoptee experiences for adoption agency agendas, especially given Cox's dual identity as an adoptee and an executive at Holt.[6]

Although many adoptees express ambivalence about their views on the ethics and politics of adoption, it is undeniable that a deep suspicion and distrust of adoption agencies has come to mark adult adoptee discourse. Not only are agencies often uncooperative gatekeepers to adoptees' "files" and to treasured information about their pasts, but also it is believed that they have profited from the commodification of children's bodies and experiences. There is a growing suspicion that agencies are businesses that privilege the needs and desires of adoptive parents, and there is shared cynicism about social workers' real commitments to the best interests of the child. Even while adoptees employed at agencies feel that they are on the front lines acting as advocates for fellow adoptees and trying to change the system from within, being on an agency payroll can have a stigmatizing effect for them in adoptee circles.[7]

The sense that the 1999 Gathering was guided by adoption agency agendas played out in the workshops where adoptees shared intimate and painful memories of Korea, thus complicating the narratives of success and achievement that characterized the speeches during the opening plenary. In the workshop I observed, adoptees discussed painful memories of their childhoods and the negative experiences of living in a white culture with a white name and family but an Asian physiognomy.

Participants were especially outspoken in group 2, which was comprised of adoptees born between 1960 and 1966. Mark Hagland recounted to me what he had heard about the group 2 workshop during my interview with him at his apartment in Chicago in November 2003. Although he was not at the Gathering and thus not a part of the original group 2, he was soon afterward invited to join the group's exclusive electronic mailing list and quickly became a core member and celebrator of the subsequent mini-gatherings. Mark's twin, Pauline Park—a transgender activist from New York—was at the group 2 meeting and, according to Mark, was the first to stand up and introduce herself as a transgendered Korean adoptee. After Pauline spoke, another person told the group about the sexual abuse she suffered from her father throughout her childhood. For Mark, the significance of meeting lay in the ways that the adoptees' testimonies confounded the expectations of the naive adoption agency facilitators:

> [The event] was sponsored by Holt and [the adoptees] basically got the impression [that Holt] wanted us to be nice and well groomed with

> scrubbed faces . . . and [to be able to say] "Look what happened to these beautiful little babies, and they're all wonderful and happy." And the group 2 people stood up and said [things like] "I had abuse issues and [other] issues." Again I wasn't there, but I heard universally that the . . . facilitators were just like aghast. And so that energy really led to . . . the whole [mini-gathering] phenomenon, so it was a good thing.

Maureen Grimaud, one of the original members of group 2, described her experience as follows:

> [As members of the group we] finally got to meet someone just like ourselves. There were a lot of the hurts and pains we experienced growing up that we could never share, even though some had it worse than others growing up—though we all shared the similar prejudices and being odd, being an oddity in society, always being on display, everywhere, and I mean *everywhere* we went. Always being asked a lot of questions. So we shared that unity amongst ourselves. And it's so nice to hear it from somebody else, not ourselves. So, the instant bond was immense, very quick and intense. . . . Some people shared some really deep-seated experiences that they had never shared with anyone else. It kind of just broke the tip of the iceberg and then we had to leave.

Because of the intense bonds that formed among the group's participants they decided to form an email list. They agreed that it would only be for adoptees—there would be no spouses, agencies, or anyone else allowed into the group except for those who had been at the Gathering. This decision to make the list exclusive to adoptees was motivated in part by the resentment that many of the group 2 adoptees, in their thirties and forties, felt toward the facilitators, who were adoption agency social workers and adoptive parents. As Maureen explained, "That was . . . the consensus we realized by having this social facilitator that was not an adoptee in the room. The direction he was going in, he wasn't on the same level as us. . . . They think differently, they think they know what we're feeling, but they don't really know. Like you go into a Native American tribe, and you try to describe what Native American way of life is, you don't really know, you can only write what you see." The presence of facilitators who weren't "on the same level" was also experienced as infantilizing, and it conveyed a sense of being "put in a test tube" and "tested for your experiences again." This discomfort with connotations of social engineering and scientific examination was what led to the mini-gatherings, the first of which, KADapalooza, was organized in direct response to the fact that the Gathering was orchestrated by Holt.

It cannot be merely coincidental that Maureen used the analogy of Native Americans being observed by social scientists to illustrate to me, an anthropologist, the positivist fallacy and ocularcentrism of unreflexive participant observation. In fact, the ontological and epistemological unrepresentability and incommensurability of adoptee personhood are, at times, held up as roadblocks to prevent incursion by nonadoptees, and, at other times, objectified and mutually marveled at. The shared sense of isolation, alienation, and loss that characterizes adoptee narratives speaks to the vital importance that adoptees attribute to safeguarding their exclusive spaces of full and uncontested belonging.[8] The planning committee of the 2004 Gathering worked to create these protected spaces of public intimacy for the adoptee participants but also had to manage the collective image of adoptees in the context of the dominant Korean public and prevalent discourses about international adoption.

STAGING A KOREAN GATHERING

The Gathering in Seoul was conceived as a symbolic homecoming, a fitting culmination for the Gathering conferences. In addition, because of its postponement for one year it ended up coinciding with the fiftieth anniversary of the first official overseas adoptions of children from Korea, thereby contributing even greater symbolic weight to its historic significance. The idea for a Gathering in Korea had germinated during discussions at the 2001 Oslo conference, and the thirteen adoptee groups in attendance became part of the original planning committee for the 2003 Gathering. A core group of organizers from the first and second Gatherings eventually replaced the original committee, and they faced the task of rebuilding sponsor contacts and trust after the conference plans were aborted in 2003.

A dispute between the Korean adoptee organization Global Overseas Adoptee's Link (GOA'L), headed by Ami Nafzger, and other organization leadership over hotel venues was in part the cause of the withdrawal of GOA'L from the planning committee. Thus, a rift had emerged early on between adoptees living in Korea and the Gathering committee. The Gathering was promoted as an opportunity to show the Korean public that adoptees had grown up and were now adults, but for Ami Nafzger, the founder of GOA'L, this was just another indication that "the Korean adoptees [in the United States] don't know what's going on in Korea."

After the initial setback, the new planning committee, with administrative and operational support from the Overseas Koreans Foundation, monetary donations from the Ministry of Health and Welfare, and in-kind support from Samsung and the Jeontae Buddhist order, managed to pull the conference together in the first few months of 2004. Like other adoptee conferences, the Gathering included panel discussions about race and ethnicity, dating, visiting and living in Korea, and searching for and reunions with birth family. It also continued the workshop model instituted at the first Gathering, where adoptees were separated into age cohorts, but the agency facilitators were replaced by adoptee moderators.

In adhering to the traditions established by the first Gathering, the third Gathering placed the building of community and the fostering of networking over any political or ideological agenda. The planners also refused to highlight any one individual over the group, and they considered the adoptees themselves to be their own experts. For the journalists covering the event, the planners' reluctance to articulate or define adoptees as a whole and their resistance to articulating a clear or political message to the Korean public or government made it difficult, according to a reporter for Korea's Yonhap News Service, to report on the Gathering—especially in Korea where the adoption issue (*ibyang munje*) is a controversial and highly sensationalized topic often enfolded into polemics of national pride and shame. The planning committee deliberately sidestepped the polarizing moral debate to highlight instead the obvious and relatively unnewsworthy fact that adoptees are now independent adults as well as to underscore their communitarian desire to get together and share stories.

At the press conference, held on the afternoon before the opening reception, a reporter from the *JoongAng Daily* asked the planning committee what they would want the Korean government to do to help adoptees, and also to comment on some of the issues or problems Korean adoptees have with "the adoption system." Susan Cox was quick to respond that the conference was "not organized around political agendas." Deflecting attention away from the government, she interjected her own moral perspective: "We need to ask, what can *Koreans* do to open up their experience to pting children? In a perfect world, there would be no need for inter-onal adoption. . . . When judging adoption, we have to ask, compared to what? Children belong in families."

These questions and answers touched upon latent tensions within the planning committee around the expectation of a political response to the Gathering that had become prominent during the lead up to the conference. As a quasi-public affair it existed on the borders between different audiences and competing publics. For some adoptees in Korea, especially those affiliated with the new group Adoptee Solidarity Korea (ASK) and GOA'L, the Gathering was seen as an opportunity to direct a collective adoptee message to the Korean public. Anticipating the media frenzy that would accompany the event, they wanted to capitalize on the heightened attention to make a political statement about the continued practice of adoption from Korea.

At the same press conference, for instance, the siblings HyoJung and HyoSung Bidol, who were attending as interested observers, were interviewed by the reporter from the Yonhap News Service, which they took as an opportunity to announce the establishment of ASK—an "organization that is starting a movement against overseas adoption," as it was reported in the following morning's papers. The wire report attracted attention from other journalists since it was the first to offer a "hook" on the Gathering, and the sibling pair and other members of ASK thus gained a number of opportunities to speak with Korean reporters about their opposition to the adoption system. In the next day's article printed in *The Metro*, a free daily tabloid, HyoJung Bidol was quoted as saying, "Since Korea has entered a stage of $10,000 per capita income, overseas adoption is unacceptable," a statement that was clearly imagined as being addressed to "the Korean public," which was already accustomed to critiques of adoption as reflections of the incomplete nature of South Korea's economic and social development.

Whereas politically mobilized adoptees living in Korea, like HyoJung Bidol, saw the anticipated media blitz around the Gathering as an opportunity to present critical viewpoints on Korea's ongoing adoption system to an unknown and anonymous Korean public or Korean society, the planning committee considered the primary public of the conference to be adoptee participants who had traveled far and paid money to attend. In addition, they believed that many of the adoptees would have no interest in or perhaps no agreement with the more politicized opinions of the adoptees in Korea. The original planning committee had negotiated this tension with GOA'L, which had also wanted to make a political statement, and members like Liselotte, who, as she told me in 2005, felt it would be unfair to "use other people for that. They have to agree on it, and you cannot abuse the fact that people are totally inexperienced and totally emotional over the situation and just use them for some political game."

Thus, anxieties on the part of the planning committee led to attempts to manage and contain political interpretations of the event, and in this way reflected some of the divisive politics among adoptees and the limits to the "romance of community" (Joseph 2002). Whereas external boundaries were maintained through the exclusion of nonadoptees, multiple internal differences were finessed through invocations of community and its diversity. The suppression of discourse and dialogue around the politics of international adoption, however, has proven to be the most divisive for those who participate in and hold stakes in this collective formation.

Miranda Joseph (2002) offers an incisive critique of the "romance of community" for recent identity-based social formations by drawing attention to the embeddedness of community in capitalist relations of power, which are often occluded in the fetishization of communities as natural or given. The invocation of community to silence or exclude other identifications in Joseph's ethnographic study of "homosexist" tendencies among gay and lesbian community theater players, is also evident in adoptee social practices wherein community has served to silence alternative views or identifications in the name of adoptee identity politics. The planning committee foregrounded the collective identity of adoptees in a rational-critical manner considered to be germane in the public sphere, and they suppressed those whose emotional, irrational, or inappropriate outbursts might have undermined the legitimacy of the adult adoptee community. The projection of a positive image of adoptees was largely centered around an image of the adult adoptee who was fully capable of participating in global civil society as a normal but also privileged citizen. This image, however, was threatened by adoptees whose political projects interpreted adoptees as victims of cultural and economic imperialism, and which were considered to be motivated by negative, irrational, or angry sentiments.

PRIVATE POLITICS: MANAGING DISSENT

Throughout the spring months before the Gathering, members of the planning committee visited Seoul to meet with sponsors and adoptee advocacy groups to discuss their financial needs and to organize volunteer support. They also wanted to make sure that adoptees living in Korea would attend the conference, despite the fact that GOA'L was no longer involved. In April, the planning committee scheduled an informational meeting for adoptees in Korea, and around twenty adoptees showed up.

Liselotte Birkmose, representing the committee, explained what the Gathering was and summarized the conference itinerary. She said that there were three adoptee organizations involved with the planning committee: Also-Known-As from New York, Adult Asian Adoptees of Washington (AAAW), and Korea Klubben from Denmark. She expressed the "hope [that] it will reflect the different things going on in our community." The registration fee was set at $150 and hotel rooms were priced at $100 with up to three occupants allowed per room. Traditional Korean dresses, or *hanbok*, were available for purchase, and adoptees could select and have theirs fitted on the first afternoon of the conference. Aside from the workshops, the programming for the four-day event included adoptee artist performances and exhibitions, an open mic session, a makeup and style class, a Korean tea ceremony, Korean cultural performances, a visit to the presidential residence, and a leadership meeting for adoptee organizations. She suggested that adoptees wear their *hanbok* for the final gala dinner, which was sponsored by Samsung. After the conference there were a number of tours of Korea that adoptees could take, one organized by OKF, another by AAAW, and yet another by Shilla Travel, a company founded by a Dutch Korean adoptee.

When the floor was opened for questions, a male adoptee who had been living in Korea for two years asked, "It seems that the programs are oriented for people's first visits to Korea. Are there any specific things planned for adoptees living in Korea?" Liselotte encouraged the discussion of topics relevant to adoptees living in Korea in the workshop sessions because "many adoptees will be interested to hear about living in Korea." Another adoptee wondered about whether adoptive parents or native Koreans would be included. Liselotte responded in the negative, but noted, "It's not our intention to close off everything to the society. There will be other opportunities for people to do things together." She emphasized that the Gathering was meant to "prove that we are adults, that we are capable of doing this. We have no political agenda." When pressed, she continued by stating, "Korean society should have an idea that we are in a special kind of community. It's hard to send out one message because we are all very different."

The adoptees I spoke with afterward were not impressed by the presentation. For them it was clear that the Gathering planning committee was marginalizing their perspectives. Not only did they feel that the conference would not be reflective of the community but also that the members of the planning committee had been chosen by fiat rather than democratically. Moreover, the meeting itself was not, as adoptees had been led to believe, a consultation with Korea-based adoptees about how to meet their expectations but rather a report from the committee about the decisions already made about the conference and how it would reflect the community—a community in which the Korea-based adoptees no longer felt included.

According to HyoJung Bidol, this meeting became the impetus for ASK:

> I think it was people's understanding that, at that time, she [Liselotte] was asking for feedback for what we wanted to happen at the Gathering . . . [But] when people started asking questions it was clear that that was not what she was looking for but that she was just there to represent the Gathering committee, to say this is what we are going to do, and this is what kind of help we need from you, and we're not really looking for input for the Gathering *from* [you]. And I think that was very upsetting for a lot of people in realizing that this Gathering, that was supposed to be for us, was not about us being heard. And so after that is when we started kind of bringing people together and started talking about how [we] want this to be something different for us. *Substantive,* rather than just a getting together of adoptees.

At its origin ASK was a reading group attended by a handful of politically progressive American adoptees in their thirties who were living in Korea. After the informational meeting with Birkmose it transformed into a social justice project with the short-term goal of opening up a discussion around the political economy of adoption from Korea. The members began planning a meeting for the final day of the conference in order to provide a space for a discussion of the political dimensions of adoption, a topic that the conference organizers had been unwilling to engage. On the second day of the Gathering, ASK distributed a flyer announcing the meeting, which read, "ASK stands in opposition to international adoption; addresses the political, social, and economic context of adoption and accordingly seeks comprehensive solutions and alternatives; keeps members informed of policies that impact the issue of adoption; plays a role in mobilizing the community of adoptees who say enough is enough." The group also made clear that it did not intend to disrupt the Gathering but rather wanted to "create spaces for discussion and movement." Members also handed out postcards and were selling T-shirts with a design by Mihee Nathalie Lemoine, an adoptee artist and activist who was also a founding member. The T-shirt sported a cartoon image of a crying baby being held upside down by its ankles, as if newly born, with a large plunger-like stamp printing on its buttocks the words "Made in Korea."

Before the flyers were handed out, and even afterward, there was a swirl of rumor and suspicion about the group regarding whether or not it would be disruptive of the Gathering's main ethos of community, and what it was planning to do exactly. By stirring up latent feelings among adoptees who held divergent views on the pros and cons of adoption, ASK's meeting became a source of anxiety for the organizers of the Gathering. Given the two years of intense effort and labor that went into planning the conference, some of those involved reportedly felt personally affronted by the suggestion of dissent.

As was the case at the previously held Gatherings in Washington, D.C., and Oslo, the workshops at the Korea conference were organized according to age in order to divide the 430 adoptee participants into several cohorts. The planning committee had for each group preselected adoptee facilitators to help guide the discussions. The groups spent three hours discussing a range of topics related to adoption—their personal histories growing up as ethnic and racial minorities, their feelings about natal family and experiences with search, their involvement with adoptee organizing, and their interests in Korea and Korean culture.

Sarah Dankert, a recent political science graduate of Barnard College, had been involved with the New York City-based group Also-Known-As before she moved to Korea. I had met Sarah in New York before she had moved to Korea, and she was working with Also-Known-As to extend the reach of the organization onto college campuses. She was also active in educating Korean American campus groups about the particular experiences of transracially adopted Koreans. Because of her close ties with Also-Known-As, the Gathering planning committee asked her to serve as a facilitator of the workshop group for those born between 1978 and 1986—one of the largest cohorts at the conference. After moving to Korea, however, Sarah had become a core member of ASK. This fact placed her in a conflicted position with the planning committee, which was deeply concerned about containing "political" discourse.

On the evening of the second to last day of the conference, Sarah arrived at a bar where a large group of adoptees was socializing. She had just come from a meeting with the planning committee and was agitated and upset because, as she told us, she had been blamed for allowing the discussion in her group to become "political." In fact, she told us, it was another adoptee who was well known for being particularly vocal about the ethics and politics of adoption who had raised the questions and pushed the discussion toward "political" topics. The planning committee members, however, assumed that she held two competing allegiances, one to the Gathering and one to ASK, and accused her of inappropriately using her role as facilitator to push her own (or ASK's) agenda. The next day's morning session, which was open to the general public, was to feature presentations by the facilitators from each group who were to summarize what had been discussed in each of the workshops. To resolve the matter, the planning committee decided that Sarah would have to "cover the political stuff" because no one else was "comfortable" discussing it.

The next morning, as scheduled, the facilitators from each of the workshops were seated on the stage, some visibly tired from jet lag or, more likely, a late night of drinking and socializing. Each of them discussed in brief the highlights of their group's discussion from the previous day. Sarah arrived late and appeared somewhat defiant as she strode across the stage to take her place next to her copresenter, an adoptee from Australia. The Australian listed off the issues that had been discussed: identity, racism on the part of both whites and Koreans, and feelings toward biological family and adoptive family. She concluded by mentioning that after someone raised the question of what the Korean government should do to end overseas adoption, the discussion "did become very political." Sarah then took the microphone and, in an off-handed way, commented as follows: "We started trying to bring up the topic of search and reunion but it ended up getting diverted by [that] question, and [the discussion] ended up taking on as a tool of Western countries—that are, quote-unquote, more countries—as a form of modern day colonialism. And that [led] questions about Korean adoptees being white people, [adoption] ...ng a form of institutionalized colonialism, the process of adoption changing and the power structures [behind] why white people would adopt Asians in general." She then went on to list the issues that had been discussed, including the exoticization of Asian American women, the commodification of children in adoption, the exploitation of adoptee labor in Korea, and how adoptees could contribute to a changing Korean society. Her presentation was received with polite applause, as the others had been, and the reporter from the next group took his turn.

As discussed above, whereas some of the more radical adoptees consider the adoption system, including postadoption services, culture camps, and other agency-coordinated activities, to constitute the perpetuation of a deeply flawed system of adoption, if not outright imperialism, most adoptees express ambivalence about the politics of adoption, and its costs and benefits. Sarah herself, in an interview several months prior to the third Gathering, expressed in halting terms her own mixed feelings about adoption:

> I don't know how I feel about adoption. At this point in my life the ideal would not be adoption. I feel awful about saying that. Maybe because of the feeling of loss I feel toward my birth family. Not that my life is horrible or difficult. It's weird. I'm trying to think of a p.c. way to configure my thoughts on adoption because I feel horrible saying that. My parents did a very good job. . . . I know adoption is good; my family is fabulous. . . . At the same time I think I'm still frustrated with the idea of loss and [the] odd motivation of people who adopt. I don't understand fully. Why are you adopting? Do you want to feel better about yourself?

Sarah's conflict with the planning committee as well as the general anxiety over introducing a political discussion into the space of the Gathering indicated clearly that this vector of difference was considered to be so threatening that it had to be actively marginalized and disciplined, if not prohibited. The question of whether adoptees should project a positive or a negative view of adoption has been a recurrent issue in countless group discussions. From the standpoint of adoption advocates, a call to end adoption is reactionary and discounts the benefits of adoption for indi-

10. A one-person demonstration outside the Ambassador Hotel in Seoul, August 2004. The sash under the tree reads, "End the overseas adoption of our children." (Photo by author)

vidual children. For critics of adoption, however, broader structural inequalities and political circumstances inform their own moral perspective, whether they see it as an imperfect system that is in dire need of reform or as an unconscionable practice grounded in colonial power relations and centuries of white privilege.

The planning committee believed that there was going to be an organized protest, and in that event they wanted to make sure that their hosts, the Korean sponsors and government officials, would be whisked through the hotel entrance. There was, in fact, an organized protest, but it was not organized by adoptees. Indeed, it was the most unobtrusive protest imaginable: next to a tree approximately one hundred yards away from the hotel entrance a middle-aged Korean man stood with his seven-year-old son. He wore a plastic banner on his torso, and on the tree was another banner that read, "End the overseas adoption of our children" (figure 10).

A handwritten sign in English on the ground attested allegiance to adoptee activism: "We love GOA'L adoptees." "ASK" had been written in as well, with an arrow pointing to two ASK postcards. The man was part of Chamah (Cham Sarang Moim, or True Love Association), a small group of Korean Catholic parents who had adopted domestically. The head of the group, known as Mr. Hong, was a strong advocate for adoptees in Korea who ran an online chat board called "AntiBabyExport" and who was engaged in his own counterpublic struggles to change Korean attitudes about adoption.

CONCLUSION

The consolidation of the adoptee counterpublic around the Gathering conferences has been an unprecedented and novel phenomenon. The stigma of racial difference and anomalous kinship histories have bound a disparate and highly deterritorialized group into an imagined community that exists in a subordinate relationship with respect to other dominant cultural forms and publics. One can also view adoptee conferences as rites of passage that are marked by strict boundary maintenance that fashion categorical purity out of adoptee-only spaces and institute a boundary between adoptees and nonadoptees. These rites of passage bring isolated and formerly infantilized adoptees together to articulate a version of adoptee personhood that is collective, empowered, and independent.

The intermittent nature of adoptee sociality is an important factor for understanding the success of these events. The ability to participate in an intensely intimate public and then to return to one's "real life" means that differences that are more difficult to broach among adoptees can be celebrated as part of the community's strength in diversity rather than as threats to the coherence of the collectivity. The politics of adoption, however, are the most divisive aspects of this community. As I have suggested in this chapter these political views are forced to be privatized either by undermining or silencing adoptees' critiques of the system by construing them as individualized expressions of personal pathology or psychic angst, or by forcing those debates and conversations to the margins and apart from the spaces and practices already designated as being representative of the "community." In this dynamic one can see a classic tension between the politics of recognition and the politics of redistribution (Fraser

1997), wherein the symbolic celebration of a collective identity comes up against a demand to address and remedy material inequalities. By and large, adoptee conference participants are middle class and their collective identification is grounded in a shared class disposition, yet politically motivated adoptees in Korea have been able to articulate the embeddedness of the adoption system in fundamental classed and gendered inequalities.

The adoptee community as designed by IKAA is not manifestly counter-hegemonic in its organizing principles. Rather, it is focused on producing spaces for the exploration of group identity and the celebration of its uniqueness. Even as the counterpublic production of belonging around adoptee kinship and adoptee cultural citizenship is a consequence of transnational biopolitics, global capitalism, and social inequality, these aspects of their shared condition cannot be broached in the process of producing a vision of adult adoptee identity that still hews to normative modes of social discourse and decorum.

This project is organized around a "politics of recognition" (Taylor 1994) in which social personhood entails an acceptance of adoptees as normal, or just like everyone else, but also as distinctive and global. As Tim Holm told a reporter from the *Kukmin Daily*, when asked what he would tell Korean society, "Tell them we are normal, not different, not special. We're everyday people just like everyone else. Maybe we were disadvantaged when we started, but we're not disadvantaged now." For those members of the community who want to push the politics of recognition toward more radical ends—that is, a social justice movement with transformative rather than accommodationist goals—new spaces of organizing had to be produced outside of the community. Contingent essentialism means that the adoptees who were aligned with ASK were naturally part of the community, yet they could still be disciplined and marginalized for disseminating alternative political views.

The members of ASK developed their critiques out of their experiences as adoptees in Korea, where cultural citizenship was as problematic, if not more so, than in their adoptive countries. In the next chapter I discuss the everyday and official relationships between adult adoptees and Korea. Much of what adult adoptees have been able to accomplish through the Gathering conferences and in the development of the global network has been due to the recognition on the part of the South Korean government of adult adoptees as Koreans and as part of the ethnic Korean diaspora. Yet for adoptees living and working in Korea, negotiating their problematic relationship to the Korean state and native Koreans has been complicated in a context of heightened globalization, neoliberalization, and multiculturalism.

Part II

5

Our Adoptee, Our Alien

Adoptees as Specters of Family and Foreignness in Global Korea

At the opening ceremony of the Gathering in Seoul in 2004, the South Korean minister of health and welfare, Kim Geun Tae, publicly delivered words uncommonly heard from the lips of a government official. He said, in Korean, "*Saranghamnida*" (I love you). This unusual melding of bureaucratic formality with intimate sentiment was addressed to the audience of 430 adoptees, who ranged in age from their early twenties to late fifties and who hailed from fifteen countries across the Western world. The rich symbolic potential of this homecoming was mined by organizers, journalists, and government officials, including Minister Kim whose presidential ambitions were as much on display as was his concern for impressing the adoptees in the audience.[1]

The minister's speech, delivered in Korean and read in English by a Korean interpreter, was carefully crafted, and in the subsequent media coverage it was highlighted as a particularly eloquent performance. Prefacing his declaration of love with expressions of ambivalence and trepidation at the thought of delivering a speech to the adoptees, the minister stumbled and halted as he spoke these words:

> I was afraid about what kind of reception I would receive. I wanted to say I love you, but I hesitated. I had to consider

> whether I had a right to say that or not. . . . I would like to tell you on behalf of the Korean people that we have tried hard to make a respectful country. However, as I stand in front of you I feel uncomfortable. I will tell you with all my courage that I love you all here. I can say to you with confidence that you will have a place in our hearts. I will try my very best to make you proud to be our daughters and sons. I am very proud of you, please remember that.[2]

The minister framed his declaration of love as an expression of the nation's paternalistic affection and pride in its children. Describing the "painful things" endured by the Korean people in the name of industrialization and democratization, he reminded the audience that their "parents, sisters, and brothers had to go through hardships, too." In conclusion he invited the adoptees to join in South Korea's future path toward "peace and unity" on the peninsula, and he closed with the following statement: "I express deep gratitude toward your adoptive parents who raised you. After all these years, you are in Korea, the place which turned you away. I would like to give you my warmest welcome. I am really proud of you all and want to confess my love for you even more."

What is striking about this speech and what, ever since president Kim Dae Jung's tearful apology in 1998 to a group of twenty-nine overseas adoptees, has proven to be characteristic of official state messages to adoptees, is the juxtaposition of discourses of economic rationality and globalization with metaphors of love, nurturance, and inalienable "roots." President Kim himself asked the adoptees who gathered at the presidential residence to "nurture [their] cultural roots" because "globalization is the trend of the times" (cited in Yngvesson 2002: 421–22).[3] Official state narratives reiterate how the tragedy of the Korean War and the ensuing poverty of the postwar years led to the heartbreaking yet necessary solution of overseas adoption. As the minister of health and welfare told the adoptees, "We could not overcome the chains of poverty and we had to send you far away." The plot of national development then predictably shifts from the third world past to the present by underscoring Korea's standing as the eleventh or twelfth largest economy in the world. The economic collapse of 1997–1998 notwithstanding, Korea is still considered to be an exemplary model of development and democratization in East Asia. It is presented as ever aspiring to first world status and striving to be a nation in which adoptees—who are now adult citizens of advanced Western nations and "daughters and sons" of Western families—can find pride. As the minister stated, "We achieved democracy as a solid political system here and are restoring the pride of the Korean people. Even though it is not enough, we are getting close to the current level of other developed countries."

In this teleological narrative, Korea's achievements as an advanced nation, while not complete, are located fully in the contemporary era of global capitalism. It paints overseas adoption as a practice of the past necessitated by South Korea's economic and political plights, and it conceals the fact that adoptions from Korea increased exponentially during the period of the nation's greatest economic strides. Even with the decline in adoptions since the 1990s, 2,258 children were sent abroad for adoption in 2004, ranking Korea fourth in the world in foreign adoptions.[4] This official narrative also effectively erases adoptees' individual pasts under the production of the "homogeneous, empty time of the nation" (Anderson 1991: 26; see also Benjamin 1968), thereby privileging kinship with the motherland over individual historical ties and obscuring the deeply felt psychic losses and historical disjunctures that shape adoptee subjectivities. Whereas in the previous chapters I focused on adoptee personhood and collective self-representation in a variety of online spaces and conference locations, in this chapter I turn the lens onto the confluence of adult adoptee returns and South Korean globalization.

Transnationally adopted Koreans are symbolically situated at the border of the nation. As specters of both family and foreignness—pitiable orphans who were abandoned by both natal family and nation—they are also repressed remainders and reminders of Korea's third world past (Hübinette 2005). As adults in the context of South Korea's self-conscious globalization drive, they are being optimistically revalued as successful, model citizens of their adoptive countries who, it is hoped, will take on roles as cultural ambassadors or civil diplomats between the West and Korea. Having overcome a traumatic developmentalist history and the shackles of authoritarian rule, Korea now enrolls adoptees into a logic of filial piety and long-distance nationalism (Anderson 1992) by rhetorically inviting them to participate in the national project of advancing Korea's standing in the world. What this would entail in actuality, however, is invariably left unaddressed.

Moreover, for adoptees themselves—whose lives have been split across two nations, two families, and two histories—the cultural capital necessary to realize their transnational potential seems to have already been forfeited. Kim Park Nelson, an adoption scholar whom I quote in chapter 3, expressed discomfort with these messages of paternalism when she stated the following: " 'Thank you for taking our children, thank you for raising our children'—it's like 'thanks for taking care of my dog for a while.' It just seems like such an *odd* sentiment, which I guess is kind of a prelude to the Korean government claiming us, because they wouldn't thank someone for taking care of [something] if they didn't think it was theirs, right?" Following the 2004 Gathering a Canadian adoptee wrote a personal essay expressing her disappointment in the event. In the essay her words suggest how "shame" lurks behind the multiple iterations of "pride" in the rhetoric of state officials such as Kim Geun Tae: "The speeches reminded us that we were abandoned, rejected, burdens to our families and country. We were poor lost souls who needed to be rescued. Sadly, for many of us, as grown adults, we are still waiting for this great salvation to come. The belief that adoptees were all adopted into rich Western families to experience prosperity and success is a lie. I think many adoptees bitterly resent this misrepresentation."

These two stereotypes, of the pathetic and pitiable orphan and of the lucky transnational émigré, also formed the background to quotidian experiences of adoptees in Korea. Adoptees who traveled to Korea and especially those who relocated to live and work there reported both forms of reception in their interactions with native Koreans. There was a marked generational distinction between reactions among older Koreans—for whom adoptees may embody an orphan history and a reminder of past poverty, thereby provoking many to say or think *pulssanghae* (poor thing) —and the reactions of the younger generation in their twenties and early thirties for whom adoptees may represent the enviable fulfillment of upward mobility and economic success (*sŏnggong*). The expectation and burden of success are reflected by young Koreans, who themselves express how they feel trapped by the nation's economic instability, limited employment options, and entrenched gender and class stratifications.

In this chapter I explore the dynamics of kinship and globalization for expatriate adult adoptees in Korea, and I situate their experiences in the context of South Korea's state-sponsored globalization project (*segyehwa*) and the recent expansion of the English-language education market in

Korea. Feminist scholars in particular have examined how the trope of the family is often mobilized by groups in making political claims, whether to buttress or challenge existing nationalisms (see McClintock 1995; Jager 1996). This familist vision of the nation has also been extended in state claims on its diasporic subjects. In Korea especially, diasporic politics are being actively mobilized and merged with transnational processes in the production of new forms of long-distance nationalism.

During the course of my research I witnessed how, against competing discourses of popular and official nationalisms, adoptees negotiated notions of kinship and relatedness in Korea. This is not to imply that adoptees did not often imbue Korea with a host of existential longings, myths of authenticity, and yearnings for wholeness and plenitude, as might be done by other diasporic or exiled persons, but rather to acknowledge how the disrupted and remade kinship narratives of adoptees complicate conventional constructions of Korea as a place of origins, roots, and ethnic attachment. Although transnational and transracial adoptions denaturalize the purported basis of kinship in biological procreation, the state's primordialist rhetoric often seeks to renaturalize adoptees as Koreans based on metaphors of biogenetic kinship. Moreover, in daily experiences with native Koreans, adoptees came up against other kinds of blood-based paradigms that attempted to include adoptees as Koreans based on consanguinity with the nation. For adoptees, however, whose backgrounds are very often unknown, a different valence of blood (*p'itjul*) and lineage (*hyŏlt'ong*) can serve as the basis for discriminatory or exclusionary practices that malign their presumed to be polluted or bad bloodlines. In contrast to these normative discourses and practices, adoptees have been engaged in their own transnational reckonings of relatedness and mobilizations of kinship ideologies in the production of adoptee kinship.

My research on Korean adoptees who return to Korea suggests how attempts to imbue adoptees with folklorized versions of Korean culture fail to grasp the other kinds of connections to place, biography, and natal family that, in their fragmentation and incompletion, haunt adoptee subjectivities and often constitute the powerful pull that motivates adoptees' returns (E. Kim 2005). This contradiction between a generic culture and particular historical connections exists in the midst of other tensions in which adoptees become entangled when they return to Korea. Neoliberal values constitute part of the contemporary backdrop to adoptees' resignifications in the Korean national imaginary in which adoptees are viewed ambivalently as victims of Korean modernity and also, increasingly, as lucky "flexible citizens" (Ong 1999) who symbolize the cosmopolitan strivings of modern Koreans. I show how adoptee social spaces in Seoul provide locations for the production of alternative forms of belonging in which intimate relations of adoptee kinship based on mutual care and shared interests are in formation, thereby superseding the more problematic kinship tropes proffered by the state or represented in popular nationalist ideologies. Hence, for adoptees, the notion of belonging in Korea increasingly signifies membership in an adoptee subculture such that adoptees who may have returned to Korea with fantasies of national or familial reintegration discover an adoptee expatriate community that supplements or even replaces other, essentialized or biologically defined forms of relatedness.

Among the adoptees I met, most had been living in Korea for one to three years, but a significant core group had been there for upward of five years. Although there are no reliable statistics on adoptee returns, rough estimates put their numbers at around three thousand to five thousand per year, the majority of which come for short visits. This is in addition to the estimated two hundred adoptees who live in Korea for extended periods of one year or longer. The significance of returning to Korea for some adoptees was made evident to me when I witnessed their sometimes surprisingly impetuous decisions to suspend their university or postgraduate schooling, to quit their jobs or career paths, or to take an extended leave from work in order to experience life in Korea or to initiate a search for their Korean family. What has made these choices imaginable is the existence of a close-knit community of adoptees in Seoul, the ease of finding work, especially for English-speaking adoptees, and legal recognition and resignification of adoptees as valuable members of the (South) Korean diaspora.

IBYANGIN, IBANGIN

The title of this chapter is borrowed from an art exhibition that opened in early August 2004 at two galleries in downtown Seoul. Co-organized and co-curated by the adoptee artist and activist Mihee Nathalie Lemoine, "Ibyangin, Ibangin / Our Adoptee, Our Alien"[5] featured the work of eleven female artists who as children had been adopted to Europe and the United States.[6] The exhibit coincided with the Gathering conference, and also, as the exhibition poster noted, with the anniversary of the fiftieth year of foreign adoptions from Korea.

In addition to playing on the homophonic resemblance between the Korean words for stranger (*ibangin*) and adoptee (*ibyangin*), "Our Adoptee, Our Alien" also ironically appropriates the pattern of ethnonationalist expressions ubiquitously employed by Koreans: our nation (*uri nara*), our race (*uri minjok*), our language (*uri mal*). The show's title is thus suggestive of the ambivalent relationship that overseas adoptees (*haeoe ibyangin*) have to the Korean nation and the myth of ethnic homogeneity that characterizes state discourses and other dominant representations (see Grinker 1998).

This relationship is one that Mihee, who was adopted in 1969 to a Belgian family and who lived in Korea for twelve years, has a particularly intimate understanding. Since the early 1990s, adult adoptees have been introduced to Koreans through sensationalizing media coverage and melodramatic film and television narratives. These media accounts have proliferated, especially as an increasing number of adoptees have turned to the Korean news media for help in locating birth relatives.[7] The accounts are typically portraits of adoptee groups visiting the motherland (*moguk pangmun*) to explore their roots (*ppuri ch'atki*), or else they train a voyeuristic eye on adoptees reuniting with their birth families (*ch'in kajok sangbong*) (Hübinette 2005: 89–106). Adoptee reunions with birth families also exist within a broader mediascape of sensationalized and sentimentalized reunions of war-separated families (*isan kajok*), foundlings, and long-lost friends, lovers, and beloved teachers. Television is a major "search technology" in South Korea where the modern family has been profoundly marked by separation and displacement, and there is now a veritable genre of family reunions programs, especially following the mass-mediated reunions in 1983 of thousands of families who had been separated during the Korean War (C. S. Kim 1988). Despite all this media attention, the existence of an active, if fluid, community of overseas adoptees living and working in Seoul is largely unknown to most Koreans.

Mihee and other adoptees were the initial pioneers of what has become for adult adoptees a kind of mass pilgrimage to their country of birth. These adoptees, most of whom arrive with few if any personal contacts and with rudimentary cultural knowledge or language ability, often encounter discrimination or rejection by Koreans who are confounded by the Korean appearance (*oemo*) of these coethnic foreigners. In defying expected isomorphisms between race, culture, family, and nation, adoptees are thus as much border denizens "beyond culture" (Gupta and Ferguson 1992) in Korea as they may have felt in their adoptive countries. To address the specific issues that adoptees face in Korea, Mihee and eleven other adoptees founded the group Global Overseas Adoptees' Link (GOA'L) in 1998, which they envisioned as a home base for adoptees. Ami Nafzger from Minnesota also joined this effort, and even though the original group disbanded due to conflicts in leadership and personality, Nafzger took up the frayed reins and, with the help of the media, was able to attract a group of dedicated Korean volunteers to help her get the fledgling organization on its feet (see chapter 6).

FROM ABANDONED CHILDREN TO VALUABLE ASSETS

The 1990s witnessed the resignification of adoptees from that of abandoned children (*pŏryŏjin ai*) to "valuable assets." This took place in the context of Korea's state-sponsored globalization drive (*segyehwa*), which was initiated during the presidency of Kim Young Sam and expanded under Kim Dae Jung. The economic and cultural segyehwa project opened up new legal provisions for adoptees to travel to Korea and stay for extended periods of time, and the transformation of the private education sector created economic opportunities for adoptees to commodify their "Westernization" through English-language teaching. These emergent spaces of labor and capital reflect global hierarchies of nation, race, and gender that stratify both overseas Koreans (H. Park 2001, 2005; Park and Chang 2005) as well as adoptees, whose relative privilege depends upon their proximity to centers of American economic and cultural influence. In addition, adoption itself has become resignified in the context of the neoliberal logics of upward mobility and "cosmopolitan striving" (Park and Abelmann 2004), which stand in marked contrast to the histories of abandonment and loss that adoptees are actively confronting and constructing through their collective social practices.

Announced during the APEC summit of 1994, in anticipation of Korea's matriculation into the OECD and its achievement of $10,000 per capita income, Kim Young Sam's segyehwa project was a proactive and symbolic appropriation of globalization discourse aimed to boost the nation's competitiveness in light of new global economic pressures. Harnessing the power of the then 5.3 million ethnic Koreans (now 7 million) resid outside of the peninsula was key to realizing this project (see S. S. K 2000).[8] As a form of diaspora politics, the segyehwa policy endeavored to assist overseas Koreans with their economic and social status in their host countries and to foster ethnic ties to Korea, as well as to "encourage and facilitate overseas Koreans' economic activities related with the homeland" (cited in Yoon 2002: 134). The Overseas Koreans Foundation (OKF) was established in 1997 as "a nonprofit public organization" affiliated with the Ministry of Foreign Affairs and Trade. Today, OKF administers educational programs, funds cultural events, and invites overseas Korean CEOs and "meritorious" Koreans to Korea for networking conferences and cultural exchange. It also hosts youth programs and leadership forums, and it has offered a motherland tour for adult overseas adoptees since 1998 (see chapter 6).[9]

Under Kim Dae Jung's presidency, the segyehwa policy was expanded to actively include the overseas Korean population. In 1999, the Korean government passed the controversial Overseas Koreans Act (OKA), which officially extended recognition to ethnic Koreans who were foreign nationals or permanent residents in other countries.[10] Coming on the heels of the devastating economic crisis of 1997–1998 (the IMF crisis), this legislation was broadly considered to be a government attempt to attract foreign investments from wealthy Korean Americans. Modeled on China's policy for overseas Chinese (H. Park 2005), the OKA grants eligible Koreans privileged visa designation that allows them to stay in Korea for up to two years and includes rights to work, make financial investments, buy real estate, and obtain medical insurance and pensions. It replaced the term *kyop'o*, which always connoted a sense of distance in referring to overseas Koreans who had left Korea, with *tongp'o*, which has become the more modern and politically correct term because it refers to overseas Koreans as "compatriots" with the same ethnic origins and blood (*hyŏlt'ong*). The law, as Jung-Sun Park and Paul Chang (2005) argue, "utilizes legal categories to define 'Korean identity,' [but] it also entails the construction of a Korean identity based on 'primordial' ethnic ties and the belief in shared blood and heritage (*hyŏlt'ongjuŭi*). Thus, legal national identity is confounded with ethnic identity."[11]

As the law was being deliberated in the National Assembly, GOA'L and other adoptees were active in making sure that adoptees would be included in the proposed legislation. Their efforts paid off, and they were able to secure recognition as long as they could prove Korean birth by obtaining their records from their Korean adoption agencies. In fact, Korean American adoptees were addressed explicitly in an official press release announcing the Overseas Koreans Act, which mentioned the "increasingly important role" that adopted Koreans will play in "bridging Korea with the global community." As the press release stated: "Such individuals are unique and valuable assets to Korea. While they are Korean in a biological sense, their American culture and lifestyles serve as a precious resource for the international development of Korea." Along with these visa rights, the opening in 1999 of the Adoption Center (Ibyang Chŏngbo Sent'ŏ)[12] by the Ministry of Health and Welfare and the inauguration in 1998 of the OKF Cultural Awareness Training Program for Overseas Adopted Koreans (Kukhoe Ibyang Tongp'o Moguk Munhwa Yŏnsu) were further gestures by the government to acknowledge the needs of adult adoptees. In addition, representatives of the Korean state have regularly appeared at each of the major adoptee conferences, thus reiterating the state's interest in and inclusion of adoptees in the broader global Korean community.

As other scholars have noted, Korean-style globalization demonstrates how state power and practices can be applied to the production of an expanded vision of the nation such that, rather than presenting a threat to the legitimacy of the nation-state, globalization in Korea is mobilized to underwrite state power and build a deterritorialized nation-state (Park and Chang 2005; Shin 2003; H. Park 2001, 2005; see also Schiller and Fouron 1998). In addition, the self-consciousness of the Korean state about its global position now includes a distinct reflexivity about its people and their *cultural* representation in the world's eye. A concern with Korean people's cosmopolitanism and their ability to act as model global citizens while still retaining a strong sense of ethnic nationalism was explicit in state discourses following the "coming out" of the Korean public en masse during the 2002 World Cup Games as well as the anti-American demonstrations that drew worldwide attention in 2003.

Especially under President Kim Dae Jung, the Korean diaspora of roughly 7 million individuals became a vital part of this vision, and their long-distance nationalism (Anderson 1992), as demonstrated by the global wave of Korean fans sporting red T-shirts and chanting "Taehanmin'guk" (the Republic of Korea) for the South Korean soccer team during the

World Cup, was seen as a repository of greater Korean collective identity (*hanminjok*) from which Korea could draw upon to further its own national project. As the president of OKF stated in 2003, "The World Cup has sharpened the sense of our nation, and shown to the world the potential of our people."

Of course, the subjectivities and sentiments of ethnic Koreans around the world often exceed and defy state designs. For adoptees, in particular, who have little to no knowledge or memory of Korea or of Korean culture, official inclusion as overseas Koreans has entailed their cultural normalization and incorporation into this globalized vision of the Korean nation through the trope of the motherland.[13] In the case of adoptees, the motherland is a distinctly modern, transnational projection of the nation that naturalizes and sentimentalizes the presumed to be biological and emotional ties that adopted Koreans must feel for the nation. Yet for adoptees, going back is not always experienced as a warm homecoming; in fact, it can be a disorienting journey through space and time, and it often results in the disruption of idealized expectations and longings. Confronted with Korean ethnonationalisms and xenophobias, adoptees, like other transnational subjects who return, face the impossibility of true repatriation in the form of seamless belonging or full legal incorporation (see H. Park 2005 on similar dynamics among ethnic Koreans from China).

The longings for origins on the part of adoptees resonate with the romantic yearnings for homeland associated with diasporic subjects, and, because adoptee genealogical and cultural origins are often conflated, the notion of Korea can take on a heavy symbolic significance. Adoptees' identifications and disidentifications with Korea are, however, multiple and heterogeneous and can hardly be contained within static typologies or nationalist constructions of diaspora. In a global context in which diaspora is no longer simply an analytic category but a social category as well, diasporic claims made by nation-states, individuals, and transnational subjects of all kinds often jettison the constructivist definition of diaspora (as identification in flux; cf. Hall 1991 and Gilroy 2000) in favor of one promoting cultural nationalism based on a notion of primordialism.

As Aihwa Ong notes, "Given its currency in the age of transnationalism and multiculturalism, 'diaspora' should not be considered as an objective category, but rather treated as an ethnographic term of self-description by different immigrant groups or publics. More and more, diaspora becomes an emotional and ideologically-loaded term that is invoked by disparate transnational groups as a way to construct broad ethnic coalitions that cut across national spaces" (2003a: 90). For these reasons I avoid using the term "diaspora" as an analytic shorthand to frame adoptee subjectivities and instead consider it to be a social category and set of ideological and affective tropes that, like ethnicity or identity, comprise a discursive repository from which social actors draw to make political claims to recognition and belonging in both essentializing and cosmopolitan ways. Although return, or its possibility, is a crucial part of adoptee experiences, I consider this to be, as Ong rightly notes, a matter of transnational processes rather than of diasporic identification. Especially given the South Korean government's self-conscious appropriation of diaspora discourse to further its own neoliberal projects, diaspora ceases to be a purely descriptive category and instead enters into a politicized and positioned set of representations.

In addition to diaspora politics, recuperative historical projects have also framed adoptees as part of the Korean people (*minjok*) who share histories of oppression with other groups whose victimization by the authoritarian regimes of the past grant them a redemptive form of cultural citizenship under the liberal democratic administrations of the present. With the lifting of authoritarian state control over free speech and public discourses, a range of formerly repressed social justice issues was unearthed in the 1990s. Called by some academics a "coming to terms with the past" (*kwagŏ chŏngsan*) (see Ahn 2002), or "the straightening up of history" (*yŏksa paro sewugi*) as it was called by President Kim Young Sam (S. N. Kim 2000), a process of historical reckoning brought marginalized and stigmatized groups into the public sphere: the Korean women conscripted as sex workers by the Japanese imperial army ("comfort women"), the civilian victims of the Korean War, including the state-sponsored massacre of civilians in a "communist" uprising on Cheju Island in 1948, and the civilian victims of the 1980 Kwangju Uprising. It was in this context that adoptees and the adoption issue surfaced in the mid-1990s, especially as the clock was ticking down to the planned suspension of the adoption program in 1996.

Jaeeun Kim argues that the 1990s in Korea witnessed the rediscovery and official recognition of two types of victims who were "suddenly rescued from decades of invisibility and silence." Those two groups were comprised of "those who were victimized *directly* by the anti-human righ crimes committed by the *repressive authoritarian state*" and "those victimized *indirectly* by the inability of the *shamefully weak and helpless state* in the past" (2006: 41–42). Kim counts the prodemocracy activists who were falsely imprisoned and tortured in the former category and adoptees and so-called comfort women in the latter category.

I argue, however, that adoptees cannot be so easily accommodated into dominant periodizations of postmodern and postcolonial Korea, and in fact they recall the failures and incomplete nature of both processes. Thus, part of the ambivalence that characterizes the state's discourse of transnational adoption is attributable to a problem of temporality. Unlike other "rediscovered" overseas coethnics, such as Korean Chinese or Korean Russians, adoptees are not displaced casualties of Japanese colonialism who are construed as returning family. Neither can they be recuperated as victims of the repressive state apparatus like the prodemocracy movement activists or migrant workers sent to Germany and South America in the 1970s. And the fact that adoptions are continuing to take place means that one of the symptomatic practices of the "weak state" has yet to be reformed.

Moreover, the links of adoptees to the nation are genealogical but their adoptions complicate lineage-based reckonings of kinship in both official and popular nationalist logics. Thus, the legal and cultural incorporation of adoptees is problematized by their adoptions into white Western families and nations. In my observations, official messages from the government present maternalistic or paternalistic desires to embrace adoptees as family, but these expressions are shot through with ambivalence about who adoptees are (Korean/Western, children/adults, tragic/lucky), and whether or not they will be able to forgive and forget enough to accept their role as ambassadors and bridges connecting Korea to the West. As HyoJung Bidol concisely asserted regarding Koreans' reactions to adoptees in Korea, "They don't know what to *do* with us."

ADOPTEES IN THE MOTHERLAND

The Overseas Koreans Foundation, since establishing its annual summer Cultural Awareness Training Program for Overseas Adult Adoptees in 1998, has been the main government entity dealing with returning adoptees. Adoption agencies offer postadoption services for birth family search and reunion as well as motherland tours, and they sometimes permit adult adoptees to volunteer or work in their orphanages or baby reception centers. All of these services presume that adoptees are short-term visitors to Korea, and it is on those terms that the state has until very recently recognized them as "overseas Koreans."

The adoptees who started streaming back to South Korea after the 1988 Olympics largely took the South Korean government and adoption agencies by surprise. Adoption agency professionals especially were not prepared to deal with the large number of requests by adoptees for information about their birth families. But the government began to nominally address the increasing adoptee presence with provisions in the 1995 Special Act Regarding Adoption Promotion and Procedure (Ibyang Ch'okchin Mit Chŏlch'e Kwanhan T'ŭngnebŏp) that stipulated the establishment of programs and services to help returning adoptees. Programs, including cultural education, language training, preferential job recruitment, and birth family reunions, were further outlined in 1996, and over the past decade they have been slowly realized by adoptee advocacy groups such as GOA'L and a handful of recent NGOs (see chapter 6).

The mission of GOA'L was to provide a "home away from home" in order, as Ami Nafzger told me, to "provide a connection for adoptees who have nothing, no family" in Korea. In the first couple of years after GOA'L's founding in 1998, Nafzger was contacted by over two hundred adoptees, mostly by word of mouth, and many of them stayed with her in her tiny, one-room apartment in Seoul.[14] Today, one of GOA'L's most important functions is to provide an instant community for adoptees who arrive in Korea, and its members do so through weekly weekend get-togethers, monthly meetings, seasonal retreats, and holiday parties. As Nafzger explained to me after her return to the Twin Cities in 2004, "It's like another family . . . you don't really have a place in Korea, you don't really have a place here, but you have a place with each other, when you meet each other—your own community, your own unique society."

With the passage of the OKA and the circulation of information among adoptees around the world about the possibilities for finding birth family members and the feasibility of returns to Korea, adoptees have been returning in larger numbers and staying for longer periods of time. This estimation was verified by Kim Dae-won (Jan Wenger), GOA'L's secretary general, who kept an up-to-date list of adoptees in Korea stored in his mobile phone. In spring 2004 he had 40 active names on his group list, and by January 2005 there were nearly 100. And at GOA'L's holiday party in December 2005 it was reported that more than 150 adoptees attended (S. J. Kim 2005).[15]

The means by which adoptees traveled to Korea were varied. Those who went for a short stay might have been participating in a motherland tour offered by their Korean or Western adoption agency, by the government, or by one of five NGOs with adoptee-related programs (see chapter 6). Others returned during the summer months to learn the Korean language, to engage in cultural education tours, or simply as individual tourists. The adoptees spending a longer period in Korea were generally those in their twenties and thirties who could find employment as an English language instructor or who were able, as in the case of a few European adoptees, to work for a Korean company or for a foreign company's Korean branch. Their motives for going to Korea were likewise quite varied. Some reported having been encouraged and cajoled by their adoptive parents, whereas others came despite the fact that their adoptive parents felt threatened by their interest in Korea. One adoptee described how she had for many years "pushed Korea to the back of her mind," but then, like some other adoptees, she eased herself into imagining a trip back after encouragement from her friends and family. Others had met Korean exchange students or immigrants in their adoptive countries who helped them to consider Korea in more concrete terms, or met other adoptees who had been back and who could provide contacts and advice.

First trips to Korea could be complex and potent emotional and psychological experiences that unmoored identity and dislodged narratives of coherent selves. One might say that for some adoptees travels across geographic space entail journeys back through time, thereby effectuating a temporalization of space or what Barbara Yngvesson and Susan Coutin, in the context of adoptee and deportee returns, call "planar time": "Traveling such a temporal path entails multidirectional movements, not simply from present to past or future, but sometimes from one present to another" (2006: 184). Against the impersonal symbolism and generalized state rhetoric of the motherland, therefore, Korea as place and nation holds specific meaning for adoptees as they locate their particular origins and the places of their prior presences, which often are mediated through the "paper trails" (Yngvesson and Coutin 2006) left by their adoption documentation.

Yet there are no clear correlations between adoptees who return to Korea and the desire to search for birth family, though that desire is undoubtedly a strong motivation for some. While many adoptees claimed to have always fantasized about Korea as a site of plenitude and true familial or ethnic belonging, this fantasy may also be precisely what they hope to protect by not going to Korea or searching for natal family. Moreover, a fear of experiencing a second rejection also counteracted other desires for connection to Korea, whether cultural or biological. I also met a number of adoptees who found themselves in Korea almost accidentally: two such American adoptees had joined the army and were stationed in Korea either by request or chance; others had found themselves there on business-related trips. As stories of birth family searches and reunions and other experiences in Korea have circulated among adoptees, they have composed an increasingly vibrant transnational social imaginary and common storehouse of knowledge about what it means to be adopted and Korean. In addition, adoptees are influenced by an adoption industry that has emerged around the recognition of roots and cultural identity as important aspects of adoptee subjectivity and the adoptee journey (see chapter 3).

The adoptees I met traveled to Korea for a myriad of reasons and with a range of expectations, yet despite the diversity in their experiences those who spent even a short amount of time in Korea often told me of what Maya Weimer terms, in her film *Rendez-vous* (2006), the "remarkable feeling of being unremarkable." In finally "looking like everyone else," they marveled at their ability to blend into the homogeneous social fabric of Korea. However, the novel feeling of belonging among other co-ethnics was also likely to be rapidly followed by the realization that the gaps in language and culture create moats of miscommunication and incomprehension that rendered them foreigners in their birth country. Moreover, any fantasies that adoptees may have harbored about their ability to be Korean or to be fully accepted in their homeland were easily disrupted by their encounters with the dominant ethnic nationalism that equates Koreanness with cultural, linguistic, and ethnic homogeneity based in shared blood and the myth of a five thousand year old history.[16] Adoptees, like other transnational subjects who return to purported homelands, confront the impossibility of true repatriation in the form of seamless belonging or full legal incorporation and may discover that their hybridity, which is marked by racial difference in their adoptive countries is, in the context of

Korea, inverted, thus swinging them to the other side of what one adoptee described as a "pendulum" from Korean to Danish or American (cf. Roth 2002 and Tsuda 2003).

PASSING AND FAILING IN KOREA

It could be argued that South Korean taxi drivers are the unacknowledged legislators of Korean ethnic identity. In the course of my research with adult adoptees who had repatriated to Korea, the talk about taxi *ajŏssi* (taxi drivers, or *unjŏnsa*) ranged from complaints about their hair-raisingly reckless driving practices, to suspicions of having been overcharged, to grumblings about invasive questions regarding nationality and ethnicity. For diasporic Koreans who travel to their natal or ancestral land, taxi drivers have retained curious power as representatives of Korean (patriarchal) ethnonationalism and gatekeepers to cultural authenticity.

Elaine Kim, in a discussion of the Korean American writer Theresa Hak Kyung Cha's *Dictée*, writes about the shame and rejection that is at the heart of the encounter between the Korean taxi driver and his ethnic Korean (American) passenger: "The Korean American visiting South Korea is harshly berated for not being fluent enough in Korean because the taxi driver imagines her as solely and exclusively Korean and views her broken Korean language as a betrayal of the nation state. Her shame at not being fluent emerges from a similar, if not the same, viewpoint" (2002: 30). For adoptees, who left Korea at a young age and who very rarely had (re)gained mastery of the Korean language, taxi driver stories were emblematic of Korean society's inability to understand their position as individuals who are "genetically Korean" yet "culturally Western." At the same time, however, surprising variations in the expected pattern of these encounters served as barometers for how conventional understandings of cultural identity and national belonging were being stretched in increasingly multicultural Korea. The issue of taxi drivers came up during my fieldwork in everyday conversation and in interviews as illustrations of adoptee disidentifications with dominant notions of Koreanness. These anecdotes of taxi drivers offered quick illustrations of how Koreans and Korea were as ethnocentric as ever, or else of how the nation's globalizing consciousness seemed to be loosening deeply entrenched ethnocentric assumptions.

As a relatively cheap and routine form of transportation in Seoul and most cities in Korea, taxis also provide intimate spaces of dialogic encounter and can be opportunities for intercultural exchange and ethnographic discovery. Many Koreans ride in the passenger-side seat next to the driver and engage in lively discussions and conversations about politics or personal matters. Adoptees who enter a taxi often expect to be questioned about the dissonance between their appearance as Koreans and their linguistic incompetence. Some may simply say that they are a kyop'o or second-generation Korean, usually from the United States. Others might feign Chinese or Japanese origins, while still others might use the taxi ride as an opportunity to challenge culturalist expectations by telling the driver that they are adopted and therefore cannot speak fluent Korean.[17]

For Seung-pyo, a Korean American male adoptee in his mid-twenties who was adopted at the age of five to parents living in a small town in New Hampshire, an exchange with a taxi driver represented a poignant moment of cultural acceptance and legitimacy. Living in Pusan at the time, he asked the driver to take him to Gimhae airport:

> I guess my pronunciation was wrong, so he was taking me to the park. I said *Gimhae konghang* [Gimhae airport] and he thought I said *Gimhae kongwŏn* [Gimhae park]. So I was like, "Sir, I have to catch a plane." And he was like, "Ohhh, the *airport*, the *airport*" [*kong*hang, *kong*hang]. So he asked, "Where are you from?" and I was like, "I'm from the States" [*Migukehsŏ wassŏyo*]. And he said, "So there's this thing—I think when foreigners come to Korea they should speak in Korean!" And I said, "Yeah, I agree with you." So he said, "Right, right, right!" It was really funny. Then he was like, "So how come you can't speak Korean? [*Wae han'gukmalŭl chal mot hannya*?] I was like, "I was adopted, that's why." And he said, "Well, there's no difference [*sanggwan ŏbsi*]. You're Korean, then, aren't you? If you were born in Korea, you're Korean." I was like, *wow*. He was in his late fifties, early sixties, [from] around the time adoption started. It was *great*. I mean this person doesn't even know me and is working—this is an [everyday] conversation; this isn't him trying to kiss my ass, it was *real*. So it was *great*.

Seung-pyo had been living in Korea for around two years, and he performed the dialogue in Korean by mimicking the taxi driver's southern dialect (Kyŏngsangdo sat'uri) and his own polite standard Korean—code switching with remarkable ease. Indeed, this exchange may have only been possible because Seung-pyo had an adequate command of Korean, one that could help transform an episode of miscommunication into an opportunity for ethnic identification and legitimization—from being a foreigner to being a Korean in the eyes of the taxi driver. But the affective valence of the story, what made it "great" can only be understood in the context of other, less than positive encounters that adoptees have had with native Koreans, ones in which adoptees may be subject to the same treatment as the Korean American in Elaine Kim's example but whose particular histories of adoption complicate the ethnocentric assumptions that underwrite the dynamics of betrayal and shame in encounters between Koreans and the cultural others in their midst.

INSIDE OUTSIDERS

When adoptees arrive in Korea they are like "inside outsiders," as the memoirist Katy Robinson described the experience to Mark Hagland. In a personal essay for *Korean Quarterly* about his first visit to Korea, Hagland explained that an "inside outsider" is "essentially Korean-looking, like these other ethnic Koreans, yet inside, as American as they come." He continued by stating, "And though I feel the cultural gulf quite profoundly, I also feel a kind of fraternity with the Koreans. I am in a sense one of them, and in another sense not. I will always be physically one of them, and culturally not one of them" (2002: 20).[18] Adoptees could try to "pass" in Korea, and although their bodily comportment, physique, and clothing might have given them away as foreigners, with the increasing homogenization of global fashion trends and brand names by the early 2000s, they were less conspicuous than they might have been in the past. Often limited in their language and cultural knowledge, however, adoptees had to confront their failure to fully be accepted as Korean, especially when subject to xenophobic or discriminatory treatment as foreigners (*oegukin*). Some adoptees who had left Korea in their infancy did not even consider their returns to be returns because they doubted they had any real connections to Korea or anything to return to. For others, however, especially those who had left as toddlers or young children, frustration at their inability to assimilate into Korean society suggested a deeply felt desire for acceptance and belonging in their birth country, thereby making them particularly sensitive to encounters with ethnocentrism and xenophobia.

Craig Adams was adopted at the age of eight to an upper-middle-class family in Wisconsin. In his late twenties, he was an accredited ESL teacher in the United States. In spring 2004 he had traveled to Seoul with the intention of staying for at least one year to teach English and experience life in Korea. He told me about a disturbing encounter he had while riding the subway with his English-speaking companions. In the middle of a conversation with his friends, he was sharply reprimanded in Korean by a middle-aged man who quickly became verbally and physically aggressive when Craig tried to ignore him. As Craig said to me, "I just wanted to be able to tell him, 'I'm sorry, I was adopted. I can't speak Korean.'" Thus, instead of the shame that the Korean American might feel for not living up to the ethnonationalist and ethnocentric expectations in encounters with Koreans, Korean adoptees may instead feel a sense of injustice for being blamed for their lack of cultural knowledge. As another adoptee declared, "It's not my fault."

Craig, who felt silenced and disempowered by his encounter with the Korean man on the subway, might have benefited from the "spontaneous empowerment tool" that adoptee artist kate hers (Hershiser) attempts to provide for adoptees (figure 11). She composed and distributed this calling card as a response to similar experiences she had in Korea in 1998. Written in Korean and in English, it literally translates the adoptee's identity for the Korean public by challenging dominant assumptions about ethnicity that equate blood with culture and nation.[19] It also makes an important distinction between adoptees and kyop'o, who share some similarities but who often differ in terms of having knowledge about the "culture and language of [their] own people."

When adoptees first began coming back to Korea as adults in the late 1980s and early 1990s, they coincided with a wave of return migrations among Korean American emigrants, as well as return visits by their grown children. Thus, adoptees were often assumed to be kyop'o, which refers to any overseas Korean but in common usage usually implies Korean American. Yet unlike those second-generation Koreans who were raised by ethnic Korean parents (who might, more than their children, be held accountable for failing to transmit ethnic and national pride to their offspring), adoptees had been removed involuntarily from Korea and transplanted into a Western environment, raised by white parents, and most often provided little to no exposure to cultural ways of "being Korean."

For instance, Sarah Dankert, who left Korea when she was six and was adopted with her twin sister to a family in a rural town in Minne-

© Kate Hershiser Aka / 박경희 1998

친구에게,

네, 그렇습니다. 영어하고 있습니다. 당신의 반응 때문에 저는 교포라고 말씀드리고 싶습니다. 당신은 잘 모르시겠지만 저는 어렸을 때 입양되어서 외국으로 건너갔습니다. 따라서 우리나라 말을 잘 못합니다. 모국에 돌아온 이유는 한국문화와 한국말을 배우기 위해서입니다. 그래서 당신의 행위로 인해 한국사람들에 대한 편견을 가지고 싶지 않고 당신도 저, 즉 교포들에 대한 선입견을 가지지 않기를 바랍니다. 내가 영어를 써서 당신을 불편하고 언짢게 만들었지만 당신도 마찬가지로 저를 불편하게 만든 것에 대해 유감입니다.

안녕.

Dear Friend,

Yes, I am speaking English. Your comments prompt me to tell you that as you probably guessed I am a kyopo(overseas korean). However, what you probably aren't aware of is I was adopted from Korea when I was young. Consequently, my language skills aren't up to par. My reasons for my return to the motherland are to learn about the culture and language of my own people. Please don't let your behavior be reason for me to stereotype Korean people's attitudes, just as I do not wish for you to have prejudices towards myself, a kyopo. I am sorry if my speaking English offended or threatened your being, just as I am sorry your behavior made me feel uncomfortable.

Sincerely,

11. Kate Hershiser (kate hers), "Calling Card (after Adrian Piper)." (Reproduced with permission from kate hers and Yeong and Yeong Book Company)

sota, returned twelve years later and spent most of her time with second-generation Korean-Americans: "I had Korean features, but I didn't share the experiences that they had, I couldn't share the culture with them. The kyop'os had never been [to Korea], but could understand the cultural stuff. It was so frustrating for me there. I had spent a third of my life there, but I couldn't understand." In addition, unlike second-generation kyop'o who have family connections in Korea, adoptees lack kinship networks. Further, they may find themselves at a greater disadvantage than other foreigners who are racially distinguished as non-Korean and thus not subject to the same culturalist expectations.

Thus, because of their interstitial identities, adoptees trouble dominant understandings of ethnic and national identity not only in their adoptive countries but also in Korea. Ami Nafzger, for instance, was told repeatedly by Koreans that she was a *oeguk saram* (foreigner). As she told me, "It was drilled into my head so many times that I was a oeguk saram. And that was it. And you are—you are a foreigner. And you really come to feel like you really, really are a foreigner there." Yet in the same breath, she stated, "But it's convenient for them, when [you're] a Korean, for them to say, oh, you're really Korean, you're a real Korean because you eat kimchee—That doesn't make me a real Korean!" Or, as a Danish adoptee told a group of native Korean volunteers at a training workshop for the adoptee service provider International Korean Adoptee Services (INKAS), "If I learn one word of Korean, Koreans expect me to learn ten more words, and they expect me to be more Korean. But Danishness is not something I can get rid of . . . there are such high expectations from Koreans, it's easier not to meet them at all."

Male heterosexual adoptees were sensitively attuned to the global hierarchies of race and gender when they returned to Korea, especially when they witnessed the elevated status of white men in Korea who were treated with deference and granted special treatment as privileged foreigners. Seeing Korean women date white men could be particularly galling to some male adoptees who realized that the heterosexual stratifications that have emasculated them in their adoptive countries were also mirrored and replicated in Korea. They thereby witness how neocolonial relationships with the United States have produced a sexual economy in Korea in which it seems that white men, no matter how physically unattractive or morally repugnant, possess greater social capital than do Korean men (see Kelsky 2001 on Japanese women and Western men).[20]

Adoptees, who are "culturally white" but "genetically Korean," unlike their white male counterparts, were expected to assimilate to Korean ways and could be subject to diminished status because of their lack of Korean cultural authenticity. Aaron, a male adoptee from Wisconsin, came to Korea as a college exchange student in 2001. He explained to me in August 2003 his own disidentificatory practices: how he actively refused to speak Korean in resistance to the cultural pressure to conform to Korean ways simply because he "looks Asian." During a street-side campaign for the 2001 "Hi Seoul" tourism promotion, the tag line of which was "Seoul Welcomes the World," he was passed over by employees of the Korean National Tourism Organization who were handing out brochures and free trinkets to passersby. He approached one of them who explicitly told him that the campaign was not directed at someone like him. Given the assumptions that the desirable tourist is a white Western (male), he said caustically, "They should call it 'Seoul Welcomes the White World.'"

ADOPTEE SOCIAL SPACES IN SEOUL

In August 2003 I was staying at my cousin's apartment in the northern part of Itaewon. As a teenager in the mid-1980s I had stayed in the same area of Itaewon with my family for summer vacations. My brother and I used to walk down the steep and winding streets from our apartment to Itaewon-ro where we would go to Wendy's or Pizza Hut, which along with KFC were the only American fast food chains in Seoul at the time. The street also featured discount furriers and leather goods purveyors, as well as piles of fake Polo shirts and Fila socks that we would inevitably wear back home. These were the years of intense demonstrations by the student movement for democratization, but one would never have known about it in Itaewon.

My brother and I recognized that Itaewon was a different place than other parts of Seoul, since our neighbors included a Korean woman and her African American husband and all the shop owners spoke English. It also had a palpably seedy feel. The anthropologist Eun-Shil Kim calls Itaewon a deterritorialized place and describes how it was known as the "'Las Vegas of Seoul'—a recreation center and place of cultural consumption for American soldiers. . . . where [they] engaged in hedonism, prostitution, illegal drugs, and criminal activities" (2005: 38). In her study Kim analyzes the transformation of Itaewon from an exotic "foreigner's district" that served as the sexual playground and shopping mall for American soldiers stationed in Korea in the 1970s and 1980s to the "multicultural village" of today.

By the late 1990s, Itaewon, which is bordered by the American military base in the adjacent Yongsan district and by the embassy district of Hannam, had become home to a growing expatriate community of African and South Asian migrant workers, embassy people, business people, English teachers, and adoptees. In 2003 the seedier clubs were being replaced by more sophisticated establishments and European or "ethnic" Asian restaurants, and the hawkers of imitation handbags and fake brand-name clothing competed with the legitimate franchise outlets of companies like Adidas, Nike, and Rockport. The real estate market reflected the foreign origins of the area's residents, including the use of monthly leases rather than ones based on the large investment deposits, or "key money," required by landlords in other neighborhoods.

Mihee Nathalie Lemoine had been based in Itaewon for the twelve years she lived in Korea. Her close friend, the fellow Belgian adoptee Vincent Sung, who worked as a fashion photographer in Europe and in New York, later started managing a new bar, Spy, in Itaewon. A small group of lesbian adoptees socialized in some of the gay bars and lounges on "Homo Hill," which has been a place where gay and transgender Korean men have, according to Eun-Shil Kim, been able openly to express their sexuality given the unique atmosphere in Itaewon marked by a "tolerance of things generally deemed socially unacceptable" in mainstream Korean life (2005: 57). Sung opened up another bar, Chez Vous, in early 2004, and the exposed balcony and variety of wines and Belgian beers made it a popular destination for some adoptees, especially during the 2004 Gathering conference.

For others, however, Chez Vous was too expensive, and they disliked going to Itaewon because they considered it to be an inauthentic cultural space that symbolized Korea's neocolonial relationship with the United States. Adoptees were also less likely to frequent the more affluent parts of Seoul, located south of the Han River, where the hyper-elite transnational Koreans reside. There, the sons and daughters of wealthy Seoul residents, who are educated in American high schools and universities, are known to spend their summers hanging out in expensive clubs and restaurants, peppering their speech with English idioms, and flaunting their wealth through conspicuous consumption of brand-name European and American luxury goods and Westernized haute cuisine.

Many other adoptees preferred to hang out in the cheap bars (*hop'ŭ*, based on the German word *hof*) in the university areas of Hong-ik University and Shinch'on. There, adoptees from GOA'L would congregate on the weekends around large wooden tables, and order pitchers of *saengmaekchu* (beer on tap) and mixed drinks like "lemon soju" (sweet potato liquor combined with powdered lemonade mix) for as little as 3,000 won (US$2.50). Hippo Hof in Hongdae in particular became a regular place for adoptees to meet up on the weekends during the summer months. A typical weekend night would involve three or four stops, with the first in a barbeque restaurant, followed by drinks at a hof, then dancing at a nightclub or singing karaoke at a *noraebang*, and finally ending with a salty, spicy snack at an outdoor street vendor (*p'ojangmach'a*). Under Kim Dae-won's watch as secretary-general of GOA'L, these get-togethers became a key form of community building by providing a regular set of meeting points and watering holes for adoptees, and they might be considered to be the spaces that constitute alternative spaces of belonging for the expatriate adoptee community.

ENGLISH FEVER

The resignification and revaluation of adoptees by the Korean state and as experienced in their everyday lives in Korea revealed the ongoing ambivalence that surrounds them as co-ethnic foreigners. But with the transformation of parts of Seoul into multicultural spaces a shift became palpable for many adoptees. Taxi drivers, who might have in the past asked why adoptees couldn't speak Korean, could just as easily respond, "So, now that you know English, you can come here and make lots of money?" If essentializing stories of taxi drivers can serve as any kind of measure, it seems that neoliberal economic logics were dislodging culturalist expectations.

Part of the globalization drive initiated by President Kim Young Sam included a plan to extend English-language education to elementary school classrooms. This extension of the public school curriculum to reflect the exigencies of a new global order, along with the lifting of government restrictions on private after-school education, contributed to the near ubiquity of English-language learning among Korean school-age children.[21] Despite, or perhaps due to, the devastating effects of the IMF crisis in 1997, as well as a three-year ban (1997–2000) on private after-school English institutes (*yŏngŏ hagwŏn*), the market in English-language education grew exponentially for students of all age groups.[22] As So Jin Park and Nancy Abelmann explain, "In the new millennium, market principles and the consumer demand for education triumphed over state regulation. To wit, by the end of the decade, South Korea boasted one of the world's most vibrant private after-school educational markets, with few limits in the name of equality" (2004: 649).

The expansion of English language education in Korea is part of the broader "education fever" (*kyoyuk yŏl*) that has characterized South Korean modernity and gripped the country's middle class with even greater force in the post-IMF era (Seth 2002). According to a recent market report,

Korea spends 7 percent of its GDP on educational expenditures, which is one of the largest percentages among nations in the world (*Korea Times* 2005). As middle-class mothers strive to educate their children for an increasingly globalized and competitive job market, English has become accepted as *the* requisite skill for future success. To fill the need for English-language teachers in primary and middle schools, the Korean government through the Ministry of Education began recruiting English teachers from English-speaking countries in 1995 through a program called EPIK (English Program in Korea). The Fulbright English Teaching Assistant (ETA) program, administered by the Korean office of the United States–Korea Fulbright Program, began in 1992 with eight teachers and by 2007 was placing up to eighty American college seniors or recent college graduates across the country. Around the same time, the expanding *hagwŏn* (after-school study institutes, or "cram schools") market was seeking English teachers, often without regard to their qualifications or prior experience. This development, along with the establishment of the Overseas Koreans Act and the extension of visa privileges for overseas Koreans, created new possibilities for adoptees to return to Korea and to live there for extended periods of time.

Kelli Donigan first came to Korea on the EPIK program in 1997 after graduating from the University of Michigan. She was also one of the first adoptee members of GOA'L, and she served as employment coordinator from 2000 to 2003. When she first took on that position, she said that the organization was receiving many inquiries from hagwŏns and Korean companies seeking native English speakers. As the country recovered from the IMF crisis, Donigan observed that a new entrepreneurial spirit (*pench'ŏ*, or "venture"—short for "venture capital") had taken hold of Koreans who could no longer rely on lifetime employment and security at one of the nation's conglomerates (*chaebŏl*). Koreans began investing in after-school instruction schools and were soon recruiting heavily for native English speakers by offering full competitive salary packages, including airfare, accommodations, and benefits.

By the late 1990s, information about teaching English in Korea became widely available on the Internet. Adoptees like Robert Sullivan from Nebraska were able to apply online for work at an English hagwŏn. Robert, who was unsuccessful in his attempts to get information about his Korean family from his adoption agencies in the United States and in Korea, decided in 2001 that getting an English teaching job would give him the opportunity to go to Korea and find out more about his past. He applied and was immediately offered a job by a hagwŏn and had a flight booked to Seoul. The night before his scheduled departure he received a phone call from the hagwŏn informing him that the offer had been rescinded. Robert had sent a photo of himself to the school so that the escort who was being dispatched to pick him up at the airport would be able to recognize him. Apologizing, the hagwŏn representative said that the school had made the decision on the assumption that he was white, but seeing that he was Korean they could no longer hire him.[23]

It was ironic for adoptees to be on the one hand considered oeguk saram, while on the other hand have their Korean appearance serve as a liability on the job market where whiteness is valued as a sign of (American) cultural authenticity and nativeness. In another ironic twist, however, and one that might suggest how Korean mothers' preferences have been changing, one hagwŏn owner, a former volunteer at GOA'L, told me that Korean mothers were requesting that he hire kyop'o teachers because they felt that Caucasian Americans were too lenient. In this case, he asked, "Are adoptees kyop'o or white?"

For nonnative English speakers, job opportunities were much more scarce, a situation that had created new hierarchies of value and stratifications among different groups of adoptees. It was thus difficult for European adoptees to spend extended periods of time in Korea unless they could secure corporate-sector positions, which generally require advanced degrees or specialized experience. In fact, one Scandinavian adoptee I know who has a good command of English took on an American-sounding name in order to work at an English hagwŏn. For Francophone and German adoptees whose accented English marked them more clearly as nonnative English speakers, this strategic move would have been impossible, and their job prospects were thereby much more limited and more dramatically segmented and stratified. The Europeans I knew, for example, were unemployed, enrolled in language programs, working for European companies, or self-employed.

More than a few adoptees were deeply cynical about the ways in which the global economy had structured their ability to return to Korea, requiring them to participate in the reproduction of Koreans' middle-class status and the entrenchment of American cultural imperialism. One American adoptee I met was adamant about not working at a hagwŏn and chose instead to take a less-well-paying position at a public elementary school. He understood that the same economic logic that shapes the state's representation of adoptees as "successful global citizens" failed to grasp their social and cultural marginalization in Korea, where their loss of membership in a linguistic and national community has been ironically transformed into a gain—in a context where (American) English-language ability has become a commodity of significant exchange value and a sign of cosmopolitan privilege.

BRINGING ADOPTEES HOME

Mihee Nathalie Lemoine's installation piece in the "Ibyangin, Ibangin" exhibition was called "I Wish You a Beautiful Life." It borrowed its title from a well-known book in Korean American adoption circles, *I Wish for You a Beautiful Life* (1999), which features Korean women in a home for unwed mothers who have written letters addressed to their as-yet-unborn and soon-to-be-relinquished infant children. Mihee began her project by sending out an email to her contacts and posting it to electronic mailing lists used by adoptees. The email announced the "Korean Adoptee Suicide Memorial Project," and a call was made for submissions to commemorate adoptees who had committed suicide. A request was made for the victim's Korean and Western names, dates of birth and death, and name of the adoption agency, as well as any message that friends or family of the deceased would want to include in commemoration. Mihee underscored the fact that she was not intending to place blame on adoptive parents but rather only to "voice [the] memory" of adoptees.

Using the materials she collected, Mihee created a piece composed of five shiny Mylar squares that were hung on the gallery wall like reflective tombstones. A banner with the title of the piece was placed over the set of squares. The squares themselves were printed with the Korean name of the deceased adoptee transliterated into English, the years of birth and death, the name of the adoption agency, the adoptive country, and the year of adoption. Surrounding these squares were email responses that Lemoine received from members of the French adoptee group Racines Coréennes, after her request was posted to their chat board. Some members were offended by her request, such as one person who wrote, "What kind of idea is this? And why not a memorial for the ethnic Uzbekistanian Koreans living in Morocco? I have absolutely no interest." Another wrote, "I do not believe that it would please me to know that my name was placed on a memorial because I had committed suicide, particularly if I was adopted." Out of a broad range of opinions, from outrage to curiosity, Mihee included responses that reflected the shadow of ambivalence that adoption casts. The messages were printed on white fabric and were hung like pieces of cloth off of a drying line, suggesting the airing of (dirty) laundry (see figure 12).

The author of one of the messages wrote as follows: "This project challenges me and without a doubt makes me uncomfortable. It is because this subject is terribly painful, and none among us can say that it will not confront us one day." Another wrote, "We do not hide the fact that adoption is associated with experiences that are positive and enriching and, also, unfortunately, with unhappy experiences, which can lead to the worst acts. Let us not be like the ostrich. Even if the unhappy are a minority (everything is relative), we cannot escape them."

Mihee explained her intentions in an artist statement, which appeared in the exhibition catalogue:

> This piece is a critique of what Korea has not given its overseas adoptees: a sense of identity. The tragedy of adoptees that have committed suicide has haunted me especially during the first years of my activist involvement in the Korean adoptee community. . . . I hope that Korea will understand that globalization should not include displacing its orphans in the Western world without their consent, and to consider the human rights of children. Sending children abroad for the benefit of their well-being does not always result in their success as adults. I wish for Korea to not forget those who had less of a chance to survive in their overseas adoption experience.

Mihee's provocative piece brings a repressed history of adoption to the surface by insisting, against the optimistic vision of the adoptee as a cosmopolitan global citizen, "cultural ambassador," or "diversity mascot" (Ruth 1997) that the unlucky adoptees—those who did not "succeed"—be counted and remembered.[24]

The adoptee art critic Kim Stoker has written about the "artivism" of adoptee artists like Mihee and kate hers whose socially and politically engaged artistic work is also a form of cultural activism. In Stoker's words,

12. Mihee-Nathalie Lemoine, "I Wish You a Beautiful Life," installation view. (Courtesy of the artist)

"Artivism takes these notions a step further by its essential quality of public 'roguishness,' meaning that the act of the art itself, its existence and its presentation, mischievously confronts and subverts expectations of the intended audience" (2005: 230). In the case of "I Wish You a Beautiful Life," Mihee's action was to publicly air out adoptee suicide as a social fact rather than as a set of private and inexplicable individual tragedies. As such, it was an act that touched a sensitive nerve among adoptees (cf. Durkheim 1951 [1897]).[25]

A few weeks after the art exhibition closed, news of an adoptee's suicide began circulating among members of the adoptee community in Seoul. As the local authorities sought more information about the case, I received phone calls from directors at OKF and the adoptee advocacy organization KoRoot asking me if I had known the twenty-seven-year-old male adoptee from San Francisco who had been found dead outside of his apartment building in Seoul early one morning in late August. I had never met him, and it appeared that no one in the closely networked group of adoptees had either. Later on, it surfaced that a member of ASK had met him briefly when working for a short time at the same English hagwŏn. But the member had not known him well and could only say that he seemed to be friendly and cheerful. Although foul play had not yet been ruled out, and there was no evidence such as a suicide note, it was generally assumed that his death had been intentional and self-inflicted.

A few days later I received a group text message from Dae-won announcing an impromptu memorial service at the city coroner's office. Afterward, KoRoot, along with GOA'L, ASK, and INKAS, decided to organize a more formal memorial service for the deceased before his body was repatriated to the United States. On the evening of September 3 I arrived at KoRoot to see that the garden had been set with a table covered in a white cloth. On this altar were placed two large arrangements of white flowers typical of memorial services (*ch'umosik* or *ch'udosik*), between which were tall white candles on either side of a framed photo of the departed.[26] The front panel of the altar was covered by a South Korean flag and an American one hanging side by side.

As the ceremony began, the forty-five people in attendance—Korean adoptees and a handful of Korean volunteers—stood where the family would usually be positioned during a formal memorial service. Each person was given a white carnation. Standing on the lawn to the right side of the altar, I interpreted for Reverend Kim who opened the service by recounting the initial sorrow and confusion he experienced upon hearing the news of the adoptee's death, and how, when he and Dae-won first went to the city morgue, they found that, in place of his name, the tag on the casket had been labeled simply with the word *oegukin* (foreigner). Dismayed by this, they decided to hold the impromptu service at the coroner's office, and after receiving permission from the deceased's parents in the United States, they organized this, more formal, memorial service.

The news of the suicide and ensuing activities and talk made the outlines of the community and its importance, especially following the Gathering conference, strongly palpable. Many regretfully observed that "he wasn't connected to the community," implying that, had he been, the social support he needed might have helped prevent his suicide. The sad news brought home for many the reality that suicide and depression are significant issues that many adoptees confront. For Dae-won it raised anxieties about a possible copy-cat effect. It also provoked reflection on the "community" and its role in providing kinship, social support, and informal peer counseling for adoptees who generally lack language skills, family connections, or basic cultural knowledge in Korea. The community was acknowledged as being especially vital for those who return to Korea already estranged from their adoptive families or countries and with fragile hopes of finding a place of authentic belonging.

The memorial service was organized quickly, to take place before the body was repatriated to the United States. I interpret the service as a symbolic attempt to recuperate and repatriate the adoptee's (absent) body into the adoptee community. The suicide not only brought the hidden histories of adoptees who, in Mihee's words, "had less of a chance to survive" but also a recognition of the limits of cultural citizenship for adoptees in Korea—who, caught between nation-states and cultural locations, can die as foreigners in their so-called motherland. It also demonstrated clearly how adoptee kinship fills in for the absence of genealogical ties to family and nation for adoptees in Korea.

KINSHIP AND GLOBALIZATION IN AN AGE OF NEOLIBERALISM

Early in 2006 stories of "study abroad adoption" (*ibyang yuhak*)—Korean parents sending their young children to be legally adopted by American citizens—made the news in Korea and the United States. It was reported that these parents had calculated that, given the competitiveness of the South Korean school system and the lack of guaranteed job security, it was best for their children to be educated in America. Legal adoption granted their children citizenship, a better education, and brighter economic prospects, and for their sons it was a reprieve from mandatory military service. In return, however, it required the parents to relinquish all legal ties to the child. This new trend in strategic "education emigration" (see Abelmann 2003) was brought to light by parents who had been victims of fraud by "adoption brokers" who are paid up to $40,000 to find an American family, oftentimes retired Korean American couples, willing to legally adopt the child. Not only were parents vulnerable to swindlers, but the children, it was reported, also exhibited emotional distress and difficulties in adjustment to their new lives (A. Lee 2006).

Although these cases represent an extreme example of the extent to which some Korean parents may be willing to go in order to educate their children and to either maintain their social status or to gain upward mobility, they are part of a range of strategies that parents have devised to take advantage of legal loopholes and global trends to grant their children and themselves a more flexible and transnational future. Indeed, a survey in March 2006 by the *Dong A Daily* newspaper found that, given the opportunity, one out of four Koreans said they would emigrate for education (*imin kyoyuk*) (Lee and Park 2006).

Early education adoption is but one trend in disembedded and deterritorialized kinship practices among Korean families that have produced phenomena such as the "wild geese families" (*kirŏgi kajok*) in which fathers stay in Korea to earn money to support the wife and children living overseas for better educational opportunities. Korean children often are sent to live with relatives in America to attend high school or boarding school and return home on vacation. There is also a network of businesses that caters to Korean exchange students by offering homestays and support services for young Korean students abroad. Like the "parachute kids" and "astronaut wives" of the Chinese diaspora (Ong 1999; Yeoh, Huang, and Lam 2005), Korean transnational families are also finding ways to flexibly insert their children into the global economy, and in the process, stretching dominant definitions of the nuclear family, Korean kinship, and Confucian values (see Ong 1999: 128). Thus, even as the Korean state is extending the bounds of the nation across transnational space, based on blood and inalienable kinship ties to the ethnic nation, Korean families are seeking to evade state regulation and the obligations entailed with citizenship.

Economic instability in Korea and a hypercompetitive educational system have created the conditions for both informal and legal adoption to be practiced as a strategy of transnational social and economic capital accumulation. In this neoliberal context of every child for himself, transnational adoptees who were adopted overseas from the 1950s to the 1980s are resignified as lucky, thereby replacing problematic projections of shame and pity with equally distorted ones of envy. One male adoptee in his early thirties from rural Wisconsin, who first came to Korea as an enlisted soldier with the United States Army, talked to me about how Korean mothers hired him to edit their children's personal essays for their applications to elite American boarding schools. For this adoptee, being considered lucky by those mothers was not such a bad thing:

> We are really looked at as lucky. A lot of the families, especially the upwardly mobile families who are trying to get their children into the biggest schools and create wealth for generations, they're saying, "You got a good deal." But then we come back [to Korea] and whine and [say], "Oh, I don't know who my mother is." On a very human level, that's important, but also on a very human level I gotta eat, man, and I really like my high-speed Internet connection on my fat-ass computer. It's a huge trade. When I'm in a situation where I don't know my parents anyway, I don't know my parents in Korea or in the States, it's all a plus to me.

This rather flippant characterization depends upon a neoliberal logic of rational self-actualization that radically downplays the importance not only of state regulation but also of social relations and intimacy. For other adoptees, however, the ease with which this equation or "huge trade" can be drawn, from needing to eat to wanting a "fat-ass computer," and from severed kinship ties and knowledge to a "high-speed Internet connection," points to some of the moral and ethical dangers in uncritical celebrations of transnational adoptees as exemplars of globalization.

A Korean elementary school English teacher in her late twenties, who had spent a summer volunteering for an adult adoptee motherland tour, told me over ice cream at a Baskin Robbins in southern Seoul that her friends thought that adoptees had enough money and therefore shouldn't be receiving help from the Korean government. As she explained, "Korean life is really limited. Most people have a regular life—if we live a regular life then we're lucky—school, marriage, children. If we go another way [take an unconventional path], people think you've failed in your life. From American movies, we think [Americans] enjoy their lives. We just work and study." Her thoughts, albeit somewhat simplistic, may reflect the sentiments of young Koreans who feel limited in their life possibilities and whose imaginaries are shot through with generations of mobility stories (Abelmann 2003), transnational families, and global mediascapes (Appadurai 1996). For them, adoptees who are free to travel to Korea, make money, and return to their Western lives may very likely appear to be quite "lucky."

HyoJung Bidol, who had been living in Seoul for four years, found these perceptions by young Koreans to be woefully misinformed: "People in their twenties say, 'Oh, you're so lucky. You get to be an American. You speak perfect English.' So then [for them] the most important thing is that I got to grow up in America and speak English fluently? [They're] missing the whole experience." And as Mihee Lemoine cautioned in her statement to Korean supporters of KoRoot at the organization's first anniversary fund-raising event: "If you send Korean babies to foreigners, don't think that you are sending them for *yuhak* [overseas education]. It's not *yuhak* education; it's adoption, which means that it's not reversible."[27]

Thus although some Koreans may believe that adoptees have fared well by having entered into a privileged Western world, with all the opportunities for education and advancement it can afford, this crude calculation often discounts the pain and loss of family, belonging, and history that adoptees must often grapple with. For many adoptees, comparing the opportunities they've gained to the things that they've lost—natal family relations, genealogical knowledge, culture, language, and national belonging—only points out their profound incommensurability. As Sebastian Hootele, a thirty-three-year-old Belgian adoptee who had moved to Korea in summer 2004, told me, "I got love, a family, an education, and all those things, but the fact that I'm here says something—there's something missing."

Sebastian met Mihee Lemoine, whom he affectionately called his "sister," in 1987 at a Korean-language program run by a Korean immigrant church in Brussels. The ten adoptees who met there formed a tight-knit group and became founding members of the Korean Belgium Association (KoBel) in 1991. It was through a summer camp organized by a Korean church that Sebastian, who knew very little English, had a chance to move to Los Angeles to live with a Korean host family for six months. Several years later he was nearly fluent in English, and in a meeting with me at the coffee shop of the Ambassador Hotel during the Gathering conference, he stated: "What would I be if I stayed? I wouldn't have the opportunity to travel as I have for ten years. . . . Would you stay in an orphanage and live like a bum and have no future or choose to be in a family and receive everything I have had?"

Sebastian embraced his cosmopolitan privileges and his pride in being Belgian. In the exhibit room on the top floor of the Ambassador Hotel during the Gathering, KoBel's booth was the most artfully designed and colorful. On the walls of the display were posters of Belgian beer and the Belgian cartoon character Tintin, and the table sported glossy books about Belgium, Belgian chocolates, and bottles of Chimay and other beers. The other tables were bland in comparison, with simple banners, flyers, and publications about the organizations, but nothing culturally specific that suggested any identification with the adoptive countries. Sebastian took this as an indication that the other adoptees had not "accepted where they came from. They're not 100 percent Belgian and not 100 percent Korean. I take part of both, and make 100 percent of myself."

When I saw Sebastian again in January 2005, he was busy preparing a major project called the Adoptee Awareness Wall, which was to be composed of a series of posters featuring three thousand photographs of adoptees who'd been sent overseas. The plan was to line the walls of subway stations in Korea's major cities with posters stretching a length of five hundred feet in order to present a stunning visual representation of the vast extent of Korean adoption over the past fifty years. Intended to bring visibility to adoptees in Korea and to raise awareness among Koreans about adoption-related issues, the project carried high ambitions and reflected a growing consensus among many adoptees about the troubling aspects of the ongoing practice of overseas adoption. The project's Website, Ibyang.com, stated the following: "Adoption is a key social issue. We adoptees are the result of past and [ongoing] social dysfunction, yet it still continues, into the year 2005! This situation can be addressed by educating the public and, we hope, Korean society will then begin to ask itself questions about why adoption continues and will resolve to do something about it. We adoptees can be the spark to trigger the social consciousness of the Korean society."

While working on this project and encountering difficulties with fund-raising and sponsorship, Sebastian had settled into life in Seoul. He lived in Itaewon in a shared apartment with a young Swedish adoptee, and he had a Korean girlfriend. In addition, I was surprised to hear, he was in the process of surrendering his Belgian citizenship and European Union membership to reclaim his Korean citizenship.[28] We had shared a long subway ride back to the Noksapyong subway station from Kangnam, and as we walked up the hill through the bone-chilling winter wind I questioned his rationale about the citizenship issue. I asked why he didn't simply take on his Korean name as a symbolic act of claiming identity, as many other adoptees I know have done, since giving up his European citizenship would surely limit his future abilities to work and travel.

He replied with gravity: "I'm not going to change my name or get rid of my Belgian identity. That's who I am. I am Sebastian Hootele." What was meaningful for him was to be fully present in Korea, where he was born and where he can now, by his own choice, stay and live. He was not, he told me, going to renounce his adoptive family or his identity and history as a person raised in Belgium, but, having traveled extensively and lived in Europe and the United States, he was certain that he didn't want to go back to Belgium. He wanted to be a Korean in Korea. He tried to clarify it further for me by stating, "Koreans look at me, and they don't understand that I'm Belgian. Now I can say that I'm Korean." The Adoptee Awareness Wall was also part of Sebastian's desire to be a part of Korea, to work, as a legal Korean citizen, toward progressive social change and greater cultural citizenship and visibility for adoptees in Korea.

As "study abroad adoptions" and "wild geese families" stretch and distort normative kinship practices among Koreans, a network of Korean obstetricians and travel agencies streamline the process for expectant Korean couples to give birth in Hawaii to take advantage of the American citizenship principle of jus soli. In the context of these and other strategic maneuvers to manipulate citizenship and kinship, the idea that someone would choose to renounce citizenship to a Western country struck me as being highly unusual. Yet for Sebastian, whose "discrepant cosmopolitanism" (Clifford 1997) had led him from Korea to Belgium to the United States and then back to Korea again, legitimizing his presence in Korea had clear and present value. He was choosing to dwell and to be fixed in a world in which flexibility, movement, and deterritorialization are the rules governing the global economy. Against a neoliberal logic that trades kinship for globalization, in which the cultural losses of adoption and abandonment are easily resignified as individual economic gains, this adoptee was trading in his cosmopolitan citizenship for a sense of locality and kinship in order to restore national belonging in the face of his own foreignness.

CONCLUSION

The specific time-space compression of adoptees who return to Korea—even those, or especially those, who are reunited with natal family—forces them to confront the losses of time, memory and the accumulation of daily intimacies that make family and culture. Thus the frustrations at being unable to ever really fit in Korea or in the West, and the seemingly insurmountable hurdles of language and difference, contribute to the deeply felt desire to carve out a space of adoptee kinship and belonging, whether at a hotel conference or in the bars of cosmopolitan Seoul. Many adoptees also reflect on their relative privilege and the gains of material comfort, love, and family life that adoption afforded them, and some come to realize how large the cracks can be in the social welfare system in Korea and how harrowing it is, especially for those born into poverty or nonnormative family situations. As adoptees increasingly return to Korea they thus confront not only their own pasts but also the political-economic circumstances and inequalities that made it necessary for them to be adopted.

With the rise of global English, adoptees and other English-speaking expatriates have found an economic niche that enables them to travel to Korea and stay for extended periods of time. Hence, rather than merely a situation of freely chosen family, adoptee kinship is also structured by the nation-state and the global political economy—specifically South Korea's own proactive globalization project that recognizes overseas coethnics as part of the deterritorialized nation and the lucrative market in global English. In this process, new stratifications that reflect the broader global hierarchy of nation-states are reproduced among adoptees whose value is differentially determined in terms of economic and social capital. In addition, adoptees' desires for citizenship and state recognition exist within the context of the heightened commodification of kinship among affluent South Koreans who view adoptees enviously as they themselves engage in strategic forms of "familial governmentality" (Ong 1999) to evade state control in the neoliberal pursuit of upward mobility and cosmopolitanism. The emergence of an active, if fluid, community of adopted Koreans in Seoul demonstrates how new kinds of relatedness are being formed in the midst of other, increasingly transnationalized, kinship practices and nationalist claims.

The repatriations to Korea by adoptees suggest that there's something missing, but this search for missing pieces, as Sebastian's story suggests, should not lead us to presume that adoptees' returns can be regarded as straightforward attempts to replace an imposed identity with a natural one by rejecting adoptive family and adoptive nation in favor of the imagined plenitude of Korean birth mothers and motherlands. Rather, Sebastian reminds us of other possibilities—that one's relationship to nations and families can be fluid, expansive, and additive rather than fixed, narrow, and exclusive. In opposition to some critics of the adult adoptee counterpublic who presume that adoptees' interests in their roots are signs of failed assimilation, biologistic reductionism, or regressive nationalism, adoptees in Korea suggest quite the opposite. Adoptee contingent essentialism opens up possibilities for a "diasporic citizenship" (Siu 2005), in which partial belonging to two (or more) nation-states constitutes full belonging to the adoptee community. Yet these connections are not only symbolic but also, as I show in the next chapter, continually emerging out of material and social relations as adoptees enact their national belonging through everyday forms of political participation.

6

Made in Korea

Adopted Koreans and Native Koreans in the Motherland

At the Gathering conference in Seoul in 2004 it was the so-called native Koreans or "Korean Koreans"—as they are often referred to by adoptees in Korea—rather than adoptive parents or adoption agency social workers who constituted the excluded other. As the conference was being held in Korea with South Korean government and corporate support, there were many Koreans at the conference, but their presence was restricted to specific settings. Korean sponsors and government dignitaries, for instance, were honored in the official ceremonies, and local NGO supporters were permitted to set up information booths on the top floor of the hotel. Throughout the conference a battalion of Korean volunteers was kept on the ready to ensure that things ran smoothly, but the volunteers mainly circulated in the hallways and on the top floor. They were not allowed to attend the workshop sessions, which were designated as being for adoptees only.

Among the other nonadoptees who showed up at the hotel were the birth parents hoping to locate children sent for adoption many years earlier, and the dozen or so who were found wandering the hotel, stopping random adoptees to ask if they knew their children, were directed upstairs to the Adoption Information Center, which was staffed by social workers from the four Korean adoption agencies. Reporters also hovered, hoping to locate scintillating rags-to-riches success stories or to get the first scoop on a dramatic family reunion. Given the planning committee's concern over the potentially disruptive presence of the Korean media, which have a reputation for being insensitive toward and exploitative of adoptees, the reporters' access was tightly policed.

In one workshop session, a reporter from one of the major daily newspapers tried to pass as an adoptee participant but was quickly caught out and roundly dismissed. When we spoke at the Gathering, the Belgian adoptee Sebastian Hootele was critical of this as separatist behavior that he surmised would negatively affect the way that journalists represented adoptees to the Korean public. He told me that if adoptees wanted to "have recognition from Korea, we need to stop separating and putting walls up—that creates differences. We are putting in place the feeling of differences."

As I described in chapter 4 the adoptee conferences were intermittent sites of intersubjective sociality that were managed and designed to produce safe spaces for the performance of community and to give shape and coherence to a deterritorialized group of highly diverse individuals. In strictly delimiting the participation of native Koreans, the Gathering carved out a peculiar social space in Korea that reterritorialized the "non-place" (Augé 1998) of the hotel into a performative site of adoptee cultural production. This boundary maintenance was rationalized as a necessary measure to shield first timers, who, it was anticipated, would be culturally disoriented and emotionally vulnerable on their first journeys back to Korea. The planning committee had, in part, conceived of the role of Korean volunteers, who were recruited from the different NGO adoptee advocacy groups, as buffers between adoptees and insensitive Koreans. As such, they occupied a liminal position within the adoptee-dominated space, and circulated in the in-between places of the hotel—lobbies, elevators, hallways, and registration desks.

The topic of the exclusion of Korean volunteers from adoptee-only spaces had been a point of contention during the first planning meetings for the 2003 Gathering when Global Overseas Adoptees' Link (GOA'L) was still involved. A Korean volunteer who had worked closely with GOA'L during the late 1990s told me over dinner in August 2003 that, in the first stages of planning that conference, the adoptees discussed excluding native Korean volunteers from the main auditorium. She couldn't understand their logic at all; as she stated, "The volunteers are doing all the work!" Likewise, in an interview a few weeks before the Gathering, the main volunteer and interpreter for the adoptee service provider International Korean Adoptee Services expressed her displeasure at the exclusion of Koreans from the Gathering: "They should open the hotel so that *more* Koreans can know about adoptees. . . . That's a *very* good chance for Koreans to know about adoptees and how they feel." Indeed, the strict boundary maintenance at the Gathering was felt by some dedicated Korean volunteers to be a harsh rejection of the friendship and support they had extended to adoptees to help them feel welcome in Korea.

In contrast to the spatial and temporal boundedness of the conferences, adoptees living in Korea were able to engage in sustained sociality and interaction not only with each other but also with the native Koreans who wanted to help them. A range of social spaces and nonprofit organizations in Seoul had been established by 2004 and comprised a distinct social field of adoptees and their advocates. In addition to GOA'L, there were two other nonprofit organizations: International Korean Adoptee Services (INKAS) which offers a summer camp, scholarships for language programs, and assistance with birth family search, and KoRoot (Ppuriŭi Chip), a European-style hostel run by a Korean couple who spent more than twelve years in Europe. KoRoot provides low-cost accommodations for adoptees, and it has also become a meeting place and community center by hosting events and courses that are designed to help short-term and long-term returnees to learn about Korean culture and to adjust to everyday life in Korea.

These organizations provided spaces and events for adoptees and native Koreans to meet and develop friendships or even romantic relationships. Given the fact that most adoptees have little Korean-language ability, they depend greatly on the assistance and support of native Korean advocacy groups and their volunteers, especially when tackling the challenges of searching for birth family. As I discussed in the previous chapter, given the magnified importance of English in the global economy, many young Koreans were initially drawn to volunteer for adoptee advocacy groups because they wanted to practice their English skills with native speakers. Thus, a common perception among adoptees was that Korean volunteers, who tend to be university students or recent graduates, are less interested in helping adoptees than they are in finding free English-language partners. Longtime Korean volunteers, in turn, critiqued the tendency of adoptees to hold them to unrealistic expectations and of exhibiting a sense of entitlement and cultural superiority with little concern for the personal sacrifices the volunteers make on their behalf.

Even as the organizations offered opportunities for cultural exchange and the development of intimate relationships, the language barriers and culturalist preconceptions were not always easy to overcome. Skepticism among some adoptees about the native-Korean NGOs that were established to help those who return were particularly marked during the time I was in Korea. At a post-Gathering discussion hosted by GOA'L, the facilitator Cory Tomcek noted that "adoptees are always wary of 'Korean Korean' adoptee advocacy groups—What's your interest in helping adoptees? Who's funding you? Are you just part of the system? That sort of thing. The first step is to investigate these groups."

In this chapter, I answer some of the basic questions voiced above by Cory about adoptee-advocacy groups and their relationship to "the system." Taken together they constituted an increasingly interconnected, intercultural, and transnational field that drew together adult adopted Korean returnees and the Koreans who helped them. During my fieldwork between February and September 2004, in addition to socializing with and interviewing adoptees living in Seoul, I volunteered at the different advocacy groups, became acquainted with the founders and head administrators, interviewed Korean volunteers, and distributed a questionnaire to Korean volunteers. Because many of these groups have relatively short histories and the language barriers made it difficult for adoptees to conduct their own investigations, adoptees sometimes asked me to address similar questions to those raised by Cory during the meeting. I was asked about the motivations of native Koreans and the government in helping adoptees, where the money was coming from, and what stance the organizations took toward adoption. In addition to suspicions about Koreans using adoptees to consolidate their own economic or social capital, an initial cynicism toward Korean Christians was also noticeable, especially among European adoptees with secular outlooks.

Whereas in the previous chapter I examined the South Korean government's legal recognition and symbolic embrace of adoptees as overseas Koreans, in this chapter I bring ethnographic focus to the relationships between native Koreans and adoptees as they were mediated by the NGOs that emerged in response to the return of adult adoptees to Korea since the late 1990s. I analyze how adoptees' disidentification with dominant ways of being Korean and their incomplete cultural citizenship in Korea were understood and negotiated by native Korean organizations and volunteers.

In addition, I contextualize these relationships within the recent history of South Korean democratization and the expansion of neoliberal governmentality. With the transfer of power from a succession of authoritarian regimes to a civilian government in 1993, civil society organizations and NGOs proliferated in South Korea. Adoptee-related nonprofit organizations (*piyŏngni tanch'e*) and NGOs (*min'gan tanch'e*) are among those groups, and they have served as forums for Korean volunteers in their twenties and thirties to meet and learn about adoptees as well as to expand their own civic participation and senses of national belonging and international connectedness in contemporary Korea.

Many Korean volunteers are motivated by religious idealism and Christian values, and they earn social capital in the form of "good works" or grace for the assistance they extend to adoptees. But if the interest of native Koreans in helping adoptees can be calculated at all (some adoptees wondered if the organizations were making money off of them, for instance), my research suggests that one must take into account conceptions of Korean civil society, democratization, and the transformations of Korean citizenship vis-à-vis the nation, within the context of economic and cultural globalization.

I underscore how these NGOs not only mediate the experiences and cultural incorporation of adoptees in Korea but also how they mediate contemporary modes of citizenship for South Koreans by providing them opportunities to perform and actualize their own belonging to the postcolonial, postmodern nation, imagined as an active civil society in which participation in social issues through volunteerism is a defining feature of contemporary personhood. These processes, however, retain adoptees as others to the nation whose marginalized status makes them ideal objects of civic paternalism and charity for Korean volunteers. At the same time, however, adoptees are intervening into dominant conceptions of Korean culture and personhood through everyday interactions with these native Korean volunteers. Moreover, they are taking on force as agents of social change through multiple forms of counterpublicity that are invested in the improvement of adoptee lives in Korea and a desire to participate in Korean society as fully recognized members.

FILLING GAPS IN "THE SYSTEM"

In Cory's comment cited above he asked what relationship the "Korean Korean" advocacy groups had to "the system." For adoptees, the system refers to the congeries of adoption agencies and government bureaus that deal with overseas adoption, and which, from the perspective of not a few adoptees, are engaged in a self-protective process of reproducing their own institutional legitimacy and structural power. In addition, they stand in the way of adoptees who struggle to assert their rights to basic information about their adoption histories and desire to make contact with their Korean parents.

As civil society organizations have emerged in other national contexts in the gap between services provided by state welfare programs and those offered by international aid organizations (Fisher 1997), in the case of Korean adoptees, adoptee advocacy NGOs fill in gaps by providing services and support that are outside of the purview of existing state institutions and adoption agency programs. There has been a close if poorly understood relationship between the Korean state and the four government-approved adoption agencies, which since 1976 have been the only licensed agencies permitted to process overseas adoptions.[1] According to one former social worker, these agencies are not dissimilar to the state-supported, family-run conglomerates (*chaebŏl*) that had close ties to the authoritarian regimes of the 1970s and 1980s.

It was during the 1980s, in fact, when overseas adoption was actively encouraged by the state as a form of "emigration" and tied to the state's population control project. This policy also construed overseas adoption as a form of "civil diplomacy" (*min'gan oegyo*) prefiguring a surplus population of children as future bridge builders and eventually as productive suppliers of Western knowledge and skills to further South Korea's economic development. Given this checkered past, it is not surprising that the agencies were viewed with some suspicion by adoptees—who are at once privileged enough to question yet relatively powerless to make immediate interventions, and who may have brought to these perceptions ethnocentric notions of backward and corrupt third world governments and bloated bureaucracies.[2]

Some adoptees now view adoption agencies as seeking to reproduce their own existence and legitimacy rather than uphold the best interests of the child in ways that resonate with the description of "goal displacement" in South Korean adoptions offered by the social work scholar Rosemary Sarri and her colleagues. Goal displacement describes a condition in which "organizations are under pressure to secure resources to maintain themselves":

> They do this by conforming to the demands for external funding or legitimization. In the case of intercountry adoption of Korean children, the original goal of attempting to solve the social problem of orphaned and abandoned multiracial children was gradually displaced by continuance of the practice long after the original problem no longer existed, because it served organizational maintenance needs of adoption agency administrators and because it relieved the South Korean government of having to establish domestic programs. In this case, private child placing agencies have actually promoted these practices in South Korea because there was a market of persons in the U.S. who wished to adopt these children. (89–90)

The adoptees who were sent overseas during the 1970s and 1980s were products of an underfunded welfare system and a cold war developmentalist state that equated low population growth with economic progress and invested heavily in military spending to ensure "national security" at the expense of social programs.[3] These adoptees constitute the great majority of the adult returnees of the past several years.[4] As many of them engage in searches for their birth families they also come to recognize themselves as products of a system that encouraged adoption as a quick fix social welfare solution (Sarri, Baik, and Bombyk 1998) in which adoption agencies acted as influential brokers of "biopower" (Foucault 1990).

As a result, some adoptees view adoption agencies less as the private social welfare institutions they purport to be and more as extensions of the South Korean state. Because of their investments in reproducing the system, agencies are not trusted as having adoptees' best interests in mind. As adoptees returned in increasing numbers in the early 1990s, agencies were caught off guard by the thousands of requests first arriving by fax and phone and then by email and cell phone. Resources were strained and, consequently, so were relations with adult adoptees.

The reform of adoption legislation since 1996 has required Korean agencies to set up postadoption services (*sahu kwŏlli saŏp*). There is no specification, however, as to what those programs should entail aside from motherland visits.[5] In response to the legal reform, the four adoption agencies have slowly and unevenly implemented services and programs that include motherland tours and homestays, counseling on birth family search, and the facilitation of communication or reunions between birth families and adoptees.[6] Since 1998, GOA'L and other adoptee advocacy NGOs have stepped in to supplement postadoption services offered by adoption agencies and the government, with the additional goal of educating Korean society to alter public consciousness (*ŭisik pyŏnhwa*) on the "adoption issue" (*ibyang munje*).

THE STRUGGLE OVER RIGHTS AND RECORDS

Of the many gaps that NGOs attempt to fill, assistance with the birth family search has struck the most sensitive emotional and political chords. Highly sensationalized by the Korean media, reunions are often assumed to be the main reason that adoptees return to Korea, even though many adoptees come with different motivations or degrees of interest. In spite of the diversity in attitudes toward searching, it is undeniable that a sea change took place in the late 1990s for a critical mass of adult adoptees who grew up believing that they were true orphans with no living parents or who could not fathom undertaking a search in a distant country and a foreign culture. As dramatic stories of search and reunion circulated at conferences and through the media, what was once considered to be impossible or unimaginable has become increasingly feasible and desirable.[7]

Prior to the 1996 legislative reforms, adoption agencies were simply "placement agencies" (*ibyang alsŏn kigwan*) that focused on processing paperwork and preparing children to be legally adopted overseas. The 1996 legislation changed their designation to "adoption agencies" (*ibyang kigwan*) and stipulated the provision of postadoption services, which includes oversight of the adoption placement for six months following an adoption as well as motherland visits (I. Park 2000). The issue of birth family search was not addressed, however, and agencies are under no legal obligation to help adoptees with their searches. Out of necessity in the past few years, though, given the pressure from the thousands of adoptees, adoptive parents, and birth parents coming to find information (13,068 in 2005, with 316 reunions [Overseas Koreans Foundation 2006]), the agencies have developed internal policies that are intended to balance the rights to privacy of the birth families with adoptees' rights to information.

A typical initial visit to an adoption agency involves sitting down with a social worker from the postadoption services bureau and reviewing one's adoption file. Each agency has a different reputation when it comes to birth family search, and treatment by social workers can sometimes seem wholly arbitrary and their attitudes fickle. Holt adoptees have often reported that when they go to view their adoption file they are forced to sit a considerable distance from the social worker's desk, and that only select portions of the file are shared with the adoptee. This selective viewing may be especially noticeable if the adoptee comes with a Korean speaker or demonstrates the ability to read Korean. Very often, adoptees have been disappointed to find that the information they are given is what they already have seen in their files at home—copies of their adoptive parents' home studies or other documentation from the Western counterpart agencies.[8]

In one case I accompanied an adoptee friend to view her file at her adoption agency, and in so doing I witnessed how this rite of passage can be at once powerfully emotional yet peculiarly impersonal. Adoptee artists have poetically represented the potent materialization of the adoptee's preadoption past in the bureaucratic form of paperwork, but what is less often captured in these accounts is the authoritative control that agency social workers wield over adoptees' access to these documents and over their interpretations. The subjugated position of the adoptee comes through strongly in adoptee narratives of visits to adoption agencies in which social workers stand as unpredictable gatekeepers to valuable knowledge about the adoptee's identity as represented by her past life and genealogical origins. These social workers thus come to represent the system and the agencies' quasi-governmental roles. The wide-ranging inconsistencies in treatment by agencies suggest to many adoptees that unethical and possibly illegal adoptions are being covered up.[9]

These suspicions have been supported by stories that have emerged from adoptees who have reunited with birth family and learned of the circumstances that surrounded their adoptions. Some have found that they were relinquished by grandparents, jealous stepparents, or well-meaning relatives, thus suggesting how easily the legal and social connection between Korean parents and their children could be manipulated in a system that seemed to lack adequate oversight.[10] Children who were recorded as foundlings, for instance, have discovered that they were dropped off at an orphanage or adoption agency by grandparents who believed it would be impossible for their widowed daughters-in-law to raise the children alone. Mothers, especially working-class widows or abandoned women, were convinced by well-meaning social workers, neighbors, relatives, or religious figures that the best they could do for their child was to send her abroad for better opportunities. All of these cases reveal how agencies focused less on family preservation than on processing children, often on the basis of minimal background investigation, to shuttle them quickly through the system to new parents overseas. Because of this situation, case files filled with misinformation and spotty or incomplete data are commonplace.

It is not surprising, therefore, that rumor and conspiracy theories characterized many narratives about searches among the adoptees I spoke with. Korean adoption agencies (as well as their counterpart Western ones) were frequently construed as corrupt institutions in the business of protecting their own reputations rather than helping adoptees. Already having profited from the commodification of adoptee bodies, agencies that charge adoptees for viewing their own files or for conducting a preliminary family search were considered to be especially contemptible. Adoption agencies, for their part, claimed that they are legally bound to protect the identities of Korean parents and would be subject to large government fines if they released identifying information to adoptees. Moreover, they asserted that they simply do not have the resources or personnel to help the overwhelming number of adoptees who come to their offices, often without a prior appointment. The lack of systematic protocol at agencies invariably added more provocation to an already difficult and anxious process that holds no guarantees for success or happy outcomes.

Due to these circumstances, many of the pioneers who navigated the straits of "search"—as it is referred to by adoptees—and who found adoption agency social workers to be unsympathetic or uncooperative, took on the role of guide and advocate for others who wanted to search. For instance, the American adoptee Wayne Berry, shortly after locating his birth family in 1995, established a birth search registry to try to link adoptees with birth parents who might be searching for them. And Mihee Nathalie Lemoine, who was reunited with her Korean mother in 1991 and moved to Korea in 1993, has helped more than five hundred adoptees search for natal family through her organization Korean Overseas Adoptees (or KOA, which is also a transliteration of the Korean word for orphan).

Mihee's work in particular was motivated by a desire to wrest exclusive control over the search process from the adoption agencies, which she strongly believes privilege their own reputations over adoptees' best interests. She attempted to make the process less agonizing and frustrating for those already at a disadvantage in terms of language ability and cultural knowledge. Unlike the agencies, she refused to charge fees to adoptees, and in countless instances in which adoption agencies told an adoptee that there was no information or that it would be impossible to find any relatives Mihee, who picked up the Korean language in the process, was able to track down leads through police departments, orphanages, or media contacts and thus facilitate the reunions of more than two hundred adoptees since 1991.

The distrust of adoption agencies and the recognition of the need for adoptee-centered search services also informed the efforts of other adoptees who worked with Mihee to establish GOA'L. In addition, the group's founders wanted to reach out to the Korean public to improve the social status of adoptees in Korea and to help destigmatize the image of adoption and adoptees. Addressing these problems was a considerable challenge for the adoptees who started GOA'L, especially because of their marginalization in Korean society and their lack of Korean-language fluency. As I discuss in the next section, a conjuncture of the adoption issue, the coming of age of adoptees, and the emergence of a self-consciously vibrant civil society in Korea in the mid-1990s made it possible for the founders of GOA'L to make crucial links with powerful figures in the growing NGO movement.

GOA'L AND THE EMERGENCE OF NONGOVERNMENTAL ORGANIZATIONS IN KOREA

Adult Korean adoptees were first invited back on a government-sponsored motherland tour in 1989, and some of those adoptees went on to become founders of adoptee associations in their adoptive countries and to serve as the first sources of information about Korea for other adoptees, especially in Europe (see chapter 3). By the mid-1990s, returning adoptees were appearing frequently in South Korean media reports, and, by the late 1990s, with the economic crisis taking its toll and orphanages overflowing with children, the adoption issue had once again become a topic of major political and public attention.

The "adoption problem" (*ibyang munje*) has been commonly construed in the media as an issue that continues to reflect poorly on Korea's international status as an advanced nation. In addition, the arrival of adult adoptees recalls the repressed or shameful histories that lie behind the celebratory master narrative of Korea's "economic miracle." With the IMF crisis looming and the sudden reversal of an eleven-year decline in overseas adoptions, the plan to suspend the international adoption program in 1996 was also abandoned. Adoption appeared again in the South Korean press as a sign of how fragile Korea's modernization achievements were in actuality.[11] It was around this time that a group of a dozen European and American adoptees first met in Seoul to discuss the possibilities of starting an organization for returning adoptees in Korea.

As outlined in the previous chapter, GOA'L was envisioned as a home base for adoptees returning to Korea. When it first gained momentum in 1998 it was not only the first adult adoptee organization in Korea but also the first adoptee-related organization aside from the four state-designated overseas adoption agencies. An important piece of prehistory to GOA'L's establishment is the effort of one of its original members, Don Roloefs. In 1996 at the age of twenty-four, Don first began cooperating with the South Korean civil society organization Citizens' Coalition for Economic Justice (CCEJ; Kyŏng Sillyŏn) in an effort to develop a global network of adoptees.

Don's first visit back to Korea was in 1993. Prior to this, he had had little interest in Korea or adoption, even though his brother, with whom he had been adopted, was active in Aerirang, the Dutch Korean adoptee association. After Don returned from Korea, he began participating in Aerirang activities, and on a whim in 1995 he decided to join others from the organization traveling to Düsseldorf to attend the conference for European adoptees. As noted in chapter 3, the Düsseldorf conference was sponsored by CCEJ and organized with help from Reverend Kim Do Hyun, who was based in Switzerland at the time. The conference was the first to bring adult adoptees together under the umbrella of the global Korean diaspora. Don attended the conference even though his main interest at the time was in Korea rather than in adoptees per se. Without a clear career path after his university graduation, he thought, "Why not go to Korea and spend some time [there]?" Having been active with Aerirang, he agreed to try to work for the organization while staying in the country: "That's how this idea started off of the kind of network. At that time Kyŏng Sillyŏn offered a desk [in their office] . . . And that's how I started, and I started with a *lot* of energy and a *lot* of enthusiasm."

The organization CCEJ, which was established in 1989 by some five hundred Korean lawyers, professors, and ministers under the leadership of Reverend Sŏ Kyŏng Sŏk, is widely regarded as the first civic organization in postauthoritarian South Korea. Throughout the 1970s and 1980s, student- and worker-led pro-democracy movements (*minjung undong*) were the primary forms of a resistant civil society that opposed the authoritarian state and its collusion with the nation's conglomerates (*chaebŏl*) (Koo 1993). With the democratic transition in 1987, followed by the establishment of the first civilian government in 1993, these student- and worker-led antigovernment formations gave way to more moderate, middle-class civil society movements, of which CCEJ is widely considered to be an important forerunner.

One of CCEJ's early projects, the Global Korean Network, was intended to develop mutually beneficial relationships among diasporic Koreans around the world. Adoptees were included in that vision, and they were identified early on as long-neglected members of the overseas Korean population. In 1996 CCEJ's English-language newsletter, *Civil Society*, announced the support of overseas adoptees as one of the main projects of CCEJ's International Affairs Department, and it included a report called "Plans for Global Network of Overseas Korean Adoptees" that listed Kim Dong-Sik (Don Roelof's Korean name) as a contact.

It was the specific conjuncture of adoptees' returns to Korea, the rise of the "civil society movement" (*simin sahoe undong*), and the public reckoning with the nation's historical traumas (*kwagŏ chŏngsan*; see chapter 5) in postauthoritarian Korea that animated the interest of middle-class civic activists in the 1990s.[12] Thus, adult adoptees were first identified and acknowledged by the new civil society movement rather than by the government, but eventually, close ties between those grassroots movements and the civilian administrations helped adoptees to gain legal status as "overseas Koreans."

The legitimacy of GOA'L as an autonomous organization in the eyes of Koreans and also of adoptees has been slowly earned. Although it garnered intermittent interest from politicians, their agendas, ultimately, were focused on the needs of Korean voters rather than on noncitizen Korean adoptees. And without connections to secure corporate funding, the volunteer-run organization survived precariously for many years on membership dues, small grants from individuals, and nominal donations from the four adoption agencies. Gaining legitimacy was also hampered by the prevalent perceptions of adoptees as children, which were only exacerbated by the limited Korean-language ability and cultural knowledge of most adoptees.

ADOPTEE ACTIVISM AND CULTURAL CITIZENSHIP: FROM *IBYANGA* TO *IBYANGIN*

According to Ami Nafzger, GOA'L was launched on 5 March 1998, but a schism and literal fistfight among two factions in the group led to a dramatic breakup. Ami was living in the remote eastern city of Gumi at the time, and in the aftermath she found herself the only one willing and able to take up leadership of the group. She picked up the tattered remains of the organization and slowly worked to build up adoptee and Korean support.

A major break for GOA'L came in November 1998 when the Korean Broadcasting Service aired a "huge documentary" about the organization, which in turn inspired an overwhelming number of native Koreans to come to support the fledgling organization. As Ami recalled, "There were so many people, I didn't know what to do with them. It was the blind leading the blind." One reason for the surprising volunteer response to GOA'L may have been the high unemployment rates and grim job prospects that hung over Korea during the 1997–1998 IMF crisis. Many of the core volunteers for GOA'L in 1998–1999 were well-educated and competent Koreans in their mid to late twenties who were unemployed when they first saw GOA'L in media reports and thus had ample time and energy to devote to developing the organization.[13]

Yet struggles over leadership, exacerbated by language barriers, were an issue from the beginning. As Ami, who didn't speak Korean, noted: "It was so frustrating, because the Koreans would be sitting there and I didn't know what was going on. They started making their own social network and started doing their own thing. There was a language and cultural difference." The issue of language came up again shortly after the founding of GOA'L, when the subject of birth family search and adoptees' rights to information was addressed at the first Policy Symposium of the Human Rights Forum at the South Korean National Assembly in April 1998. Scholars, agency workers, and government officials spoke on the topic of adoptees' human rights, especially with respect to birth family search.

Three overseas adoptees were invited to speak on the opening panel, yet none of the proceedings, which all took place in Korean, were translated for the adoptees in the audience. As Ami, who was one of the speakers, told me, "There were thirty adoptees we invited. [After the adoptee panelists spoke] the rest of the conference was in Korean, and no one knew what was going on. It was an adoption conference about Korean international adoptees. That's where [we got upset]: We're not children, you need to treat us like human beings. If you're going to have a conference and it's about us, we deserve to have the right to know."

It is not an understatement to say that adoptee belonging and cultural citizenship have been profoundly circumscribed by adoptees' inability to communicate in Korean. Whereas growing numbers of adoptees are enrolled in Korean-language classes at various universities in Korea, some of which offer tuition discounts or scholarships for overseas adoptees, the great majority of adoptees have been continually challenged by their limited Korean-language ability. Thus, with the category "adoptee" (*ibyanga*) already stigmatized in Korea, the language issue has aggravated the adult adoptees' sense of infantalization and partial citizenship, thus imposing limits on their self-empowerment and political agency.

Asserting adoptee citizenship and personhood were major items on GOA'L's initial agenda. The organization sought to establish adoptees as *legally* recognized Koreans included in the Overseas Koreans Act of 1999 and as *culturally* legitimate Koreans who are *ibyangin* (adopted persons), not *ibyanga* (adopted children). When in 2003 I asked Ami about the status and perception of adoptees in Korea, she said, "It's changed a lot. I think adoptees had a reputation of infighting, and that we're children: ibyanga, instead of ibyangin, because ibyangin is not a word. The First Lady is starting to use this word now [i.e., ibyangin], so we've taught them different languages; we've taught them lots of things."

As Ami noted, the term "ibyangin" is not considered a word in Korean. It is a neologism that replaces the diminutive character "a" for "child" in the word "ibyanga" (adopted child) with "in," the character for person. When I would describe my research to Koreans unacquainted with adoptee-related issues, they would sometimes gently correct me by saying, "It's not ibyangin, but ibyanga" (*Ibyangin malgo, ibyanga rago hayo*). In those instances I would explain to them that because adoptees are no longer children they feel that ibyangin is a more appropriate word with which to refer to them—that is, as adopted persons.[14]

The term "ibyangin" is troubling not only because of its semantic irregularity but also because, following dominant ideologies of kinship in Korea, adoption has long been a stigmatized form of social reproduction. When practiced, therefore, adoption is often a closely guarded secret, even from the child himself or herself, although a movement supporting "public adoptions" (*konggae ibyang*)—in which adoptions are not kept secret from the child, family members, or community—has been active for the past decade.[15]

The secrecy that still characterizes adoption means that the term "ibyanga" cannot denote a distinct social identity or subject position as much as a liminal stage between two families—that is, from being the child of another (*namŭi ai*) to being a child treated as if it were biologically related to its parents (*uri ai, nae chasik*) (cf. Modell 1994). In this light, ibyangin might be seen as a social impossibility. Ibyangin is itself an intercultural invention that weds a Western notion of the individuated and autonomous person with a Korean understanding of adoption, which inherently connotes a dependent relation of a child to its parents, whether natal or adoptive. Thus the problematic forging of the word and concept ibyangin helps us to comprehend how the term "adult adoptee" in Euro-American contexts might also present an oxymoronic semantic construction that in many ways linguistically encapsulates the paradoxes of Korean adoptee personhood and politics.[16]

In addition to the conflation of adult and child categories, adult Korean adoptees also call forth the contradictory valences of blood in Korea: on the one hand they are embraced as co-ethnics for sharing the same blood (*hanp'itjul*), yet on the other hand they are considered polluting due to the probability of a "bad bloodline" under a dominant cultural belief in the ineluctability of genealogical inheritance and blood as a predictor of character, health, and fate. In speaking to an audience of volunteers at an INKAS workshop, a male Danish adoptee in his thirties succinctly captured how, although blood is deployed to embrace adopted Koreans under an ethnocentric banner of Korean pride, the exclusionary power of bloodlines limits the full inclusion of adopted Koreans: "Koreans say, 'We can see that you're Korean, you have Korean blood, you should marry a Korean woman,' but I know they're just saying that—they don't want their daughter to marry me."

As GOA'L's efforts demonstrated, asserting adoptee personhood and belonging in Korea required tackling the issue of infantilization and partial personhood in the context of historically entrenched ethnonationalisms. These adoptee cultural politics engage issues of social power, recognition, and representation, yet in these efforts language is a key obstacle in adoptees' claims to political agency. Because of the organization's dependence upon Korean volunteers, for instance, some Koreans and even adoptees I spoke with felt that GOA'L could not rightfully claim to be an adoptee organization since they had the impression that it was really being run by native Koreans. At the same time that adoptees were attempting to overcome these challenges to create their own home base in Korea, the South Korean state was identifying and defining adoptees as uniquely positioned overseas Koreans whose ethnic attachment to the nation could be recuperated and fostered to promote the interests of the state.

ADOPTEES BECOME OVERSEAS KOREANS

By the late 1990s, the South Korean state, primarily through OKF, began to include adoptees as members of the "global Korean family" (Kim 2005), but official recognition was predicated on the idea that they were short-term visitors or tourists to Korea and not long-term sojourners or return migrants. As described in chapter 5, OKF was established in 1997 as part of the state's proactive *segyehwa* (globalization) policy, which was intended in part to consolidate the economic and social capital of Korean overseas populations for the benefit of political and economic development, especially on the heels of the 1997–1998 financial crisis. As a semi-autonomous government body, OKF calls itself "a nonprofit public organization affiliated with the Ministry of Foreign Affairs and Trade" (Overseas Koreans Foundation 2003) whose mandate is to extend the state's reach beyond its sovereign borders to animate the ethnic sentiments of Koreans who are citizens of other nation-states. It may be viewed as an extension of the nation's diplomatic reserves, and many of its higher-ranking employees were formerly stationed at different embassy posts. The group keeps track of ethnic Koreans around the world and works to foster a sense of shared personhood among the nation's compatriots (*tongp'o*).[17]

In addition to the summer program for adult adoptees, OKF's international exchange bureau also sponsors tours and targeted programs for ethnic Koreans from Kazakhstan, Korean American youth, and international conferences for ethnic Korean writers and artists. Other groups that are courted by OKF are international Korean CEOs and businessmen, "estimable Koreans" (*yugong tongp'o*), leaders of international Korean immigrant organizations, and overseas Korean journalists, who OKF hopes will help promote Korea's brand image. An implicit hierarchy that maps easily onto a neoliberal vision of the global economy emerges among the various overseas Koreans groups, depending upon their economic and social capital and their potential contributions to the motherland. Adoptees, who are often rhetorically celebrated as bridges and ambassadors by government officials, are, however, typically lacking the necessary cultural capital to make significant economic or political contributions to Korea.[18]

Aside from the motherland tour, OKF also supports postadoption services by donating money to the four adoption agencies and funds events that foster Korean identity held by adult adoptee groups in Europe and America. Since becoming a major sponsor for the 2004 Gathering, OKF has also taken a central role in helping the development of the International Korean Adoptee Associations (IKAA), the umbrella group of adoptee organizations, which is the foremost representative for the global adoptee community. In this capacity OKF also extends its reach across national boundaries by helping to ensure that adoptees have an ongoing connection to the motherland. Yet the cooperation of the state with adoptee organizing is understandably a cause of concern for some adoptee activists, especially those not included in the umbrella, and also for the NGOs in Korea that are in an unavoidable competition for limited government funding.[19]

Jeannie Hong originally began working with adoptees as a key volunteer for GOA'L in 1998. Even though she was trained as an architect, based on her extensive experience with adoptees, she was hired in 2001 by OKF to be director of adoptee affairs in the department of international exchange. Her primary responsibility was to run its summer motherland tour for adoptees, but she also oversaw the expansion of OKF support for adoptees through IKAA and other international adoptee associations. As a *kongmuwŏn* or government worker, she was the only bureaucrat to directly work with overseas adoptees. Her own status as a single woman in her mid-thirties working under a series of male department heads made her a relatively low-ranking employee with little or no opportunities for advancement, yet she wielded considerable influence as the in-house specialist on adoption and adoptees. This expertise granted her leeway in making decisions about adoptee affairs, since no one on staff at OKF had much experience with or knowledge of adoptees, and many of them were uncomfortable communicating in English.

Despite her long association with GOA'L, that relationship soured shortly after she was hired by OKF, in part because her inability to direct funds to the struggling organization was interpreted as an intentional betrayal. It also aggravated the tendency of adoptees to fetishize the state as a repressive monolithic entity co-opting adoptee resources and agendas.[20] Moreover, having gained valuable knowledge about adoptees and important adoption agency and government contacts through her work with GOA'L, Jeannie was seen as capitalizing on adoptees for her own career advancement and social power. OKF's influence, however, is limited in scope to populations of Koreans residing in foreign countries, and its projects are focused on cultural diplomacy through fostering warm feelings for the motherland and the development of "model citizens" who will reflect well on Korea's own international image. With this mandate, Jeannie had little power to divert funding to NGOs that worked to support adoptees within Korea. Her primary responsibility was to provide a safe and educational cultural experience for adoptees on the ten-day motherland tour, the Summer Cultural Awareness Program for Overseas Adopted Koreans.[21]

The motherland tours provided by OKF, as well as those offered by agencies, introduce adoptees to Korean traditions, customs, and official history, and while they are not entirely without value these programs assume that cultural training can "recuperate ethnic identity" (*tongjilsŏng hoebok*) in the adoptee's postadoption phase.[22] Adoptees are construed as deserving of OKF support on the basis of their Korean origins, and thereby become objects of pastoral projects in which ethnic sentiments and pride are considered to be latent, needing only be released and fostered to promote the psychological well-being of the adoptee and the image of the nation. However, instead of elaborate meals and costumed displays of traditional Korean culture, adoptee activists have suggested that money and effort would be better spent guaranteeing access to birth family records, providing discounted or free programs for language training, and expanding citizenship rights to grant adoptees greater agency over their everyday lives in Korea.

As the primary state agency that deals with adult adoptees, OKF grants them limited recognition as being of but not in the nation. For long-term sojourners, programs like the motherland tour fail to address the gaps in legal citizenship (despite their F-4 visa status they are still considered to be foreigners when it comes to basic services) and cultural belonging that they face.[23] In contrast to this limited recognition on the part of the state, adoptee advocacy NGOs like GOA'L and KoRoot foster community building and empowerment of adoptees living in Korea. KoRoot, for instance, established in 2005 a weekend workshop to help adoptees with long-term employment and career building strategies, and the topics covered at GOA'L's annual conferences—including panels on domestic adoption, adoption and social welfare reform, and business entrepreneurship—reflect the evolving concerns of adoptees beyond racial and ethnic identity and birth family search and reunion. In the following section, I unpack the interests of Korean advocacy organizations to explore how adoptee belonging and cultural citizenship in Korea are entangled with shifting definitions of citizenship and moral personhood for native Koreans.

NEW OBJECTS OF CHARITY AND CHANGING THE WORLD

KoRoot, a guest house in Seoul for adult adoptees, was established in 2003, and in April 2004 I heard that Kim Do Hyun, the minister who'd assisted CCEJ in organizing the 1995 Düsseldorf conference, had recently taken over as its director. Since that time, it has become one of the main NGOs for adult-adoptee returnees. Cory, whose questions regarding native Korean adoptee advocacy groups appeared earlier on in this chapter, may very well have had KoRoot in mind when he asked, "What is their interest in helping adoptees?" Whereas state interest as exemplified by OKF focuses on the human capital of adoptees as economic and cultural ambassadors, NGOs like KoRoot or INKAS focus on adoptees as innocent victims of the state, who are deserving of aid based upon their forced migration and involuntary alienation from Korea. Moreover, the interests of advocates such as Kim Do Hyun are deeply articulated with the democratization movement and the subsequent transformations of liberal citizenship in South Korea.

I went to visit Reverend Kim at KoRoot shortly after hearing about his directorship. KoRoot is located in a two-story stone house down a peaceful side street a few miles west of the central downtown intersection of Gwanghwamun. In contrast to the ubiquitous high-rise apartment buildings that comprise Seoul's cityscape and that can be a visually assaulting introduction to South Korea's compressed modernity and rapid urbanization, this affluent section of Seoul suggests a different time and place. Like the other single-family residences in the area, KoRoot's property is walled off from the street by a gate that opens onto a well-tended lawn and garden. As I walked up the short path to the house, I saw Reverend Kim (Kim *moksanim*) through the glass panel of the front door as he struggled with what was a new lock that had to be unlatched by punching in a preset code. As I learned later, installing the code key was one of his first changes to KoRoot, as the previous managers had imposed a strict curfew system that often left tardy adoptees homeless for the night—incidents that did not foster much goodwill between KoRoot and its guests.

The house was sunny and tidy and held up to its description as a "European-style guesthouse." Reverend Kim had already had an exhausting morning in which he gave two interviews, one to the editor of *Korean Quarterly* and another to the Korean Broadcasting Station. He seemed flustered and a bit annoyed, and he told me straightaway that he had a headache from doing so many interviews. After that inauspicious beginning, I learned about his work in Switzerland helping Kim Dae-won (Jan Wenger) found the adoptee association Dongari, and then how he was asked to come back to Korea to run KoRoot.

Reverend Kim had spent the past eleven years in Europe, eight in Basel, Switzerland, and close to three at Birmingham University in the United Kingdom where he worked on a graduate degree in divinity. When problems arose with KoRoot's prior management, the assistant pastor of his church in Seoul, who was on the board, sent him an urgent request asking if he would return to Korea to take over the running of KoRoot, which otherwise, they feared, would fail. He accepted on a provisional basis as he was also pursuing a position with the government's bureau of ecumenical affairs, although he had heard just ten days before we met that he had not been selected. He thus officially accepted the post at KoRoot, and he and his wife, Kong Jung Ae, moved into a room on the first floor.

I quickly ascertained that Reverend Kim had been uncharacteristically grumpy when I first arrived. By the end of our conversation, I was charmed by his warm and generous personality, and I was impressed by his understanding of and dedication to adoptees. We agreed that I would come to KoRoot once a week to help with Website translation and other English-language related needs.

During that first conversation Reverend Kim expressed his concerns about fostering an active civil society (*hwalbalhan simin sahoe*) in Korea and changing public consciousness about adoption (*uisik pyŏnhwa*). He had already composed a list of projects he wanted to accomplish through KoRoot to make it more than just a guesthouse, and to also meet the actual needs of short- and long-term returnees with processes of acculturation and language acquisition. To inform and educate Koreans, who he thought were generally ignorant (*musikhan*) about adoptee issues, he also planned to translate and publish adoptee memoirs into Korean. To accomplish all of these goals, he needed to be able do more than simply meet his monthly operating costs, which were barely covered by the per day fee of 12,000 won (US$10) paid by adoptee guests and by donations from KoRoot sponsors and supporters.

A week later Reverend Kim took me out to lunch near KoRoot and told me about his involvement in the student democratization movement in the 1970s and 1980s. Following the establishment of President Park Chung Hee's "reformist" Yusin Constitution, the amendment in 1972 that established a military state and granted Park nearly unlimited dictatorial powers, Reverend Kim became involved in the T'alch'um Tongari (Traditional Mask Dance Group), which was a key group for the most radicalized student organizers at Seoul National University. After the leaders of the T'alch'um Tongari were arrested and imprisoned, Reverend Kim also went into hiding for a short period. Later on he switched his major from literature to theology, with a focus on minjung theology.[24]

Reverend Kim's background in minjung-inspired activism suffused his work with adoptees. His masters thesis conceptualized a theology of birth mothers by drawing upon minjung and feminist theologies to argue that Korean birth mothers are part of the minjung, and as such they should be liberated from their guilt by reframing the relinquishment of their children from being an individual sin to one that is embedded in structures of inequality—namely those of capitalism and patriarchy. Viewing the mothers as victims of South Korea's economic and political dependence on the

United States and their oppression under a Confucian patriarchal system, as well as in the context of hegemonic Eurocentrism, permits Reverend Kim to argue that the Christian church needs to open itself up to the experiences and suffering of birth mothers rather than requiring them to repent for their past sins before being permitted into the church.

Reverend Kim envisioned KoRoot as a place through which to provoke social change by encouraging a redefinition of the family and the place of birth mothers in Korean society and by altering the consciousness of Koreans regarding adoption and adoptees. At the first anniversary fund-raising event for KoRoot in July 2004, for instance, he made a decidedly minjung statement to compel the attendees to donate money to KoRoot's cause: "Adoptees are the center of the world" (*ibyangindŭli segye chungsim imnida*). He concluded by stating, "Through KoRoot, we can change the world!"

Although at that event Reverend Kim made explicit references to God and named his work for adoptees as a "calling from God" (*purŭm*), in his everyday work with adoptees he scrupulously placed into the background his own role and identity as a religious figure. He explained to the dozen Korean volunteers who had come to KoRoot to help out at the fund-raising event that members of the Saemunan Church (New City Church) would be holding a worship service in the second-floor sitting area a half hour before the start of the program.[25] As he explained, even though KoRoot's leadership was made up of people who identified as Christians (he and two members of the board of directors are ministers), the organization itself was not a Christian or religious organization. Moreover, he told the volunteers that the opening ceremony for KoRoot the year before had begun with a worship service that foregrounded the Christian color of the organization, which, he added somewhat vaguely, wasn't such a good idea. This year, the church members would quietly hold a worship service in the second-floor lounge so that non-Christian attendees would be able to relax and socialize before the event officially began.

Aside from respecting the individual choice and religious affiliation of KoRoot's guests, another reason that may help explain why the worship service was quietly conducted on the second floor is the objectifying and infantilizing cast that Korean Christian renderings of adoptees can take. The worship service, which was led by a female elder of the New City Church, recalled depictions of unhappy (*purhaenghan*) adoptees in media representations and in everyday discourse in which adoptees may be thought of as pitiable (*pulssanghan*). Following the reading of a biblical passage that described Christ's tending to the indigent (*kananhanja*), the elder made a direct connection between Christ's mercy toward the poor and the adoptees at KoRoot: "I don't need to remind you why we are here today—to reflect upon these people who were adopted overseas [*haeoe ibyang toen jadŭl*], as they are thinking about their birth parents [*saeng pubu*] and returning [to Korea]. KoRoot tends to adoptees [*ibyanga*], who are those needy people [*kananhanja*]."

The elder then concluded by leading a prayer: "We hope that you will please remember the most important people here, the precious people [*kuihan saram*], the pitiable people [*pulssanghan saram*]. Truly, what have they done wrong? It is the failing of our people [*minjok*]; it is the failing of adults through which they have suffered so much [*manŭn kasŭm ap'ŭmŭl an'go issŭmnida*]. Through KoRoot, please relieve their suffering."

Reverend Kim held a heightened sensitivity to adoptees' sense of being used by Koreans, especially Christians. This sensitivity developed especially during his time in Switzerland, where in his initial attempts to reach out to adoptees he identified their "anti-religious" sentiments, as he called them. The skepticism among adoptees about religiously motivated aid led him to literally put away his religious persona by removing his theological texts from the main room of KoRoot to a back corridor. In place of the texts, he displayed adoption-related books, adoptee memoirs, and scholarly work on adoption. And when a box of English-language novels and trade books was donated by Holt, Reverend Kim asked me to go through them all to pick out the ones that I thought would seem too religious (which included almost all of them, since it appeared that they had been donated by evangelical Americans).

The religious motivations of Reverend Kim were, however, inseparable from his political roots in the anti-authoritarian minjung movement. Rather than being an evangelical mission to save adoptees through religious conversion, Reverend Kim's calling was to serve adoptees who were the unacknowledged minjung, victims of a patriarchal and authoritarian state that privileged national security over social welfare and that made it impossible for class- and gender-subordinated women to keep their children. Perhaps more difficult for Reverend Kim than placing his religiosity into the background was squelching his political opinions, which he sometimes mistakenly believed that other adoptees and even adoptive parents would naturally share. For some more moderate adoptees, such as those on the Gathering planning committee, his views seemed incompatible with his job as a service provider whose proper role they believed was to help adoptees and not peddle his political views.

As this example suggests, the personal motivations of Koreans, especially those of Reverend Kim's generation, are entirely shaped by their membership in the Korean nation, local and national politics, and a moral vision for the future of the world, as well as of democracy in Korea. In contrast to Reverend Kim, for whom adoptees represent unacknowledged victims of the authoritarian state, a younger generation of Koreans who desire to help adoptees are influenced less by the unfinished business of the democratization movement and more by dominant values of civic engagement in contemporary South Korea and their own "cosmopolitan striving" (Park and Abelmann 2004) in the context of globalization. Both of these generations gain social capital through their work with adoptees, and ironically need to sustain a view of adoptees as Koreans who are fundamentally alienated from Korea in order to maintain the logic of paternalism that lies at the basis of the volunteer ethos. Even if adoptees as objects of pastoralism and paternalistic "helping" are framed as victims, however, the encounters between them and native Korean volunteers also open up possibilities for alternative conceptions of belonging to the nation in the context of global capitalism and multiculturalism. It is to these dynamics that I now turn.

TRANSFORMATIONS OF *CORÉENITÉ*

For KoRoot's first anniversary event, Reverend Kim asked three adoptees to deliver statements to the mostly Korean audience. He had been hoping that they would present strong messages, but it was only after Nicole Sheppard, as a representative of GOA'L, introduced the organization and talked about the material needs of adoptees who come to Korea, and Daniel Avril, a French adoptee, spoke of his personal history and desire to learn more about Korean culture and traditions, that Mihee Lemoine delivered her own pointed message.

With a calm demeanor and soft-spoken voice Mihee addressed the audience in French, which was translated into Korean by Reverend Kim's daughter. Mihee began by reminding the audience that 2004 marked the fiftieth anniversary of Korean adoption, and that although Korea is a "rich country" it has sent two thousand children overseas every year for the past ten years to white families. She asked that should any of them meet an adoptee who doesn't speak Korean or doesn't understand what it means to be Korean ("qu'il parle pas bien corréen ou qu'il comprendre pas le corréenité") instead of treating him as if he's not Korean they should try to imagine a broader concept of Koreanness ("un coréenité plus large").

The "corréenité plus large" that Mihee asked of her Korean audience may be seen as one that is beginning to be fostered among the native Korean volunteers who work with adoptees. Between the reductive representations produced for quick consumption in the Korean media that vacillate between reinscribing stereotypes of the "*pulssanghan ibyanga*" (pitiable adopted child) or the "*tahaenghan haeoe ro ibyang toen han'gukin*" (fortunate overseas adopted Korean), and the state project of imbuing adoptees with cultural roots, Korean volunteers come up against the diversity of adoptee experiences and their discrepant cultural locations by recognizing them as being simultaneously of the nation and outside it, as Koreans who are both similar and different from them.

Each of the NGOs claimed to have more than one hundred volunteers on their rosters, though the number of active volunteers was considerably lower. Many of the most involved volunteers I met were those who could communicate well in English and who had extended experiences working or studying abroad. Some of them said they felt a sympathetic connection to adoptees because they had similar experiences with cultural displacement when living abroad and also upon returning to Korea. Kim Jong Hyock, for instance, attended both college and business school in the United States, and when he returned to Korea during the IMF financial crisis he saw a report about GOA'L on TV and thought that volunteer work with them would be a good way to maintain his English skills. What he discovered, however, was that his own felt disconnection from Korea made it more comfortable for him to hang out with adoptees than with his Korean peers.

This identification with the cultural displacement of adoptees was also shared by James Ko, who had spent twelve years in Australia with his younger brother as an exchange student and then returned to Korea at the age of twenty-seven after completing a master's degree in information technology at an Australian university. He was working in the IT department of Philip Morris's Seoul office, and he began helping out at GOA'L when a friend who volunteered there told him that the group needed help with its Website. He explained to me how he could relate to adoptees who also "had no choice" in being sent abroad, and he felt he understood their feelings of being racially isolated by his own experience in Australia. When he returned to Korea, moreover, he felt different from Koreans, who treated him as a kyop'o and wanted to practice their English with him. Thus, his own hybrid cultural position drew him to other kyop'o or adoptees, even though he did not consider himself to be a kyop'o.

Despite similarities between adoptees and *yuhaksaeng* (overseas exchange students), we might recall Mihee Lemoine's cautionary words, quoted in chapter 5, to the Korean donors of KoRoot: "It's not yuhak education; it's adoption, which means that it's not reversible." Aside from the remaking of primary kinship relationships entailed by adoption, another major difference that distinguishes the experiences of Koreans like James from those of adoptees is his ability to speak Korean. Therefore, although he may feel betwixt and between in Korea, and also holds a foreign passport, he enjoys greater cultural citizenship as a Korean than do the majority of adoptees. For James and for Jong Hyock, adoptees represent one pole along a spectrum of Korean identifications and disidentifications against which they measure their own senses of belonging or alienation.

A questionnaire I distributed to volunteers at OKF and GOA'L asked respondents whether they believed that overseas adoptees were Koreans. Out of eighteen responses, eight answered unequivocally that adoptees are Korean, with one twenty-one-year-old university student writing, "Even though they were raised in different places, aren't they the same race, sharing our same blood? [*Uriwa kat'ŭn p'irŭl nanun hanminjok anikkayo?*]" Two respondents didn't believe that they were Korean at all, but the remaining eight demonstrated more flexibility in reckoning national and racial belonging, with four attempting to quantify their partial Koreanness (e.g., "half half" [*pan pan*] and "20 percent"). Four others suggested that it would be unfair to impose a national or ethnic identity upon adoptees and that, based on their own identities, adoptees themselves can decide which nationality they belong to (*sŭsŭroŭi chŏngch'esŏngi nationality-rŭl kyŏljŏng*). Adoptees may be understood as being "both people of our country and also foreigners" (*uri nara saram igo oeguk saram igo*) as one twenty-six-year-old female volunteer told me, for whom the basis for helping them rests on the fact that they are Korean by birth and were sent without choice as babies to foreign countries.

Yet for other volunteers, grasping the notion of the identity in difference of adoptees presented a profound contradiction between the ideologies of *hanminjok* (Korean race) or *han p'itchul* (one blood) and the acceptance of adoptees as Koreans who are also foreigners. The examples I offer below are drawn from conversations with male volunteers, a fact that may suggest how ideologies of citizenship and family are differently gendered for young Koreans. Confronted with the various ways in which adoptees disidentify with dominant ways of being Korean, volunteers were sometimes forced to question their own naturalized and deeply entrenched notions of cultural and national belonging—the very Koreanness upon which they rationalized their volunteer work for adoptees in the first place.

During an initial meeting of volunteers for the 2004 OKF summer program I asked each person to introduce himself or herself and to explain his or her reasons for volunteering. One young man, a university student, began by stating that the OKF program was intended for overseas Koreans, but, he admitted, he was confused about whether adoptees are Korean or not. He related two personal encounters with adoptees to illustrate the conflicting and contradictory ways in which they are and are not Korean. As an exchange student in Sweden, he said, he noticed an Asian woman in one of his classes. He thought she might also be an exchange student from Korea but since she didn't act like a Korean he assumed that she was Chinese or Japanese. The two eventually met and he learned that she was Korean but had been adopted to Sweden as an infant. Thus, despite her outer appearance (*oemo*), on the inside (*sogesŏ*) there was not one thing Korean about her. In the end they became friends and he told her about Korea and tried to introduce her to Korean culture.

His second example was drawn from his visit to Amsterdam during the 2002 World Cup, which was cohosted by Japan and South Korea. He and his friend ran into a group of Korean-looking men carrying a Korean flag, and it turned out that they were adoptees. They all went to a pub together and cheered for the Korean soccer team, and in so doing bonded together as Koreans (*chŏngi tŭrŏdda*). He concluded the story by saying, "So, I can't figure it out—are they Korean or not?" For this Korean volunteer, being Korean engaged physical and racial appearance, gendered assumptions, cultural knowledge, language, and (sport) nationalism all in a framework of ethnonational identity. The first example presented an instance of a disturbing disconnect between the expected isomorphism between Korean bodily form and cultural content, and the second provided one of surprising mutual understanding and spiritual connection. In both cases, he was seeking a fixed identity that would help him understand adoptees as a group in relation to an essentialized and naturalized model of Koreanness.

Another interview suggested to me how the destabilization of taken-for-granted categories of national belonging that adoptees provoked could yield processual and historically contingent models of ethnic or national identity among native Korean volunteers. Ben, a student at Korean Catholic University double majoring in international studies and English language and culture, had been a volunteer for the adoptee advocacy group International Korean Adoptee Services (INKAS) for four years when we met. He and his friend Bruce, another INKAS volunteer, who was training to be a pilot at Korea Aviation University, met me for an interview at a coffee shop near Yongsan in July 2004. Bruce was running late that morning, and as we waited for him Ben and I drank coffee and chatted. He was particularly passionate about child welfare issues related to adoption because he had a vivid memory of meeting his mother's friend, a foster care mother tending to babies before they were sent overseas for adoption. This was during the IMF crisis, and the woman was taking care of five or six babies at once. She wept as she told Ben's mother that they would all be going overseas the next day. This memory stuck with him, and in his narrative it served as a primary reason for his decision to volunteer for INKAS. But he also admitted that, like most volunteers, he was initially drawn by the opportunity to improve his English, with the added benefit of being able to help others.

Although Ben didn't have much time to devote to INKAS in the beginning, he socialized with adoptees and guided them around Seoul to "introduce them to Korean culture," he said. I was curious about what he found important about teaching adoptees Korean culture and I asked him to elaborate. My question, however, cast him unexpectedly into confusion:

> Personally, I think they have the same blood, right? So inside their heart they are Korean . . . their appearance is also Korean. But they need to

> know about Korean culture, because . . . [this issue] is so confusing!. . . . it's hard to [find an] appropriate answer. But personally I think they are Korean because they have the same blood flowing in their body.
>
> *Do you think they would agree with you?*
>
> I don't think so. But that's why I'm confused. They think they are American or Danish or [some other nationality] . . . When they get to Korea I see they have some conflict in their mind, they are confused about their identity: Am I Korean, am I American? But I think it's an inevitable process. What they learn, what they achieve, is *their* culture, but inside their heart they are Korean, I think. That's why they are confused, I think.

When Bruce arrived I filled him in on my discussion with Ben, and then I asked him what he thought about Ben's confusion:

> Bruce: In my point of view the identity question is more of a personal thing, so I never ask them about their identity. It's like asking about age or marriage.
>
> *But do you think adoptees are Korean? Ben said that he thinks that adoptees have Korean blood, and in that way they're Korean.*
>
> Bruce: But I don't think they are Korean. They are so different from kyop'o. They were raised by white . . . parents, so I don't think they are Korean.

Ben then interjected, stating,

> But I feel the same thing . . . when I meet adoptees. I feel the same thing as I do with Koreans. You are adoptees, but you are just like one of the Koreans to me—"Oh, my friends, how are you doing?" That's why I think that.

Like the confusion that the OKF volunteer expressed over the Koreanness of overseas adoptees, Ben was attempting to reconcile his embodied understanding of being Korean—the affective recognition that makes him "feel the same thing" with adoptees as he does with other Koreans—with what he knew of adoptees' own feelings of being unfixed or caught between categories.

In many ways Ben's dilemma is based on the same contradictory preconditions that underlie the logic of the OKF project: the Korean identity of adoptees is taken to be biologically inherited yet is also constructed as something that needs to be culturally acquired through NGO or state-sponsored pastoral projects. Official OKF documents refer to this as *tong-jilsŏng hoebok*, or restoration of (homogeneous) ethnic identity. In official speeches given by the first ladies of Korea, who present a face of the motherland to adoptees, the Korean state has encouraged adoptees to forget their difficult past but also to remember their roots in order to move in step with the Korean nation that is setting its sights on a per capita income on par with that of the most advanced economies.

In contrast, Bruce, who told me that he didn't "believe in *hanminjok*" (Korean race) because it was simply a rhetorical tool for politicians to draw upon, also didn't think that adoptees are Korean because they had been raised by white parents. For him, the government is still accountable for adoptees' welfare on the basis of their "difficult pasts"—their personal histories of displacement—rather than on a reified notion of blood. Thus, what makes adoptees deserving of government and NGO services and attention is their involuntary exile by the nation.

To clarify this point, Bruce brought up a statement made by a Danish adoptee at a training workshop for INKAS volunteers a few weeks earlier. According to Bruce, this adoptee expressed his belief that children should continue to be sent abroad through international adoption to ensure that those children who had already been adopted would not be forgotten. Bruce then followed this comment by asking me if I had heard about the Koreans in Mexico, who are the most recently "discovered" members of the Korean diaspora. Members of this group were first stumbled upon by South Korean missionaries in the Yucatan Peninsula in the early 2000s. They had been living in Mexico for nearly a century after being sent as indentured laborers by the Japanese government in 1905 (Patterson 1994). Bruce had seen a television documentary about them, and he described them as "forgotten":

> Several hundred [Koreans] immigrated to Mexico and then they were just forgotten, so the people in Mexico married Mexicans or each other. So, still, their facial appearance is more Asian, and they still remember "Arirang" [an iconic Korean folk song]. They still remember Korean words like *harabŏji* [grandfather] or *abŏji* [father]. . . . They still think

> they are Korean, but the Korean government doesn't think that they are Korean [and] can't give them a passport or any rights. So the same thing will happen to adoptees as [in] the Mexican Korean story—they were just abandoned.

Whereas the Korean government claimed that the Koreans in Mexico had been sent there under the Japanese colonial authority and therefore were not the responsibility of the South Korean state, for Bruce, these ethnic Koreans in Mexico remain Korean by dint of racial appearance and extant cultural memory.

Unlike the Korean Mexicans described by Bruce, adoptees may not believe that they are Korean. And although they may look Asian, they may not know any Korean words or folk songs. But Bruce believes that the Korean government should acknowledge both groups and ensure that they be remembered as Koreans. What makes these two cases comparable, therefore, is not an essentialized Koreanness as reflected or expressed in cultural traits but rather common histories of involuntary displacement and exile. Against the cooptation of various diasporic formations into a homogenous identity equated with the South Korean state and its official nationalisms, Bruce promoted the reinscription of diasporic Koreans like the Korean Mexicans and adoptees into Korean social memory.

Yet Bruce's view of forgotten Koreans is different from that of the Danish adoptee—he did not, for instance, recommend the continuation of forced labor migration of Koreans to Mexico in order to maintain the Korean Mexican population. The Danish adoptee, however, feared the demise and eventual extinction of the Korean adoptee community should overseas adoption from Korea eventually be suspended. Adoptees, who were once nonpersons disposed of by the state as surplus population and then converted into a special category of overseas Koreans, are, in this vision, reified as a distinct diaspora that needs to be sustained and reproduced for its own sake.

Continuing to send children overseas, which is a dystopic reality of how women and children are devalued by the nation-state, thus becomes part of a strangely utopic vision of social reproduction. Although the Danish adoptee's views may be unique to him, and they gave pause to other adoptees I mentioned them to, they are not wholly irrational or unimaginable, especially from the perspective of Scandinavia where Korean adoptees, who constitute the majority Asian population, are threatened with becoming an "endangered species." Thus, adoptees who are outspoken activists for the suspension of overseas adoption from Korea, are, within this logic, implicated in the eventual demise and extinction of their own people and the hard-won achievements of community. For the Danish adoptee, not being forgotten means continuing the reproduction of adoptees as a unique population; for Bruce, it is the symbolic recognition of them as involuntarily exiled; and for adoptee activists, beyond the discursive work of articulating adoptee counterhistories, addressing the specific material needs and rights of adoptees through legal state recognition must be the basis for their reconstitution as part of the nation.

FROM *KUNGMIN* TO *SIMIN*

Seungsook Moon (2005) tracks the emergence of a vision of active citizenship in Korea since the transition to procedural democracy in 1987 and the installation of the first civilian administration in 1993. Moon's account shows how gendered constructions of citizenship have shifted from the state-dictated role of the citizenry as subordinate to the state (*kungmin*) to the assertion of a new citizenry that embraces civic responsibility and works toward progressive social justice and equality (*simin*). As the anthropologist Jesook Song states: "The 1980s political movements engendered a new generation of identity politics and civil/human rights activism in the 1990s. This new direction partially passed down the spirit of resistance [i.e., of the radical democracy movement and labor activism of the 1980s] toward diverse arenas of social movements beyond class, labor, and reunification issues" (2006: 42).

In the mid-1990s, adoptees drew attention as highly sentimentalized objects of national shame and guilt and became one of many human rights projects taken up by civil society organizations. Adoptees, once the youngest victims of South Korea's authoritarian developmentalist state, might now be seen as among the most privileged objects of charity for the newly democratized citizenry in the context of state-supported globalization. But it should be stressed that adoptees' embodied histories and cultural activism are simultaneously widening dominant conceptions of Koreanness and calling forth a diversity of marginalized histories against the national master narrative.

As the South Korean state offers vague and imprecise messages of welcome to adoptees as ambassadors and bridges, thereby leaving their specific relationship to the nation ill defined, I offer another metaphor and interpretive framework. The bridge metaphor presupposes two fixed and culturally distinct territories or nation-states that the adoptee links together, and it conjures backbreaking (emotional) labor, just as the notion of ambassador can suggest the challenges of negotiating between competing agendas rather than glamorous cosmopolitanism or good-humored détente. Based on my analysis of adoptees in Korea and their relationships with native Koreans and NGOs, I suggest that adoptees are not so much bridges as they are catalysts for social transformation and the expansion of civil society in Korea. The interest of Korean NGOs and volunteers is thus shaped by a broader social ethos in post-1987 Korea to expand participatory citizenship, build civil democracy, and articulate a moral vision.

These organizations frame adoptees as Koreans who were forcibly sent overseas as children and who are thereby deserving of aid and assistance upon their return to the country. To meet the needs of returning adoptees, NGOs have worked to fill in the gaps between the adoption agencies, which are unable or unwilling to provide adequate assistance in birth family search or basic guidance, and the state, which dedicates only one person to handle adult-adoptee affairs. In contrast to training to be culturally Korean by letting their Westernized bodies be dressed up in traditional Korean hanbok, for instance, adoptees, as the return of the repressed and the intrusion of the "constitutive outside" (Butler 1993), are provoking an expansion of Koreanness—Koreanness in a foreign tongue, or "un coreénité plus large"—by troubling the normative bounds of family and national belonging.[26] A core group of adoptees in Korea are engaging in cultural activism, adoption reform, and social justice movements, and alongside native Koreans they are contributing to the expansion of civil society—not through the rhetoric of bridges but through their everyday practices and political projects.

Yet these processes need to be understood within the context of South Korea's post-IMF cultural and economic neoliberalization. With these concerns in mind, one can appreciate how discourses of participatory democracy and civil society may be seen as overly invested in naive and celebratory representations of agency and self-empowerment, failing to take into account the multiple vectors and circuits of state power within a transnational frame. With OKF and IKAA now representing the community and the legitimation of GOA'L as a South Korean NGO, the incorporation and naturalization of adoptees as a new and self-empowered category of the Korean diaspora, along with the institutionalization of postadoption services and adoptee service providers, might be considered a welcome development. For some other adoptees, however, it signals a dangerous flirtation with the very process of "goal displacement" that reproduced the adoption system beyond its rational limits and perpetuates Korea's dependence on overseas adoption as a social welfare policy solution (Sarri, Baik, and Bombyk 1998). The work of organizations like GOA'L to establish adoptee presence in Korea risks naturalizing the adoptee community and perpetuating the system by making the "post" of "postadoption" a retroactive compensation for the original and involuntary forfeiture of language, culture, nation, and citizenship.

The secretary-general of GOA'L, Kim Dae-won, in particular, discussed with me his concerns that GOA'L, by making it easier for adoptees' needs to be met in Korea, might also be making it easier for the government to defer the reform of social welfare programs in general and overseas adoption in particular. What Dae-won articulated is similar to what Julia Paley in her study of social movements in postdictatorial Chile calls "paradoxical participation," in which the encouragement of civic participation actively recruits individuals into the neoliberal rollback of state services and thereby displaces state accountability onto self-regulating, "responsibilized" subjects: "Participation offered a sense of meaning to citizens at the same time as it limited avenues through which citizens could act" (2001: 146).

In 2004 GOA'L gained full recognition as a South Korean NGO, and it received its first major grant from the Ministry of Health and Welfare in 2005. By giving GOA'L a substantial sum the state may finally be acknowledging the ongoing presence of adoptees within the national borders as well as recognizing the organization's services as increasingly necessary as the next and largest wave of adoptees comes of age. KoRoot, for its part, has begun to address the practical ways in which adoptees are able to capitalize on their bridge potential. The Hibsok program was started in spring 2005 as a ten-week-long weekend "business school" that helps long-term returnees adapt to Korea and to "construct a career path in [their] field." The course, which includes lectures by small businessmen, employees of foreign and Korean corporations, professors, and tourism experts, was partly funded by the Seoul metropolitan government with a grant specified for "government participation projects for NGOs [*piyŏngni tanch'e sichŏng ch'amyŏ saŏp*]."[27]

One can see how the work of NGOs and the increasing visibility of adoptees in the Korean media can work to naturalize and normalize the return of adoptees to the motherland as an expected part of the adoptee lifecycle. And adoptees, who constitute their own special subcategory of the global diaspora, are being actively trained to assimilate to Korean culture and economy. As government-funded postadoption services are increasingly institutionalized they extend state biopower, which rationalized the export of adoptees as excess bodies, into techniques of government in the "post" period through the restoration of Korean identity and other incomplete restitutions for prior sacrifices of language, culture, and family. Even as children continue to be sent abroad every year, the institutionalization of postadoption services helps to guarantee that those children will have an easier time identifying with Korea and an easier time returning to the motherland, especially as adult adoptees begin to take on greater responsibility to help fill in the gaps—in services and in personal and national histories—that the state and adoption agencies have demonstrated little will to directly address.

Here I would like to recall the "tragic irony" of child sponsorship as identified by Erica Bornstein (2001), with which I concluded chapter 1. She describes how child sponsorship programs, as humanitarian gestures of Christian charity for needy children, create intimate relationships yet also produce distance and differences between children and their local communities as well as between recipients and donors. When they return to Korea, adult adoptees, who were once those child beneficiaries, confront and sometimes attempt to rebridge the distances and disparities in social, economic, and cultural capital that were set into motion through their adoptions. The work of GOA'L and the other NGOs that help adoptees attempts to rectify those distances and differences within a context of postcolonial aspirations for democratic participation, emergent neoliberal rationalities, and cosmopolitan striving. The "time-space compression" of adoptee returns thereby reanimates the tragic irony as well as sets in motion possible transformations in the understanding and practice of transnational adoption, paradigms of citizenship, and the re-membering of the national body.

CONCLUSION

In 2007 GOA'L started a campaign to promote dual citizenship for adoptees. The desire for citizenship is entangled with concerns around adoptee rights in Korea and the ability of foreigner-established organizations like GOA'L to function on equal footing with native-Korean NGOs in terms of government grants and fund-raising. As I have argued, GOA'L is part of an emergent field of cultural production in which Korean adoptees who live in Korea are articulating their alternative subjectivities and cultural identities as members not only of the global Korean family but also as participants in the nation with particular stakes and interests in maintaining their presence there. This articulation of an alternative Korean subjectivity is coincident with the emergence of a range of other groups now residing within South Korea and making claims on the state—Amerasians, migrant laborers, multicultural families, return migrants, and other overseas ethnic Koreans. In this way, adoptees living in Korea are participating in Korea's globalization from within rather than as metaphoric bridge builders or ambassadors linking the West with Korea, which in dominant narratives is imagined to be a homogeneous nation united in its desire for advanced nation status.

As Korea enters into an increasingly multicultural and multiethnic global era it would be rather easy to assert that hegemonic ideologies of cultural and racial homogeneity are giving way to more expansive notions of who counts as Korean. This conclusion, if indeed supportable, can only be a partial one. What seems more likely is that increasingly economistic views of personhood are influencing the cultural modes of incorporation available to differently stratified groups. Participation in contemporary Korea may be entering into a postidentity phase in which one's cultural citizenship and incorporation in the nation is determined not solely through essentialized blood identities and assimilation into the dominant culture but also through views of personhood increasingly inflected with neoliberal rationalities in which citizenship and well-being are measured against free-market logics of economic self-regulation and entrepreneurship.[28]

In the context of Korean civil society, Korean volunteers and adoptee advocates have been able to modify their more radical projects for revolutionary social change into moderate forms of participatory democracy that rely on the incomplete membership of adoptees who exist as unassimilable others to the Korean nation. Adoptee NGO projects also become modes of self-governance in which adoptees themselves provide the services that the state is unable to furnish. These might be regarded as successful campaigns for self-empowerment, yet without full citizenship rights adoptees continue to be marginalized as others to the nation by the very NGOs that attempt to ameliorate the conditions of their daily existence in Korea. Moreover, adoptee recognition is increasingly predicated on the localization of neoliberal values in which entrepreneurship and economic bridge building are offered as the idealized models for the roles that adoptees can play as members of global Korea. In the context of adoption politics these discourses and projects reinforce the notion that adoption is an acceptable social welfare policy solution in which original sacrifices of language, family, and culture can be recovered in the postadoption phase. They also shift focus away from the ongoing and unresolved "adoption problem" (*ibyang munje*) by foregrounding a partial view that equates adoptee upward mobility with the success of adoption.

7

Beyond Good and Evil

The Moral Economies of Children and Their Best Interests in a Global Age

While the recognition that their lives could have been different is common to many transnational adoptees, the story each tells himself or herself about what that difference would have meant is intensely personal. The narratives are often fiercely owned and held on to: an individual dispossessed of his or her past can at least have control over a narrative of possibility. . . . Each stage of life generates new narratives that are always only fictions but they are strong fictions, fictions through which identity is tested, adjusted and redefined.—ELIZABETH HONIG, "PHANTOM LIVES, NARRATIVES OF POSSIBILITY"

In summer 2004 a new TV reality series took South Korea by storm. *Foster Mother of Love* (*Sarangŭi witakmo*; translated by the English-language press as *Celebrity Foster Mom*) featured famous female stars who served as temporary caregivers to an infant for two weeks before the child was sent to its new adoptive family. The show was part of a domestic adoption campaign that was spearheaded by the California-based Mission to Promote Adoption in Korea (MPAK)—a Christian organization founded by a Korean American adoptee. Viewers watched these young, single women bond with an adorable infant, while the show's host, a famous comic in his own right, flirted with the mother and doted on the child, thereby fulfilling the role of "daddy" in these domestic scenes.

In advancing MPAK's aims, the show provided various pieces of information to its audience, including the eligibility requirements to be a short-term foster mother and the latest tips on child rearing and development, and it also satisfied its spectators' voyeuristic curiosity by offering glimpses into the personal residences and domestic lives of these pop culture figures. It also exerted subtle moral pressure on viewers to consider the problem of overseas adoption and the imperative that Koreans take responsibility for the raising of Korean children.[1] As the time approached for these temporary mothers to see their children off at the airport or to hand over the child to domestic adoptive parents, sentimental music accompanied by melodramatic text ("The day has arrived"; "The moment of parting") primed viewers for the inevitable tragic finale. The foster mothers were invariably overcome with sorrow, often to the point of inconsolable weeping.

A major omission in these narratives of love and loss, however, was the prequel: the episode that told the story of the biological mother, who was also, according to statistics, most likely a young, single woman. But unlike the high-profile stars of the show, the birth mother was rendered invisible by the long shadow of stigma associated with unwed motherhood in Korea. In the show's choreography of domestic normativity, the birth mothers were rarely if ever mentioned, let alone pictured. Rather, the celebrity mother literally performed the emotional role of the birth mother by caring for and bonding with the child, undergoing the trauma of separation, and, in the end, expressing hopes and fears about the child's unknown future with another family, possibly in another country, as well as the desire to reunite with the child when he or she was grown up. Behind the emotional potency of the series was not only the celebrity embodiment and enactment of the birth mother's subjectivity and grief but also the embodiment and display of national grief over the abandonment of these children —or "our children," as the show continually reminded its viewers.

As I have shown, the issue of adoption in Korea has been an ongoing topic of public debate, with periodic calls for policy reform and political intervention. The sting of being dubbed "the orphan-exporting nation" by the international media during the 1988 Seoul Olympic Games still lingers, in part because overseas adoptions from Korea continue unabated today. *Foster Mother of Love* capitalized on this national shame, giving the national guilt trip a makeover through its top-billed movie starlets. Yet the program also reinforced notions of "right" families through the mock portrayal of a domestic heterosexual idyll that represents the modern ideal and that implicitly restigmatizes nonnormative familial arrangements, especially those of unmarried mothers and their children.

The unwed mother and especially the teenage unwed mother (*sipdae mihonmo*) have been identified since the early 1990s as objects of social welfare concern that necessitate the continuation of South Korea's controversial transnational adoption program. Conventional wisdom in Korea and in the Western countries to which adoptees are sent blames the persistence of Confucian family values and preoccupations with patrilineal bloodlines for the reluctance among Koreans to adopt "their children." This perspective, however, obscures other salient factors that contribute to the problem of adoption in Korea, ones that place the burden for child welfare less on the Korean family—in this case, the family that doesn't adopt—and more on the state, which has so far failed to promote family coherence, provide adequate financial support for single mothers, or tackle the problem of inadequate sex education. Korea today shares the same demographic stresses prevalent in other so-called advanced nations: a precipitously low birth rate and high rates of abortion, divorce, and infertility, and their concomitant effects of a shrinking workforce and an aging population. What it does not share with its global economic peers is a welfare system that aids single women in raising their children or a system that holds the fathers of these children accountable for their well being.[2] The erasure of the birth mother (and birth father) in this reality show thus reflects the profound marginality of the birth mother in Korean society at large.

NEW VOICES

The past few years have witnessed an unprecedented degree of visibility for the Korean birth mothers of an earlier period. Their stories have often been filtered through sensationalizing depictions in the Korean media or through the moralizing discourses of adoption agencies, but now birth mothers are addressing adult adoptees directly in discussion groups coordinated by adoptee advocacy organizations. One cannot assume that all birth parents want to be found by their children, and a good number, no doubt, prefer to forget and move on with their lives. But the parents who come out publicly to tell their stories suggest how powerfully the media has functioned as a kinship technology in Korea (H. Kim 2007) and also how profoundly these separations have affected their lives. For instance, in the midst of the media blitz surrounding OKF's motherland tours the organization was inundated with phone calls by desperate and grieving birth parents who wondered if one of the adoptees they'd seen on TV or in the newspaper was the child they relinquished many years ago. Some were so desperate that they dialed the phone number on their television screens or at the end of the newspaper article because they simply had nowhere else to turn for sympathy or advice. Like one of the birth mothers that Laurel Kendall met in the course of her fieldwork in Korea, many of these parents reveal the long-term emotional consequences of "a painful choice that was not [theirs]" (2005: 169).

The few generalizations that can be drawn from the stories women tell of relinquishing their children must be made cautiously, and more ethnographic research will be necessary to adequately contextualize their easily melodramaticized and romanticized accounts. Dominant representations suggest that adoption is a significantly feminized practice and reflect the degree to which "universal motherhood" is fetishized and the mother-child bond imbued with sacral value in the West and in Korea. Even with these caveats in mind, it is nevertheless difficult not to be struck by the emerging narratives, appearing with increasing frequency in the media, from adoptees who have reunited with biological relatives and from newly vocal birth mothers. They paint a dark picture of the compromising effects of industrialization, modernization, and specific gendered modernities (Kendall 2002) on individual Korean women. From their accounts it is clear that economic, social, and political oppression, in conjunction with practical forms of euphemized violence, made adoption the only possible or responsible choice. In addition, these accounts reveal ways in which rapid urbanization and the nuclearization of families undermined the ability of extended family networks to provide daily care for children of working-class families struggling to survive in harsh economic environments.

These stories tell of the constraints experienced by women who were beholden to an entrenched patriarchal system—marked by the "cult of domesticity" and son preference—that placed immense reproductive burdens on them. Birth mothers tell of the shame of giving birth to another girl in a long series of attempts for a son, and others speak of being widowed or abandoned and attempting to balance work and caregiving without familial support or public childcare providers. Some of these women left their children in the care of relatives who, for the mother's and the children's "own good," shuttled the children off to orphanages or adoption agencies while the mother was at work. Still others were victims of domestic abuse and had little hope for their own survival, and thus sent children for adoption to literally save their lives. And others were young women who moved to the city to find work in a factory and were raped or entered into relationships with little understanding of their own sexuality. Some were romantically involved with married men who promised to leave their wives but never did. Others were in stable marriages but hit tough financial straits and had no other means of feeding themselves or their children.

The story of one Mrs. Kim is particularly telling and resonates with other stories, including that of Deann Borshay Liem who documented her reunion in the film *First Person Plural* (2000). Mrs. Kim appeared at the 2004 Gathering conference bearing a poster-sized photograph of her daughter, Sumi, whom she had sent for adoption thirty-two years earlier. According to an article in the *Dong-A Daily* newspaper, she, like many poor women in the 1970s, had a child while she was in a consensual union with the man she planned to marry.[3] Unfortunately, however, the father of the child died suddenly. Determined to raise her daughter on her own, Mrs. Kim found work in a factory and asked her mother to care for Sumi. Mrs. Kim's mother, however, concerned about her daughter's future, pushed for the child's adoption.

As Mrs. Kim told the reporter, "The people around me convinced me (*sŏldŭk*) that if I raised my daughter she would always go hungry, and that there would be almost no way that she could be educated. They said it would be so much better if she was sent to a good place to be adopted." She began looking for her daughter in 1979 with the support of her new husband and family, but it wasn't until a few days before the Gathering conference in 2004 that she found out from the adoption agency that had placed Sumi that her daughter had come looking for her in 1995. For Mrs. Kim, poverty, early widowhood, and social pressure made adoption seem like the best, and indeed, the only option for her to be a good mother to her child. But under the "clean break" paradigm instituted by international adoption law, being a good mother also required the full surrender of her child and taking on a lifetime of guilt and uncertainties.

PHANTOM LIVES AND OTHER POSSIBILITIES

Just as Mrs. Kim reportedly spent thirty-two years of sleepless nights wondering about the fate of her daughter, adoptees have similar thoughts: What if I had stayed in Korea, who would I be? What would my life have been like? These "what-ifs" and "phantom lives" (Honig 2005) of adoptees are also imagined by adoptive parents and adoption agencies who help adoptees frame the reasons for their adoptions but often take a limited and stereotypic view of Korean kinship and patriarchy to construct answers to the what-ifs. These constructions of Korean culture, envisioned as an unchanging same of Confucian patriarchy, construe adoption as a necessarily moral and pragmatic solution.[4]

Motherland tours sponsored by adoption agencies frequently bring adoptees to orphanages and homes for unwed mothers, thereby providing historically disembedded narratives or "imagined antiautobiographies" (Kendall 2005) that encourage adoptees to connect their adoption origins from a generation earlier to what they see today. These become opportunities for adoptees to witness firsthand and to project directly onto the children and women they meet (but with whom they cannot communicate directly) how differently their lives might have turned out if they had stayed in Korea. These visits may be seen as extensions of the "euphemized violence" to which Korean birth mothers were subjected—the nonchoice between adoption or something worse for themselves and their children. An adoptee from Minnesota who went to Korea on an agency motherland visit described how the Korean social worker told the participants after a visit to an orphanage, "Don't you feel lucky? That could've been you." Yet the visit had a different effect on the adoptee: rather than making her feel grateful for having been saved from the fate of the children at the orphanage it provoked a desire for other alternatives. As she told me, "I just wish it wasn't always a choice between being adopted or being in an orphanage."

Adoptee activists are increasingly attempting to widen the scope of possibilities; not only do many seek out answers to questions about their own pasts and reasons for adoption but also a number are engaging in discussions about the future of the international adoption system. Their critique of the political and economic realities of adoption is a direct challenge to the humanitarian altruistic discourses that weigh institutional life in an orphanage against adoption into a loving family, and upon which rest notions of children's best interests and injunctions to be grateful. For these adoptees in particular, making claims to political voice and agency forces them to contend with dominant representations that, despite evidence to the contrary, continue to equate transnational adoption with the humanitarian rescue of orphans.

Borrowing from Giorgio Agamben's critique of modern state sovereignty (1998), I argue that the humanitarian orphan in transnational adoption is constructed as a figure of "bare life" that the adoptee must pass through in order to be included in the political life guaranteed by the adoptive family and the nation-state. In the contemporary world, Agamben argues, humanitarianism is increasingly separated from politics. Just as humanitarian organizations "can only grasp human life in the figure of bare or sacred life" (133), I suggest that adoption agencies are unable to grasp the orphan as anything but bare life, thereby "maintain[ing] a secret solidarity with the very powers they ought to fight" (133). In other words, the orphan, especially as a highly mediated, sentimentalized image, obscures the very structures of power and global inequalities that produce the problem of the orphan in the first place.

When Molly Holt, the daughter of the founder of Holt International Children's Services, tells adoptees that they would have died had they not been adopted, she deploys the figure of the orphan as bare life and its symbolic violence to subvert adoptees' attempts to frame adoption in political terms. Likewise, female adoptees frequently report having heard cautionary tales from parents and agency workers about how, if they had stayed in Korea, they would have been prostitutes and effectively reduced to a dehumanized and commodified body. These salvation narratives require adoptees to be grateful for having been rescued from a life of abjection, and they reinscribe a line between the dehumanized and excluded lives of orphans and prostitutes and the political lives of adoptees as members of first world nations. In this logic, the orphanage is, like the camp, a zone of indistinction in which children "die" or are "next to nothing," and from which children must be "rescued" in order to become full persons (Agamben 1998). By invoking the orphan as a figure of bare life, opponents of adoptee political projects attempt to undermine the activists' claims to political subjectivity based on their experiences of displacement.

Moreover, because the promise of happiness is implicit in the narrative of the orphan "saved" by adoption, adoptees become, like other oppressed people, "perceived as mean, bitter, angry or dangerous" if they do not demonstrate "anything but the sunniest countenance" (Marilyn Frye, cited in Ahmed 2008: 127). The discursive logic that pits the happy, well-adjusted adoptee against the unhappy malcontent obscures broader social injustices by reducing structural relations of power and economy to individual biography and psychology. It is a residual aspect of a once dominant assumption that the interest of adoptees in roots was a rejection of assimilation and thereby a symptom of the failure of the adoption placement. Both of these frameworks give rise to the conflict felt by adoptees who fear that they are negating themselves if they take a positioned stand against the inequalities of the adoption system.

During the 2007 Gathering in Seoul, for instance, a newly formed group of activist birth mothers known as Mindulae (dandelions) staged a protest at the nearby subway station. As adoptee activists enlisted conference attendees to support the demonstration, a Korean American adoptee whose own birth mother was a main organizer of the event experienced the paralyzing ambivalence of feeling a kinship obligation to support his Korean mother yet worrying that he would be "negating [his] own existence" by attending an "anti-adoption" rally.

For the most politically oriented adoptees, therefore, crafting a germane public discourse for discussing the politics of adoption has been a difficult process, especially given the intensely personal nature of the narratives and fictions that adoptees construct of their "phantom lives" and adoption realities, as Elizabeth Honig eloquently describes in the epigraph to this chapter. Because these narratives are expressions of agency, they are "fiercely owned and held on to" (2005: 215), yet in many discussions among adoptees, and especially between adoptees and adoptive parents, experience proves to be double edged: at once reified and used as incontrovertible evidence of political victimhood, it is also vulnerable in its particularity and can be disregarded as merely biographical, a pathological exaggeration, and too private to be of public concern.

The logic of humanitarianism, coupled with the injunction to be grateful, compels adoptee activists to separate their pasts as orphans and their present lives as adult adoptees. They foreclose any association that would frame them as objects of charity or fetishize them as vulnerable, childlike victims in their attempts to claim agency, recognition, and full personhood in politically legitimate registers. In doing so, however, they sacrifice the affective power of their stories, the pathos that makes abandonment and adoption stories such prevalent sources of inspiration for melodramatic films and soap operas the world over. In the next section, I describe how, at the 2004 Gathering, members of ASK attempted to circumvent these dominant logics to avoid getting trapped by reporters who sought causal linkages between possible negative childhood experiences and their current political stances. As became apparent, however, this resistant strategy could be considered counterproductive in a discursive economy that requires personal stories to authenticate political claims.

INCOMMENSURABILITY, REFUSAL, AND MORAL AUTHORITY

On the second day of the Gathering conference a radio reporter from the Korean Broadcasting Station sat down with a member of ASK to interview her for the show *Minority Report.* The ASK representative presented the group's position on international adoption by pointing out how the social welfare problems of Korea are inadequately addressed by sending children overseas, by mentioning the political opposition to the adoption of black children by white families in the United States, and by emphasizing the need to support single women to raise their children. The reporter, however, wanted to know about the representative's personal history and tried to elicit a story about her childhood growing up in the American Midwest. She became quiet, conferred with her fellow ASK members, and finally responded that her personal experiences were not relevant and that she would only answer questions related to the group and its political position. The reporter insisted that there must be, nevertheless, a personal reason for her political views. When pressed further she conceded that she had been subjected to racism when growing up. But she quickly stressed that it was more crucial to understand the structural inequalities of the adoption system than it was to focus on her adoption biography.

Afterward, I asked the reporter what he thought of the interview. He admitted that he was sympathetic to ASK's political argument, yet without a personal story, or a feeling-rich connection (*chŏng*) to touch a Korean audience, he was afraid that he wouldn't be able to do much with the recording. Like another reporter who was frustrated that she hadn't been able to get her adoptee interviewee to shed any tears for the television camera, this reporter was likewise frustrated that he hadn't gotten a more "emotional" story. He predicted that the interview would not air, and in fact it did not. In this case, ASK's strategy to decouple the personal and the political in order to project an unequivocally political argument backfired because it refused to deliver what the media need and desire—a story. It also highlights how ASK adoptees, as activists who seek to intervene in the dominant public, struggle to develop modes of address and speech that will be recognized as "rational-critical" even as the media can only recognize them through hyperexpressive, particular, and emotional testimonies.

After the Gathering, I sat down with core members of ASK and asked them to comment on the tendency to pathologize politicized adoptees as angry or resentful. I also asked them how they coped with the binary logic that governs the discourse around adoption. What follows are several of the responses to my questions:

> HyoJung Bidol: I think that we've actually, as a group, tried to be really clear that we don't *care* if you had a good adoption experience or a bad adoption experience. I mean, we do in that that's your experience, but we're not talking about this as an individual experience, that adoption happens in this much larger context. And you can still be against international adoption and have had a wonderful adoption experience. . . . But that again is really hard for people to get there.

> Su-Yoon Burrows: Adoption at the bottom line is emotional and hard to separate. If they made a choice to say I'm against adoption then it's an insult to their parents.

> Sarah Dankert: That's why groups fell apart when they got political. It's because adoption, in so many ways, is connected to a personal or an emotional experience, so it's really awfully hard to separate. And to say, you know, that's your experience and that's fine, but when it comes over on to this half, you have to separate—that's why people sometimes have almost a violent reaction to some of the stuff that's going on with us because it's really hard for them—for us also—to separate the emotional from what we think is political.

> HyoJung: But I think it's something we as a group need to figure out how to do. To understand their personal experience and figure out how to actually move them to look beyond that.

These adoptees are negotiating a complex set of boundaries between private and public in which the emotional, the personal, and experience need to be separated from the political—not only to articulate a more rational and legitimate discourse but also, I would add, to excerpt the orphan that undermines the adoptee as a political agent. In extracting adoption discourse from binaries of happiness and unhappiness, success and failure, or luck and misfortune, the members of ASK resisted attempts to reduce the relevant scope of adoption to personal biography or psychology and concomitant attempts to abstract individual experience from broader political structures and historical injustices (see Ahmed 2008). Although my primary contention is that the remembering of a collective sense of displacement among adopted Koreans constitutes the affective basis of collective personhood, what I have just described suggests that memory's mobilization in processes of social reclamation is more complicated than a simple choice between forgetting or remembering.

Personal memory, commonly considered to be located in an intensely private domain of the self, has become increasingly commodified, publicized, and politicized in late capitalism, especially in recent local and global cultures of trauma and public therapy (e.g., Berlant's intimate public sphere [1997]). In attempting to move beyond personal experience and refusing to comply with dominant representational regimes that require suffering victims in order to tell an effective story, activists in ASK are implicitly extracting themselves from the voyeuristic economy of public trauma and continually redrawing boundaries between what is public and what is private. In encounters with the media I see the refusal to perform memory as a kind of claim making in which retaining a focus on the *political* means the active rejection of the Korean media's commodification and depoliticization of their *personal* histories, whether spun as tragic or successful. So rather than a choice between remembering or forgetting the past, these adoptees suggest that memory and its performance must be mobilized selectively and strategically. In making this claim adoptees deter representations that either infantilize them as pitiable orphans or depoliticize them as successful transnational subjects—both are forms of symbolic violence that cancel the inherent complexity and ambivalence of adoptees' experiences.

Like the AIDS activists that Ann Cvetkovich describes, adoptee activists are attempting to construct a political culture out of "a trauma culture that is not about spectacles of wounded helplessness but about trauma as the provocation to create alternative life-worlds" (2003: 453). Against an airbrushed substitution for a birth mother's grief or the latest political jockeying around the "adoption issue," adult adoptee activists are asserting themselves as *historical* subjects. While in some situations they may acknowledge that their orphan pasts inform their personal and political subjectivities, in other instances, they struggle to evade the overdetermining constraints that those pasts have on their claims as political subjects. They seek to address the present conditions of gendered inequality and social injustice that continue to make overseas adoption the "best" and only solution for women and children in South Korea and other nations around the world.

By declining to perform grief or pathology for Korean journalists who regularly fetishize or try to elicit visibly emotional performances, however, these adoptees demonstrate the difficulty faced by members of subordinated groups when their social personhood and modes of address continue to be misrecognized and discounted, even when they attempt to engage in the "rational-critical" discourse required for participation in dominant publics (Warner 2002; Fraser 1997). In conforming to the model of the disinterested, rational-critical member of a general public, they risk losing the affective potency of their stories and their moral authority as adoptees, as well as the potentially transformative and subversive power of their personal histories and particular personhood (Warner 2002; Fraser 1992), as demonstrated by the radio report that never aired.

Many adoptees, especially those adopted at older ages, live with the split between who they were and who they might have been. Expanding the possibilities of that sphere could yield alternatives to the existing tradeoffs between bare survival or a fully realized life, between dying or living, and between being neglected in an institution or adopted into a loving home. Toward this end GOA'L, ASK, and other adoptee activists in Korea have been working with birth mothers—both those who gave up or lost their children over the past fifty years and the young women today living in homes for unwed mothers who are making the "terribly constrained type of 'choice'" (Gailey 2000) to relinquish their children. Other adoptees are lobbying the Korean government to reform the social welfare system and to devise better programs to furnish women with the economic and social support necessary to raise their children. These adoptee projects are finding allies among Korean NGOs and activists who are promoting reform of adoption, child welfare, and family policy. Adoptees, who have had the chance to tell their stories, have been seeking out the unrecognized histories of these women whose productive and affective labor has long been obscured.

These collaborations and coalitions are unprecedented and are raising novel tensions around power, representation, and spectacles of suffering. Activist birth mothers, for instance, are engaged in strategic essentialist projects in which their status as the "true" victims of the patriarchal and misogynistic adoption system reproduces a narrative of oppression and disenfranchisement that threatens to homogenize the discrepant histories of all birth mothers into a single narrative. In addition, adoptees sometimes look upon these newly vocal victims with fetishizing and romanticized gazes. Nevertheless, these developments are indicative of how adult adoptees are constructing social justice projects that intervene into existing structures, moving beyond concerns with their personal histories to the broader political economic conditions that fuel the adoption system in Korea.

REVISITING ORPHANS

In 2008 a UNICEF press release identified "a growing consensus on the need to revisit the use of the term 'orphan' and how it is applied" due to the common use of the word to refer to children who are living with surviving parents or other family members. Of the 132 million children who are counted as orphans by UNICEF only 13 million have lost both parents, and UNICEF has acknowledged that a misunderstanding about the actual number of children in need of immediate care "may then lead to responses that focus on providing care for individual children rather than supporting the families and communities that care for orphans and are in need of support" (UNICEF 2008). Moreover, 95 percent of those 13 million children are over the age of five, which contrasts starkly with transnational adoption statistics in which the vast majority of adopted children are infants. Thus a basic premise of international adoption, which proponents insist serves the greater good by providing care for orphaned children, needs to be reconsidered. Some critics would argue that humanitarian motivations are secondary to egocentric desires for "family" and "maternal citizenship"

(Anagnost 2000), but the orphan figure nevertheless continues to inform the moral semiotics of transnational adoption.

The orphan in the West was once associated with the inhumane travesties of the industrial revolution, Dickensian children's asylums, poverty, and backwardness. In literature and film it has often been embedded in narratives of social uplift, heroic rescue, and Romantic self-invention (Auerbach 1975), and as a classic liminal figure existing on the edge of society the orphan embodies both purity and danger (Douglas 1984 [1966]). With the deinstitutionalization of the child welfare system in the early twentieth century, the word has lost currency in American contexts where most children are currently accounted for. For instance, children in foster care are framed as victims of familial abuse or neglect but not as orphans. Moreover, the privileging of biogenetic relations in American legal precedence has made domestic adoptions in the United States seem perilous because of the assumption that birth parents and others could challenge the rights of the adopting parents.

The orphan could be construed as the ultimate figure of global humanitarianism. And legal norms, social conventions, and cultural representations in the Euro-American West reinforce the idea that children who are adopted are orphans in need of immediate rescue. The orphan myth has not only misrepresented adoptees—many of whom long believed that they were true orphans but have come to realize that they have existing parents and relatives in Korea—it also erases history and power. Ever since the war orphans of the 1950s, the orphan in Korean and other transnational adoption has obscured the structural violence of the cold war and neoliberal economic policies, thereby permitting Americans in particular to "save" children who are themselves often victims of American foreign policy decisions (Briggs 2006).

Thus in the early twenty-first century orphans and orphanages only exist "elsewhere"—in poor or developing nations—where poverty, corruption, war, and the disorderly processes of modernization contribute to the suffering of innocent children. Third world orphanages proliferated under twentieth-century developmentalist regimes as the effects of global capital and cold war conflicts created new crises for families and children and new opportunities for missionary and international aid projects. Neoliberal structural readjustment policies have made the lives of poor people increasingly precarious, and the effects have become tragically obvious in the numbers of children housed in orphanages throughout the non-Western world. The conditions at these facilities are often sadly inadequate, and I do not take lightly the reality of human suffering, but my critique of the cultural politics of the orphan figure emphasizes that the disappearance of orphans and orphanages in the West reinforces a modernist teleology of progress and development that constructs third world orphans, like the former "primitive," in a place and time distant from our modern world (Fabian 1983). The reasons for their suffering are made invisible and inconsequential in light of the urgency of their rescue.[5] In this way the highly mediated orphan, a simulacrum of universal affect and pure humanity, becomes a "tranquilizing convention" (Malkki, cited in Bornstein 2001) that itself becomes abstracted from the realm of politics. Whether or not these children have kinship relations with parents or other caregivers has proven to be largely irrelevant when conventional wisdom and international conventions privilege Western-style nuclear families over other family arrangements, and when notions of "right childhoods" equate "material poverty with inner deprivation" (Stephens 1995; Boyden 1990).

Orphans, in this framework, are children in need of immediate rescue, no longer through imperialistic paradigms of civilization but through neoliberal notions of opportunity. Supported by Eurocentric moral values, adoption thereby often privileges modernist goals of liberal subjectivity against community sustainability and preexisting relations of kinship and care. For instance, anthropologists of Latin America (Scheper-Hughes 1990; Fonseca 2003; Leinaweaver 2007) have documented how indigenous modes of survival and child circulation are devalued and usurped when the state and the international adoption system normalizes the removal and exporting of a child as "moral and beneficial" (Leinaweaver 2007: 175).

Many adoptees have had to confront the psychic effects of these dominant narratives, whether within their adoptive family relations or in more public domains. Typically, the adoptee could only feel gratitude and indebtedness for having been given "life" and "opportunity" through inclusion in the bourgeois nuclear family, and more complex feelings of ambivalence, mourning, or resentment were suppressed, condemned as ungrateful, or pathologized. Recent dispensations in social work practice now attend to the losses inherent to adoption. Related to this view, children are no longer seen as tabula rasa but as arriving from the birth country with a "backpack" full of preadoption psychological traumas and possible genetic disorders (Howell 2007). As I discussed earlier in this book, recognition of the psychological effects of separation on even those adopted in infancy is now viewed as central to adoptee identity, and the exploration of roots is encouraged as part of the multicultural turn in adoption policy and practice. Yet these models fall short of acknowledging power and history in the making of (adoptive) family relations and "the family" as the site for the production and reproduction of intersecting race, class, and gender ideologies.

Ann Stoler's "tense and tender ties" of empire (2006) remind us of how microprocesses of power reinforce or reproduce relationships of inequality in the most private realms of the family and the household. This orientation helps move our thinking beyond the sentimentalization and universalizing of the child as a symbol of innocence to ask more critical questions about the ambivalence and ambiguity wrought by intimate relations embedded in and structured by state power and dynamics of domination and resistance. The tragic irony of transnational adoption is that family intimacy is made possible by the vast inequalities of the global political economy, and for some adoptive parents recognizing their implication in relations of stratified reproduction (Colen 1995) has been a radicalizing experience (Register 2005; Cornell 1999). Hegemonic narratives of adoption, however, continue to reinforce the moral value of adoption through the figure of the orphan, which is in turn reinforced by ideologies of American exceptionalism.

Indeed, despite the changing circumstances of adoption and reproductive politics in the West and in South Korea, the figure of the orphan has had an enduring legacy in the dominant social imaginaries about child welfare in a global context.[6] The orphan prevails as a sentimental object of Western humanitarianism and in Korea as a pitiable symbol of the nation's incomplete modernization. This legacy has direct bearing on adult adoptees' contemporary struggles to assert agency as full persons and as political subjects. Given the reductive inaccuracies of the orphan label and the depoliticizing effects of the orphan figure, adoptee activists in particular have actively distanced themselves from those sentimentalizing representations.

CONCLUSION

The photo series by the adoptee artist Soon Ja Terwee (figures 13 and 14) visually captures the ambivalence of adoptee "contingent essentialism" by

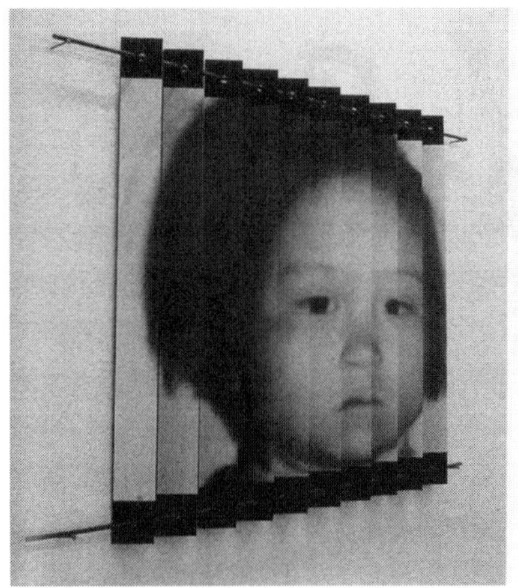

13. Soon Ja Terwee, "Irene." (Reproduced with permission of the artist from the exhibition catalogue *Our Adoptee, Our Alien*)

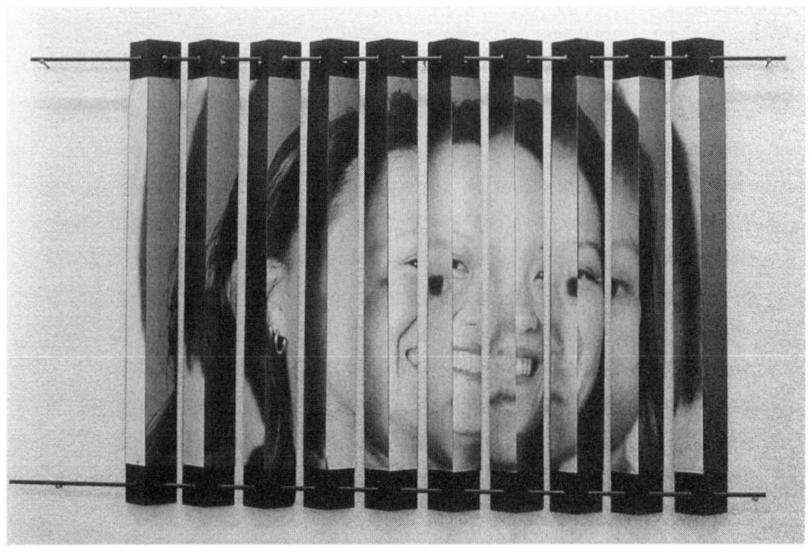

14. Soon Ja Terwee, "Irene." (Reproduced with permission of the artist from the exhibition catalogue *Our Adoptee, Our Alien*)

presenting ruptured portraits of adoptees assembled out of before and after images. These assemblages are like analog versions of a holograph in which depending upon where one stands in relation to the work one can see either the orphan whose arrival photos capture the "fear, uncertainty, fatigue, puzzlement" of the child entering into an unknown world, or the adoptee as "young, independent grown ups" (Terwee 2004). But the images comprise two parts of a whole like the adoptee herself, who represents both a third world subaltern and a privileged global citizen. As Terwee writes in an artist's statement, "I feel that the emotions that caused these facial expressions have moved and settled somewhere inside and are something that every adoptee is carrying with him/her and probably stored in a deep and far place in the heart where it won't cause any obstacles in their lives (anymore)." By bringing the orphan into the same spatial and temporal frame with the adoptee, Terwee literally fragments and disrupts the portrait of the adoptee. In doing so, she projects into a transnational public sphere a representation of the constitutive liminality and disjunctiveness of the adoptee by fracturing the linear and progressive narratives that reinforce the moral and market logics of transnational adoption. Adoption is often framed as the happy ending to a sad story, but Terwee and other adult adoptees suggest that the ending is not an ending at all. Rather, it is the middle of an ongoing narrative that offers no predictable resolutions.

The creative work and expressive cultures of adult adoptees constitute the most publicly available articulations of Korean adoptee personhood and may circulate more widely than other kinds of adoptee representations, but they should be seen as part of a broader continuum of adoptee counterpublic interventions. Adoptees voice their ambivalence in the liminal, deterritorialized, and ephemeral spaces of global capitalism in which these "obstacles" and "subjugated knowledges" (Foucault 1979) can be articulated in "adoptee-only" zones of public intimacy. Through both cultural production and social practice, adult adoptees have fundamentally altered transnational adoption in the West and in South Korea by insisting upon their recognition as a uniquely situated group of individuals whose personhood and citizenship entail particular needs and rights.

As children whose lives were shaped by global economic inequalities and hierarchies of race and power, Korean adoptees possess a constitutive transnationality that demonstrates the ways in which belonging is always a contingent and historical process. Moreover, they exemplify how kinship is practiced and performed within structures of international law and state power that legitimate certain relationships as kin and disallow others, even in light of the heightened geneticization of relatedness. Thus adoptees denaturalize both kinship and citizenship, but rather than representing the global or the potentiality of postnational cosmopolitanism they more often reveal the limitations of that vision in a world order that is profoundly organized around exclusionary boundaries of nation-based citizenship and blood-based kinship. The inequalities that contribute to the problem of abandoned children—poverty, stratified reproduction, global hierarchies of class, race, and gender—are not solved by adoption. Instead, they are replicated across transnational space and interpellate adoptees into dominant ideologies of self, family, and nation.

Notes

NOTES TO INTRODUCTION

1. For the text of this convention, see Hague Conference on Private International Law, http://www.hcch.net.
2. In demographic terminology, "lowest low" refers to countries with total fertility rates below 1.3, which are predicted to experience a 50 percent reduction in the population in less than 45 years. It was first identified as a phenomenon in Western European countries in the 1990s (Kohler, Billari, and Ortega 2002), and since the 2000s, it has come to characterize East Asian fertility patterns, especially in Japan, Taiwan, and South Korea.
3. The policies implemented in January 2007 succeeded in reducing international adoptions dramatically that year. The number of adoptees sent to the United States, which receives the majority of children from Korea, shrank by 30 percent. In 2009 American agencies also slowed Korean placements by restricting their programs to "Korean heritage" families and those who had already adopted internationally. An exception to this was made for adoptions of "waiting children"—that is, noninfant children and those with correctable medical conditions or more severe disabilities.
4. An "eligible orphan" is a child who has lost both parents to death, abandonment, or separation, or who has lost one parent to death, abandonment, or separation, with the remaining parent legally releasing the child for overseas emigration and adoption.
5. Plenary adoption (*adoption plenière*) terminates the original parent-child relationship, and in France this form is contrasted with "simple adoption" (*adoption simple*), which is additive—that is, it retains the validity of the original parent-child relationship and also recognizes the new adoptive relation with respect to inheritance rights and parental authority. Both forms can be distinguished from "open adoptions" (as they are practiced in the United States), in which birth parents and adoptive parents agree to maintain varying degrees of contact for the benefit of the adopted child, but no legally binding contracts are involved.

6. I borrow the idea of missing persons from the Korean adoptee artist kate hers's installation and video *Missing (No Chim)*.
7. Although I cannot attend to all of them, significant differences exist among European adoptees and their American counterparts with respect to dominant racializations, nationalisms, and conceptions of cultural difference and citizenship. Adoptees themselves theorize about the differences between European and American adoptees, often eliding the significant variations that exist within those two geographic categories.
8. "Circumstantial activism" is a term that Marcus (1998) defines as "quite specific and circumstantial to the conditions of doing multi-sited research itself. It is a playing out in practice of the feminist slogan of the political as personal, but in this case it is the political as synonymous with the professional persona, and within the latter, what used to be discussed in a clinical way as the methodological" (98). Marcus distinguishes circumstantial activism from affiliations with or progressive commitments to a particular social movement or the activism of academics claiming a vanguard status within the discipline.
9. Adoptee activists and their advocates often round up this total number to 200,000 based on their own independent research that takes into consideration the higher numbers of incoming adoptees recorded by receiving countries and the fact that many informal adoptions, especially in the first couple of decades, were never officially tabulated.
10. In the context of China's stringent population policy, Ann Anagnost describes the work of government "birth-workers" who use "persuasion through 'thought work' and social pressure, the approved methods of obtaining compliance with what is still policy rather than law," and which are "supplemented by direct appeal to coercive possibilities." Moreover, "coercive measures are made to look not only like persuasion . . . but even like nurturance" (1997: 131). These examples resonate with the narratives that Korean birth parents now tell about how they relinquished their children.
11. Kim and Henderson further argue that Japanese colonialism "delayed any ongoing evolution of an indigenous response to the issue of displaced children. It also opened Korea to a host of foreign social-care interventions, which would ultimately become the methods of intervention employed to the present time. Unfortunately, this fact has confounded the realization of a system that draws on the peculiar strengths and possibilities that existed indigenously thoughout the Chosun Dynasty" (2008: 16).
12. Michel Foucault describes "state racism" as instituting "a break into the domain of life that is under power's control: the break between what must live and what must die" (1997: 254). Thus, sovereign power uses race to justify the death of its own subjects.
13. The South Korean government also classified the statistics of international adoption in 1974, thereby making it impossible for South Korean researchers to

conduct studies of the program. These figures were also kept separately from statistics of emigration and overseas Koreans (cited in Hübinette 2004).

14. According to Wun Jung Kim, the prenatal care for these children was instituted in "response to demand from abroad, mostly from the U.S. and other Western countries" (1994: 143).

NOTES TO CHAPTER 1

1. The adoption of children across national borders goes by several different terms. For Korean terminology, see "Notes on Transliteration, Terminology, and Pseudonyms," in the frontmatter of this volume. In the United States, during the period following the Second World War, the terms "inter-country" and "intercountry" adoption (ICA) were most frequently used to refer to these adoptions. "International adoption" came into usage in the 1970s and is the most commonly cited term today. ICA in the 1950s and 1960s was predominantly "kinship adoption" in which European children were sent for adoption to their extended families due to the social disruptions and dislocations of the Second World War or for greater economic and educational opportunities (Hochfield 1954: 145). A smaller proportion of these children were nonrelative adoptions in which parents in the United States decided to adopt a needy foreign child. International adoption today generally refers to the transfer of nonrelative children into white American homes. The vast majority of these adoptions are also transracial adoptions, a term that came into usage around the adoptions of black and mixed-race children into mostly white families in the United States during the 1960s. In this chapter I will follow the conventions of the period by using intercountry or international adoption interchangeably.
2. As Bertha Holt wrote in the preface to *Bring My Sons from Afar*: "In 1955, when Harry was on his way to Korea, God showed him his directions. In a Tokyo hotel the verses of *Isaiah 43:5, 6 & 7* were revealed to him when he asked for confirmation. 'Fear not, for I am with thee: I will bring thy seed from the east and gather thee from the west; I will say to the north, Give up: and to the south, Keep not back: bring my sons from afar and my daughters from the ends of the earth: Even everyone who is called by my name; for I have created him for my glory. I have formed him; yeah, I have made him' " (1986: iii).
3. Following Harry Holt's death in 1964, Bertha Holt assumed the helm at Holt Adoption Agency (which is now Holt International Children's Services). Following her death in 2000, one of their daughters, Molly Holt, became chairman of Holt Children's Services, which is now an independent entity from the American-based agency (see the Website at www.holt.or.kr). Both Harry and Bertha Holt are buried on the grounds of Holt's Welfare Town in Ilsan, Korea, a facility for disabled children. Holt currently has intercountry adoption programs in fourteen countries and has placed over one hundred thousand children into new families. The Holt mission is still clearly a Christian one: "Holt

International Children's Services is dedicated to carrying out God's plan for every child to have a permanent, loving family" (www.holtintl.org/intro.shtml).

4. See, for instance, some of the critiques published on the Website Transracial Abductees (www.transracial abductees.org).
5. On 16 February 1959 the *Honolulu Star Bulletin* published an article titled "South Korea 'Exports' Children." Thirty years later it would be precisely echoed by Western journalists critiquing South Korea's adoption of children overseas as its largest export commodity. See Choy 2007 on the proxy adoption controversy.
6. The terms "waif" and "mascot" were also common in the Second World War when American soldiers stationed in Europe befriended child victims of the war.
7. The first children were evacuated from Britain in 1940, and after an extended effort by concerned Americans to sway the United States Congress to lift quota restrictions to permit the entry of Jewish children from continental Europe, a few hundred were allowed entry from France. A third effort was made under the Displaced Persons Act of 1948 which privileged the entry of orphaned children, the majority of whom were Jewish children from Eastern Europe. American sectarian organizations took responsibility for the care and placement of these children after their arrival in the United States, often leaving unrepresented children (those not of Jewish, Catholic, or Lutheran affiliation) at a disadvantage. The Church World Service stepped in to help these children, but it is striking how centrally defining religious affiliation was to the matching of these children to institutions and families. An International Social Service internal memo cites that 90 percent of telephone inquiries came from Jewish couples who hoped for the chance to adopt Jewish children. Because Jewish children were not available from Europe or Israel, these couples were asked to think about adopting Korean Amerasian children, especially those who had not been baptized (International Social Service 1957). See also Herman 2001 on the history of religious matching in New York City adoption placements.
8. Goodman 2000 also notes that three hundred Japanese children were adopted overseas annually during the 1990s, with around 20 percent adopted into American homes. An article in the *Daily Yomiuri* on 20 September 2004 about allegations of improper practices by Japanese adoption agencies unduly profiting from overseas adoption reported 106 overseas adoptions between 2000 and 2003.
9. The numbers of mixed-race children in both postwar Japan and postwar Korea were roughly estimated by the government and foreign aid organizations. As reported in the *Chicago Daily Tribune* on 18 February 1952, the *Yomiuri Shinbum* outrageously claimed that there were two hundred thousand "half Japanese waifs" born to Japanese prostitutes and American soldiers and called for America to take up its moral responsibility for these children by adopting them. Abandoned by their mothers, an estimated four thousand of these "occupation

orphans" were being raised in sectarian orphanages by 1952. Moreover, as the children approached school age they provoked social anxiety about their ability to integrate into mainstream Japanese institutions. Against these figures, Graham 1957 cites Japanese government statistics from 1953 that counted three thousand mixed-race children who were not supported by their fathers.

10. For children considered hard to place, usually for reasons of age, two different schemes to relocate them to South America were devised. Miki Sawada, the wife of a Japanese diplomat and founder of the Elisabeth Sanders Home in Tokyo, tried to export young Amerasian men to Brazil. Holt explored a similar plan to send mixed Korean children to Paraguay in the early 1960s. Despite their similar historical origins, Japanese international adoption never attained the scale, scope, visibility, or attendant political controversy that Korean adoptions have garnered over the years.
11. According to Katharine Moon, many women of the first generation of Korean military prostitutes were from poor rural families. They followed the troops during the Korean War and some had been widowed, orphaned, or lost while fleeing during the war. They may have "considered themselves 'fallen women' even before entering prostitution because they had lost social status and self-respect from divorce, rape, sex, and/or pregnancy out of wedlock" (1997: 3). See Yuh (2002) on military camp towns and military brides.
12. The term "GI babies" refers to children fathered by American servicemen and "UN babies" refers to children fathered by members of the UN forces, although the terms were often used interchangeably. In Korean these children were referred to as *honhyŏla* (mixed-blood children), and the term *chŏnjaeng koa* referred generally to war orphans.
13. North Korea also publicly condemned South Korea in 1977 and 1988. Both instances led to reconsideration by the South Korean government of the "adoption problem" (*ibyang munje*). North Korea also had many needy and orphaned children following the war, and they were sent to eastern bloc countries or to Mongolia to be adopted or fostered. According the *Washington Post*, a home was being built to house two hundred North Korean children scheduled to arrive in East Germany in November 1952, with two hundred more soon expected. These children were eventually repatriated to North Korea as adults, and they were honored as war heroes and granted high-ranking government posts.
14. According to records held by the Korean American Voluntary Associations, foreign organizations donated close to $350 million in monetary and material donations between 1950 and 1970 (cited in W. K. Choi 1995: 72).
15. The film, directed by Douglas Sirk, was an opportunity for the South Korean state to capitalize on the photogenic sentimentality of Korean orphans, and twenty-five "real-life" orphans from the original evacuation were flown to Hollywood to appear in the film (*Los Angeles Times* 1956). See the Website of

the Korean War Children's Memorial Project for more details about Operation Kiddy Car (www.koreanchildren.org) and its "real hero," army chaplain Russell Blaisdell.

16. A Proquest search for "Korean orphan" or "Korean waif" brings up more than three hundred articles in major United States newspapers for the decade 1950–1959 and a similar number for the decade 1960–1969.
17. On the Korean end, prior to the writing of a law for the adoption of children by foreigners, releases of the children were obtained from the child's parents or guardians (orphanage directors) and adoptions were certified by local government officials. The Ministry of Foreign Affairs then issued a passport for the child and the United States Consular office issued visas (Minutes of the 25th Meeting of the Joint ROK/KCAC/UNKRA Committee for Child Welfare, 8 April 1954, Seoul, South Korea).
18. As Ota adds further: "Convincing Congress that race neutrality, not race separation, is consistent with American ideals meant shifting the collective notion of belonging to America by highlighting a common humanity that overpowered racial differences. Petitioners, ineligible for membership in the American community, could individually take advantage of the changing tide by portraying themselves as a member of a nuclear family, or an antifascist or anticommunist hero" (2001: 210–11).
19. American military personnel who adopted mixed-race children in Japan accounted for 90 percent of intercountry adoptions in 1954.
20. Mrs. Hong was the director of Child Placement Service (CPS), the government-approved agency that worked closely with ISS to place the first Korean children in American families (Susan T. Pettiss to Ellen T. Visser, 3 February 1955, International Social Service, American Branch papers, Box 35, folder "ISS–Branches Korea 1954-Dec. 1955," Social Welfare History Archives, University of Minnesota). See Berebitsky (2000) on the history of singles adopting in America.
21. And in its final report, the administrator of the Refugee Relief Act described the "Orphan Program" as not only providing new homes for over four thousand destitute children and bringing happiness to many childless American homes, but "the friendly international relations engendered by America's helping hand stretched out to these children were a forward step toward better international understanding and lasting peace in the world" (quoted in Pettiss 1958: 28).
22. Public Law 203, 83rd Congress, H.R. 6481, passed 7 August 1953.
23. Many German children, for instance, were adopted to the United States after the Second World War, but unless the quota for German immigrants was oversubscribed they would not have entered the United States through the RRA (Pettiss 1958). Not only were the immigration laws of the day racist and exclusionary but anti-miscegenation laws in some southern states prohibited adoption across racial lines and segregation laws even prevented some "half-

Oriental" adoptees from attending white-only public schools (Susan T. Pettiss to Grace Rue, 10 August 1955, International Social Service, American Branch papers, Box 35, folder "ISS–Branches Korea 1954–Dec. 1955"). It was not until the *Loving v. Virginia* decision in 1967 that the Supreme Court declared anti-miscegenation laws to be unconstitutional.

24. International Social Service (ISS), first established in Geneva in 1914, was, since the Second World War, a main advocate for refugees and displaced persons. International Social Service–American Branch (ISS–AB) is the main office in the United States. It coordinated the fostering of British children by American families and helped with refugee relocation, but during the twenty-five years following the Second World War, intercountry adoptions became its primary focus. World Adoption International Fund (WAIF) was started in 1954 and became the main fundraising arm for ISS–AB (Ostling 1978: 367–71). Much of its work in the mid to late 1950s was focused on finding and establishing appropriate legal and procedural channels to regulate international adoption and to ensure that these adoptions met basic standards of child welfare. In this chapter ISS refers to the American Branch.
25. As Elaine Tyler May writes, "With the onset of the Cold War, the family surfaced as the ideological center of national culture, while public and community life declined. . . . The fierce pronatalism of the baby-boom years marked infertility as profoundly tragic and voluntary childlessness as downright subversive" (1995: 18).
26. The specter of infertility, or "childlessness" as it was euphemistically referred to, had to be addressed openly by couples, often in embarrassing detail, with social workers who questioned them about their sex lives.
27. Birth mothers who relinquished children in those years organized a support group in the 1970s that openly critiqued the culture of secrecy in American adoption, advocated for opening birth records and reunions, and aimed to debunk the myth that forgetting and moving on after relinquishing a child was "healthy" (Modell 2002). See Solinger 1994 on the implications of race and gender in the treatment of illegitimacy among young black women.
28. Although some cases of single adoptive parents were allowed in Korean adoption, the Korean government's regulations today require couples to be married for at least three years and to demonstrate a stable relationship. Single persons wanting to adopt through state welfare agencies in the 1950s were turned down as they would be "unable to offer a real 'family' to a child," according to one California state social worker in 1957.
29. According to a study in 1956 of children from Europe and Asia who had been placed in white homes by a Boston-based agency, those who expressed interest in "American-Oriental" children were usually couples with children who had a "spiritual motive" to help the child "suffering the social ostracism" (DiVirgilio 1956: 18). But the letters from prospective parents that I read from the South

Korean state archives were often from childless couples or from those hoping to add to their families, sometimes to replace children who had died or even to replace a loved one, either husband or son, who had died in the Korean War.

30. Korean children were adopted exclusively by American families until CPS started a program with Sweden in 1966. Following this program, other European countries began receiving Korean children.
31. Phyllis Woodley to Dr. Howard Rusk, 24 November 1953, Syngman Rhee Documents, VI-4, File 7 #11750086, Yonsei University Library, Seoul, South Korea.
32. Syngman Rhee to Im Byung Jik, 8 April 1954, Syngman Rhee Related Correspondence 6 (1954), "Orphan Adoption Issue" (*koa ibyang munje*), National Institute of Korean History (Kuksa P'yŏnch'an Wiwŏnhoe). Ironically, Syngman Rhee and his Austrian wife never had biological children but instead adopted two full-Korean sons.
33. Syngman Rhee Documents, VI-4, File 6, #11750041.
34. Syngman Rhee Documents, VI-4, File 6, #11750046. This family-centric approach to child preference, that is, designing the family to have the child "fit" by age and gender with the other children, is corroborated by Kim and Reid's study of adoptive families in Minnesota (1970).
35. Syngman Rhee Documents VI-4, File 7, #11750068.
36. Syngman Rhee Documents, VI-4, File 7, #11750072.
37. Syngman Rhee Documents, VI-4, File 7, #11750076.
38. Syngman Rhee Documents, VI-4, File 7, #11750086.
39. Syngman Rhee Documents, VI-4, File 9, #11750186.
40. Syngman Rhee Documents, VI-4, File 9, #11750191.
41. Syngman Rhee Documents, VI-4, File 9, #11750198.
42. A follow-up article in *McCall's*, "Adoption by Picture: A Childless Couple Found the Little Girl They Wanted in the Pages of *McCall's*" (Reid 1958), presents a different story. It claims that Sul Ja was welcomed "home" by the Caseys two years after the initial inquiry. The girl adopted by the Caseys was reunited with her sister and other former orphanage children nearly fifty years later. She learned from them that she was not in fact Sul Ja, but that Sul Ja had stayed at the orphanage.
43. *Oegyo anbu yŏnguwŏn* (Institute of Foreign Affairs and National Security), *Kyung Mu Dae* (Office of the President), "Koa kugoe ibyang 1956–60" (Overseas adoption of orphans, 1956–60), Microfilm roll no. P.0002, File 18, Frame 0001–0250.
44. Syngman Rhee Documents VI-4, File 11, #11750358.
45. In 1949, Pierce founded Great Commission Films, which later became World Wide Pictures under the Billy Graham Evangelistic Association (Hamilton 1980).
46. Syngman Rhee Documents, VI-4, File 11, #11750358.

47. Im Byung Jik to Syngman Rhee, 7 May 1956, Syngman Rhee Related Correspondence 8 (1956), "Report on the Discussion of the Problem of Unwed Mothers and Mixed-Blood Children" (*mihonmo mit honhyŏla munje t'oron pogo*), National Institute of Korean History (Kuksa P'yŏnch'an Wiwŏnhoe).
48. Katharine Moon's work on military camptown (*kijich'on*) women provides a parallel example of how military prostitutes were enrolled by the South Korean state as "instruments of foreign policy," through "people-to-people diplomacy" intended to foster improved relations between the U.S. and South Korea (1997: 84).
49. "There is quite a bit of rivalry and competition among the different agencies, and it is not beyond agencies to bribe or pressure the mothers for the release of these children, and agencies including ISS have to go to find the Korean-Caucasian children by visiting prostitute areas, as it is not a common practice for the mothers to approach the agencies for the release of their children" (SWHA, Box 35, "Korea: Reports and Visits to Korea 1956–," Report on Korea, August 1966, p. 6).
50. Han Hyun Sook, a Korean social worker and longtime adoption professional with Children's Home Society of Minnesota, writes with some remorse and ambivalence in her memoir about her role in intercountry adoptions as a young social worker for ISS in the 1960s: "I misunderstood my job and thought I was supposed to make the birth mothers relinquish their children; I pushed those mothers to sign the papers. . . . The way I tried was to convince those mothers that their children were better off coming with me and being adopted internationally. . . . Back then, the area of social work was relatively new to Korea and so we had no models to follow" (2007: 100–1).
51. SWHA, Box 35, "Korea: Reports and Visits to Korea 1956–," Patricia Nye, Report on Korea, 23–26 March 1976, p. 3.
52. Social Wefare History Archive (SWHA), Box 35, Korea: Reports and Visits to Korea 1956–," Activity Report of ISS Korea, 15–16 April 1966, Geneva, p. 5.
53. SWHA, Box 35, "Korea: Reports and Visits to Korea 1956–," Report on Korea, August 1966, p. 8.
54. But see Han 2007 for a description of the first domestic adoption program in Korea, the Christian Adoption Program of Korea (CAPOK)—an American missionary project that eventually merged with Holt Adoption Agency. Han, through CAPOK, also began the first program for unwed mothers in 1970 and helped to establish Ae Ran Won in 1971 as the first home for unwed mothers.
55. SWHA, Box 35, "Korea: Reports and Visits to Korea 1956–," Patricia Nye, Report on Korea, 23–26 March 1976, p. 2.

NOTES TO CHAPTER 2

1. Other adoptees of the war generation who are exemplars of American success stories are Paul Shinn, a former Washington State senator; Dominic Pangborn,

an artist and the CEO of Pangborn Productions; and Susan Soon-Keum Cox, vice president of Holt International Children's Services. They often serve as representatives of Korean American adoptees in official functions. Paul Shinn was nominated to be the American ambassador to South Korea, and he holds an honorary position on the South Korean National Assembly. Susan Cox has testified to the United States Congress on international adoption, was appointed to President Clinton's Advisory Commission on Asian Americans and Pacific Islanders, and sits on an advisory committee to the UN Hague Convention on Intercountry Adoption.

2. Goffman refers to moral careers in his treatise on stigma in which he states, "Persons who have a particular stigma tend to have similar learning experiences regarding their plight, and similar changes in conception of self—a similar 'moral career' that is both cause and effect of commitment to a similar sequence of personal adjustments" (1963: 32).
3. As Sandra Lee Patton, who is adopted, writes in her study of transracial adoption, "The sense of difference adoption typically fosters makes many of us feel that we constitute our own race or ethnicity, or even that we belong to a separate ontological category of humans" (2000: 6).
4. Kaja Finkler (2001) also notes that the adoptees in her study indicated that they felt like "aliens" due to their lack of information about their biological family medical history.
5. See Volkman 2005b on the construction of "birth culture" by adoptive parents with children from China.
6. As Catherine Ceniza Choy and Gregory Choy note in their analytic treatment of the first anthology of Korean adoptee writing, *Seeds from a Silent Tree* (Bishoff and Rankin 1997), the experiences of growing up in white homes make adoptee narratives of the "Asian face staring back from the mirror" distinct from those of (other) Asian Americans: "While the scholarly contributions of Asian-American studies and other ethnic studies scholars render the cultural meanings of this racialized face (i.e., not white, not American) seemingly obvious, for adopted Koreans, the face in the mirror is also a touchstone of memory—for some, literally—of a place they once called home" (2003: 271).
7. The moral careers of adoptees have taken on a normative dimension in which particular stages are taken to be typical and predictable. A common story of early alienation, for instance, is related to first experiences in primary school in which adoptees learned that they were different from other students. As one adoptee from Denmark recounted in Nathan Adolfson's film *Passing Through*, she couldn't understand why other students teased her because she could only see the ways in which she looked the same as her classmates—"I was counting eyes, and noses, and mouths. I just couldn't understand how they could tell I was different . . . But, well, I know now."

NOTES TO CHAPTER 3

1. A survey from 1999, as reported in the conference program for the Gathering of the First Generation of Korean Adoptees, found that out of 167 respondents, 80 percent of female adoptees and roughly 50 percent of male adoptees had spouses or partners who were "Caucasian," and that 45 percent of men and more than one-third of women thought of themselves as "Caucasian" when they were adolescents. As many reported, they did not have the opportunity to meet and date Asians or Asian Americans in the homogeneously white suburbs and towns where they were raised, so what demographers might regard as a hypergamous strategy to partner with whites was not seen as a choice at all. Whereas one-dimensional theories of immigration assume that outmarriage, based on a norm of co-ethnic marriage, is an indicator of racial integration, for adoptees their dating and marriage preferences were an effect of the reproduction of hegemonic racializations in their white families and communities. As Jiannbin Shiao and Mia Tuan find in their study of Korean American adoptee dating patterns, the majority "treated dating Whites as endogamous and dating Asians as exogamous" (2006: 20). Yet these patterns are beginning to change, especially among those who are currently involved in adoptee activities. As adoptees have had more opportunities to meet and date each other, other Korean ethnics, or people of Asian descent, marriages have also followed.
2. These countries are the United States, France, Sweden, Norway, Denmark, the Netherlands, Belgium, the United Kingdom, Luxembourg, Germany, Italy, Switzerland, Canada, Australia, and Korea.
3. As a percentage of the total adoptee population, ten thousand participants comprises just 5 percent, but as a percentage of the total adult population these individuals represent closer to 20 percent of those adopted between 1953 and 1980.
4. Dani Meier (1998) uncovers some of the historical, institutional, and cultural reasons for Minnesota's high rate of adoptions from Korea. Notable is the pivotal role that a United States–trained social worker, Mrs. Han Hyun Sook, played in linking Korean agencies with the Minnesota-based Children's Home Society of Minnesota. In addition, Minnesotan parents were pioneers in transracial domestic adoptions from the 1950s, and when those adoptions contracted due to political controversy in the early 1970s agencies began expanding their overseas programs to satisfy the demand for adoptable children (see Han 2007).
5. That Savasta's reputation as the "Italian kid" serves as a sign of his fully American socialization demonstrates how Asians, unlike prior waves of European immigrants such as Italians have not, despite their class mobility, become assimilated through a process of whitening but rather continue to be positioned as aliens, or "forever foreigners" (Tuan 1999).

6. Korean immigration to the United States totaled 35,800 in the 1960s and exploded to more than 270,000 by the 1970s.
7. "Nostalgia without memory" is a phrase used by Arjun Appadurai (1996) to describe how global mediascapes (re)produce mythic origins and collective memory for diasporic social formations.
8. The adoptee David Miller's poem "Tightrope" (1997) suggests the treacherousness of this position: "Walking a tightrope / Pulled on both sides / Korea / America / For if I fall either way / I lose a part of me."
9. Recently, as the next generation of adoptees has come of age, adoptees in their twenties have begun to take on larger leadership roles.

NOTES TO CHAPTER 4

1. The Hague Convention has provided a standard in international adoption policy, but each signatory nation determines how it will implement the convention's recommendations and how it will enforce adoption standards via existing immigration laws and social welfare policies.
2. At the 2004 Gathering in particular, repeated iterations of "for adoptees, by adoptees" obscured the actual reliance by the planning committee upon larger (nonadoptee) institutions and entities for sponsorship and organizational expertise.
3. The Gathering program was designed by the Korean American adoptee Laura Ganarelli.
4. Adoptees from several European countries were also present.
5. I thus view in retrospect my access to the workshop in 1999 as being exceptional and an effect of the counterpublic's then emergent nature.
6. There is a range of opinions about adoption agencies that have become increasingly polarized in recent years, especially regarding Holt International Children's Services. Holt is the largest and longest-running international adoption agency in the world, and it has placed more Korean children in the United States and Europe than any other agency. At one extreme, adoptees may express a sense of kinship with the Holt family, which was headed for over four decades by Bertha, or "Grandma," Holt after the passing of Harry Holt in 1957. These adoptees are proud of being a "Holt baby," and they participate enthusiastically in Holt-sponsored Korean culture camps, motherland tours to Korea, volunteer work at the Holt facility in Ilsan, South Korea, and trips to escort babies from Korea to the homes of their new adoptive parents—thus participating in the reproduction of their own transnational journeys. On the other extreme some, like the adoptee activists of the Website Transracial Abductees, compare Holt and its range of postadoption services to the prison-industrial complex—a system that "incarcerates" adoptees and prevents them from recognizing their own subordinate position in colonialist and imperialist structures of power.

7. Susan Cox told me that she is well aware of adoptee feelings toward agencies and her own role as a target of criticism: "And I will admit that there are times that that is really hurtful. What people don't know is how hard [I]—fight may be too strong a word, but—continue to raise the flag, that there are so many of the things that would not have happened if there wasn't someone from the inside making sure that it did. And I don't say that except to just explain that sometimes it really is difficult. There was a time when I was much more pro-agency than I am now. . . . I mean, I understand, I fully understand why there is this agency-them vs. us kind of thing, and it's because I think agencies haven't done a very good job of really *truly* taking adoptees seriously."
8. This kind of entrenchment among adoptees recalls Edward Said's "Reflections on Exile" in which he locates a connection between the painful loss of exile and the powerful pull of nationalism: "Exiles feel . . . an urgent need to reconstitute their broken lives, usually by choosing to see themselves as part of a triumphant ideology or a restored people. The crucial thing is that a state of exile free from this triumphant ideology—designed to reassemble an exile's broken history into a new whole—is virtually unbearable, and virtually impossible in today's world" (1990: 360).

NOTES TO CHAPTER 5

1. As Arthur Kleinman and Veena Das note, "In our contemporary political context, with its emphasis on the 'politics of recognition,' such work is oriented toward creating a public sphere in which the hurts of the victims may be voiced: dramatic gestures in which representatives of the state have offered 'regrets' or 'apologies' for historical wrongs committed on behalf of the state come to mind. At one level such gestures are important because they signify an acknowledgment of the 'crimes' of the state even when it has acted within the 'law.' As performative gestures, however, the 'apologies' acquire force only if notions of 'sincerity' and 'authenticity' can be read in these gestures and if there can be an agreement on the identification of communities as perpetrators and victims as these are crafted through such gestures" (2000: 13).
2. The quotes from the minister's speech are taken from the English version that was read by the official interpreter of the Gathering to the adoptee audience.
3. President Kim included adoptees in his inaugural address as one of the twenty-five points that his administration would address. The apology and recognition of adoptees need also be contextualized within other repressed counternarratives to the nation that emerged following Korea's transition to a democratic government. Comfort women, labor movement organizers, North Korean sympathizers, student radicals, divided families, and other groups have had their histories legitimized and aired publicly since the early 1990s.
4. In 2006 Korean adoptions were outpaced by adoptions from Ethiopia.
5. The phrase "Our Adoptee, Our Alien" was first used in 1999 for an art action

and awareness-raising campaign organized by Mihee and kate hers, an adoptee performance artist, as part of their KimLeePark Productions artivist collective. KimLeePark combines the three most common surnames in Korea. The collective's art interventions have included street theater performances that depict an allegorical story of a displaced adoptee returning to the place of her birth and a petition-signing campaign to support the inclusion of adoptees in overseas Koreans visa legislation.

6. The exhibit was co-curated with Hyung-Mi Gwon, an art student at Kyung-hee University. It was sponsored by Kyung-hee University's graduate school of NGO studies, and the galleries that hosted the exhibitions, Keumsan Gallery and Dongsanbang Gallery. In the past decade, there has been an efflorescence of artwork by adopted Korean artists working in poetry, film and video, painting, mixed media, photography, textile design, and animation. Notably, all but a few of the artists are female.
7. For a comprehensive account of pop cultural representations of Korean adoptees in Korea, see Hübinette 2005.
8. There are an estimated 7 million ethnic Koreans residing outside of Korea. The greatest numbers are in China (2.4 million), the United States (2 million), Japan (900,000), the former Soviet republics (532,000), and Central and South America (107,000) (Ministry of Foreign Affairs and Trade 2005). Approximately half of the 107,000 estimated overseas Koreans living in Europe are adoptees.
9. Under the leadership of Lee Kwang Kyu since January 2004, OKF has expanded its programs to include formerly "alienated" (*sooedoen*) Koreans—that is, Korean women who married American soldiers (*kukche kyŏrhonja*), their Eurasian or Amerasian children, and Korean adoptees.
10. The OKA's criterion for determining eligibility for the status of overseas Koreans initially excluded those Koreans who had left Korea before the national division and the establishment of the Republic of Korea in 1948 by requiring proof of former South Korean citizenship. Because it effectively excluded Korean Chinese and Korean Russians, the law was deemed illegal in 2001 for violating the equality principle in the national constitution. For a discussion of the controversy over the constitutionality of the OKA, see Park and Chang 2005, which includes the results of a survey that asked Koreans their opinions of whether or not various categories of overseas Koreans were "Korean," to which more than 76 percent responded that adoptees are "Korean."
11. In addition to facilitating the financial investments of Korean Americans, the law was related to the influx of ethnic Koreans from China who filled in the increasing labor shortages in the so-called 3-D jobs (dirty, dangerous, and demeaning) (see H. Park 2005).
12. In 2005, the Adoption Information Center was renamed Global Adoption Information and Post Service (GAIPS). As an attempt to centralize information for returning adoptees searching for biological family as well as part of the

government's efforts to promote domestic adoption, GAIPS services overlap with those of preexisting NGOs and adoption agencies (see chapter 6).

13. Korea is also referred to as the "motherland" (*moguk*) in contemporary usage for 1.5-generation and second-generation Koreans, and perhaps most commonly when referring to Korean as one's mother tongue (*mogukŏ*). But *choguk* (often translated as fatherland, and literally meaning ancestral land) is also found in media reports that refer to adoptees' or other overseas Koreans' relationships to Korea. It is most often associated with patriotic discourse, such as *choguk t'ongil*, or national reunification. *Koguk*, literally the "native country," carries a sentimental valence and is sometimes employed to describe the nostalgic return of elderly Koreans.

14. Mihee Nathalie Lemoine also served as a major hub for adoptees, especially for adoptee artists and those from Europe. In addition, through her organization KOA, she has helped more than six hundred adoptees search for biological family.

15. It is impossible to determine how many adoptees return to Korea every year, or how many are living there on a long-term basis, as Korean immigration records track entry by nationality and do not treat adoptees as a separate category. In 2001, the Ministry of Health and Welfare reported nearly three thousand adoptees visiting their adoption agencies (which would also include younger adoptees traveling with their parents), and these numbers are undoubtedly growing.

16. Scholars of Korean nationalism (Em 1999; Grinker 1998; Jager 1996; Robinson 1988; Shin, Freda, and Yi 1999) have discussed the powerful ideology of ethnic homogeneity that has its roots in the Japanese colonial era, during which anti-imperialist nationalist movements drew strength from a belief in the distinctiveness of Korean personhood, race, and nation, despite the lack of territorial sovereignty. The notion of *minjok* thus encompasses conceptions of both nation and race, and it is grounded in a history (the origin myth of T'angun), language, and culture considered to be unique to the Korean people. Following the national division, Korean cultural nationalism became a key part of the ideological struggle between North and South Korea, with both states drawing upon the notion of unitary nation (*tanil minjok*) and shared blood (*hyŏlt'ong*) to argue for the legitimacy of either the ROK or the DPRK as the sovereign representative for the Korean people (Shin, Freda, and Yi 1999). Moon 1998 provides a necessary feminist intervention into dominant constructions of the nation, in which the purported homogeneity of the people obscures the marginalization of women to the private realm of the family, subordinate to family patriarchs. Under constant attack by feminists since its legislation in 1960, the patriarchal Family Law, which in 2004 was finally deemed unconstitutional, has legitimated male dominance through the family head system (*hojujedo*), thereby underwriting a nationalist vision of the nation as a community of men. Throughout

Korea's modern history, feminist opposition to the law has been countered by neoconservative politicians who argue that the family head system is embedded in Korea's Confucian tradition and acts as a bulwark against the encroachments of Westernization. As Seungsook Moon writes, in this view "the Korean nation is essentially a familial community in which members have collective orientation as opposed to 'Western individualism' " (1998: 54).

17. Indeed, in my own experience as a passenger I was also sometimes questioned about where I was from, and often used it as an opportunity to talk about my research and gain insight into everyday perceptions of the "adoption issue" (*ibyang munje*).
18. Hagland, who was adopted as an infant with his twin brother in 1961, went to Korea at the age of forty-two. He had no memories of Korea and few expectations of assimilating into Korean society. In fact, similar to other adoptees—some adopted at older ages, some like Hagland, as infants—he had traveled widely in his life, and, in part a strategy to deal with his own racial difference and semiforeignness, he explored and immersed himself in European cultures. As he put it, he had "gone through all the philiae"—Francophilia, Hispanophilia, even Germanophilia.
19. The "Korean public" is a phrase often used by adoptees when discussing strategies for changing the status and perceptions of adoptees in Korea. The South Korean media has been a key player in helping to bring adoptee voices and critiques to the public, as well as in helping adoptees to locate biological family. What is interesting about the expression the "Korean public" is that it indexes the felt marginality of adoptees from the national imaginary or public sphere, the "we" of *uri nara* (our nation), of which they are distinctly not a part.
20. In early 2005 a scandal broke out around English Spectrum, an employment and information Website for English teachers in Korea. A column titled "Ask the Playboy" offered advice and salacious anecdotes about the "playboy's" exploits with Korean women (see Choi 2005).
21. For a detailed historical context and analysis of English-language education in Korea, see Park and Abelmann 2004. Collins 2005 explores the contradictory cultural significance of English in colonial and postcolonial Korea. In 2006 the Ministry of Education further amplified English instruction programs in the public schools by extending the start of English education from elementary school to primary school.
22. According to Michael Seth, *hagwŏn*, or cram schools, especially those concentrating on English education, expanded dramatically in the early 1990s. Seth cites statistics that show that whereas only 4 percent of elementary school students were enrolled in private English-language *hagwŏn* in 1990, by 1997 that figure had risen to 50 percent (2002: 188).
23. In 2006 a *Korea Times* article described the formation of the first ever English teachers' union in Korea, which was mobilized after the founders' employer,

Berlitz Korea, announced that it would only hire Caucasian teachers from North America (Drechsler 2006). Although outrageously discriminatory, Berlitz Korea's proposed hiring policy simply made explicit what many adoptees and foreigners in Korea already recognize to be a tacit and widely applied hierarchy based on race, nationality, and gender. Native speakers of English are assumed to be white North Americans, and they are the most highly sought after and well compensated, followed by Korean Americans and adoptees. Men seem to be more highly valued than women in all racial and national categories.

24. As the responses to Mihee's email query revealed, the subject of suicide and depression in the adoptee community is highly controversial and touches upon a more divisive debate among adoptees about the politics and moral value of international adoption.

25. The most comprehensive epidemiological study of suicide among international adoptees in Sweden was published in 2002 by a group of Swedish researchers who found that international adoptees were three to four times more likely to have serious mental health issues, including suicide and suicide attempts, than were native-born Swedes. A subsequent study examined suicide among domestic Swedish adoptees, nonadopted native-born Swedes, and internationally adopted Swedes for the entire cohort born between 1963 and 1973 and living in Sweden since 1987. This study has forced the rethinking of adoption policy in Sweden, and it also has served to fuel adoptee critiques of transnational adoption (see Hjern, Lindblad, and Vinnerljung 2002; von Borczyskowski et al. 2006).

26. Confucian ancestral rites, referred to generally as *chesa*, have been adapted and altered significantly under the influence of Christianity. As Okpyo Moon (2003) demonstrates through ethnographic case studies, *ch'udosik*, or Christian-style ancestor ceremonies, introduce a newly invented ritual practice that exists in tension with traditional Confucian rites. *Ch'umosik* and ch'udosik are used interchangeably to refer to Christian memorial services, with some confusion regarding the distinction between them. Public memorial services in cases of national tragedy such as the Kwangju Massacre on 18 May 1980 are referred to as ch'umosik, and memorials held by family members for departed loved ones are referred to as either ch'umosik or ch'udosik.

27. Mihee's original statement, in French, is as follows: "Si vous envoyez les infants corée aux etrangés, ne pensez pas que vous faîtes de *yuhak*. C'est pas du tout le *yuhak*; c'est l'adoption. Ça veut dire, c'est pas réversible."

28. Korea's citizenship policies are based on the model of jus sanguinis, or blood-based national belonging. According to Eungi Kim, despite Korea's below-replacement fertility rate, which reached a low of 1.13 in 2003, the government "still clings to nearly a zero-immigration policy, shaped by the . . . cultural ideology that extols Korea's ethnic and linguistic homogeneity and cultural uniqueness and accordingly disdains foreign workers as permanent residents,

let alone citizens. Though the government willingly exploits foreign workers for domestic economic growth, it extends no welcome to join the national community" (2005: 16–17).

NOTES TO CHAPTER 6

1. Those agencies are Holt Adoption Agency, Social Welfare Society (SWS, formerly Child Placement Service), Korea Social Service (KSS), and Eastern Social Welfare Society (ESWS).
2. A central question that arises is one of profit motive and the "best interests of the child." The low rates of domestic adoption are attributed in part to the profit motive and "goal displacement" since, at $2,000 per domestic adoption, agencies have less fiscal incentive to find domestic adopters. In addition, an audit in 2001 of the four agencies found that some of the fees (for foster care, medical expenses, and hospital delivery expenses, among other things) that are paid for by the central government were also being charged to domestic adoptive parents.
3. South Korea's development rested on a tightly collusive relationship between the state, banks, and *chaebol* (multinational business conglomerates).
4. During this period, according to Myungsook Woo, social welfare expenditures were heavily weighted toward education rather than health or social security. In addition, President Park Chung Hee promoted personal thrift and diligence as solutions to poverty as the welfare budget was drastically reduced, which in part was influenced by antagonistic relations with North Korea and the equation of welfare generosity with communism (2004: 30). Thus, Woo concludes that welfare policies during South Korea's industrialization were "biased toward the better-off who were critically important to the maintenance of state power and the achievement of state policy" (69).
5. Postadoption services in the United States primarily are composed of programs designed to help adoptees connect to their cultural heritage or "birth culture" (Volkman 2005b). In Europe (the Scandinavian countries in particular), postadoption services have a stigmatizing connotation as they tend to be equated with mental health counseling and failed adoptions. The Danish adoptee Kirsten Sloth (2007) has been critical about the overemphasis on adjustment in transnational adoption research in which any deviation from the "normal" family is considered to be pathological.
6. The Adoption Information Center, which was officially opened in 1999, was to be jointly run by the four adoption agencies. It remained largely inactive for five years, however, until it was renamed Global Adoption Information Post Services (GAIPS) in late 2004. In 2009, GAIPS, which was also largely inactive, was renamed K-Care, in preparation to become the central authority for international adoption, in compliance with the Hague Convention, which South Korea had yet to ratify.

7. Susan Cox described how hearing stories from adoptees who had found Korean family at the first Gathering provoked many adoptee participants to begin to wonder about their own possibilities for finding family members in Korea. As Cox noted: "In those workshops, when they were hearing—most of them, for the first time—[statements like] 'Well, actually, people have been able to find family,' [or] 'Well, yeah, there [was information about birth family] we were able to learn about,' [there was] kind of an excitement, or an 'aha' moment like, 'Really, you could do this?' "
8. A social work student who was considering a focus in adoption volunteered at Holt's summer program and became close friends with a number of adoptees in the early 2000s. She told me that she was asked to leave the program because the administrators felt that she had become too close with the adoptees. She could only speculate that the reason was that her boss feared that she would share information with her adoptee friends.
9. The improvement in record keeping since the late 1980s, when the majority of children relinquished for adoption were born to unwed mothers, has made it somewhat easier for these adoptees to conduct searches as adults.
10. Nancy Scheper-Hughes describes the Brazilian adoption system of the 1980s wherein poor *favela* women were tricked or coerced into sending their children for a better life in foreign families. In like manner Korean women as well may not have easily, or fully consciously, given up their children for adoption. In ways that resonate with the Korean adoption system, Scheper-Hughes suggests that "the altruistic and religious ideology of the adoption institution masked the social process that allowed the 'rescue' of children from women, who, given the choice and material support, might have preferred to raise them themselves" (1990: 62).
11. Also in 1996 the dramatic and highly symbolic case of Brian Bauman hit the newsstands. Bauman, a Korean American adoptee and United States Air Force cadet, was diagnosed with leukemia in 1995 and was in desperate need of a bone marrow transplant. His search for Korean relatives or possible donors was highly publicized by the Korean media, which provoked a massive blood drive. In the process, he found four half-siblings. The eventual donor was a member of the South Korean military who, in a display of transnational military solidarity, was found in a blood drive during which every member of the military was tested (Vickery 1998).
12. Don eventually withdrew from the group that would become GOA'L in March 1998, but the organization continued to have a relationship with Sŏ Kyŏng Sŏk.
13. Official unemployment rates during the crisis were 8 percent (up from 3 percent before the crisis), although studies that incorporated women at home and students who wanted to work into their calculations estimated the unemployment rate to be closer to 20 percent (Song 2006: 41–42). Several years after the economic crisis, the high rates of unemployment among young Koreans con-

tinued to be a cause for concern. In 2003 the base unemployment rate was 3.3 percent, but the category of unemployed youth (those in their twenties) was 7.1 percent with male college graduates and female high school graduates identified as those having the most difficulty finding work (Choi 2004).

14. The terms "ibyangin" and "ibyangdoen han'gukin" (overseas adopted Korean) have almost entirely replaced "ibyanga" in media accounts about adult adoptees since the late 1990s.

15. Tai Soon Bai 2007 attributes shifts in adoption consciousness in Korea to the highly publicized returns of adult adoptees in the 1990s. Overseas adoptee stories influenced adoptive parents in Korea to consider their children's desire and rights to know their origins, thus paving the way for the open adoption movement.

16. To further illustrate this point, when describing my research as a study of adult adoptees to people in the United States I was sometimes asked whether I meant that they had been adopted as adults.

17. In the statistics of overseas Koreans, however, it is notable that whereas other ethnic Koreans are divided up and categorized by nation of residence, adoptees are counted in a separate category. Hence, despite differences in culture and language among them, they are taken to comprise a distinct subset of the Korean diaspora.

18. In 2004 one of Lee Kwang Kyu's first steps upon taking the helm at OKF was to bring so-called international brides (*kukje kyŏrhonja*) and their mixed-race children into the overseas Koreans category. Thus, alongside adoptees these women and their offspring are now incorporated as other formerly estranged (*sooedoen*) Koreans who have been excluded from official accounts of Korean history. This group includes women who married Europeans after emigrating for work as nurses in Germany as well as Korean women who married American soldiers, who are often assumed to be former military camp town sex workers and thus largely marginalized or shunned by other Korean immigrants (see Yuh 2004).

19. Regarding Korean NGOs, Pan Suk Kim writes the following: "Generally, an NGO's financial resources come from membership fees, profits from projects grants, donations, and financial assistance from institutions, but most NGOs experience financial troubles. Except for a few large NGOs, most have relatively small numbers of members and low membership fees" (2002: 287).

20. The Ministry of Foreign Affairs and Trade does not oversee adoption policy but seeks to count, regulate, and discipline, through OKF, overseas Koreans. The Ministry of Health and Welfare (reorganized and renamed the Ministry for Health, Welfare and Family Affairs in 2008) handles actual overseas adoption policy, collects statistics about adoption placements, oversees the four adoption agencies, and makes policy recommendations to the government. Nevertheless, one French adoptee I spoke with was convinced that the state would

be able to silence anyone it wanted to should the OKF participants articulate anti-adoption or anti-government sentiments.

21. As I argued in an essay written shortly after the 2001 tour (E. Kim 2005), adoptees were included in a newly expanded vision of the global Korean family. But given their histories of displacement, cultural training through folklorized versions of Korea served less to create identifications among adoptees with Korea and Korean culture than it did to highlight adoptee difference and disidentification with official Korean histories and nationalisms.
22. Finding Korean family for adoptees is not included in this agenda. Under pressure from adoptee participants, however, the OKF program, which began as a motherland tour that was identical to those for other kyop'o groups, now also offers birth family search options, including adoption agency consultations and visits to orphanages and homes for unwed mothers. Jeannie Hong also, as she puts it, "as a human being" rather than as an employee of the government, helped dozens of adoptees with their searches.
23. For instance, adoptees who come to Korea without any relatives, Korean contacts, or without a Korean corporate sponsor encounter difficulties with basic services—buying a cell phone contract or opening a bank account—which require a native Korean guarantor.
24. Often compared to liberation theology, minjung theology is a people's movement indigenous to South Korea that emerged in the late 1970s as part of the left-wing Korean Protestant response to the repressiveness of the Park Chung Hee regime. Minjung theology promotes social justice by actively grounding its perspectives in the experiences of the minjung (common people) with oppression and alienation.
25. According to Chung-Shin Park (2003: 194), Saemunan Church was one of the main churches that functioned as a gathering place for anti-government activities and democratic organizing following the installation of the Yusin Constitution.
26. Judith Butler describes the "constitutive outside" in the context of the normative injunctions of sexed identities. Performativity does not denote a free play of willful and agentive identifications but rather is a discursive process constrained by the historicity of discourses and norms that "circumscribe the domain of intelligibility." The constitutive outside, she writes, is "the unspeakable, the inviable, the nonnarrativizable that secures and, hence, fails to secure the very borders of materiality. The normative force of performativity—its power to establish what qualifies as 'being'—works not only through reiteration but through exclusion as well. And in the case of bodies, those exclusions haunt signification as its abject borders or as that which is strictly foreclosed: the unlivable, the nonnarrativizable, the traumatic" (1993: 188).
27. Don Roloefs has, in fact, been successful in his own forays into the tourism business with the company he founded in 2003 that specializes in tours to

South and North Korea. Catering to adoptees and non-adoptees alike he also makes special efforts on behalf of adoptee clients who are interested in viewing their adoption files or in finding more information about their Korean family.

28. I follow Aihwa Ong's definition of neoliberal rationalities in which "cultural discourses converge with the rationality of the market, conflating the moral value of liberal egoism with one's command over capital. The neoliberal discourse that increasingly defines citizenship in economic terms, by insisting that citizenship is the civic duty of individuals to reduce their burden on society and to build up their human capital, becomes a vital supplement to the classic liberal rights–based definition of citizenship" (2003b: 15).

NOTES TO CHAPTER 7

1. MPAK promotes domestic adoption but does not oppose international adoption. The founder, Steven Morrison, is concerned that the quota system, which ties the number of international adoptions in one year to the number of domestic placements in the previous year, will result in an overall decline in adoptions, unless the domestic numbers are improved.
2. South Korea's child welfare spending in 2007 was equivalent to 0.2 percent of the GDP, which was the lowest amount among OECD members (Bae 2007, cited in Kim and Henderson 2008).
3. Laurel Kendall (1996: 123) describes how cohabitation before marriage had become a common practice by the 1970s among rural and working-class urban Koreans. Rather than the "traditional" arranged marriages, this new generation entered into love relationships and often postponed the marriage ritual due to limited financial resources.
4. See Brian 2004 for adoption agency practices in the United States.
5. Following Liisa Malkki I would argue that the issue is not one regarding compassion or the lack thereof but rather it is one of recognizing the dehistoricizing *effects* of "humanitarianism" on individuals—namely, that of "producing anonymous corporeality and speechlessness" (1996: 389). Humanitarianism itself, Malkki underscores, must be contextualized within complex histories of charity, international relations, colonialism, missionization, development, and peacekeeping interventions that have reproduced these effects over time.
6. South Korea's rapid modernization and economic development confounds the modernist teleology at the heart of transnational adoption, making the ongoing practice of overseas adoption problematic and a seeming contradiction. This contradiction destabilizes the logic of humanitarianism and empowers adult adoptees, liberated from the myth of the orphan, to critique the system. Nevertheless, as I demonstrate, the orphan legacy continues to affect adoptees' political subjectivity, in part because dominant discourses of adoption recall Korea's not-so-distant third world past.

Works Cited

Abelmann, Nancy. 2003. *The Melodrama of Mobility: Women, Talk, and Class in Contemporary South Korea*. Honolulu: University of Hawaii Press.

Abelmann, Nancy, and John Lie. 1995. *Blue Dreams: Korean Americans and the Los Angeles Riots*. Cambridge, Mass.: Harvard University Press.

Adolfson, Nathan. 1998. *Passing Through*. Video. San Francisco: Center for Asian American Media.

Agamben, Giorgio. 1998. *Homo Sacer: Sovereign Power and Bare Life*. Trans. Daniel Heller-Roazen. Stanford, Calif.: Stanford University Press.

Ahmed, Sara. 2008. "Multiculturalism and the Promise of Happiness." *New Formations* 63:121–37.

Ahn, Byung-ook. 2002. "The Significance of Settling the Past in Modern Korean History." *Korea Journal* 42 (3): 7–17.

Altstein, Howard, and Rita Simon. 2000. *Adoption across Borders: Serving the Children in Transracial and Intercountry Adoptions*. Lanham, Md.: Rowman and Littlefield.

Anagnost, Ann. 1997. *National Past-Times: Narrative, Representation, and Power in Modern China*. Durham, N.C.: Duke University Press.

——. 2000. "Scenes of Misrecognition: Maternal Citizenship in the Age of Transnational Adoption." *positions: east asia cultures critique* 8 (2): 389–421.

Anderson, Benedict. 1991. *Imagined Communities: Reflections on the Origin and Spread of Nationalism*. New York: Verso.

——. 1992. "The New World Disorder." *New Left Review* 193 (May/June): 3–13.

Appadurai, Arjun. 1996. *Modernity at Large: Cultural Dimensions of Globalization*. Minneapolis: University of Minnesota Press.

Asbury, William F. 1954. "Military Help to Korean Orphans: A Survey Made for the Commander-in-Chief, United Nations Forces, Far East, and for the Chief of Chaplains of the United States Army." Richmond, Va.: Christian Children's Fund, www.koreanchildren.org.

Auerbach, Nina. 1975. "Incarnations of the Orphan." *ELH* 42 (3): 395–419.

Augé, Marc. 1995. *Non-Places: An Introduction to an Anthropology of Supermodernity*. Trans. John Howe. New York: Verso.

Bai, Tai Soon. 2007. "Korean Child Welfare: The Practice of Overseas Adoption." In *International Korean Adoption: A Fifty-Year History of Policy and Practice*, ed. K. J. S. Bergquist, M. E. Vonk, D. S. Kim, and M. Feit. New York: Haworth Press.

Barthes, Roland. 1957. "The Great Family of Man." In *Mythologies*. Trans. Annette Lavers. New York: Noonday Press.

Basch, Linda, Nina Glick-Schiller, and Cristina Szanton Blanc. 1994. *Nations Unbound: Transnational Projects, Postcolonial Predicaments, and Deterritorialized Nation-States*. Langhorn, Pa.: Gordon and Breach.

Benjamin, Walter. 1968. *Illuminations*. New York: Schocken Books.

Berebitsky, Julie. 2000. *Like Our Very Own: Adoption and the Changing Culture of Motherhood*. Lawrence: University Press of Kansas.

Berlant, Lauren. 1997. *The Queen of America Goes to Washington City: Essays on Sex and Citizenship*. Durham, N.C.: Duke University Press.

Bhabha, Homi. 1994. *The Location of Culture*. London: Routledge.

Bishoff, Tonya, and Jo Rankin, eds. 1997. *Seeds from a Silent Tree*. San Diego: Pandal Press.

Bornstein, Erica. 2001. "The Verge of Good and Evil: Christian NGOs and Economic Development in Zimbabwe." *PoLAR: Political and Legal Anthropology Review* 24 (1): 59–77.

Borshay Liem, Deann. 2000. *First Person Plural*. Video. San Francisco: Center for Asian American Media.

Bourdieu, Pierre. 1991. "Rites of Institution." In *Language and Symbolic Power*. Cambridge, Mass.: Harvard University Press.

Bowie, Fiona, ed. 2004. *Cross-Cultural Approaches to Adoption*. London: Routledge.

Boyden, Jo. 1990. "Childhood and the Policy Makers: A Comparative Perspective on the Globalization of Childhood." In *Constructing and Reconstructing Childhood*, ed. Allison James and Alan Prout. London: Falmer Press.

Brettell, Caroline. 1993. *When They Read What We Write: The Politics of Ethnography*. Westport, Conn.: Bergin and Garvey.

Brian, Kristi. 2004. "This Is Not a Civic Duty: Racial Selection, Consumer Choice, and the 'Multiculturalist' Bind in the Production of Korean-American Adoption." Ph.D. diss., Temple University.

———. 2007. "Choosing Korea: Marketing 'Multiculturalism' to Choosy Adopters." In *International Korean Adoption: A Fifty-Year History of Policy and Practice*, ed. K. J. S. Bergquist, M. E. Vonk, D. S. Kim, and M. Feit. New York: Haworth Press.

Briggs, Laura. 2003. "Mother, Child, Race, Nation: The Visual Iconography of Rescue and the Politics of Transnational and Transracial Adoption." *Gender and History* 15 (2): 179–200.

———. 2006. "Making 'American' Families: Transnational Adoption and U.S. Latin

America Policy." In *Haunted by Empire: Geographies of Intimacy in North American Empire*, ed. Ann Stoler. Durham, N.C.: Duke University Press.

Bruining, Mi Ok Song. 1989. "The Politics of International Adoption: Made in Korea." *Sojourner: The Women's Forum* 14 (9): 18.

Brysk, Alison. 2004. "Children across Borders: Patrimony, Property, or Persons?" In *People Out of Place: Globalization, Human Rights, and the Citizenship Gap*, ed. A. Brysk and G. Shafir. New York: Routledge.

Butler, Judith. 1993. *Bodies That Matter: On the Discursive Limits of "Sex."* New York: Routledge.

——. 2003. "Afterword: After Loss, What Then?" In *Loss: The Politics of Mourning*, ed. David Eng and David Kazanjian. Berkeley: University of California Press.

Carbado, Devon W. 2005. "Racial Naturalization." *American Quarterly* 57 (3): 633–58.

Carp, Wayne. 1998. *Family Matters: Secrecy and Disclosure in the History of Adoption*. Cambridge, Mass.: Harvard University Press.

Carsten, Janet, ed. 2000. *Cultures of Relatedness: New Approaches to the Study of Kinship*. Cambridge: Cambridge University Press.

——. 2004. *After Kinship*. Cambridge: Cambridge University Press.

——. 2007. "Constitutive Knowledge: Tracing Trajectories of Information in New Contexts of Relatedness." *Anthropological Quarterly* 80 (2): 403–26.

Cartwright, Lisa. 2003. "Photographs of 'Waiting Children': The Transnational Adoption Market." *Social Text* 21 (1): 83–109.

——. 2005. "Images of 'Waiting Children': Spectatorship and Pity in the Representation of the Global Social Orphan in the 1990s." In *Cultures of Transnational Adoption*, ed. T. A. Volkman. Durham, N.C.: Duke University Press.

Castañeda, Claudia. 2002. *Figurations: Child, Bodies, Worlds*. Durham, N.C.: Duke University Press.

Chakerian, Charles. 1968. *From Rescue to Child Welfare*. New York: Church World Service.

Chappell, HyunJu Crystal. 2004. "A Common Thread: Korean Adoptee Networks Growing Worldwide." In *Community: Guide to Korea for Overseas Adopted Koreans*, ed. E. Kim. Seoul: Overseas Koreans Foundation.

Chicago Daily Tribune. 1952. "Jap Paper Says Yanks Father 200,000 Waifs: Asks Homes in America for Such Children." 18 February, 16.

——. 1953. "Brings Home Orphan." 12 November, C15.

Children's Bureau. 1955. *Protecting Children in Adoption: Report of a Conference Held in Washington, June 27 and 28, 1955*. Washington, D.C.: U.S. Department of Health, Education and Welfare, Social Security Administration.

Chira, Susan. 1988a. "Seoul Journal; Babies for Export: And Now the Painful Questions." *New York Times*. 21 April, A4.

——. 1988b. "The Seoul Olympics: U.S. Olympic Reporting Hits a Raw Korean Nerve." *New York Times*. 28 September, A1.

Choi, Sun-young. 2005. "Web Messages Draw Koreans' Wrath." *JoongAng Daily*, www.joongangdaily.joins.com, 17 January.

Choi, Won Kyu. 1995. "Oeguk min'gan wŏnjo tanch'e hwaltonggwa han'guk sahoe saŏp palch'ŏne mich'in yŏnghyang" (Activities of foreign voluntary agencies and their influences upon social work development in Korea). Ph.D. diss., Seoul National University.

Choi Youngsup. 2004. "Structural Factors behind Korea's Youth Unemployment." *Korea Focus* 12 (1), http://www.koreafocus.or.kr.

Choy, Catherine Ceniza. 2007. "Institutionalizing International Adoption: The Historical Origins of Korean Adoption in the United States." In *International Korean Adoption: A Fifty-Year History of Policy and Practice*, ed. K. J. S. Bergquist, M. E. Vonk, D. S. Kim, and M. Feit. New York: Haworth Press.

Choy, Catherine Ceniza, and Gregory Paul Choy. 2003. "Transformative Terrains: Korean American Adoptees and the Social Constructions of an American Childhood." In *The American Child*, ed. C. Levander and C. Singley. New Brunswick, N.J.: Rutgers University Press.

Christian Science Monitor. 1953. "GIs Clothe South Korean Waifs." 17 October, 6.

———. 1956. "President Widens Door for Korean Orphans." 30 October, 16.

Clement, Thomas Park. 1998. *The Unforgotten War: Dust of the Streets*. Bloomfield, Ind.: Truepeny Publishing Company.

———. 2005. "Not Bad, for a War Orphan." *Korean Quarterly* 9 (1): 39–40.

Clifford, James. 1988. *The Predicament of Culture: Twentieth-Century Ethnography, Literature, and Art*. Cambridge, Mass.: Harvard University Press.

———. 1997. "Traveling Cultures." In *Routes: Travel and Translation in the Late Twentieth Century*. Cambridge, Mass.: Harvard University Press.

Close, Kathryn. 1953. *Transplanted Children: A History*. New York: United States Committee for the Care of European Children.

Colen, Shellee. 1995. "'Like a Mother to Them': Stratified Reproduction and West Indian Childcare Workers and Employers in New York." In *Conceiving the New World Order: The Global Politics of Reproduction*, ed. G. Ginsburg and R. Rapp. Berkeley: University of California Press.

Collins, Samuel Gerald. 2005. "'Who's This *Tong-il*?' English, Culture and Ambivalence in South Korea." *Changing English* 12 (3): 417–29.

Cornell, Drucilla. 1999. "Reimagining Adoption and Family Law." In *Mother Troubles: Rethinking Contemporary Maternal Dilemmas*, ed. J. Hanigsberg and S. Ruddick. Boston: Beacon Press.

Cox, Susan Soon-Keum, ed. 1999. *Voices from Another Place: A Collection of Works from a Generation Born in Korea and Adopted to Other Countries*. St. Paul, Minn.: Yeong and Yeong Book Company.

Cvetkovich, Ann. 2003. "Legacies of Trauma, Legacies of Activism: ACT UP's Lesbians." In *Loss: The Politics of Mourning*, ed. D. L. Eng and D. Kazanjian. Berkeley: University of California Press.

Daily Yomiuri. 2004. "Government to Probe Kids' Adoptions Overseas." 20 September, 1.

Deuchler, Martina. 1992. *The Confucian Transformation of Korea: A Study of Society and Ideology*. Cambridge, Mass.: Harvard University Press.

DiVirgilio, Letitia. 1956. "Adjustment of Foreign Children in their Adoptive Homes." *Child Welfare* (November): 15–21.

Dong A Ilbo (*Dong A Daily*). 1952. "Honhyŏla ch'ongsu chosa ttaro suyonghal kyehoek ch'ujin" (Research on the total number of mixed-race children; Plan for separate accommodation pushed through), 18 August.

——. 1953. "Honhyŏla silt'ae chosa hŭk baek hwang sam saek ŭro" (Research on the actual situation of mixed-race children, following three colors, white, black, yellow). 29 July.

——. 1955. "Hŏyŏnge ttŭn imin hŭimang" (Vainglorious hope for emigration). 10 January.

Dorow, Sara, ed. 1999. *I Wish for You a Beautiful Life: Letters from the Korean Birth Mothers of Ae Ran Won to Their Children*. St. Paul, Minn.: Yeong and Yeong Book Company.

——. 2006. *Transnational Adoption: A Cultural Economy of Race, Gender, and Kinship*. New York: New York University Press.

Douglas, Mary. 1984 [1966]. *Purity and Danger: An Analysis of the Concepts of Pollution and Taboo*. London: Ark Paperbacks.

Drechsler, Geoff. 2006. "English Teachers' Union Wins Concessions." *Korea Times* (English edition). 1 March, 5.

Durkheim, Emile. 1951 [1897]. *Suicide: A Study in Sociology*. New York: Free Press.

Ebony. 1955. "How to Adopt Korean Babies: Three Hundred Oriental-Negro Foundlings Are Available for Adoption by Americans." September, 30–33.

Edstrom, Eve. 1955. "Agencies Troubled by Independent Adoptions." *Washington Post* and *Times Herald*, 18 October, 29.

Ehrenreich, John. 1985. *The Altruistic Imagination: A History of Social Work and Social Policy in the United States*. Ithaca: Cornell University Press.

Ekbladh, David. 2004. "How to Build a Nation." *Wilson Quarterly* (winter): 12–20.

Em, Henry. 1999. "*Minjok* as a Modern and Democratic Construct: Sin Ch'aeho's Historiography." In *Colonial Modernity in Korea*, ed. G. W. Shin and M. Robinson. Cambridge, Mass.: Harvard University Asia Center.

Eng, David. 2003. "Transnational Adoption and Queer Diasporas." *Social Text* 21 (3): 1–37.

Escobar, Arturo. 1995. *Encountering Development: The Making and Unmaking of the Third World*. Princeton, N.J.: Princeton University Press.

Fabian, Johannes. 1983. *Time and the Other: How Anthropology Makes Its Object*. New York: Columbia University Press.

Fassin, Didier. 2007. "Humanitarianism as Politics of Life." *Public Culture* 19 (3): 499–520.

Finkler, Kaja. 2001. "The Kin in the Gene: The Medicalization of Family and Kinship in American Society." *Current Anthropology* 42 (2): 235–63.

Fisher, William. 1997. "Doing Good? The Politics and Antipolitics of NGO Practices." *Annual Review of Anthropology* 26: 439–64.

Fonseca, Claudia. 2003. Patterns of Shared Parenthood among the Brazilian Poor. *Social Text* 21 (1): 111–27.

Foucault, Michel. 1979. "Governmentality." *Ideology and Consciousness* 6: 9–21.

——. 1990. *The History of Sexuality: An Introduction.* New York: Vintage.

——. 1997. *"Society Must Be Defended": Lectures at the Collège de France, 1975–1976.* New York: Picador.

Foucault, Michel, Luther H. Martin, Huck Gutman, and Patrick H. Hutton. 1988. *Technologies of the Self: A Seminar with Michel Foucault.* Amherst: University of Massachusetts Press.

Fraser, Nancy. 1992. "Rethinking the Public Sphere: A Contribution to the Critique of Actually Existing Democracy." In *Habermas and the Public Sphere,* ed. C. Calhoun. Cambridge, Mass.: MIT Press.

——. 1997. *Justice Interruptus: Critical Reflections on the "Postsocialist" Condition.* New York: Routledge.

——. 2005. "Transnationalizing the Public Sphere." Republic Art project, http://www.republicart.net.

Gailey, Christine Ward. 2000. "Ideologies of Motherhood and Kinship in U.S. Adoption." In *Ideologies and Technologies of Motherhood: Race, Class, Sexuality, Nationalism,* ed. H. Ragoné and F. W. Twine. New York: Routledge.

Gallagher, Ursula. 1958. *Social Workers Look at Adoption: A Report of a Meeting on the Role of the Social Agency and the Social Worker Called by the Children's Bureau, May 27–29, 1957.* Washington, D.C.: U.S. Department of Health, Education, and Welfare, Social Security Administration.

Gill, Brian. 2002. "Adoption Agencies and the Search for the Ideal Family, 1918–1965." In *Adoption in America: Historical Perspectives,* ed. E. W. Carp. Ann Arbor: University of Michigan Press.

Gilroy, Paul. 2000. *Against Race: Imagining Political Culture beyond the Color Line.* Cambridge, Mass.: The Belknap Press of Harvard University Press.

Ginsburg, Faye. 1989. *Contested Lives: The Abortion Debate in an American Community.* Berkeley: University of California Press.

Ginsburg, Faye, and Rayna Rapp. 1991. "The Politics of Reproduction." *Annual Review of Anthropology* 20: 311–43.

——. 1995. "Introduction: Conceiving the New World Order." In *Conceiving the New World Order: The Global Politics of Reproduction,* ed. F. Ginsburg and R. Rapp. Berkeley: University of California Press.

Global Korean Network of Los Angeles (GKN-LA). 1997. *Proceedings of the Second Annual GKN-LA Winter Conference, 22–23 February 1997.* http://www.gkn-la.net.

Goffman, Erving. 1963. *Stigma: Notes on the Management of Spoiled Identity*. New York: Simon and Schuster.

Goodman, Roger. 2000. *Children of the Japanese State: The Changing Role of Child Protection Institutions in Contemporary Japan*. Oxford: Oxford University Press.

Graham, Lloyd B. 1957. "Children from Japan in American Adoptive Homes." Paper presented at the National Conference on Social Welfare, 84th Annual Forum, Philadelphia, 19–24 May.

Grinker, Roy Richard. 1998. *Korea and Its Futures: Unification and the Unfinished War*. New York: St. Martin's Press.

Gupta, Akhil, and James Ferguson. 1992. "Beyond 'Culture': Space, Identity and the Politics of Difference." *Cultural Anthropology* 7 (1): 6–23.

——, eds. 1997. *Anthropological Locations: Boundaries and Grounds of a Field Science.* Berkeley: University of California Press.

Ha, Kyu-man. 2002. "Rethinking the Government's Role in Overseas Adoption" (Kukche ibyangŭlwihan chŏngbu yŏkhalŭi chaego). Paper presented at the Korean Association for Public Administration, Spring Conference, Chŏ'nan, South Korea, 19–20 April.

Habermas, Jürgen. 1989. *The Structural Transformation of the Public Sphere: An Inquiry into a Category of Bourgeois Society*. Trans. Thomas Burger with Frederick Lawrence. Cambridge, Mass.: MIT Press.

Hagland, Mark. 2002. "Seoul Train." *Korean Quarterly* 6 (2): 20–23.

Hall, Stuart. 1991. "Old and New Identities." In *Culture, Globalization and the World System*, ed. Anthony King. Minneapolis: University of Minnesota Press.

Hamilton, John Robert. 1980. "An Historical Study of Bob Pierce and World Vision's Development of the Evangelical Social Action Film." Ph.D. diss., University of Southern California.

Han, Hyun Sook. 2007. *Many Lives Intertwined: A Memoir.* St. Paul, Minn.: Yeong and Yeong Book Company.

Harvey, David. 1990. *The Condition of Postmodernity.* Cambridge, Mass.: Blackwell.

Helmreich, Stefan. 1992. "Kinship, Nation, and Paul Gilroy's Concept of Diaspora." *Diaspora* 2 (2): 243–49.

Herman, Ellen. 2001a. "The Difference Difference Makes: Justine Wise Polier and Religious Matching in Twentieth-Century Child Adoption." *Religion and American Culture* 10 (1): 57–98.

——. 2001b. "Families Made by Science: Arnold Gesell and the Technologies of Modern Child Adoption." *Isis* 92 (4): 684–715.

——. 2002. "The Paradoxical Rationalization of Modern Adoption." *Journal of Social History* 36 (2): 339–85.

——. 2008. *Kinship by Design: A History of Adoption in the Modern United States.* Chicago: University of Chicago Press.

Herrmann, Kenneth J. Jr., and Barbara Kasper. 1992. "International Adoption: The Exploitation of Women and Children." *Affilia* 7 (1): 45–58.

Hershiser, Kate. 1998. "Calling Card (after Adrian Piper)." In *Voices from Another Place*, ed. Susan Soon-Keum Cox. St. Paul, Minn.: Yeong and Yeong Book Company.

Hjern, A., F. Lindblad, and B. Vinnerljung. 2002. "Suicide, Psychiatric Illness, and Social Maladjustment in International Adoptees in Sweden: A Cohort Study." *Lancet* 360:443–48.

Hochfield, Eugenie. 1954. "Problems of Intercountry Adoptions." *Children* 1 (4): 143–47.

Hollingsworth, Leslie Doty. 2003. "International Adoption among Families in the United States: Considerations of Social Justice." *Social Work* 48 (2): 209–17.

Holm, Tim. 2005. "President's Corner." Asian Adult Adoptees of Washington (AAAW) http://www.aaawashington.org.

Holt, Bertha. 1956. *The Seed from the East.* As told to D. Wisner and H. Albus. Eugene, Ore.: Holt International Children's Services.

——. 1986. *Bring My Sons from Afar.* Eugene, Ore.: Holt International Children's Services.

Honig, Elizabeth. 2005. "Phantom Lives, Narratives of Possibility." In *Cultures of Transnational Adoption*, ed. T. A. Volkman. Durham, N.C.: Duke University Press.

Honolulu Star Bulletin. 1959. "South Korea 'Exports' Children." 16 February.

Howell, Signe. 2001. "Self-Conscious Kinship: Some Contested Values in Norwegian Transnational Adoption." In *Relative Values: Reconfiguring Kinship Studies*, ed. S. Franklin and S. McKinnon. Durham, N.C.: Duke University Press.

——. 2007. *The Kinning of Foreigners: Transnational Adoption in a Global Perspective.* Oxford: Berghahn Books.

Hübinette, Tobias. 2004. "Korean Adoption History." In *Guide to Korea for Overseas Adopted Koreans*, ed. E. Kim. Seoul: Overseas Koreans Foundation.

——. 2005. "Comforting an Orphaned Nation: Representations of International Adoption and Adopted Koreans in Korean Popular Culture." Ph.D. diss., Stockholm University.

International Social Service (ISS). 1960. *Adoption of Oriental Children by White American Families.* New York: Child Welfare League of America.

Jager, S. M. 1996. "A Vision for the Future; or, Making Family History in Contemporary South Korea." *positions: east asia cultures critique* 4 (1): 31–58.

Jo, Sunny (Sunny Johnson). 2004. "The Creation and Rise of KAD as a Separate Identity and Nation." In *Community: Guide to Korea for Overseas Adopted Koreans*, ed. Eleana Kim. Seoul: Overseas Koreans Foundation.

Joseph, Miranda. 2002. *Against the Romance of Community.* Minneapolis: University of Minnesota Press.

Kane, Saralee. 1993. "The Movement of Children for International Adoption: An Epidemiologic Perspective." *Social Science Journal* 30 (4): 323–39.

Kelsky, Karen. 2001. *Women on the Verge: Japanese Women, Western Dreams.* Durham, N.C.: Duke University Press.

Kendall, Laurel. 1996. "Getting Married in Korea: Of Gender, Morality, and Modernity." Berkeley: University of California Press.

——. 2002. "Introduction." In *Under Construction: The Gendering of Modernity, Class, and Consumption in the Republic of Korea,* ed. L. Kendall. Honolulu: University of Hawaii Press.

——. 2005. "Birth Mothers and Imaginary Lives." In *Cultures of Transnational Adoption,* ed. T. A. Volkman. Durham, N.C.: Duke University Press.

Kim, Choon Soon. 1988. *Faithful Endurance: An Ethnography of Family Dispersal in Korea.* Tucson: University of Arizona Press.

Kim, Dong Soo. 1978. "Issues in Transracial and Transcultural Adoption." *Social Casework* (October): 477–86.

Kim, Eleana. 2001. "Korean Adoptee Autoethnography: Refashioning Self, Family, and Finding Community. *Visual Anthropology Review* 16 (1): 43–70.

——. 2004. "Gathering 'Roots' and Making History in the Korean Adoptee Community." In *Local Actions: Cultural Activism, Power, and Public Life in America,* ed. M. Checker and M. Fishman. New York: Columbia University Press.

——. 2005. "Wedding Citizenship and Culture: Korean Adoptees and the Global Family of Korea." In *Cultures of Transnational Adoption,* ed. T. A. Volkman. Durham, N.C.: Duke University Press.

Kim, Elaine H. 2002. "Teumsae e-kki-in yosong: Korean American Women between Feminism and Nationalism." *Review of Korean Studies* 5 (2): 29–44.

Kim, Elaine H., and Chungmoo Choi. 1998. *Dangerous Women: Gender and Korean Nationalism.* New York: Routledge.

Kim, Eun-Shil. 2005. "Itaewon as an Alien Space within the Nation-State and a Place in the Globalization Era." *Korea Journal* 45 (3): 34–64.

Kim, Eungi A. 2005. "Low Cultural Receptivity to Foreigners in Korea: The Case of Transnational Migrant Workers." *Korea Observer* 36 (1): 1–20.

Kim, Hi Taik, and Elaine Reid. 1970. "After a Long Journey: A Study on the Process of Initial Adjustment of the Half and Full Korean Children Adopted by American Families, and the Families' Experiences with These Children during the Transitional Period." Masters thesis, University of Minnesota.

Kim, Hosu. 2007. "Television Mothers: Lost and Found in Search and Reunion Narratives." In *Proceedings of the First International Korean Adoption Studies Research Symposium,* ed. Kim Park Nelson, Eleana Kim and Lene Myong Peterson. Seoul: International Korean Adoptee Associations.

Kim, Hyuk-Rae. 2000. "The State and Civil Society in Transition: The Role of Non-Governmental Organizations in South Korea." *Pacific Review* 13 (4): 595–613.

Kim, Inchoon, and Changsoon Hwang. 2002. "Defining the Nonprofit Sector: South Korea." Working Papers of the Johns Hopkins Comparative Nonprofit Sector Project, no. 41. Baltimore: Johns Hopkins Center for Civil Society Studies.

Kim, Jaeeun. 2006. "Incorporating Koreans Abroad: The Politics of Membership in the 'Divided Nation.'" Paper presented at the seminar Theory and Research in Comparative Social Analysis, University of California, Los Angeles, November 16.

Kim, Jung Woo, and Terry Henderson. 2008. "History of the Care of Displaced Children in Korea." *Asian Social Work and Policy Review* 2 (1): 13–29.

Kim, Kyŏng Su. 2004. "50 Years of Overseas Adoption" (*Haeoe ibyang 50 nyŏn*). *Weekly Chosun* (*Chugan Chosun*). 12 August, 38–42.

Kim, Pan Suk. 2002. "The Development of Korean NGOs and Governmental Assistance to NGOs." *Korea Journal* 42 (2): 279–303.

Kim, Penny, Richard Shaefer, and Charles Mills. 2003. *Though Bombs May Fall: The Extraordinary Story of George Rue, Missionary Doctor in Korea.* Nampa, Idaho: Pacific Press.

Kim, Samuel S. 2000. *Korea's Globalization.* Cambridge: Cambridge University Press.

Kim, Seong-Nae. 2000. "Mourning Korean Modernity in the Memory of the Cheju April Third Incident." *Inter-Asia Cultural Studies* 1 (3): 461–76.

Kim, Soe-Jung. 2005. "Overseas Adoptees Find Mutual Support." *JoongAng Daily* (English edition). 19 December, 6.

Kim, Wun Jung. 1994. "International Adoption: A Case Review of Korean Children." *Child Psychiatry and Human Development* 25 (3): 141–54.

Kim, Young-Hoon. 2003. "Self-Representation: The Visualization of Koreanness in Tourism Posters during the 1970s and the 1980s." *Korea Journal* 43 (1): 83–105.

Kim Harvey, Youngsook. 1983. "Minmyŏnŭri." In *Korean Women: View from the Inner Room*, ed. Laurel Kendall and Mark Peterson. New Haven, Conn.: East Rock Press.

Kim Yi, Eunhee. 2001. "Mothers and Sons in Modern Korea." *Korea Journal* 41 (4): 5–27.

Klein, Christina. 2003. *Cold War Orientalism: Asia in the Middlebrow Imagination, 1945–1961*. Berkeley: University of California Press.

Kleinman, Arthur, and Veena Das. 2000. "Introduction." In *Violence and Subjectivity*, ed. Veena Das, Arthur Kleinman, Mamphela Ramphele, and Pamela Reynolds. Berkeley: University of California Press.

Kohler, Hans-Peter, F. C. Billari, and J. A. Ortega. 2006. "Low Fertility in Europe: Causes, Implications, and Policy Options." In *The Baby Bust: Who Will Do the Work? Who Will Pay the Taxes?*, ed. Fred R. Harris. Lanham, Md.: Rowman and Littlefield.

Koo, Hagen. 1993. "Strong State and Contentious Society." In *State and Society in Contemporary Korea*, ed. Hagen Koo. Ithaca, N.Y.: Cornell University Press.

Korea Times. 2005. "Korea's Private Education Bill, 2.9% of GDP." 14 September, 1.

Lankov, Andrei. 2008. "Miss Mom Symbolizes Dynamic Family Change." *Korea Times*, 24 March. http://www.koreatimes.co.

Latour, Bruno. 1993. *We Have Never Been Modern.* Trans. Catherine Porter. Cambridge, Mass.: Harvard University Press.

———. 1995. *Reassembling the Social: An Introduction to Actor-Network-Theory.* Oxford: Oxford University Press.

Lee, Aruna. 2006. "New Immigration Strategy: Koreans Send Children to America for Adoption." *New America Media,* 25 January. http://news.newamericamedia.org.

Lee, Inch'ŏl, and Minhyŏk Park. 2006. "If They Could, 25% of Koreans Say They Would Migrate for Education" (Kungmin 25% kyoyuk imin, kihoe toemyŏn kagetta). *Dong A Ilbo.* 31 March, 1.

Lee, Kwang Kyu. 1999. *Overseas Koreans.* Seoul: Jimoondang Publishing Company.

Lee, Richard M. 2003. "The Transracial Adoption Paradox: History, Research, and Counseling Implications of Cultural Socialization." *Counseling Psychologist* 31 (6): 711–44.

Leifsen, Elsbeth. 2004. "Person, Relation and Value: The Economy of Circulating Ecuadorian Children in International Adoption." In *Cross-Cultural Approaches to Adoption,* ed. Fiona Bowie. London: Routledge.

Leinaweaver, Jessica. 2007. "On Moving Children: The Social Implications of Andean Child Circulation." *American Ethnologist* 34 (1): 163–80.

Lemoine, Mihee Nathalie, ed. 2001. *Overseas Korean Artists' Yearbook (OKAY Book).* Seoul: JinSol Books.

———. 2004. "Artist's Statement." In *Our Adoptee, Our Alien.* Exhibition catalogue. Seoul: Art Camp.

Lewin, Tamar. 1990. "South Korea Slows Export of Babies for Adoption." *New York Times.* 12 February, B10.

Lifton, Betty Jean. 1994. *Journey of the Adopted Self: A Quest for Wholeness.* New York: Basic Books.

Los Angeles Times. 1953a. "Korean Waif Becomes Real American Boy." 10 January, 19.

———. 1953b. "First Korean War Baby Brought Here by Nurse." 21 December, 6.

———. 1956. "Korean Orphans Arrive and Meet New Parents." 13 June, 1.

Louie, Andrea. 2000. "Re-territorializing Transnationalism: Chinese Americans and the Chinese Motherland." *American Ethnologist* 27 (3): 645–69.

———. 2004. *Chineseness across Borders.* Durham, N.C.: Duke University Press.

Lovelock, K. 2000. "Intercountry Adoption as Migratory Practice." *International Migration Review* 34 (3): 907–49.

Lowe, Lisa. 1996. *Immigrant Acts: On Asian American Cultural Politics.* Durham, N.C.: Duke University Press.

Maira, Sunaina. 2002. *Desis in the House: Indian American Youth Culture in New York City.* Philadelphia: Temple University Press.

Malkki, Liisa. 1994. "Citizens of Humanity: Internationalism and the Imagined Community of Nations." *Diaspora* 3 (1): 41–68.

——. 1995. *Purity and Exile: Violence, Memory, and National Cosmology among Hutu Refugees in Tanzania*. Chicago: University of Chicago Press.

——. 1996. "Speechless Emissaries: Refugees, Humanitarianism, and Dehistoricization." *Cultural Anthropology* 11 (3): 377–404.

Mannheim, Karl. 1993 [1952]. "The Problem of Generations." In *From Karl Mannheim*, ed. K. H. Wolff. 2nd ed. New Brunswick, N.J.: Transaction Publishers.

Marcus, George. 1998. *Ethnography through Thick and Thin*. Princeton, N.J.: Princeton University Press.

——. 1999. "Critical Anthropology Now: An Introduction." In *Critical Anthropology Now: Unexpected Contexts, Shifting Constituencies, Changing Agendas*, ed. G. Marcus. Santa Fe, N.M.: School of American Research Press.

Masson, Judith. 2001. "Intercountry Adoption: A Global Problem or a Global Solution?" *Journal of International Affairs* 55(1): 141–66.

May, Elaine Tyler. 1988. *Homeward Bound: American Families in the Cold War Era*. New York: Basic Books.

——. 1995. *Barren in the Promised Land: Childless Americans and the Pursuit of Happiness.* New York: Basic Books.

McCall's. 1953. "Warmth for the Orphans of Korea." October, 16.

McClintock, Anne. 1995. *Imperial Leather: Race, Gender and Sexuality in the Colonial Contest*. New York: Routledge.

Meier, Dani. 1998. "Loss and Reclaimed Lives: Cultural Identity and Place in Korean-American Intercountry Adoptees." Ph.D. diss., University of Minnesota.

Miller, David. 1997. "Tightrope." In *Seeds from a Silent Tree*, ed. Tonya Bishoff and Jo Rankin. San Diego: Pandal Press.

Ministry for Health, Welfare and Family Affairs (MIHWAF). 2009. "The Current State of Domestic and International Adoption" (*kungnaeoe ibyang hyŏnhwang*). Seoul: Ministry for Health, Welfare and Family Affairs.

Ministry of Foreign Affairs and Trade, South Korea (MOFAT). 2005. "The Current State of Overseas Koreans, 2005" (*2005 nyŏndo chaeoe tongp'o hyŏnhwang*). Seoul: South Korean Ministry of Foreign Affairs and Trade.

Mitchell, Timothy. 1991. "The Limits of the State: Beyond Statist Approaches and Their Critics." *American Political Science Review* 85 (1): 77–96.

Modell, Judith S. 1994. *Kinship with Strangers: Adoption and Interpretations of Kinship in American Culture*. Berkeley: University of California Press.

——. 2002. *A Sealed and Secret Kinship: The Culture of Policies and Practices in American Adoption*. New York: Berghahn Books.

Modell, Judith S., and Naomi Dambacher. 1997. "Making a 'Real' Family: Matching and Cultural Biologism in American Adoption." *Adoption Quarterly* 1 (2): 3–33.

Modell, Judith S., and John Terrell. 1994. "Anthropology and Adoption." *American Anthropologist* 96 (1): 155–61.

Moon, Katharine H. S. 1997. *Sex among Allies: Military Prostitution in U.S.-Korea Relations.* New York: Columbia University Press.

Moon, Okpyo. 2003. "Ancestors Becoming Children of God: Ritual Clashes between Confucian Tradition and Christianity in Contemporary Korea." In *Korean Anthropology: Contemporary Korean Culture in Flux*, ed. Korean National Commission for UNESCO. Elizabeth, N.J.: Hollym International.

Moon, Seungsook. 1998. "Begetting the Nation: The Androcentric Discourse of National History and Tradition in South Korea." In *Dangerous Women: Gender and Korean Nationalism*, ed. Elaine Kim and Chungmoo Choi. New York: Routledge.

——. 2005. *Militarized Modernity and Gendered Citizenship in South Korea*. Durham, N.C.: Duke University Press.

Nelkin, Dorothy, and M. Susan Lindee. 1995. *The DNA Mystique: The Gene as a Cultural Icon*. New York: W. H. Freeman.

New York Times. 1953. "Waiting for that Letter" (photo). 20 October, 5.

——. 1954. "Korean Orphan Baptized Here." 11 January, 16.

——. 1958. "Korean Orphan, 9, Gets Fresh Start." 21 January, 33.

Nopper, Tamara Kil-ja Kim. 2004. "Transracial Adoptions, White Supremacy and the Communities that Suffer." Solidarity, Yahoo! Groups, groups.yahoo.com.

Novas, Carlos, and Nikolas Rose. 2000. "Genetic Risk and the Birth of the Somatic Individual." *Economy and Society* 29 (4): 485–513.

Oh, Arissa. 2005. "A New Kind of Missionary Work: Christians, Christian Americanists and the Adoption of Korean GI Babies, 1955–1961." *Women's Studies Quarterly* 33 (3/4): 161–88.

Oh, John K.-C. 1999. *Korean Politics: The Quest for Democratization and Economic Development*. Ithaca, N.Y.: Cornell University Press.

Ong, Aihwa. 1996. "Cultural Citizenship as Subject-Making: New Immigrants Negotiate Racial and Ethnic Boundaries." *Current Anthropology* 37 (5): 737–62.

——. 1999. *Flexible Citizenship: The Cultural Logics of Transnationality*. Durham, N.C.: Duke University Press.

——. 2003a. "Cyberpublics and Diaspora Politics among Transnational Chinese." *Interventions* 5 (1): 82–100.

——. 2003b. *Buddha Is Hiding: Refugees, Citizenship, the New America*. Berkeley: University of California Press.

Ostling, Mary L. 1978. "The International Social Service–American Branch (ISS–AB)." In *Social Service Organizations*, vol. 1., ed. Peter Romanofsky. Westport, Conn.: Greenwood Press.

Ota, Nancy K. 2001. "Private Matters: Family and Race and the Post–World War II Translation of 'American.'" *International Review of Social History* 46 (supplement): 209–34.

Overseas Koreans Foundation (OKF). 2003. "Summer Cultural Training Program for Overseas Adopted Koreans." Brochure. Seoul: Overseas Koreans Foundation.

——. 2004. *Community: Guide to Korea For Overseas Adopted Koreans*, ed. Eleana Kim. Seoul: Overseas Koreans Foundation.

——. 2006. *International Korean Adoptee Resource Book.* Seoul: Overseas Koreans Foundation.

Paley, Julia. 2001. *Marketing Democracy: Power and Social Movements in Post-Dictatorship Chile.* Berkeley: University of California Press.

Park, Chung-a. 2006. "Singles Can Adopt Children." *Korea Times.* 18 July. http://www.koreatimes.co.kr.

Park, Chung-Shin. 2003. *Protestantism and Politics in Korea.* Seattle: University of Washington Press.

Park, Hyun Ok. 1998. "Ideals of Liberation: Korean Women in Manchuria." In *Dangerous Women: Gender and Korean Nationalism,* ed. Elaine Kim and Chungmoo Choi. New York: Routledge.

——. 2001. "Segyehwa: Globalization and Nationalism in Korea." *Journal of the International Institute* 4 (1). http://hdl.handle.net/2027/spo.4750978.0004.105.

——. 2005. "Repetition, Comparability and the Indeterminate Nation: Korean Migrants in the 1920s and 1990s." *boundary* 2 32 (2): 227–51.

Park, In Sun. 1998. "People Who Search" (Ppurirŭl ch'atnŭn saramdŭl). Seoul: Hana Medical Publishing.

——. 2000. "Looking after Our Child with Our Hands." Unpublished paper.

Park, Jung-Sun, and Paul Y. Chang. 2005. "Contention in the Construction of a Global Korean Community: The Case of the Overseas Koreans Act." *Journal of Korean Studies* 10 (1): 1–27.

Park, So Jin, and Nancy Abelmann. 2004. "Class and Cosmopolitan Striving: Mothers' Management of English Education in South Korea." *Anthropological Quarterly* 77 (4): 645–72.

Park, Soon Ho. 1994. "Forced Child Migration: Korea-Born Intercountry Adoptees in the United States." Ph.D. diss., University of Hawaii.

——. 1995. "Spatial Distribution of Korea-Born Adoptees in the United States." *Journal of the Korean Geographical Society* 30 (4): 411–28.

Park Nelson, Kim. 2007. "Adoptees as 'White' Koreans: Identity, Racial Visibility and the Politics of Passing among Korean American Adoptees." In *Proceedings of the First International Korean Adoption Studies Research Symposium,* ed. Kim Park Nelson, Eleana Kim, and Lene Myong Peterson. Seoul: International Korean Adoptee Associations.

Park Nelson, Kim, Eleana Kim, and Lene Myong Peterson, eds. 2007. *Proceedings of the First International Korean Adoption Studies Research Symposium.* Seoul: International Korean Adoptee Associations.

Passaro, Joanne. 1997. "'You Can't Take the Subway to the Field!' 'Village' Epistemologies in the Global Village." In *Anthropological Locations: Boundaries and Grounds of a Field Science,* ed. A. Gupta and J. Ferguson. Berkeley: University of California Press.

Patterson, Wayne. 1994. *The Korean Frontier in America: Immigration to Hawaii, 1896–1910.* Honolulu: University of Hawaii Press.

Patton, Sandra Lee. 2000. *BirthMarks: Transracial Adoption in Contemporary America*. New York: New York University Press.
Perry, Twila. 1998. "Transracial and Intercountry Adoption: Mothers, Hierarchy, Race and Feminist Legal Theory." *Yale Journal of Law and Feminism* 10: 101.
Peterson, Mark. 1977. "Some Korean Attitudes toward Adoption." *Korea Journal* 17 (12): 28–31.
——. 1996. *Korean Adoption and Inheritance: Case Studies in the Creation of a Classic Confucian Society*. Ithaca, N.Y.: Cornell University Press.
Pettiss, Susan T. 1954. "Intercountry Adoptions Offer New Challenge." *Child Welfare* 32 (9): 13–14.
——. 1958. "Effect of Adoption of Foreign Children on U.S. Adoption Standards and Practices." *Child Welfare* 37 (7): 27–32.
Pupavac, Vanessa. 1998. "The Infantilisation of the South and the UN Convention on the Rights of the Child." *Human Rights Law Review* 3 (2): 3–8.
Rapp, Rayna. 2001. "Gender, Body, Biomedicine: How Some Feminist Concerns Dragged Reproduction to the Center of Social Theory." *Medical Anthropology Quarterly* 15 (4): 466–77.
Rapp, Rayna, and Faye Ginsburg. 2001. "Enabling Disability: Rewriting Kinship, Reimagining Citizenship." *Public Culture* 13 (3): 533–56.
Rapp, Rayna, Deborah Heath, and Karen-Sue Taussig. 2001. "Genealogical Dis-Ease: Where Hereditary Abnormality, Biomedical Explanation, and Family Responsibility Meet." In *Relative Values: Reconfiguring Kinship Studies*, ed. S. Franklin and S. McKinnon. Durham, N.C.: Duke University Press.
Register, Cheri. 2005. *Beyond Good Intentions: A Mother Reflects on Raising Internationally Adopted Children*. St. Paul, Minn.: Yeong and Yeong Book Company.
Reid, Bud. 1958. "Adoption By Picture." *McCall's*, January, 51.
Repetto, Robert. 1981. "Introduction." In *Economic Development, Population Policy, and Demographic Transition in the Republic of Korea*, ed. R. Repetto, T. H. Kwon, S. U. Kim, D. Y. Kim, J. E. Sloboda, and P. J. Donaldson. Cambridge, Mass.: Harvard University Press.
Riles, Annelise. 2001. *The Network Inside Out*. Ann Arbor: University of Michigan Press.
Riley, Nancy. 1997. "American Adoptions of Chinese Girls: The Socio-political Matrices of Individual Decisions." *Women's Studies International Forum* 20 (1): 87–102.
Robins, Steven. 2006. "From 'Rights' to 'Ritual': AIDS Activism in South Africa." *American Anthropologist* 108 (2): 312–23.
Robinson, Katy. 2002. *A Single Square Picture*. New York: Berkley Books.
Robinson, Michael. 1988. *Cultural Nationalism in Colonial Korea, 1920–25*. Seattle: University of Washington Press.
Roesch-Rhomberg, Inge. 2004. "Korean Institutionalised Adoption." In *Cross-Cultural Approaches to Adoption*, ed. Fiona Bowie. London: Routledge.

Roth, Joshua Hotaka. 2002. *Brokered Homeland: Japanese Brazilian Migrants in Japan.* Ithaca, N.Y.: Cornell University Press.

Rothschild, Matthew. 1988. "Babies for Sale: South Koreans Make Them, Americans Buy Them. *Progressive* 52 (1): 18–23.

Rouse, Roger. 1991. "Mexican Migration and the Social Space of Postmodernism." *Diaspora* 1 (1): 8–24.

Ruth, Kari. 1997. "Dear Luuk." In *Seeds from a Silent Tree,* ed. Tonya Bishoff and Jo Rankin. San Diego: Pandal Press.

——. 1999. "Kimchee on White Bread." In *Voices from Another Place,* ed. Susan Soon-Keum Cox. St. Paul, Minn.: Yeong and Yeong Book Company.

Ryang, Sonya. 2004. "A Note on Transnational Consanguinity; or, Kinship in the Age of Terrorism." *Anthropological Quarterly* 77 (4): 747–70.

Safran, William. 1991. "Diasporas in Modern Societies: Myths of Homeland and Return." *Diaspora* 1 (1): 83–99.

Said, Edward. 1990. "Reflections on Exile." In *Out There: Marginalization and Contemporary Cultures,* ed. R. Ferguson, M. Gever, Trinh T. Minh-ha, and C. West. New York: New Museum; Cambridge, Mass.: MIT Press.

Sarri, Rosemary C., Y. Baik, and M. Bombyk. 1998. "Goal Displacement and Dependency in South Korean–United States Intercountry Adoption." *Children and Youth Services Review* 20 (1/2): 87–114.

Schein, Louisa. 1998. "Forged Transnationality and Oppositional Cosmopolitanism." In *Transnationalism from Below,* ed. M. P. Smith and L. Guarnizo. New Brunswick, N.J.: Transaction Publishers.

Scheper-Hughes, Nancy. 1990. "Theft of Life." *Society* 27 (6): 57–62.

Scheper-Hughes, Nancy, and Carolyn Sargent. 1998. "Introduction." In *Small Wars: The Cultural Politics of Childhood,* ed. N. Scheper-Hughes and C. Sargent Berkeley: University of California Press.

Schiller, Nina Glick, and Georges Fouron. 1998. "Transnational Lives and National Identities: The Identity Politics of Haitian Immigrants." In *Transnationalism from Below,* ed. M. P. Smith and L. E. Guarnizo. New Brunswick, N.J.: Transaction Publishers.

Selman, Peter. 2007. "Intercountry Adoption in the Twenty-First Century: An Examination of the Rise and Fall of Countries of Origin." In *Proceedings of the First International Korean Adoption Studies Research Symposium,* ed. K. Park Nelson, E. Kim, and M. Peterson. Seoul: International Korean Adoptee Associations.

Seth. Michael. 2002. *Education Fever: Society, Politics, and the Pursuit of Schooling in South Korea.* Honolulu: University of Hawaii Press

——. 2006. *A Concise History of Korea: From the Neolithic Period to the Nineteenth Century.* Lanham, Md.: Rowman and Littlefield.

Shiao, Jiannbin Lee, and Mia H. Tuan. 2006. "Korean Adoptees and the Salience of Race in Romance." Paper presented at the annual meeting of the American Sociological Association, Montreal, Canada, 10 August.

Shim, Jae-yun. 2002. "Measures to Improve National Image Unveiled." *Korea Times*, 10 July. http://www.koreatimes.co.kr.

Shin, Gi-Wook. 2003. "The Paradox of Korean Globalization." Working paper, Asia/Pacific Research Center, Stanford University.

———. 2006. *Ethnic Nationalism in Korea: Genealogy, Politics, and Legacy*. Stanford, Calif.: Stanford University Press.

Shin, Gi-Wook, James Freda, and Gihong Yi. 1999. "The Politics of Ethnic Nationalism in Divided Korea." *Nations and Nationalism* 5 (4): 465–84.

Siu, Lok. 2003. "Diasporic Cultural Citizenship: Chineseness and Belonging in Central America. *Social Text* 19 (4): 7–28.

———. 2005. *Memories of a Future Home: Diasporic Citizenship of Chinese in Panama*. Stanford, Calif.: Stanford University Press.

Sloth, Kirsten. 2007. "Researching Adoption: Whose Perspective and What Issues?" In *Outsiders Within: Writing on Transracial Adoption*. Cambridge, Mass.: South End Press.

Smith, M. P., and L. E. Guarnizo, eds. 1998. *Transnationalism from Below*. New Brunswick, N.J.: Transaction Publishers.

Snyder, Rick. 2008. "'Tell Even Us': Diasporic Nostos in Theresa Hak Kyung Cha's *Dictee*." Paper presented at the American Comparative Literature Association annual meeting, Long Beach, Calif., April 26.

Social Welfare Society (Taehan Sahoe Pokji Hoe). 2004. *Taehan sahoe pokji hoe 50 nyŏn* (50 years of the Social Welfare Society). Seoul: Social Welfare Society.

Solinger, Rickie. 1994. "Race and 'Value': Black and White Illegitimate Babies, 1945–1965." In *Mothering: Ideology, Experience and Agency*, ed. E. N. Glenn, G. Chang, and L. R. Forcey. New York: Routledge.

Song, Jesook. 2006. "Family Breakdown and Invisible Homeless Women: Neoliberal Governance during the Asian Debt Crisis in South Korea, 1997–2001." *positions: east asia cultures critique* 14 (1): 37–65.

Spivak, Gayatri Chakravorty. 1988. "Subaltern Studies: Deconstructing Historiography." In *In Other Worlds: Essays in Cultural Politics*. New York: Routledge.

Stephens, Sharon, ed. 1995. *Children and the Politics of Culture*. Princeton, N.J.: Princeton University Press.

Stock, Kimberly Kyung Hee. 1999. "Rise of a Fourth Culture: Korean Adoptees." *Transcultured* 1 (4): 11.

Stoker, Kim. 2005. "Beyond Identity: Activism in Korean Adoptee Art." *Duksung Women's University Journal* 34: 223–48.

Stoler, Ann Laura. 2006. "Tense and Tender Ties: The Politics of Comparison in North American History and (Post)Colonial Studies." In *Haunted by Empire: Geographies of Intimacy in North American Empire*, ed. A. Stoler. Durham, N.C.: Duke University Press.

Strathern, Marilyn. 1999. *Property, Substance, and Effect: Anthropological Essays on Persons and Things*. London: Athlone Press.

Taylor, Charles. 1994. "Politics of Recognition." In *Multiculturalism: Examining the Politics of Recognition*, ed. Amy Gutmann. Princeton, N.J.: Princeton University Press.

——. 2002. "Modern Social Imaginaries." *Public Culture* 14 (1): 91–124.

Terwee, Soonja. 2004. "Artist's Statement." In *Our Adoptee, Our Alien*. Exhibition catalogue. Seoul: Art Camp.

Tomes, Kimberly Saree. 1997. *Looking for Wendy*. Video. New York: Third World Newsreel.

Trenka, Jane Jeong. 2005. *The Language of Blood*. St. Paul, Minn.: Graywolf Press.

Trenka, Jane Jeong, Julia Chinyere Oparah, and Sun Yung Shin, eds. 2006. *Outsiders Within: Writing on Transracial Adoption*. Cambridge, Mass.: South End Press.

Trouillot, Michael. 2001. "The Anthropology of the State in the Age of Globalization." *Current Anthropology* 42 (1): 125–38.

Tsuda, Takeyuki. 2003. *Strangers in the Ethnic Homeland: Japanese Brazilian Return Migration in a Transnational Perspective*. New York: Columbia University Press.

Tuan, Mia. 1999. *Forever Foreigners or Honorary Whites? The Asian Ethnic Experience Today*. New Brunswick, N.J.: Rutgers University Press.

Turner, Victor. 1969. *The Ritual Process: Structure and Anti-Structure*. Ithaca, N.Y.: Cornell University Press.

——. 1974. *Dramas, Fields, and Metaphors: Symbolic Action in Human Society*. Ithaca, N.Y.: Cornell University Press.

UNICEF. 2008. "Orphans." Press release. http://www.unicef.org.

Vickery, Martha. 1998. "Brian Bauman Update." *Korean Quarterly* 1 (3): 16.

Volkman, Toby Alice. 2005a. "Introduction: New Geographies of Kinship." In *Cultures of Transnational Adoption*, ed. T. A. Volkman. Durham, N.C.: Duke University Press.

——. 2005b. "Embodying Chinese Culture: Transnational Adoption in North America." In *Cultures of Transnational Adoption*, ed. T. A. Volkman. Durham, N.C.: Duke University Press.

von Borczyskowski, Annika, Anders Hjern, Frank Lindblad, and Bo Vinnerljung. 2006. "Suicidal Behaviour in National and International Adult Adoptees: A Swedish Cohort Study." *Social Psychiatry and Psychiatric Epidemiology* 41: 95–102.

Warner, Michael. 2002. "Publics and Counterpublics." *Public Culture* 14 (1): 49–90.

——. 2005. *Publics and Counterpublics*. New York: Zone Books.

Warren, Kay. 1999. *Indigenous Movements and Their Critics: Pan-Maya Activism in Guatemala*. Princeton, N.J.: Princeton University Press.

Washington Post. 1959. "North Korea Attacks U.S. on Orphans." 8 June, A6.

Waters, Mary C. 1990. *Ethnic Options: Choosing Identities in America*. Berkeley: University of California Press.

Wegar, Katarina. 1997. *Adoption, Identity, and Kinship: The Debate over Sealed Birth Records.* New Haven, Conn.: Yale University Press.

Weil, Richard. 1984. "International Adoptions: The Quiet Migration." *International Migration Review* 18 (2): 276–93.

Weimer, Maya. 2006. *Rendez-vous.* DVD.

Weismantel, Mary. 1995. "Making Kin: Kinship Theory and Zumbagua Adoptions." *American Ethnologist* 22 (4): 685–704.

Weston, Kath. 1991. *Families We Choose: Lesbians, Gays, Kinship.* New York: Columbia University Press.

Wolf, Margery. 1968. *The House of Lim: A Study of a Chinese Farm Family.* Englewood Cliffs, N.J.: Prentice-Hall.

Woo, Myungsook. 2004. *The Politics of Social Welfare Policy in Korea: Growth and Citizenship.* Lanham, Md.: University Press of America.

Yeoh, Brenda S. A., Shirlena Huang, and Theodora Lam. 2005. "Transnationalizing the 'Asian' Family: Imaginaries, Intimacies and Strategic Intents." *Global Networks* 5 (4): 307–15.

Yngvesson, Barbara. 2000. "'Un Niño de Cualquier Color': Race and Nation in Intercountry Adoption." In *Globalizing Institutions: Case Studies in Regulation and Innovation,* ed. Jane Jenson and Boaventura de Sousa Santos. Aldershot, U.K.: Ashgate.

——. 2001. "'Almost Swedish': The Body within the Body of International Adoption." Paper presented at the Traffic In Kinship Conference, New York University, 26–27 September.

——. 2002. "Placing the 'Gift Child' in Transnational Adoption." *Law and Society Review* 36 (2): 227–56.

——. 2005. "Going 'Home': Adoption, Loss of Bearings, and the Mythology of Roots." In *Cultures of Transnational Adoption,* ed. T. Volkman. Durham, N.C.: Duke University Press.

Yngvesson, Barbara, and Susan Coutin. 2006. "Backed by Papers: Undoing Persons, Histories, Return." *American Ethnologist* 33 (2): 177–90.

Yngvesson, Barbara, and Maureen A. Mahoney. 2000. "'As One Should, Ought, and Wants to Be': Belonging and Authenticity in Identity Narratives." *Theory, Culture and Society* 17 (6): 77–110.

Yoon, In-Jin. 2002. "A Comparison of the South and North Korean Policy of Overseas Koreans." In *Proceedings of the International Conference on the Korean Diaspora and Strategies of Global Network.* New Haven, Conn.: East Rock Institute.

Yuh, Ji Yeon. 2002. *In the Shadows of Camptown: Korean Military Brides in America.* New York: New York University Press.

Zelizer, Viviana. 1994. *Pricing the Priceless Child: The Changing Social Value of Children.* Princeton, N.J.: Princeton University Press.

——. 2007. *The Purchase of Intimacy.* Princeton, N.J.: Princeton University Press.

Index

Page numbers in italics refer to figures.

Eleana Kim is an assistant professor of anthropology at the University of Rochester.

Library of Congress Cataloging-in-Publication Data
Kim, Eleana Jean, 1971–
Adopted territory : transnational Korean adoptees and the politics of belonging / Eleana J. Kim.
p. cm.
Includes bibliographical references and index.
ISBN 978-0-8223-4683-8 (cloth : alk. paper)
ISBN 978-0-8223-4695-1 (pbk. : alk. paper)
1. Intercountry adoption—Korea (South) 2. Intercountry adoption—United States. 3. Adoptees—Korea (South) 4. Adoptees—United States. I. Title.
HV875.5.K49 2010
306.874—dc22 2010024148